REMAKING APPALACHIA

REMAKING APPALACHIA

ECOSOCIALISM, ECOFEMINISM, AND LAW

NICHOLAS F. STUMP

 WEST VIRGINIA UNIVERSITY PRESS / MORGANTOWN

ISBN 978-1-949199-90-1 (cloth) / 978-1-949199-91-8 (paperback) /
978-1-949199-92-5 (ebook)

Library of Congress Cataloging-in-Publication Data
Names: Stump, Nicholas F., author.
Title: Remaking Appalachia : ecosocialism, ecofeminism, and law / Nicholas F.
    Stump.
Description: First edition. | Morgantown : West Virginia University Press,
    2021. | Includes bibliographical references and index.
Identifiers: LCCN 2020051295 | ISBN 9781949199901 (cloth) | ISBN
    9781949199918 (paperback) | ISBN 9781949199925 (ebook)
Subjects: LCSH: Environmental law—Appalachian Region.
Classification: LCC KF3817 .S869 2021 | DDC 344.7304/60974—dc23
LC record available at https://lccn.loc.gov/2020051295

Cover and book design by Than Saffel / WVU Press
Cover image used under license from Shutterstock.com.

For my mother, Charlene Kay Findley Stump; and for my grandfather, Nelson Findley, who was killed aged twenty-seven in the West Virginia coal mines.

CONTENTS

ACKNOWLEDGMENTS

A special thanks to Derek Krissoff, WVU Press Director, for his expert guidance and unerring support. Derek made this project possible. Special thanks also to Anne Lofaso for her extensive guidance on this project and for her long-term mentorship. And a special thanks to Ryan Wishart for his transformative comments, and for the extensive feedback or comments from Priya Baskaran, Ryan Claycomb, Tim Cronin, Ann Eisenberg, Antonia Eliason, Atiba Ellis, Danielle Emerling, Evan Johns, Jena Martin, Patrick McGinley, Alison Peck, Jesse Potts, Matt Titolo, and James Van Nostrand. A special thanks also to all anonymous reviewers who provided invaluable comments or feedback.

Family support was crucial for this project. A deep thanks to Jen Sizemore, my spouse, who also lent her expertise on Appalachian public health. Thanks also for support from David Stump, Deborah Stump, Fay Asfour Stump, Josh Stump, Mary Stump, Rachel Stump, and from many other family members.

For core feedback or support, including through conference workshopping, a deep thanks to James Addington, Kira Allmann, Robert Bastress, Valena Beety, Victoria Bogdan Tejeda, Greg Bowman, Meghan Campbell, Kelly Diamond, Karen Diaz, Charles DiSalvo, Becca Spence Dubois, Kevin Escudero, Josh Fershee, Nathan Fetty, Sara Georgi, Tom Hansell, Jessica Haught, Barbara Howe, Michael Iafrate, James Jolly, Sarah Lamdan, Ben Manski, Nicholas Mignanelli, Angela Maranville, Jason Miller, Kathryn Newfont, Caroline Osborne, Ann Pancake, Stewart Plein, Mark Podvia, Ken Price, Will Rhee, Bryan Richards, Allison Scott, Dennis Smith, Lynne Stahl, Shine Tu, Elaine Wilson, and Alyssa Wright.

Thanks also for additional support, feedback, or guidance from Chris Carson, Lou Couch, Caity Coyne, Jessica Dai, Amy Dawson, Sally Deskins, Jennifer Dubetz, Martin Dunlap, Stephanie Foote, Sandy Fredman, Megan Heady, Rachel Holbert, Tatsu Johnson, Drew Killmeyer, Dan Kimble, Robert Kerns, Bethany Kubicar, Jane LaBarbara, Ashton Marra, Traci Mays, Stephanie Miller, Jennifer Momen, Jennifer Oliva, Sharon Ryan, Leighann Sainato,

Charles Schultz, Sherry Steadman, Beth Toren, Jessica Vanderhoff, Charlotte Vester, Joshua Weishart, Ernie Williams, and Chad Wilcox.

Much gratitude for the institutional or organizational support, including conference presentations and workshopping opportunities, from WVU Press, WVU College of Law, WVU Libraries, WVU Humanities Center, WVU Reed College of Media, WVU Appalachian Justice Initiative, WVU Library Faculty Scholarship Group, Appalachian Futures, Appalachian Studies Association, 100 Days in Appalachia, Law and Society Association, Oxford Human Rights Hub, ClassCrits Association, American Association of Law Libraries Research Crits Caucus, West Virginia Libraries Association, Southeastern Association of Law Libraries, and West Virginia Humanities Council.

INTRODUCTION

Appalachia, as an "energy sacrifice zone," has long been devastated by the coal industry and related negative actors, and environmental law has comprehensively failed to protect the region from such industry-produced harms.[1] Environmental law's failure emanates from its essential supportive role within liberal capitalism's ecologically unsustainable paradigm. This paradigm, however, has reached its limit in a world of finite resources, as illustrated by the destruction of niche sacrifice zones such as Appalachia, and more broadly, by the global ecological crisis.[2] Consequently, Appalachia does not require further environmental law reform within this unsustainable and deeply exploitative paradigm. Rather, Appalachia requires truly transformative change beyond the liberal order. *Remaking Appalachia* further contends that such transformative change should be steeped in certain strains of eco-feminism, which focus on economic degrowth, critical justice (along lines of class, gender, race, indigenous status, etc.), local-to-global connections, and deep intersections with ecosocialist approaches.[3] In this way, *Remaking Appalachia* is fundamentally concerned with the pursuit of transformative economic and socio-legal change for a region that has long been subordinated. At the same time, however, this book is concerned with how such regional change can both inform and be informed by coordinated radical transformations at the broader national and global levels.

Since the late nineteenth century, Appalachia's environment and citizenry have indeed been profoundly exploited by the fossil fuel hegemony. This fossil fuel hegemony consists principally of natural resource extractive industries—namely, the coal and oil and gas industries—as allied with complicit Appalachian elites that have facilitated and otherwise benefited from this hegemony.[4] The coal industry, in particular, has constituted the prime negative actor in the prior century and half, as it has wrought extensive (and intertwined) ecological, social, cultural, and economic devastation on the region. In the prior three decades, this phenomenon has been perhaps best exemplified by the rise of mountaintop removal mining, which has obliterated, to date, five hundred mountains and two thousand miles of ecologically crucial headwater streams, all while Central Appalachia remains among the most impoverished regions in the nation. What is more, despite the fact that coal has declined precipitously, the industry persists, and its harmful vestiges, such as unreclaimed mining sites, will long linger—even while new industrial onslaughts emerge in Appalachia; these include, among other things, the natural gas boom and a related chemical sector resurgence.[5]

The fossil fuel hegemony achieved such preeminence in part due to its historically central role within the dominant U.S. economic paradigm. Liberal capitalism—which, per the critical account, in fact drove the formation of liberal political and legal structures—is marked by the drive for ceaseless capital accumulation through multidimensional forms of oppression (i.e., of labor and nature) and a structural growth imperative.[6] Significant for Appalachia, fossil fuels have long driven the liberal capitalist paradigm.[7] Appalachian coal, in particular, helped fire the Industrial Revolution and thereafter much of the nation's twentieth-century economic "progress."[8] Other dimensions of capitalist development, however, also decimated Appalachia, such as the timber industry;[9] so, too, were even earlier development modes often ecologically problematic, with nascent transitions towards a capitalist agroecosystem in the region constituting a prime example.[10] While such phenomena are discussed in the opening chapters of *Remaking Appalachia*, the fossil fuel hegemony and coal, in particular, is indeed the overarching focal point of this book, as for the past century and a half, the fossil fuel hegemony has proven uniquely destructive in Appalachia.

Indeed, liberalism, through its various iterations—or late classical liberalism (latter 1800s–1900s), welfare state liberalism (1930s–1970s), and neoliberalism (1980s–present)—has been characterized by the state providing direct and indirect support to the fossil fuel industry. Law and policy have long constituted a core mechanism through which this phenomenon has been accomplished. As Michael M'Gonigle and Louise Takeda chronicle in "The Liberal Limits of Environmental Law," a productionist orientation has long undergirded U.S. energy policy, as it is "framed by the overriding commitment to economic development and growth based on access to cheap energy resources."[11] So, too, would environmental law, as enacted in the 1970s and subsequently refined, support economic liberalism because, while environmental regulations "mitigate some of the negative impacts of growth, they do not challenge the broad goal of expanding production" and, more broadly, of maximizing capital accumulation among elite interests.[12] Consequently, because environmental law exists as a mere internal supplement to the unsustainable liberal capitalist paradigm, the legal regime has failed utterly to halt ecological destruction in Appalachia and worldwide.

This preliminary overview of *Remaking Appalachia*'s central themes demonstrates aptly the sheer magnitude of the region's complex past and contemporary forms of subordination—and of the corresponding need for truly transformative change beyond the liberal order. Unfortunately, however, throughout the twentieth century and beyond, many reformist-minded commentators, policymakers, attorneys, and mainstream change agents, while typically acting in good faith, have nevertheless failed to identify such crucial structural issues as Appalachia's core dilemma. Rather, Appalachia has been characterized as a "land that time forgot" that has merely lagged behind the broader United States due to both infrastructural and cultural deficiencies (i.e., Appalachians having been long homogenized as a backwards, lazy, and "deviant" population)—which therefore merely requires liberal-steeped development or "uplift." [13]

The Appalachian-focused 1960s War on Poverty constitutes an exemplar of such a liberal-steeped development model. While certainly well-intentioned and humane—having been characterized as the "high point in the realization of the welfare state in the United States"—the War on Poverty ultimately failed to challenge the structurally subordinating conditions wrought by liberal capitalism (and the fossil fuel hegemony, in particular). [14] Thus, following the War on Poverty, Appalachia continued to suffer from the multidimensional destruction wrought by the fossil fuel hegemony, as exemplified by the rise of mountaintop removal, and more recently, the natural gas boom.

Like the War on Poverty, an additional example of critically flawed reform—which is of particular significance to *Remaking Appalachia*—involves long-standing efforts at environmental law reform. As broached above, environmental law is merely part and parcel of hegemonic liberalism. However, because we live in a world of bounded resources, the paradigm of ceaseless capital accumulation and "progressive commodification of everything," in addition to the growth imperative, has proven wholly unsustainable. [15] Thus, so long as environmental law remains embedded within the liberal paradigm, no amount of law reform will avert continued environmental degradation—and through phenomena such as climate change, potentially total ecological and social collapse. [16]

Remaking Appalachia will also detail more specific dimensions through which the environmental law regime has failed Appalachia. These include environmental law's disjointed nature, its reliance on non-democratic administrative agencies (which are subject to "industry capture"), legislative "outs" that explicitly facilitate continued industry-produced destruction through permit-to-pollute legal regimes; and its ultimate reliance on all branches of government, which results in the regime resisting rapid development or correction. (In this way, environmental law does not halt, but rather *organizes* and marginally mitigates liberal capitalist-produced ecological destruction.) Therefore, environmental law's deficient technical design—and more broadly, its overarching liberal character—have facilitated the fossil fuel hegemony in continuously devastating Appalachia's environment and citizenry.[17]

The central thesis of *Remaking Appalachia*, then, is that the region should eschew further incremental legal change, or "intra-systemic reform," within the critically flawed liberal capitalist paradigm—environmental law reform or otherwise. Rather, what is required is truly radical structural change—or "systemic re-formations"—beyond the liberal order.[18] Appalachian systemic re-formations would involve, by necessity, eliminating and transcending the fossil fuel hegemony in addition to the broader Appalachian neoliberal ecological political economy (of which the fossil fuel hegemony is just a cornerstone)—i.e., as necessarily interlinked with broader national and global efforts. In its place, Appalachian citizens can collectively *reconstruct* an Appalachian ecological political economy that is both critically just and strongly ecologically sustainable.

Remaking Appalachia further contends that certain strains of the ecofeminist school as intertwined with ecosocialism should closely inform such systemic re-formations in Appalachia and beyond. Ecofeminism posits that the same hegemonic patriarchal capitalist forces driving global ecological destruction are also responsible for subordination along lines of gender, race, class, indigenous status, the Global South-North divide, etc.; therefore, transformative change requires combating such forces holistically.[19] Ecofeminist strains utilized in *Remaking Appalachia* also posit that a degrowth model is required, as potentially steeped in solidarity economy, subsistence, and related approaches furthered through a bottom-up, grassroots approach. Moreover, such transformations are usefully situated in the context of closely related ecosocialist approaches, which involve, among other things, broader collective ownership of the means of production and democratic economic planning at all geographic levels (i.e., as is required to, most immediately, eliminate global use of fossil fuels).

Proposals for such radical ecofeminist- and ecosocialist-steeped transformations typically raise questions as to "political practicality" in the U.S. context—as such transitions supposedly would degrade the high quality of life that modernity has provided for many citizens; therefore, from the very outset of *Remaking Appalachia*, a response to such concerns seems necessary.

In the first place, transitions towards solidarity economy, subsistence, and related ecofeminist and ecosocialist modes aim to maintain the core, material-based quality of life provided by modernity. As *Remaking Appalachia* will discuss, community-owned clean energy systems—i.e., with "clean energy" in this book denoting renewable energy sources such as solar and wind in addition to energy efficiency modes—for instance, occupy a crucial role within such transformations. Consequently, such systemic re-formations would not qualitatively reduce the genuine benefits of modernity, including an intensively egalitarian provision of education, housing, and healthcare resources (e.g., modes of healthcare for all), as supported by a strongly ecologically sustainable and highly democratic reliance on technology.[20]

What is more, in sacrifice zone regions such as Central Appalachia—which currently is beset by severe poverty, acute environmental justice issues, crumbling infrastructure, food and healthcare deserts, and ever-diminishing social safety nets and public programs—ecofeminist- and ecosocialist-steeped systemic re-formations would very likely result in a pronounced *increase* of material-based quality of life. To illustrate this point, in 2017, the U.N. Special Rapporteur on extreme poverty and human rights toured the United States—and reported that in the Appalachian states of West Virginia and Alabama, a "high proportion of the population . . . was not being served by public sewerage and water supply services," and that neither state could proffer "figures as to the magnitude of the challenge or details of any government plans to address the issues in the future."[21] Ecofeminist- and ecosocialist-steeped transformations, in focusing on meeting community needs in an exceedingly egalitarian manner, would redress such neoliberalism-associated failures and thus likely increase material-based quality of life.

Beyond such explicit sacrifice zones, ecofeminist- and ecosocialist-steeped transformations would also likely increase material-based quality of life for vast swaths of the United States. In tandem with neoliberalism's rise, wealth inequality has reached historic proportions: currently, just 1 percent of U.S. households own 40 percent of all wealth in the nation.[22] Forty million Americans are impoverished—which is equal to the population of twenty-two West Virginias combined.[23] So, too, are such neoliberal capitalism-associated issues as an ever-shrinking social safety net, declining infrastructure, the decimation of labor forces, and profound environmental justice–based harms endemic not just to Appalachia but also the nation as a whole. And communities of color, indigenous communities, and women—among other marginalized groups—are disproportionality impacted by such collective ills of late liberalism. Thus, like with Central Appalachia, much of the United States would likely materially benefit from such ecofeminist-steeped systemic re-formations.[24]

That said, such transformations away from the hegemonic liberal capitalist paradigm would, by very their nature, curtail hyper-production and hyper-consumption modes—as the focus is on meeting basic and authentic needs through an approach based on production for "use value" rather than for "exchange value" in the market.[25] This would indeed constitute a dramatic cultural shift for Western nations (and for the United States, especially). A pertinent question, however, is as follows: do hyper-consumption modes actually increase more subjective quality of life dimensions for citizens, such as happiness, satisfaction, or meaningfulness? Plain common sense suggests otherwise. Thus, while ecofeminist- and ecosocialist-steeped systemic re-formations would require abandoning hyper-production and hyper-consumption modes, such transformations would increase those quality of life dimensions which likely many would consider to matter most (including a vast and vital increase in genuine free time).

What is more, late capitalist modes could very plausibly disappear as options altogether in the coming decades, as research on the projected impacts of the global ecological crisis indicate that the crisis constitutes a legitimate "civilizational issue." As Mary Wood chronicles in *Nature's Trust*, collective studies "project that the current trajectory of carbon dioxide pollution will trigger planetary heating on a scale that will send civilization into interminable distress" and that, further, "prevailing policies of exploitation threaten to leave 'nothing but parched earth incapable of sustaining life.' "[26] Perhaps most significantly, the watershed 2018 U.N. Intergovernmental Panel on Climate Change report—now popularized as the "Doomsday" report—argues that "rapid, far-reaching and unprecedented changes in all aspects of society" are required.[27] Thus, the political practicality critique of ecofeminist- and ecosocialist-steeped and related transformations appears increasingly out-of-touch—as mounting evidence suggests that degrowth-centered transitions are very likely required to avert total global catastrophe.

In the specific context of political practicality in Appalachia, many commentators assert that the inherent conservativeness of the region forestalls the potential for transformative change. The so-called Appalachia-as-Trump-country phenomenon that emerged during the 2016 presidential election is certainly representative of this line of critique.[28] However, Appalachia is, in fact, a remarkably heterogeneous region (in terms of both culture and politics). Of particular importance to *Remaking Appalachia*, the region boasts a long, storied, and, at times, radical grassroots activism tradition, as exemplified by the early twentieth-century "coal wars" fought over labor issues and the rich environmental resistance tradition that has persisted since the 1960s. What is more, much contemporary Appalachian grassroots activism is steeped in critical intersectionality (along lines of gender, race, etc.) and thus combats compound oppressions.[29] For instance, the famed Highlander Research and Education Center—which "serves as a catalyst for grassroots organizing and movement building in Appalachia and the South"—has a mission to "develop leadership and help create and support strong, democratic organizations that work for justice, equality and sustainability in their own communities and that join with others to build broad movements for social, economic and restorative environmental change."[30]

Similarly, Appalachian grassroots activism is marked by coalitional inter-linking, as illustrated by the recent efforts towards melding the (often histori-cally opposed) environmental and labor movements. For instance, the historic 2018 West Virginia teachers' strike—which catalyzed broader strikes across the United States—was extraordinary not only because such concerted pro-gressive activism patently disproved the homogenized "Trump country" nar-rative, but also because the strikers explicitly targeted the fossil fuel hegemony. As Sarah Jones reports in the *New Republic*, a "recurring complaint during the strike [was] the state's low severance tax of about 5 percent on coal and natural gas extraction," because higher tax rates would have accounted for the teach-ers' primary concern: a deteriorating state-provided health insurance system.[31] Thus, through coalition-building across dimensions of labor, the environment, and so forth, Appalachian grassroots activism continues to evolve as a potent force for social change—which can be tapped into in collectively exploring eco-feminist- and ecosocialist-steeped systemic re-formations. (A follow-up 2019 teachers' strike successfully defeated education-privatization legislation in West Virginia—which was notable not only for demonstrating the continued vitality of the movement, but also for what could be characterized as its multi-faceted anti-neoliberalism underpinnings.)[32]

As *Remaking Appalachia* will discuss, beyond this grassroots base, the region also is, in many other ways, ideally suited for such systemic re-formations. As a prime example, due to the region's vast and richly diverse agroecological base—e.g., studies indicate that Appalachia has the most diverse foodshed in North America—conditions are optimal for systemic re-formations involving community-based food systems.[33]

As a final point, while Appalachia is undoubtedly in need of systemic re-formations—and therefore constitutes an ideal exploratory case model for

Remaking Appalachia—comparable transitions at the national and global levels are also required; consequently, *Remaking Appalachia*'s ultimate scope extends beyond Appalachia's borders. As a baseline practical matter, for systemic re-formations to truly succeed in a region, such efforts must be intrinsically interlinked with broader transformations. As Stephen Fisher articulates in the influential *Fighting Back in Appalachia*: "Linking local fights to national and global struggles is a difficult and slow process, but it is the only approach that has a chance of bringing about fundamental change in Appalachia."[34] A single region attempting to transition towards a more just and sustainable ecological political economy is certainly desirable; but geographically interlinked projects are required—and if comparable systemic re formations are not essentially universalized, the global ecological crisis will persist as a collective "civilizational issue" imperiling us all. Similarly, to truly combat the other intertwined subordination dimensions of late capitalism—along lines of class, race, gender, indigenous status, the Global South-North divide, etc.—requires coordinated national and global re-formation efforts. Ultimately, then, while all global regions, sub-regions, and communities are uniquely situated and thus require niche needs—as collectively and democratically determined at niche geographic levels per a materialist approach—meaningful and robust local-to-global approaches are, nevertheless, imperative for truly radical change.

ORGANIZATIONAL STRUCTURE OF *REMAKING APPALACHIA*

The first chapter of *Remaking Appalachia* provides a brief overview of Appalachia's basic geography and natural resource profile before turning to the history of human communities in the region—commencing with Native American populations. The Euro-American conquest and colonization of Appalachia are then chronicled, with a special emphasis placed on the critical role market forces occupied from the earliest days of the conquest. Next, the complex character of preindustrial Appalachia is discussed, before the chapter turns towards Appalachia's late nineteenth-century period of rapid industrial growth. The coming of timber- and especially coal-based industrialization would constitute the most crucial era in the making of modern Appalachia; from this period onwards, the fossil fuel hegemony would prove remarkably successful in exploiting both the environment and citizenry in pursuing ceaseless capital accumulation. This chapter concludes, however, by tracing a more heartening phenomenon: the emergence of a robust resistance tradition in Appalachia through militant labor organizing activities.

Chapter 2 chronicles environmental law's distant historical foundations in addition to its essential liberalism underpinnings. Numerous modes of production have engendered pronounced ecological despoliation throughout history. However, as chapter 2 details, the capitalist mode of production, in particular, has produced the current global ecological crisis, due to the scope and scale of environmental destruction wrought by capitalism. While Western ideological views largely supported such devastation from the Greco-Roman periods onwards, the Enlightenment and Romantic movements would eventually introduce new cultural modes that vitally shaped environmental law. This chapter also examines two important precursors to environmental law: the conservation- and preservation-related legal regimes. That said, the common law (or judge-made law) constituted prime "proto-environmental law" in the United States, including in Appalachia. Unfortunately, as chapter 2 demonstrates, common law—namely, tort actions such as nuisance and negligence—failed utterly to protect Appalachia from industry-based harms during the period of rapid industrialization, and indeed such doctrines were explicitly transformed to support favored industries. Chapter 2 also provides an overview of economic and political liberalism—including classical liberalism's character, as historically operationalized by exploitative actors. As noted above, both proto- and modern environmental law are embedded within the (ecologically unsustainable) liberal paradigm, and thus the regimes have failed to halt the global ecological crisis.

Appalachia at the early-to-mid-twentieth-century point—particularly in the context of liberal development models and coal's continued hegemony—is explored in chapter 3. The initial Appalachian coal boom waned by the 1920s (due to, among other factors, overproduction and increased market competition). While the region retained a largely fossil fuel–based mono-economy, it would thereafter be beset by boom-and-bust cycles. Chapter 3 chronicles coal's progression throughout this period and particularly focuses on the mid-century transition to mechanization-intensive surface mining. Such a transition rapidly accelerated ecological destruction in the region and related negative human community impacts. Consequently, a rich environmental grassroots movement arose in the region that persists—in robust and multidimensional formulations—in the present era. This chapter also details the well-intentioned, if ultimately flawed, liberal development models implemented in Appalachia during this period (broadly characterized as the liberal welfare state era). Specifically, New Deal–related reforms and the Appalachian-focused 1960s War on Poverty are covered. As this chapter demonstrates, such models failed Appalachia in involving intra-systemic reform only (or mere course corrections within the liberal paradigm)—transformative change beyond the exploitative status quo, or systemic re-formations beyond liberal capitalism, were not effectuated.

Chapter 4 provides an intensive analysis of environmental law and unpacks the intersecting dimensions through which the legal regime has failed. First, the immediate social and political factors leading to environmental law's (remarkably swift) rise are discussed: the most notable direct cause was the 1960s "environmental revolution." Environmental law's essential character is then outlined: a constellation of statutes constituting the core of environmental law was enacted in the 1970s and further refined in subsequent decades. The regime predominantly relies on executive branch–related administrative agencies—to which Congress delegated extensive rulemaking authority. Environmental law's critical flaws include its overarching disjointedness; that industry and complicit lawmakers embedded nascent environmental law with legislative "outs" (thus facilitating the very industry-produced harms the regime was designed to curtail, largely through permit-to-pollute schemes); the non-democratic nature of administrative agencies, which facilitated widespread "industry capture" (or industry co-opting those agencies charged with their regulation); and environmental law's ultimate reliance on different governmental branches, thus slowing doctrinal development or course corrections. However, more fundamentally, environmental law failed due to its essential embeddedness within the liberal paradigm. That is, for over a century, the cornerstone of U.S. energy law and policy has been to support maximally cheap energy production (i.e., historically fossil fuel–driven) to the benefit of large capital interests; environmental law, which emerged long after such policy ossified, was merely designed to support and to otherwise mitigate the most egregious aspects of this paradigm. Environmental law, then, is wholly incapable of stemming the global ecological destruction wrought by liberal capitalism.

Environmental law's failures in the explicit Appalachian context are chronicled at length in chapter 5. Special exploratory treatment is provided to mountaintop removal (MTR). MTR arose as major force in the early 1990s and has continued, as an extraordinarily destructive practice, into the present era; environmental law (e.g., the Clean Water Act, the Surface Mining Control and Reclamation Act, and the National Environmental Policy Act) failed utterly to halt MTR's ravages. What is more, elements of MTR governance might indeed be characterized as the outright failure of the rule of law in the environmental governance context (i.e., as even traditionally conceived under liberalism)—which was facilitated by Appalachia's long status as a culturally marginalized energy sacrifice zone. Chapter 5 also chronicles Appalachia's more recent industry-based harms. Coal has declined precipitously in recent years due primarily to the rise of low-priced natural gas, but the Marcellus shale gas boom (and a related chemical industry resurgence) has engendered new ecological and human community-based harms in Appalachia. Beyond Appalachia, this chapter also unpacks the various dimensions of the global ecological crisis, including climate change, other pollution-based harms, and renewable resource overuse (now associated with notions of the Anthropocene or Capitalocene).

Additionally, chapter 5 provides a broader overview of Appalachia's modern social, political, and economic landscape, as perversely shaped by the coal industry's efforts to reconstruct ideological-based bonds with many Appalachian communities—i.e., following the diminishment of coal employment-based relationships. Such deeply problematic bonds have been steeped in unjust gender regimes, white supremacy, and xenophobic nationalism; and in more recent years, the Trump phenomenon and related forces have leveraged such cultural manipulation tactics in the region. Unfortunately, such collective forces likely have helped forestall efforts at grassroots-driven transformative change in Appalachia. Chapter 5 concludes, however, by discussing potential countermovements to such far-right forces; namely, the latest iterations of Appalachian grassroots movements are detailed, which, in the environmental context, arose in tandem with MTR and have been reinvigorated in the natural gas era—and which are marked by a focus on both critical intersectionality and multi-coalitional interlinking.

Chapter 6 pivots towards the prime prescriptive recommendations put forth in *Remaking Appalachia*, in focusing on the theory, practice, and praxis of pursuing transformative economic and socio-legal change. Specifically, as undergirded by critical legal theory, chapter 6 argues not for traditional environmental law reform—but rather for truly radically conceived systemic re-formations beyond the existing liberal order. This chapter further argues that contemporary ecofeminism as entwined with ecosocialism can deeply inform such systemic re-formations. Ecofeminist strains relied on in *Remaking Appalachia* focus on radical degrowth; bottom-up, grassroots approaches to solidarity economy, subsistence, and related modes; local-to-global connections; strong ecological sustainability; recommoning precepts; critical intersectionality along lines of gender, the environment, class, race, indigenous status, etc.; and deep intersections with ecosocialism (e.g., broader collective ownership modes of the means of production and democratic economic planning at all geographic levels). A materialist ecofeminist approach also is utilized, focusing on actual, lived realities within communities and regions (and which similarly eschews essentialist or homogenized notions of gender, race, etc.).

Chapter 6 also argues that, while ecofeminist- and ecosocialist-steeped systemic re-formations are required, critical legal theory–informed approaches to select environmental doctrines can nevertheless assist in effectuating, expediting, and deeply informing such re-formations. Specifically, two outliers to the environmental law regime, environmental human rights and the public trust doctrine—as radically reconceived beyond liberalism—are discussed as such "systemic stepping stone measures." Through an infusion of critical legal theory (e.g., community lawyering and radical cause lawyering precepts) such doctrines can explicitly support the movement towards systemic re-formations in Appalachia and beyond. To effectuate such post-liberalism ends, however, such systemic stepping stone measures must indeed be radically re-envisioned beyond their current paradigms—and furthered through the mass political mobilization modes that radical cause lawyering and related organizing mechanisms can help engender.

Lastly, chapter 7 applies the theoretical and praxis-based framework outlined in chapter 6 to the Appalachian region (while also drawing on pertinent Appalachian-related economic, political, cultural, and legal analyses from prior chapters). Specifically, an exploration of systemic re-formations in Appalachia is undertaken: to achieve such re-formations, the contemporary Appalachian neoliberal ecological political economy—in which the fossil fuel hegemony persists as a cornerstone—must be transcended; in its place, Appalachians can collectively reconstruct an ecological political economy along potentially ecofeminist- and ecosocialist-related lines, as interlinked with comparable re-formation efforts at other local, regional, national, and international levels. Community-based clean energy systems and local food systems are then discussed as two concrete examples of, in fact, preexisting reform sites—which, through further radical conceptualizations along ecofeminist and ecosocialist lines, are ideally suited for systemic re-formations in Appalachia.

To help effectuate, expedite, and deeply inform these and other systemic re-formations, chapter 7 then examines the systemic stepping stone measures of environmental human rights and the public trust doctrine in the Appalachian context. As infused with critical legal theory, such measures would be steeped in non-hierarchical lawyering approaches (e.g., radical cause lawyering)—and also would be truly radically reconceived, in explicitly recognizing that such measures must, through a radical "frame transformation" of the doctrines, have an overarching aim of transcending hegemonic liberalism. More specifically, a radically re-envisioned approach to the public trust doctrine as entwined with critically informed environmental human rights is explored as a novel means to help catalyze ecofeminist- and ecosocialist-steeped ecological recommoning in Appalachia as conceived of and furthered beyond the liberal capitalist paradigm.

Chapter 7 concludes by examining the recently reinvigorated Green New Deal through the lens of *Remaking Appalachia*'s prime prescriptive recommendations. Specifically, a Green New Deal will fail if formulated within liberal capitalism—but a radicalized Green New Deal could, in the alternative, help effectuate the broader collective ownership modes and democratic economic planning required for a revolutionary conversion of energy production (i.e., beyond fossil fuels) and other key sectors at all geographic levels.

Remaking Appalachia is ultimately imbued with a cautious and pragmatic sense of hope. That is, that through a collective re-envisioning of Appalachia's ecological political economy—as effectuated through mass mobilization and in conjunction with broader national and global re-formations—the region can emerge as more just and as better positioned to face the profound perils of the Capitalocene. As Maria Mies and Vandana Shiva articulate in their classic work *Ecofeminism*, all of us must endeavor to "search for an ecologically sound, non-exploitative, just, non-patriarchal, self-sustaining society." [35]

CHAPTER 1

HISTORICAL BEGINNINGS: APPALACHIAN COAL AND THE COMING OF INDUSTRIAL CAPITALISM

This chapter provides an overview of the core historical events that shaped modern Appalachia. After a brief section detailing the essential geographic and natural resource profile of the region, the development of human communities in Appalachia is explored—commencing with indigenous peoples and extending through the Euro-American conquest and colonization. The general character of preindustrial Appalachia then is covered, before this chapter turns to the late nineteenth-century period of rapid timber- and coal-based industrial growth. Indeed, the coming of industrialized coal and other industries—which occurred within the broader context of period liberal capitalism—would, in short order, create profoundly negative social, cultural, economic, and environmental conditions in Appalachia. This period's developments also set the stage for the subsequent century and a half; that is, from the late 1800s onwards, the fossil fuel hegemony would form the cornerstone of the profoundly exploitative Appalachian ecological political economy.

Appalachia's history and current landscape are intrinsically interlinked with the region's extensive mineral wealth and natural resources; indeed, "few regions in the world were as well endowed with such vast carbon deposits."[1] Appalachia coal developed over hundreds of millions of years, with deposits of anthracite coal (or "hard" coal) eventually forming in present-day Pennsylvania. Bituminous (or "soft" coal) would form throughout the region, including in Central Appalachia, a region encompassing parts of West Virginia, Kentucky, Tennessee, and Virginia.[2] The region's natural resources, however, extend beyond coal—including extensive oil and gas deposits. Also sometimes less discussed—as compared to Appalachian coal—is the former magnificence of hardwood Appalachian forests. But the early timber industry wholly razed these old-growth forests.[3] By 1920, the whole of West Virginia was "reduced to an abhorrent desert," leaving the contemporary forests a "frail shell of what they were only a handful of centuries ago."[4]

Appalachia, both historic and contemporary, also is marked by impressive biodiversity. The Appalachian mountains are among the most ancient in the world, and the mixed peaks and valleys characteristic of the region create a topography that, as paired with Appalachia's location within the temperate zone, is conducive to rich animal and plant species.[5] Appalachian biodiversity has, tragically, been much degraded—as is typified worldwide via the current (intertwined) climate change, mass extinction, and habitat loss crises, as detailed in chapter 5. And as the ecological crisis intensifies, Appalachia, like other global regions, will face increasing threats to the environment and human communities alike.[6]

APPALACHIA'S EARLY HISTORY

As Richard Drake chronicles in *A History of Appalachia*, Native Americans were the first human inhabitants in Appalachia. Indigenous populations were present in the region at least as early as 6000 B.C. Prior to the Euro-American conquest, the Cherokee people, among others, were populous in southern Appalachia, including the present-day states of North Carolina, South Carolina, and Georgia. In contrast, North Central Appalachian territories such as present-day West Virginia, Virginia, and Pennsylvania were populated, for instance, by Algonquian groups like the Shawnee and Delaware. And such groups as the Mohawk, Seneca, and Oneida populated northernmost Appalachia (e.g., New York).[7] However, these are general examples only, as, "by the time of European contact, hundreds of Native languages, cultural beliefs, environmental adaptations, residence patterns, and social orders were broadly dispersed across the region."[8]

As chapter 2 explores, human communities, as part and parcel of ecological systems, always have interacted with such systems through varying modes of production—and the diverse indigenous peoples of pre-Columbian North America were no exception to such material-historical realities.[9] However, prior to the Euro-American conquest, "the pressure on the land and resources in this period does not seem to be exceptionally great."[10] As is discussed below, though, in tandem with the Euro-conquest—and the introduction of the capitalist mode of production—Appalachia would become marked by widespread and often-irreversible ecological devastation.

The Spanish were the first Europeans in Appalachia, entering the region in the sixteenth century. It was the Spanish who applied the name *Apalchen* to the region after an indigenous people of Florida.[11] To be sure, in the subsequent century, contact between indigenous communities and Europeans, such as in the context of nascent commerce (e.g., the fur and slave trades), wrought disastrous outcomes on indigenous communities. As Wilma Dunaway notes in *The First American Frontier*, for Native Americans in southern Appalachia, "articulation with the European world economy" resulted in depopulation from such sources as "epidemics, from slavery, from warfare, from famines, and from alcoholism."[12] Thus, indigenous communities were beset by egregious and multitudinous harms at the hands of Euro-Americans.

The genocide and forced removal of Native American peoples, in Appalachia and beyond, is no doubt one of the great historical crimes. However, in a foundational sense, it must also be noted that the tragedies perpetrated on Appalachian indigenous communities served as a foundational capitalist event in the region. Put most succinctly: "U.S. capitalism is founded on the genocide of Native Americans."[13] Hegemonic liberal capitalism's core drive of ceaseless capital accumulation—and its methods in achieving such ends vis-à-vis subordination of marginalized peoples and the environment—began, in the United States, with the systemic oppression and destruction of indigenous peoples. Thereafter, U.S. economic expansion would be largely dependent on exploitation of resources seized from indigenous populations. And so, too, were indigenous populations exploited through other dimensions, as Euro-Americans also, for instance, perpetuated the historical crime of slavery on Native Americans.[14]

PREINDUSTRIAL APPALACHIA

But the comprehensive Euro-American colonization would come to Appalachia. Significantly, some debate exists regarding many core economic and socio-cultural characteristics of this era—generally termed "preindustrial Appalachia." This debate emanates from the central fact that, as Ronald Lewis notes, "Appalachia is a region without a formal history."[15] Appalachia is often said to lack a formal history because popular conceptions of the region have long been informed by pervasive—and deeply exploitative—cultural stereotypes; that is, Appalachians are homogenized as an isolated and culturally backwards people who are supposedly prone to laziness, deviancy, violence, and the like, or Appalachia as a "land that time forgot." As Lewis and others have chronicled, such conceptions were first established in the "fertile minds of late nineteenth-century local color writers."[16] An early example includes *A Strange Land and a Peculiar People*, an 1873 travelogue by William Wallace Harney. More influential, however, were John Fox Jr.'s novels centering on

Appalachia, which were a dominant factor "in the creation of Appalachian 'otherness.'"[17]

By the twentieth century, such problematic conceptions of Appalachia were firmly embedded in the national consciousness. As the decades passed, such representations would become increasingly "accepted and then reified as 'history' by subsequent reporters, scholars, and policy makers."[18] Henry Shapiro has termed this phenomenon the "myth of Appalachia"—which is a particularly apt characterization now prominent in the Appalachian studies literature.[19] Thus, the long-dominant conception of Appalachian preindustrial culture is not based on evidence; rather, the myth of Appalachia is based on "a complex intertextual reality" that approaches the "diverse preindustrial localities in the southern mountains as if each were representative of a single, regionwide folk society."[20] The myth of Appalachia persists as a toxic phenomenon—and in new, insidious manifestations—in the present era, as has recently been discussed in such works as Elizabeth Catte's *What You Are Getting Wrong About Appalachia* and the collected work *Appalachian Reckoning*. As is discussed in subsequent chapters, combating these contemporary manifestations of the myth also is an important dimension of *Remaking Appalachia*.[21]

What is more, the myth of Appalachia was also affirmatively deployed by the nascent timber and coal industries (and complicit allies) to achieve the long-term, structural subordination of the regional citizenry and environment. As Lewis writes, the establishment of the Appalachian myth by John Fox Jr. and others had the effect of facilitating "absentee corporate hegemony by marginalizing [Appalachian] residents economically and politically."[22] Thus, "'Appalachia' was a willful creation and not merely the product of literary imagination."[23] Similarly, Shannon Elizabeth Bell has noted that a "large body of scholarship has argued that the Appalachian region was, in actuality, an 'invention' of outside groups" with a significant motive including "capitalists seeking to exploit the region for its coal and timber resources."[24] The Appalachian myth was, therefore, not only false—but also explicitly formulated and deployed so as to effectuate the long-term, multidimensional subordination of the region.

The myth of Appalachia constitutes an important dimension in exploring the region as an "energy sacrifice zone." The sacrifice zone model holds that certain regions are deemed acceptable for environmental despoliation in order to serve a greater national good. In the specific Appalachian sacrifice zone context, the region's environment and citizenry are exploited via natural resource extraction in order to maintain low energy prices for the United States at large (i.e., to the ultimate benefit of elite capital interests). Stereotyping

Appalachians as an "othered" citizenry thus supports this process.[25] As Rodger Cunningham notes, "the material-historical cause of stereotyping Appalachians is, of course, that America wants our land and our resources and must therefore persuade itself that these are not presently possessed by full-fledged human beings."[26] And as Bell adds, "the social construction of Appalachia as 'premodern' or 'savage' has allowed it to serve as a 'sacrificial scapegoat' for the atrocities of capitalism, normalizing devastating practices."[27] Also under the sacrifice zone model, such cultural "otherings" are intertwined with separating out Appalachia's physical landscape from that of the broader nation, as "together, the landscape and the people are homogenized," and thus Appalachia's "destruction is imagined as not affecting the rest of the world."[28]

Numerous commentators have proffered significant work reexamining preindustrial Appalachia's characteristics. Ronald Eller published an early work as part of this movement: *Miners, Millhands, and Mountaineers.* Per Eller's influential account, period Appalachia was largely marked by agrarian self-sufficiency; Eller argues that "until the industrial transition at the turn of the twentieth century, 'few areas of the United States more closely exemplified Thomas Jefferson's vision of a democratic society.'"[29] More specifically, according to this account, in "preindustrial Appalachia mountaineers owned their own farms, worked the land as a family unit, and employed a strategy of household self-sufficiency that allowed them to avoid reliance on the market economy."[30] Eller also discusses the fact that Appalachian farms offered "full support and sustenance for mountain families" vis-à-vis garden crops, foraging (e.g., ginseng), and the grazing of livestock such as cattle, sheep, and hogs.[31] Widespread self-sufficiency was also achieved as Appalachian families devised all manner of goods required for mountain life, including tools, homespun clothing, and so on.[32] Eller also posits that areas of preindustrial Appalachia, to a perhaps remarkable degree, constituted a largely classless society—due in large part to the roughly equitable material conditions among the predominant "yeoman farmer" class. To wit, in the "rural areas of Appalachia, the lack of overt class consciousness was reflected in the emergence of strong egalitarian attitudes and beliefs."[33]

Eller's influential account is no doubt accurate in part, at least as regards certain localities and time periods. Moreover, as is argued in the latter chapters of *Remaking Appalachia*, this Appalachian tradition of subsistence farming can indeed help inform contemporary efforts towards solidarity economy– and subsistence-based transformations in the region—as is required in the age of the Capitalocene. Significantly, however, in more recent decades, the universality of such precapitalist, agrarian-ideal conceptions have been usefully challenged by many commentators. Crucial to this reexamination of preindustrial Appalachia involves claims to its precapitalist nature. As Lewis argues:

> Much recent scholarship either refutes or greatly revises the standard perspective of preindustrial Appalachia as an isolated frontier. This is particularly true if isolation is understood as the absence of commercial or cultural linkages with regional and/or national markets. Appalachians were not "precapitalist" either, strictly speaking, for even the earliest settlers emigrated from areas where capitalist terms of exchange were well understood. No one generalization holds true for the entire region or over time.[34]

Scholarship has thus demonstrated that a "wide variety of economic activities have been documented in Appalachia, taking us far beyond the marginal hard-scrabble hill farm stereotype."[35] In contrast to subsistence-based modes only, such work has documented the presence of larger-scale farms engaged in, for instance, the production of livestock for the market. Appalachian economic activities also included a manufacturing sector that arose in period Appalachia, which included gristmills, tanyards, and sawmills. So, too, were the salt and iron industries extremely important sectors in period Appalachia—and both helped catalyze early development of the coal industry. Thus, according to more recent accounts of preindustrial Appalachia, the region was characterized by more diversified economic activities.[36]

Dunaway argues from a world systems perspective that capitalism indeed was integrated into Appalachia from its outset. In *The First American Frontier*, Dunaway posits that "Appalachia was a peripheral region of an emergent world capitalist system and was linked to that system of exchange as a supplier of raw materials from its inception."[37] This occurred, even prior to comprehensive Euro-American colonization, in conjunction with indigenous populations; for instance, the Cherokee exchanged raw commodities (e.g., animal skins) with Euro-Americans as part of triangular trade-based commodity chains.[38] It was through this trade that "Cherokee village activities were restructured into an export economy" geared towards these markets.[39]

The Euro-American conquest therefore resulted in an Appalachia that "was *born capitalist*,"[40] as the settlers were largely direct descendants from earlier colonists who emigrated "from an agricultural and mercantile capitalist country about to enter into the industrial revolution."[41] And in the time thereafter, the long-term "incorporation of Southern Appalachia into the capitalist world system entailed nearly 150 years of societal, politico-economic, and cultural change," in that this incorporation entailed "creating a peripheral zone that is situated in modern times within the geographical boundaries of one of the core countries in the world system."[42] Thus, capitalism—and indeed industrialization—did not begin with the coal industry in Appalachia. Intricate market forces had long been at work in the region.

Such scholarship also raises important questions about the ecological sustainability—and thus, ultimately, the long-term viability—of Appalachian agricultural practices in this period and thereafter. For instance, in *Ramp Hollow*, Steven Stoll examines the swidden method, through which small Appalachian landowners and squatters burned forest area to create agricultural clearings for rotational planting.[43] On the one hand, Stoll notes that an overarching dependence on the surrounding ecosystem (namely, the forest) made such Appalachians "environmental managers by default."[44] However, on the other, Stoll notes that the ecological sustainability of widespread swidden technique became "a questionable strategy where a larger population made land to shift in more scarce."[45] Dunaway also asserts that Appalachian mountain agriculture, as steeped in capitalist production practices, was ecologically destructive. Specifically, as "resettlers reorganize[d] the mountains into a capitalist agroecosystem" in the latter eighteenth century, this produced the effect of "loss of biodiversity."[46] Moreover, as the "mountain ecosystem becomes increasingly articulated with and dominated by the capitalist world-ecosystem," Dunaway notes that this produces "irreversible loss of biodiversity, lability, subsidence, and climate changes that do not occur in other ecosystems."[47] (And so, too, does Paul Salstrom broach such farming-sustainability issues—as emanating from population growth and other factors—which, per his analysis, also predates the timber- and coal-based period of rapid industrial growth; Salstrom's work is discussed in chapter 3 in the context of longer-term Appalachian agricultural decline.)

Contemporary Appalachian studies work also has reexamined the demographic and cultural characteristics of preindustrial Appalachia—and has similarly produced diverse findings. As an important example, in the context of racial and ethnic demographics, much work has demonstrated that period Appalachia was more heterogeneous than popular accounts often attest—which have traditionally focused on false notions of homogenous, Scots-Irish demographics.[48] Much of the migrant population was considered of German, Italian, English, Corkian, and French Huguenot descent, among other European groups; and, of course, aside from the Euro-colonizer demographics, Native Americans also continued to populate Appalachia.[49]

African Americans—both free and slave—also populated preindustrial

Appalachia, thus implicating the region in America's second great historical crime. Slavery was exceedingly common in Appalachian areas of Virginia, Georgia, South Carolina, and Alabama, particularly where cotton and tobacco cultivation were prevalent. Slave labor was also relied on in West Virginia, Kentucky, Tennessee, and in Appalachia areas of Maryland and North Carolina.[50] Thus, broadly speaking, "slavery was entrenched across Southern Appalachia in an uneven pattern that reflected crop specializations, degree of industrialization, and commercial expansion."[51]

A central focal point of *Remaking Appalachia* is an overarching critique of both historic and contemporary liberalism—and slavery constituted a core factor in the establishment of U.S. economic liberalism. Slavery was a foundational element of classical liberalism as implemented in antebellum America: it has been convincingly argued that the "enslavement of Africans and their descendants provided the foundation of America's 'liberal' economy."[52] Slaves were central to the production of cash crops (e.g., cotton, tobacco, and indigo), then-staples of the goods on which the period capitalist markets depended. And slaves' "free labor was both the 'good' and the 'service' used to increase America's budding wealth."[53] Thus, the development of period capitalism in Appalachia—notably including the coal industry, which relied in part on slave labor[54]—was intertwined with slavery, and must be accounted for in any historical reckoning with Appalachia's economic, social, and cultural development.

Also of central importance to *Remaking Appalachia*, patriarchal conditions were the status quo in preindustrial Appalachia. Undoubtedly, Appalachian "white males held the greatest power, privilege, and freedom within the social order."[55] Adult white men, for instance, owned the most property and most often engaged in market-related work. For white men in Appalachia, work "outside the domestic realm" was their province, and "they were trained from an early age to assume the obligations and rewards of the dominant role."[56]

Appalachian women were, in contrast, often engaged in unpaid, home-related labor, and generally were subordinated by male heads of households. For instance, on smaller Appalachian farms, typical gendered work performed by women included child care, elderly and sick care, and routine maintenance of the household. Women also were responsible for "tending the family garden plot, poultry, and livestock" and were "expected to contribute labor in the fields."[57] On smaller-scale Appalachian farms, then, "poorer farm women" transitioned "back and forth continually between household subsistence work, activities to generate a few market commodities, and semiwage labor arrangements" so as to meet the "survival needs of their households."[58] As Dwight Billings and Kathleen Blee conclude in *The Road to Poverty*, "adult men were the beneficiaries of nonmarket patriarchal restrictions on the labor force participation of women and children, even in highly market-oriented economies," and the "idea of yeoman farmers as agents of a precapitalist mentalité of cooperation and egalitarianism effectively diverts attention from the patriarchal control that male farmers exercised over their wives, children, and other household members as well as the strategies of resistance exercised by household subordinates."[59]

Patriarchal conditions in preindustrial Appalachia, however, are best characterized as complex. Western society—both precapitalist and capitalist—indeed exhibits varying patriarchal modes as a central through-line. The feudal system, for instance, was fundamentally a "masculine world."[60] However, it has been observed that women often "demonstrated great productive capacity when society was organized on the basis of family and domestic industry."[61] For instance, in the Appalachian agricultural context, "women had been directly involved in all phases of rural production in farm economies."[62] Capitalism's emergence, though, resulted in individual wages displacing family earnings—with men dominating paid employment in the marketplace and women typically engaged in unpaid domestic-related work.[63]

Such a distinction implicates the important critical terminology of reproductive versus productive labor. Traditionally, male-associated productive labor involves waged work within the marketplace (i.e., the production of goods and services within the economy), whereas female-associated reproductive labor, which can be both unpaid and paid, refers to "the activities involved in maintaining and reproducing the labor force," such as childcare and domestic work.[64] As Mignon Duffy explains, because raising children creates the new workforce and because "workers would not be able to work, or at least not as productively, without being fed, having clean clothes, and having a clean bed to sleep in," as a consequence, "women's unpaid activities in the home are indispensable to the functioning of a market economy."[65] While reproductive labor generally is associated with unpaid work, even paid reproductive labor, as traditionally performed by and associated with women, is marginalized and socially devalued under liberal capitalism.[66] This gendered division of labor often was justified by the so-called natural order, but, of course, the ultimate beneficiaries were hegemonic owners of capital that exploited largely female-performed unpaid reproductive work—in addition to the environment (i.e., per the ecofeminist account, discussed more fully below)—in order to maximize capital accumulation.[67] Insofar as preindustrial Appalachia was marked by subsistence practices, then, capitalism's gendered division of labor was less fully operationalized. But the coming of industrial capitalism in Appalachia rapidly furthered such gender-based transformations.

It should also be noted that the myth of Appalachia is steeped in false notions of a universalized preindustrial Appalachian culture.[68] This supposed homogenized culture involves a complex amalgamation of essentially positive-deemed, unique traits such as egalitarian yeoman self-sufficiency—but also negative traits relating to cultural backwardness and deviancy. However, considered scholarship demonstrates that there is scant evidence "that antebellum Appalachians identified themselves as a region unified by a common culture that was distinct from the rest of the South."[69] Like other rural American areas, Appalachia constituted a diffusion of "varied cultures"—which is hardly surprising, given the diverse ethnic, racial, and cultural composition of the region (i.e., that the myth of Appalachia has long veiled).[70]

Dunaway argues that insofar as there existed a predominant cultural characteristic in preindustrial Appalachia, it was marked by capitalist-produced class subordination—wherein local Appalachian elites exploited the greater regional citizenry. As Dunaway argues, capitalism always "gives birth to a cultural sphere predominantly divided along class lines."[71] Thus, rather than "cultural differentiation," it was the "*internal cultural division of labor* between the region's elites and the masses of the population" that best characterizes preindustrial Appalachia.[72] This was because property and political power were often concentrated into the elites' hands, and so the "Appalachian minority could utilize their local positions to sustain within their communities an exploitative division of labor."[73] To this class-focused analysis we can add the other intersecting exploitative dimensions of period capitalism discussed above; that is, that economic and social systems in Appalachia were dependent on the exploitation of marginalized groups such as African Americans, indigenous populations, and women; and so, too, was Appalachia marked by compound forms of oppression, as African American Appalachian women, for instance, experienced subordination related to both gender and white supremacy.

Accordingly, a central thrust of Appalachian studies literature is that the region's long-term subordination cannot be traced to external elites only—typified by the Appalachian "internal colony model" developed in the 1970s. This is because internal elites, as embedded in hegemonic liberalism, have *always* exploited the greater Appalachian citizenry.[74] Thus, there is a fundamental flaw in characterizing all historic (and contemporary) Appalachians as homogenized victims of outside exploitative interests. Appalachian citizens are not—and have never been—separate from the ill-effects of hegemonic liberalism, as demonstrated by the interlocking systems of subordination that have been endemic to the region (albeit through various manifestations) from the Euro-conquest onwards.

APPALACHIA'S PERIOD OF RAPID TIMBER- AND COAL-BASED INDUSTRIAL GROWTH

Appalachia's first mined coal seams were, as logic might dictate, located in many of the coal-rich areas initially colonized. This included the hard coal of the Pennsylvania region in addition to the bituminous coal of the eastern-most Appalachian areas in states such as Virginia. In contrast, exploitation of Central Appalachia's immense, but more remote, bituminous coalfields occurred later in time.[75] In the early 1800s, Appalachian coal was first utilized as a domestic heating fuel and for the direct firing of forges; also at this time, rather than relying on coal, U.S. ironworks generally utilized charcoal (as derived from timber).[76] However, as the century progressed, "coal fueled the Industrial Revolution in the United States."[77] Truly explosive growth of the Appalachian coal industry occurred in the post–Civil War era. A number of factors prohibited earlier exploitation of the region's resources: lack of extensive transportation modes, massive capital requirements, an insufficient labor force, and the gathering of requisite legal title to property.[78]

Developing adequate industrial-scale transportation modes into Appalachia proved a key project for capitalists. During the early nineteenth century, modest quantities of coal and timber were essentially floated downriver. And at the mid-century point, vast swaths of North Central Appalachian territories established coal outlets largely through railroads and canals.[79] However, coalfields in more remote areas of Appalachia would not be opened until railway lines were cut through the mountains in the 1870s and 1880s, thus providing coalfield access in Central Appalachian territories in southern West Virginia, eastern Tennessee, eastern Kentucky, and southwestern Virginia.[80] Much capital was also required to open the Appalachian coalfields. Capital was required, among other reasons, to acquire coalfield lands and mineral resources, establish pertinent infrastructure, and to establish the transportation modes discussed above.[81]

As for obtaining legal title to Appalachian property, in the latter portions of the nineteenth century, preliminary steps involved prospectors identifying specific coalfields.[82] Investors next acquired property rights in coalfield resources, but Appalachia was marked by uncertain legal title, due to such factors as competing state and English grants and conflicts between large, often-absentee landowners and squatters—or "would-be yeomen without clear title" in Appalachia.[83] As Stoll explains, "the swidden-and-cabin folk hunted deer, gathered ramps, and planted corn and beans as though the forest belonged to them," and a "variety of use-right customs continued, under the awareness and without the knowledge of absentee owners"—and indeed "squatter households eventually claimed to own land they had improved, establishing boundaries with neighbors as best they could."[84] This sometimes involved squatters writing deeds and filing them in local courthouses.[85] Compounding these issues were specific legal developments such as a Virginia Land Law that enabled transfer of land grants of Revolutionary War veterans—thus resulting in absentee speculators purchasing "millions of acres from veterans, often for a mere pittance."[86]

Speculators' acquirement of Appalachian property was often carried out in a questionable ethical and legal manner, as "the mineral buyers came to the Appalachian farmer with gold, charm, legal maneuver, and sometimes fraud."[87] What is more, many speculators offered not to buy the entire land, but rather the mineral rights only. This left the surface rights, including tax liability, to the Appalachian surface landowner (this phenomenon often is termed severing the mineral rights).[88] As is discussed in chapter 3, these deeds created disastrous circumstances in time, as small landowners "not only . . . lost all rights to the minerals below the land, but they had also relinquished such other rights to the surface of the land as to limit its use for residential or agricultural purposes."[89] Therefore, during this era, millions of surface land acres in addition to both mineral and timber resources were transferred from Appalachian landowners to absentee corporate owners.[90] And as is discussed in subsequent chapters, the legacy of mass absentee ownership of Appalachian land persists as a core structural issue for the region. A minority of local Appalachians was complicit in this massive land- and mineral-transfer phenomenon. It has been observed that despite "the crucial role played by outside agents in the selling of the mountains, that played by local speculators was almost equally important."[91]

The establishment of the Appalachian timber industry has been chronicled in works such as Lewis's *Transforming the Appalachian Countryside*.[92] Generally speaking, Appalachian timber would rise in demand at the end of the nineteenth century.[93] Before large-scale industrial timbering commenced in Appalachia, there was an initial period marked by local-based cultivation practices steeped in selective cutting; however, "after 1890, most of the railroads had continued to build branch lines deeper into the mountains, enabling the lumber companies to establish their mills close to the source of the timber supply."[94] Once industrial-scale timbering commenced in the region, the decimation of Appalachian old-growth forests advanced at a rapid rate. As compared to the prior era of selective cutting, the fully industrialized timber industry, as eventually involving machine logging, was a year-round enterprise involving thousands of dedicated company loggers. Eventually, "entire mountains were clear-cut and left to erode with the spring rains," and "these logging practices [began] to take their toll on the Appalachian hardwoods," as "the cutting of commercial trees was usually carried out with little or no concern for future growth."[95] As Lewis chronicles, "two-thirds of West Virginia was still covered by ancient growth hardwood forest on the eve of the transition in 1880, but by the 1920s virtually the entire state had been deforested."[96]

The full industrial maturation of the timber industry also resulted in an early, important challenge to Appalachian agrarianism. As industrial timbering occurred year-round, many Appalachians abandoned agricultural modes in pursuit of corporate timber employment, because like the coal industry company towns, logging camps and settlements were established as housing in the region.[97] Thus, in "a comparatively few years," much of the particularly younger population "which previously had earned its living from the land," was "induced to work on the railroad or in the logging camps and lumber towns."[98] Significantly, although corporate officials—and regional elites—claimed that widespread industrialization would enhance material conditions and quality of life in Appalachia, the realities of the period labor transitions often proved otherwise. For instance, during this era, hundreds of thousands of Appalachians transitioned to mill villages, which for many constituted a substantial break from traditional yeoman culture—especially as mill village conditions often proved sub-optimal.[99]

During this time period, the timber industry and related industrial sectors indeed wrought substantial negative impacts on Appalachia.[100] However, by the turn of the century, the coal industry arose as the preeminent industrial force in Appalachia.[101] The Industrial Revolution was fueled almost entirely by coal, as Eller details that it fired factories, trains, and the like—and would in time fuel the nascent electric power plant infrastructure; so, too, would processed coal, or "coke," become central to the steel and iron industry.[102] Thus, demand for Appalachian coal radically increased, leading to the rise of a core group of mining corporations—but also of hundreds of smaller operations.[103] The Central Appalachian coalfields, which contained the largest deposits of bituminous coal, achieved market dominance at this time. Central Appalachia's coal was of a higher quality by the era's standards—and was produced at a greater profit due to favorable geographic and labor conditions (from the standpoint of the capitalists). National demand for coal steadily increased in the first decades of the twentieth century.[104]

The ascension of coal to its dominant position within the fossil fuel hegemony was achieved through the profound subordination of the Appalachian citizenry and environment. For the Appalachian citizenry, the transition to such exploitative industrial conditions is best exemplified by the so-called company town—the most notable feature of turn-of-the-century Appalachian mining life—which involved establishing communities from the ground up for miners and their dependents.[105] Company towns were a singular innovation, first and foremost, because the corporate coal operator—as compared to a state entity—was responsible for governing all aspects of mining family life, as the company owned not just the land, but also all houses, stores, churches, and so forth.[106]

Company control in some instances extended to mandatory habitation within coal housing. This was partially due to the fact that, initially, coal operators struggled with Appalachian miners abandoning mining sites to work on family farms or to engage in other seasonal activities (e.g., hunting).[107] Thus, to combat these trends, many companies often mandated company town habitation.[108] Mandatory habitation also constituted a mechanism of labor control; mining families were "concentrated so as to have proper supervision over them, to better control them in terms of labor agitation and threatened strikes."[109] Additionally, comprehensive company control notoriously involved scrip—a closed corporate currency system. Scrip was only convertible at company-owned stores, which often, given their monopoly status, adopted inflated prices. This allowed coal operators to reap yet further profits, as payments via "scrip ensured that a portion of a worker's paycheck would be funneled back to the company."[110] Because coal operator power was "pervasive, extending over almost every facet of village affairs,"[111] this has led some commentators to characterize company town life as a form of "corporate feudalism,"[112] or likewise as "oppressive serf-like conditions."[113] Due to such exploitative conditions, in a telling legal distinction, courts of the era determined that the relationship between coal operator and miner transcended mere landlord-tenant—and was that of "master to servant."[114]

Although there existed variation, Eller notes that company towns—sometimes constructed and maintained at minimum expense—could provide poor and unsafe living conditions. For instance, in 1925, the U.S. Coal Commission found that "on the whole, living conditions in the mining camps of the southern mountains were among the worst in the nation."[115] Company towns were also frequently beset by unsafe environmental conditions due to abysmal—and sometimes nonexistent—sanitation infrastructure, prevalent mine pollution, and the like; thus, corporate-managed conditions were deleterious to both the human communities and the broader environment. For instance, local streams and other waterways became polluted with refuse from coal towns and mine-produced acid runoff. So, too, did coal dust blanket company towns, and "mounds of coal and 'gob' piles of discarded mine waste" were a fixture in coalfield areas.[116] The lack of a sanitation infrastructure compounded these environmental issues in company towns, thus polluting "land and water resources in the coal districts, causing serious health problems in some areas."[117]

In the context of broader ecological damage, the nascent mining industry wrought disastrous outcomes on the region; and as will be discussed in subsequent chapters, such mining-produced devastation would only intensify throughout the twentieth century and beyond. During the early phase of industrialized Appalachian mining, Eller chronicles that the "pollution of the creeks and rivers from human waste and from the acid runoff of the mines was so great" that, in some circumstances, in the areas "around many of the streams the animal life completely disappeared."[118] As discussed in chapter 2, coal operators—through legal mechanisms such as the broad form deed—were also granted extensive rights to degrade surface owners' land in Appalachia. That is, "the sale of mineral rights also granted the coal operators the right to pollute their streams and air; destroy their spring, which may have been the only source of drinking water; and destroy the surface land through subsidence cracks, fissures, swales and floods."[119] Thus, at the turn of century period and thereafter, the coal industry wrought extensive damage to the Appalachian landscape. Moreover, as chapter 2 details, the liberal legal regime of the era was wholly ineffective in combating such destruction.

DEMOGRAPHIC TRANSITIONS DURING RAPID INDUSTRIALIZATION

Appalachia underwent dramatic demographic transitions during the period of rapid industrial growth; such changes were due, in large part, to coal industry recruitment practices. In particular, African Americans who hailed largely from the South were recruited in addition to immigrants from essentially all European regions—but of southern and eastern Europe (e.g., Italy) especially. Ultimately, due to the influx of such a diverse labor workforce, the "ethnic composition of the mountains began to change . . . almost as drastically as it had at the turn of the nineteenth."[120] However, heterogeneous coalfield populations were most notably a characteristic of Central Appalachia. In the coal regions of northern West Virginia, for instance, miners were almost universally deemed "white." And in southernmost coal regions such as Alabama and Georgia, African Americans performed the majority of coal labor. In Central Appalachia, however, coal operators cultivated a "judicious mixture" of "blacks, native whites, and foreign-born whites"—both to meet labor demands and also to create a "balance that the owners thought would keep labor most easily controlled and docile" by pitting group against group, which ultimately facilitated profit maximization.[121]

African Americans constituted a large percentage of period Central Appalachian miners. In an earlier era, slaves were utilized as Appalachian coal labor; and post–Civil War, many African Americans labored in mines that previously had worked on railway construction. However, the Appalachian African American population did not increase substantially until the coal boom intensified, when additional labor was required to supplement the ranks of the pre-existing mining workforce. By 1920, "43 percent of the black miners employed in the United States worked in West Virginia, and the vast majority of those lived in the southern part of the state."[122] Moreover, in McDowell County, West Virginia, "over 45 percent of the miners . . . were black, and one of the major towns of the county, Keystone, was predominantly black."[123]

Like many Appalachians, African American miners and their dependents would be required to adjust to a largely post-agrarian manner of life. As Joe Trotter chronicles in *Coal, Class, and Color*, as African Americans "abandoned southern life and labor for work in the coalfields . . . their rural and semirural work culture gradually gave way to the imperatives of industrial capitalism. New skills, work habits, and occupational hazards moved increasingly to the fore, gradually supplanting their older rural work patterns and rhythms."[124] Systemic racism also was a characteristic of the coalfields. In a general sense, coal operator recruitment practices for African American laborers were misleading—as the difficult and dangerous realities of the coalfields were not communicated to would-be miners. African American miners also were limited to lower-level positions and generally could not enter management.[125] (Note, though, that wages earned by African American miners in the Central Appalachia coalfields generally were equal by period expectations.)[126] Housing segregation also was endemic to Central Appalachian company towns. So, too, did Appalachian whites perpetuate racially motivated violence against African Americans in the southern Appalachia coalfields: "Incidents of racial violence were not uncommon," and "lynchings and assaults were frequently reported in the local newspapers."[127]

Significantly, industrial racism was not characteristic of the turn-of-the-century period alone. An additional and notorious exemplar of industrial racism was the Hawk's Nest Tunnel Disaster, which occurred in West Virginia in the early 1930s—and which has been characterized as "America's worst industrial disaster."[128] At Hawk's Nest, substantial African American labor was relied on for hazardous tunnel drilling in support of a large hydroelectric project. However, corporate operators knowingly exposed these workers to extreme health harms, as a dry drilling method was selected over a safer wet method. Consequently, upwards of five hundred men would perish from acute silicosis, a form of dust-caused respiratory disorder, with "disproportionate black deaths among the work crews."[129] The profound tragedy of Hawk's Nest therefore demonstrates aptly the industrial racism characteristic of the period of rapid industrialization and beyond.

European immigrants constituted the second large population of period Central Appalachian miners; foreign labor was sought due to an acute labor demand coupled with corporate dissatisfaction with the preexisting mining population. Immigrant miners hailed predominantly from southern and eastern European countries. Specifically, the "largest ethnic group to immigrate to the mountains were the Italians, although large numbers of Poles, Hungarians, and Slavs arrived as well."[130] Such European immigration increased dramatically during the first decades of the twentieth century. Some coal operators, such as the U.S. Coal and Oil Company, in fact utilized foreign-born miners as the majority workforce in some areas; by the eve of World War I, the influx of European immigrant miners peaked.[131] Similar to African American miners, many European immigrants were misled about the dangerous work conditions (and also about their ultimate geographic location). And foreign-born miners also experienced segregated housing in mining towns.[132]

By the World War I period, however, the rapid demographic transitions that had brought such diverse populations ebbed in Central Appalachia. This occurred for a variety of reasons. Numerous European immigrant miners returned to Europe; other miners left Appalachia in pursuit of employment in northern industrial centers that offered better compensation and working conditions.[133] Of course, intertwined, white supremacist–steeped Appalachian social structures also directly contributed to minority population out-migration at this time and thereafter. As a result, most recent arrivals to the Appalachian coalfields would not remain long-term: "few blacks and immigrants stayed on in the region to become a permanent part of mountain life."[134] Many, however, would remain in the region, thus contributing to an often-overlooked Appalachian heterogeneity that persists to this day (i.e., as veiled by the myth of Appalachia).

GENDERED DIVISION OF LABOR IN COAL TOWNS

A strict gendered division of labor existed in period company towns. In the first place, Appalachian women were afforded scant control over the transition to coal-based industrialization and related developments in Appalachia. By and large, Appalachian men made decisions to sell surface lands and mineral rights, and again "as the necessary infrastructure was constructed."[135] Therefore, women generally exercised minimal control over nascent coalfield development, and thereafter the company "decisions about the composition of the labor force, efficient ways to support and reproduce that labor force, and tolerable degrees of economic diversity resulted in a rigid division and valuing of labor by sex in the coalfields."[136]

Once coal towns were established, women were indeed beholden to a strict gendered division of labor. As Virginia Rinaldo Seitz writes in *Class, Gender, and Resistance in the Appalachian Coalfields*: "The gendered division of labor [was] intensified in and around the coal camps and mining towns," because while "family life was completely dominated by the coal companies through company-owned housing and stores, women were relegated to the home."[137] Women were banned from mining employment in company towns—and even their close proximity to mining sites was widely characterized as "bad luck."[138] This division of labor was not absolute, as coal town women, for instance, earned wages through such employment as nursing, running boarding houses, and working as teachers, domestic servants, and seamstresses. However, in an overarching sense, a patriarchal, gendered division of labor was the status quo.

Coal town operators benefited immensely from this gendered division of labor, which, as compared to preindustrial Appalachian modes, more radically operationalized capitalism's divide between (male-)productive and (female-) reproductive work. As introduced above, capitalism is dependent on unpaid, largely women-performed reproductive work for maximum capital accumulation: "If capitalists compensated women for all their externalized costs and unpaid labor, prices would be driven up so high that most commodities would not be competitive in the world-economy."[139] In the Appalachian coal town context, capital accumulation was thus maximized by leveraging the unpaid, reproductive work of women—in addition to (also socially devalued) paid reproductive work—such as child and elder care, cooking and cleaning, and so forth. The coal town "captured garden" phenomenon constitutes an important exemplar of exploitative unpaid labor. Coal companies variously mandated or encouraged families to plant gardens (which women often worked)—that had the effect of enhancing the health and thus efficiency of workers while also reducing "the wages they paid by shifting the burden of survival onto laboring households."[140] The ultimate effect of such exploitative conditions was that company towns could pay miners wages that fell "far below the cost of reproducing the household."[141]

This gendered division of labor had far-reaching effects on gender regimes in Appalachia. Sally Ward Maggard discusses the import of these transitions in "From Farm to Coal Camp to Back Office and McDonald's":

For men, leaving agriculture for coal mining meant working inside the coal mines in exchange for wages. Men lost control over the means of economic production, but their labor was understood as central to the economy. Women, too, lost control over the means of production. Now their economic survival depended on their connections to the men in their households who earned miners' wages.[142]

The full-scale transition to industrial capitalism in Appalachia thus had the effect generally of separating both Appalachian men and women from control over the means of production; however, men were afforded the more privileged position of wage-earning laborers (i.e., of productive labor), while women largely performed unpaid reproductive work. As Bell and York note, this "gender ideology has not only had implications for who does what work, it has also meant that men are favored as the center of community, work, and politics in Central Appalachia."[143] Coal operators then intentionally "equat[ed] masculinity with a willingness to work in dangerous conditions" and femininity with unpaid domestic labor.[144]

The ill-effects of this gender regime, in which male laborers suffered under exploitative conditions and women became dependent on male heads of households, were both insidious and manifested themselves across different dimensions. As Seitz notes, for instance, on gender-based violence: "Men released their frustrations and anger on themselves and other miners" and also "on their wives and children."[145] As is discussed in subsequent chapters, this division of labor had implications that extend into the modern era in Appalachia.

It must be emphasized from a material-historical perspective that the experience of Appalachian women was not homogenous in period coal towns. A minority of women, of course, had the benefit of higher class-based status— e.g., women in operator households—and therefore were separated in crucial dimensions from working-class women. As Shelly Romalis explains, miners generally "couldn't help comparing their hovels to grand houses, their women's threadbare clothing to operators' wives' fancy dress."[146] And as compared to women in operator households, the working-class women were indeed beset by intensive reproductive labor demands.[147] Romalis thus concludes that a "gendered division of labor . . . occurred within, as well as across, class and ethnic lines."[148] Also, the experience of African American women in company towns was unique. For instance, while African American women largely performed unpaid reproductive work such as household labor, as compared to white women, they more often performed wage-earning domestic work.[149] In fact, a higher percentage of African American women than white women overall were employed as wage earners in company towns.[150]

Broadly speaking, the experience of African American women in coal towns was deeply informed by systemic gender oppression—as compounded by both systemic white supremacy and class oppression (i.e., the latter experienced by all subordinated families in coal towns). Gender subordination also crossed class lines within African American communities, because with "gender issues, the views of the black elite men . . . converged with those of the black proletariat."[151] Like African American men, African American women thus experienced race- and class-based subordination through segregated mining camps and the like—but as further compounded by gender. As Trotter notes, in coal company towns, "white men articulated and practiced clear-cut notions of gender inequality along racial lines, placing white women of any class background on a social plane above their black counterparts," which thus illustrates "the white racist consensus" involving a "distasteful and often vicious stereotypes of black women held by whites of all classes."[152] Therefore, African American women experienced disproportionate and multidimensional subordination in coal company towns, which involved compounded gender-, race-, and class-based oppression.

Such interlocking subordination systems also had crucial intersections with industry-produced environmental devastation in Appalachia. A fundamental characteristic of liberal capitalism—as generally intrinsic in the early capitalist period, throughout the classical liberalism era, and beyond (albeit in varying manifestations)—involves interlocking subordination systems that engender compound forms of oppression along lines of not just gender, race, class, indigenous status, and so forth, but also the environment. Such an analysis is explored most fruitfully via the ecofeminist school (i.e., which is outlined more fully in the latter chapters of *Remaking Appalachia*). For preliminary purposes, however, note that ecofeminism basically holds that a core feature undergirding capitalism's logic is normative dualisms such as masculine and feminine, white and non-white, society and nature, individual and community, rationality and emotion, etc.—in which the first element in each dualism is favored. In this way, under hegemonic patriarchal capitalism, it is rational, autonomous, white male individuals who constitute the economic and political subjects of actual value, whereas marginalized populations such as women and non-whites are "othered," notions of community are generally eschewed, and the environment is exploited—all in achieving maximum profit accumulation on the part of elite interests.[153]

In the context of Appalachian coal towns, then, the industry's massive accumulation of profits was wholly dependent—indeed was only made possible—vis-à-vis intersecting forms of subordination. As examples, the dimensions of such subordination included class, as coal miners and their families were profoundly exploited; gender, through largely female-performed unpaid reproductive work; race, as African American mining communities suffered multifaceted subordination (i.e., including disproportionate impacts on African American women in particular); and the environment, which, as was explored earlier in this chapter, involved ecological despoliation through mining practices, the lack of pertinent sanitation infrastructure, and so forth. Thus, capitalist-driven accumulation of profits in period Appalachian coal towns required not just marginalizing mining communities in a general sense, but more specifically, capital accumulation was wholly dependent on the interlocking subordination systems and compound forms of oppression generally intrinsic to liberal capitalism. (And recall also that the ultimate aim of coal operators in cultivating a "judicious mixture" of mining populations in Central Appalachia was to maximize profits by pitting group against group—i.e., as was dependent on the interlocking racist, nativist, etc. ideologies that ecofeminism investigates.)[154]

COALFIELD UNIONIZING AND THE "COAL WARS"

The development of robust coalfield unionizing activities in Appalachia constitutes a foundational event for modern Appalachia—in addition to a core development in U.S. labor history at large. The industrial strife that erupted between miners and coalfield operators, as centered around unionizing efforts by the United Mine Workers of America (UMWA), would be exceedingly violent. What is more, the organizing activities of period miners was not a historically isolated event; rather, as subsequent chapters of *Remaking Appalachia* chronicle, modern liberatory campaigns in Appalachia along lines of class, the environment, gender, race, etc., echo—and continue to, in many instances, be deeply informed by—these nascent, turn-of-the-century struggles.

That unionizing activities developed early and intensively in Appalachia is logical, given the abysmal labor conditions of the region. In the Appalachian coalfields, "working conditions were miserable at worst and tolerable at best," as "mining has always been [an] inherently dangerous [industry]."[155] What is more, the mining workplace proved uniquely suitable for labor organizing: "Thrust below ground in a wilderness of mysterious tunnels, management could not possibly control labor's contacts on the job as well as they could in a more confined factory setting."[156] The first coalfield unions organized in the northern Appalachian anthracite coalfields in the mid-nineteenth century;

however, inter-union conflicts occurred and there was considerable violence during the "Molly McGuire" strikes.[157]

The historic UMWA union—still in force today—was organized in 1890. From 1890 to the early 1900s, the UMWA emerged victorious in numerous, significant strikes. That violence nevertheless became endemic to coalfield labor disputes is due in no small part to coal operator recalcitrance. For coal operators, "high on the list of activities forbidden in the company town, of course, was 'union agitation,' and most coal companies considered this form of 'mutiny' to be grounds for immediate dismissal from the mine."[158] Put plainly, "few American businessmen were more staunchly opposed to unionization than the Southern coal barons," as they "viewed the union movement as a personal threat not only to their freedom to determine business policies within the mine but to their authority within the company town as well."[159]

Appalachian coalfield conflicts escalated in the post–World War I years. Following the armistice, the UMWA demanded higher wages for miners, which was refused by the operators; a strike thereafter followed, and in time the West Virginia coalfields would become "a center for some of the worst mine violence in U.S. history."[160] Such industrial conflicts were part and parcel of the popularly termed Appalachian "coal wars," which occurred throughout the region during this broad era, and which have been chronicled in works such as Howard Lee's *Bloodletting in Appalachia* and James Green's *The Devil Is Here in These Hills*.

The West Virginia coal wars and related events of this era were marked by a series of exceptional events. One such event was the "Matewan Massacre," which occurred in West Virginia in May 1920. At Matewan, miners exchanged gunfire with agents hired by coal operators from the Baldwin-Felts agency, resulting in the deaths of more than half a dozen men—and which "made national headlines."[161] Industrial violence would later crescendo with the Battle of Blair Mountain, which unfolded as follows:

> Thousands of union miners assembl[ed] in a valley near Charleston in August 1921, armed and ready to launch their "grand offensive" on company territory. This huge uprising of citizens, unprecedented in modern American history, culminated in a three-day battle on Blair Mountain in Logan County between an insurgent army of at least eight thousand workers and a force of three thousand deputies, volunteers, and conscripts, which had been mobilized to stop the miners' army from invading company-controlled territory. The military conflict on Blair Mountain shocked the nation and embarrassed West Virginia's elected officials.[162]

The Battle of Blair Mountain only dissipated when the federal government dispatched U.S. army troops in support of the coal operator. Blair Mountain, which proved to be the largest post–Civil War American battle, demonstrated aptly the legitimate crisis engendered by a fully industrialized Appalachia steeped in the coal industry's deeply exploitative labor practices.[163] Unfortunately, following the loss at Blair Mountain, the influence of organized labor would become much diminished in the coalfields: "the 1920s . . . [were] years in which the control of the region seemed wholly within the hands of the region's coal operators."[164]

African American miners played a significant role in labor organizing during this period. This was aided by the fact that, unlike "most unions, which excluded blacks, the UMWA openly accepted them as full members"—at least in largely non-leadership positions.[165] For instance, as Trotter chronicles in *Coal, Class, and Color*, in the Paint Creek–Cabin Creek strike of 1913 and 1914, "numerous black miners joined white miners in organized confrontations with management," resulting in tangible gains for labor.[166]

Broadly speaking, commentators have observed that at least some degree of solidarity existed along race and class lines in the Central Appalachian coalfields. That is, despite the coal operators' efforts to establish a "judicious mixture" along racial and ethnic lines as a labor-control mechanism to "[play] one group off against another," coal miners nevertheless achieved some degree of solidarity based on a shared sense of exploitation at the hands of operators.[167] As Eller notes, the shared conditions of working underground was likely a great equalizer: "Working side by side in the mines, the men came to depend upon each other for their own safety," which helped give "rise to a common consciousness of class."[168] Ultimately, however, due to systemic white supremacy, such class alliances were only partially realized: "although workers resisted the inequitable demands of industrial capitalism with united action, they failed to develop a durable alliance across ethnic and racial lines."[169] This was because "American-born whites usurped the most favored supervisory positions in the coalfields, enjoyed the major fruits of welfare capitalism (especially expanding educational opportunities), and placed critical ethnic and racial limits on the progress of immigrants and blacks."[170] Tragically, then, "working-class solidarity was a highly precarious affair," because "white miners' own heritage of racism placed critical limits on their ability to identify with black workers."[171]

Similarly, the experience of Appalachian women in labor organizing was also complex in period Appalachia. For instance, commentators rightly note that "there is a history of militancy among miners' wives" and of other women in the Appalachian coalfields.[172] Notably, the role of Mary Harris "Mother"

Jones in furthering the cause of labor in Appalachia has been deeply chroni-cled. Jones, immortalized as "the most dangerous woman in America," proved a tireless and phenomenally charismatic organizer: "Jones's forte was her abil-ity to dramatize the miners' plight, creating solidarity among the workers and their families and winning support in the world beyond the hills."[173] As a prime example, Jones often would organize coal town women into "bucket and broom brigade[s]" to support strikes.[174] The work of Jones is therefore rightly touted as a core labor achievement of the era.

At the same time, Seitz argues that in the Appalachian coalfields, "class struggle in the past has been waged primarily by men."[175] What is more, in many instances, analyses of women's activism has been limited to "the persons of 'exceptional' women" such as Jones.[176] As Seitz explains:

> The image of Mother Jones casts her shadow on contemporary Appalachian scholarship that, as Sally Maggard . . . notes, "attempt[s] to recover Appalachian women as historical actors, but which misrepresents their history as a collection of a few great women of courage." As in other liberal strategies for the inclusion of a few *exceptional* women in history (the add-women-and-stir-approach), the stories of these women, "more revered that explained" . . . do not affirm *ordinary* women's place in the history of social change.[177]

Therefore, the hegemonic liberal lens can veil such material realities—with core examples including both organizing work performed by "ordinary" women and the essential reproductive labor performed by women to support that organizing.[178]

It must also be reemphasized that the experience of period Appalachian women was not homogenized—and the labor organizing context was no ex-ception. For instance, the organizing experience of African American women was unique, as organizing inherently involved niche racial concerns. As Trotter argues, for instance, African American women in company towns "perceived their class and gender interests in essentially racial terms."[179] Moreover, Trotter suggests that concerns over gender subordination "tended to give way to the imperatives of racial solidarity," because "racial hostility, along with an expanding black consciousness, helped to forge Afro-American unity across class and gender lines."[180]

In the final analysis, the historic industrial violence of Blair Mountain and related "coal wars" episodes throughout this broad era signifies the over-arching failure of period industrial capitalism to provide for the Appalachian citizenry—and to, correspondingly, adequately safeguard the Appalachian environment. It has been observed that the "bloody mine wars that rocked the mountains every decade from 1893 to 1933 reflected the miners' over-whelming desire for greater social freedom."[181] Therefore, Appalachian labor revolts during this era were indicative of Appalachians' "frustration with a subservient life" as intertwined with gender, racial, and related concerns dis-cussed above.[182] Appalachians were, of course, wholly correct in their rebellious dissatisfaction: coal operator and complicit local elites' interests were indeed diametrically opposed to those of the regional citizenry and environment, as both the period conditions and the Appalachian devastation that was to come would demonstrate.

APPALACHIA AND THE NATURAL RESOURCE CURSE

The establishment of a coal-centered industrialized Appalachia created long-term structural issues for the regional economy. In controlling essentially all aspects coalfield communities, the industry succeeded in halting the growth of a more diversified economy that would have supplemented the coal sector. Coal-based industrialization thus created an Appalachia that was extraordi-narily vulnerable to the economic vicissitudes of a resource extraction-based mono-economy.[183] Consequently, from the 1920s onwards, Appalachia was vulnerable to what are popularly termed "boom-and-bust cycles." As the name suggests, under this phenomenon, market fluctuations result in eco-nomic conditions expanding and contracting in a cyclical fashion; and when mono-economy conditions are in place, such cycles are especially devastating. Appalachian coal began experiencing boom-and-bust cycles, in the first place, due to considerable overproduction. Factors like low entry barriers, abundant labor, and high coal prices ultimately made "mining in the mountains one of the most profitable ventures in that period of capitalist expansion," thus resulting in substantial overproduction.[184] Energy market competition also contributed to the emergence of Appalachian boom-and-bust cycles.[185] After decades of uncontested coal industry dominance, the potent energy alterna-tives of oil and gas emerged following World War I; coal labor conflicts only accelerated the effects of such competition. The coal depression of 1923–25 —brought about by U.S. overproduction paired with a post-war European mining revitalization—constituted one such slump. 1927 would again send the "coal industry into the abyss of depression," and by 1930, "unemployment, destitution, and despair stalked the coal fields."[186]

The emergence of mono-economy characteristics and boom-and-bust cycles in early twentieth-century Appalachia—and the persistence of these and related structural issues—are also indicative of the "natural resource curse" model. The resource curse denotes that certain regions rich in natural resources paradoxically gain scant material benefit from those resources—as outside capital interests "[wield] power over the [region] at the expense of its citizens and the natural environment."[187] Numerous commentators have concluded that Appalachia has long experienced the negative impacts produced by resource curse conditions, as profound intersections exist "between environmental problems caused by coal operations" and "the iniquitous social and economic conditions" of the region.[188] Consequently, in addition to the energy sacrifice zone model introduced earlier in this chapter, the "resource curse" constitutes a useful exploratory device in unpacking Appalachia's long-term structural issues.

As this chapter has demonstrated, Appalachia has long been marked by complex material-historical forces; however, the coming of liberal capitalism—and especially the late nineteenth-century period of timber- and coal-based rapid industrial growth—constituted a major turning point for the region's ecological political economy. Following the Euro-American conquest of Appalachia and its subsequent colonization, the region was characterized, to a degree, by agrarian subsistence practices—but also by market-based modes, as colonized Appalachia always has been embedded in Euro-hegemonic forces. And even prior to the coming of the coal and timber industries, industrial capitalism arose in Appalachia. Nevertheless, it was indeed timber- and especially coal-based industrialization that constituted the foundational event in the shaping of modern Appalachia. Ultimately, not only would the fossil fuel hegemony, in pursuing maximum capital accumulation, wreak multidimensional forms of subordination on the Appalachian citizenry—along lines of class, race, gender, etc.—but, so, too, would the Appalachian environment become beset by intertwined harms produced by fossil fuel hegemony. And as is discussed in subsequent chapters, such conditions of structural subordination would only persist in Appalachia in the twentieth century and beyond.

CHAPTER 2

FOUNDATIONS OF ENVIRONMENTAL LAW: CLASSICAL LIBERALISM

This chapter examines the deep foundations of environmental law and also details how period legal regimes failed to protect Appalachia during its era of timber- and coal-based rapid industrial growth. First, a brief synopsis of environmental law's distant historical roots is provided, followed by the significant eighteenth- and nineteenth-century socio-cultural trends that formed its direct conceptual foundations—which were the intertwined strains of Enlightenment and Romantic thought. This chapter then details additional legal regimes that influenced the development of environmental law (which emerged from the late nineteenth century onwards), including the nascent codification of public health principles in addition to natural resource management regimes. Next, this chapter unpacks the core, hegemonic underpinnings of U.S. environmental law: the liberal paradigm. As is discussed, both proto- and modern environmental law merely support the unsustainable liberal capitalist paradigm, which has a mode of production marked by a ceaseless drive to accumulate capital via commodification of everything and which has a structural growth imperative. Thus, because both proto- and modern environmental law are merely supportive of the liberal capitalist paradigm, environmental law constitutes a wholly failed regime.

In the specific context of Appalachia's era of timber- and coal-based industrialization (as detailed in chapter 1), this chapter also discusses the primary "proto-environmental law" regime—or the legal regime governing environmental disputes—that was in force in both Appalachia and the broader United States: the common law, or judge-made law. Particularly, tort-based common law regimes such as nuisance and negligence failed to protect the regional citizenry from industrial capitalism–produced harms. As is discussed, pertinent common law doctrines were, in fact, explicitly (and perversely) modified to support favored industrial development as a supposed matter of overriding public policy. Consequently, the period legal regimes' liberal-steeped fixation on supporting favored industrial development and economic growth (i.e., as benefitting powerful owners of capital) in the context of the coal, timber, and railroad industries was achieved at the expense of Appalachia's social, economic, and ecological welfare.

HISTORICAL FOUNDATIONS OF ENVIRONMENTAL LAW

In examining the historical roots of environmental law, it is important to emphasize, first and foremost, that it was the rise of the exceedingly destructive capitalist mode of production that has resulted in the true global ecological crisis (i.e., as is discussed more fully below via the tragedy of the commodity model and notions of the Capitalocene). However, at the same time, commentators have observed that, throughout ancient history, for many societies that adopted, for instance, urbanization and intensive agriculture-based modes of production, at least some degree of pronounced ecological destruction appeared "inevitable and ubiquitous."[1] As examples, during the antiquity era, the Greek and Roman civilizations adopted agriculturally intensive modes of production—as dependent on unfree labor (e.g., slaves), and which was marked by class conflict between unfree laborers and landowners.[2] Such classical era modes of production ultimately led to extensive environmental degradation (e.g., vast Roman deforestation), thus despoiling much of Mediterranean zone.[3] As another example, evidence indicates that "rapid deforestation in early China for agricultural production, irrigation, and the production of metallic implements" ultimately "generated the conditions of ecological crisis."[4] In contrast, for those societies that eschewed intensive modes of production, the negative environmental impacts generally were less pronounced.[5]

Intertwined idelogical trends also shed important light on the foundations for environmental law. For instance, as Dan Tarlock chronicles in "History of Environmental Law," a predominant ideological view in pre-antiquity times oftentimes was that "nature was sacred."[6] The Greco-Roman worldview, however, largely "replaced reverence with rationalism," which was part and parcel of the process by which natural resources were treated as a "storehouse . . . to be exploited and transformed."[7] The explicit Judeo-Christian tradition also has long contributed to a Western ethos that eschews environmental stewardship, in holding, as a central tenet, that humans are apart from and otherwise "above" the natural world. Christianity has been characterized as especially anthropocentric, due to its reliance on Greek humanism—which centralizes humans (and men especially) within the universe. Such broad Western cultural traditions, as continually impacted by mode-of-production transitions, would certainly influence long-term development practices as steeped in radical modification of the natural world and a corresponding disregard for the long-term environmental impacts of that modification. Historical counter-examples to such worldviews do exist, most notably involving non-Western cultures such as indigenous communities in addition to some eastern religions that disrupt the human-nature binary. However, like the Greco-Romans, for many Asian civilizations, the material demands of intensive modes of production generally "overrode the ancient aesthetic and religious ideals."[8]

THE ENLIGHTENMENT AND ROMANTIC MOVEMENTS

Western environmental views would only substantially shift during the broad socio-cultural transitions that generally occurred in the eighteenth and nineteenth centuries—namely, the Enlightenment and Romantic movements, which, as Tarlock discusses, together constituted important paradigm shifts in Western society. The Enlightenment's influence emanates from its "science to understand" nature, as based on empiricism and reason.[9] As a direct result of Enlightenment thought, there arose a "growing scientific understanding of how natural systems worked, how they could be altered to serve humankind and of the adverse consequences of different types of alteration."[10] The highly technocratic character of environmental law—as is detailed in subsequent chapters—can be directly traced to this Enlightenment ethos.

The Romantic movement exerted a second major influence on environmental law's development. Romanticism arose in direct response to the Enlightenment—particularly, the Enlightenment's largely negative ramifications (e.g., the multitudinous environmental ravages wrought by industrialization). As Joanne Schneider notes, Romanticism rejected the transformations "society underwent as a result of rationalist legacies, political upheaval, technological advances, and social realignments," and instead "turned to nature for inspiration."[11] Romanticism thus constituted a radical shift in Western thought; prior to this movement, "wilderness" had wholly negative connotations (as ungodly, or as raw materials to be developed), whereas for Romanticism, wilderness transformed into "a sublime place where one could encounter the divine."[12] The end result was that social, political, and legal developments began to reflect Romanticism's influence. As Theodore Roszak notes in *Where the Wasteland Ends*, since the Romantic era, "hostility toward the artificial environment has run through our culture like a soft, lyrical counterpoint to the swelling cacophony of the machine."[13]

Both the Romantic and the Enlightenment movements indeed would produce an entwined influence on environmental law. Western approaches to environmental regulation would be informed by Romanticism's preoccupation with valuing unmodified or "pure" wilderness in addition to the Enlightenment's core contributions towards scientific examinations of the environment—which led to, in time, the development of ecology principles. This emerging—and by no means frictionless—synthesis would begin to take shape throughout the late nineteenth and early twentieth centuries.[14]

Important for Remaking Appalachia, both movements also have important gendered dimensions (which, by extension, have informed environmental law underpinnings). For instance, numerous commentators have argued that Enlightenment thought is problematic due to is implicit masculine encodings. As Noël Sturgeon notes in Ecofeminist Natures, the Enlightenment ideology often "constructed a generically masculine ideal of what it meant to be truly human," involving universalist conceptions of (positive) masculine-identified values such as rationality, objectivity, and membership of the polis.[15] Per essentialist Enlightenment thought, such masculine values were contrasted with (negative) feminine-identified values such as irrationality, emotion, subjectivity, and domestic affairs. Feminists and theoretical allies have thus sought to challenge such masculine-identified "universal, ahistorical, cross-cultural human qualities," as such "discourses collude in making invisible not only those coded as 'different,' " but that, additionally, they illustrate the "complicity of Enlightenment humanism in justifying various modes of oppressing those Others defined as less-than-human, or not-human."[16]

The Romantic movement, too, has received complex gendered treatment, including through ecological-focused feminist schools. For instance, some commentators have noted that a core characteristic of hegemonic "masculine Romanticism" is that it "celebrates the development of the autonomous self" (i.e., an individual male seeking the sublime in nature, etc.), which dovetails with masculine-liberal ideology though crucial dimensions.[17] In contrast, historically less-visible "feminine Romanticism," as associated with women Romantic authors, often "conceptualize[s] the family and the community rather than the individual as the basis of the social and political state, promoting an ethic of care in which the needs of every member of the family-politic will be met."[18] And more broadly speaking, core Romantic-associated thought—such as the primacy of intuition, emotion, the physical body, and notions of care—also can be conceived as challenging, at least in part, the hegemonic masculine value system.

The continued legacy of Romantic thought vis-à-vis contemporary ecological feminist schools has been much-debated. On the one hand, it is clear that contemporary materialist-steeped ecofeminism (i.e., as discussed more fully in chapter 6) does not constitute a mere essentialized "neo-Romantic nature ideolog[y]," as its overarching concern is in challenging interlocking subordination systems wrought by patriarchal capitalism and on "reconstruct[ing] our *social* world on egalitarian principles."[19] However, commentators such as Mary Mellor have noted that " 'Romantic' ideas" cannot "be so easily dismissed" in the context of a materialist ecological feminism, as "we cannot ignore emotional ties and caring if we are to theoretically integrate reproduction and production."[20]

More specifically, Mellor emphasizes that material concerns indeed ought to constitute the core of both a feminist- and environmental-related critique, and that this must involve theorizing around the "the very real question of the finite nature of planet and the biological differences between women and men," as there exists a "direct connection between the biological differences between men and women" and "the social construction that is put on them: between the forces and relations of reproduction."[21] Thus, the complex gendered legacies of both the Romantic and Enlightenment movements have significant implications for *Remaking Appalachia*—i.e., with its focus on systemic re-formations beyond late liberalism, including transformations of gender regimes.

LEGAL FOUNDATIONS OF ENVIRONMENTAL LAW

Nascent legal foundations of environmental law also emerged during this era. Early development of U.S. public health law constitutes one such legal regime. Buoyed by the Enlightenment-produced ascendancy of the germ theory, fledgling public health and sanitation laws were established, with examples including treatment of wastewater before discharge and pre-treatment of drinking water.[22] Also during this era, urban municipal areas enacted fledgling pollution-control laws in response to industrial-produced noise and air discharges that were demonstrably degrading public health and welfare. For instance, as Richard Lazarus chronicles in *The Making of Environmental Law*, by 1912, nearly two dozen of the largest U.S. cities had enacted abatement laws for smoke—although "these regulations saw limited enforcement and, presumably, minimal compliance."[23]

Natural resource management constitutes a second legal regime that laid the foundations for environmental law. In the latter half of the nineteenth century, legal regimes increasingly established public management of natural resources (i.e., as compared to unregulated private control)—such as through designating lands such as national parks, forests, and the like.[24] As Tarlock argues, the rationale for emerging state-controlled natural resource management regimes was twofold. The first aspect was rooted in efficiency (and thus largely Enlightenment dictates): experts urged that a rational-based approach to resource use was more "efficient" than uncontrolled private practices. The second pertained to pure preservation principles (and thus more Romantic dictates), and held that vast tracts of wilderness should be managed for the benefit of the citizenry.[25] These two strains would eventually lead to two essentially separate—and ultimately, to a large extent, conflicting—schools of resource movements, and the tension between the two "still reverberates within the environmental community."[26]

Resource conservationism was largely concerned with efficient environmental exploitation. The overarching precepts of conservationism were that resource exploitation should be steeped in highly technical approaches—and that, moreover, public ownership and management of natural resources would maximize efficiency.[27] In the context of the forest tracts, this involved establishing, essentially, "timber factories," wherein the state exploited forests in a technocratic fashion.[28] For Appalachia, an important example of the conservation movement was West Virginia's Monongahela National Forest, which was created by authority of the federal Weeks Act of 1911.[29] Thus, conservationism, at its core, generally promoted development of natural resources, not protection from environmental harms; nature was indeed to be "conserved"—but only "as a stock of resources for human use."[30] Such an explicitly exploitation-focused policy goal was telling—and as subsequent chapters of *Remaking Appalachia* demonstrate, remains a central (albeit insidious) ultimate aim of environmental law. That is, despite superficial appearances, environmental law, too, is essentially concerned with *organizing* natural resource exploitation only (e.g., through permitting schemes)—rather than in halting ecological destruction in a meaningful sense. Note, however, that such period aims were not universalized. For instance, some radical undercurrents did exist within the conservationism movement, such as the socialism exhibited by "a radicalized faction of the forestry profession"; Cade Jameson discusses such phenomena in "Radical Conservation and the Politics of Planning."[31]

In contrast to the Enlightenment-inspired, scientific underpinnings of resource conservationism, the preservation movement was steeped more in spiritualism and aesthetics. The movement's progenitors posited that "wilderness was America's cultural heritage of equal dignity to Europe's cities," and that national parks—as analogous to the cathedrals of Europe—could function as "places where the individual could get close to God or him or herself."[32] The Romantic influence on the preservation movement is therefore readily apparent. The naturalist John Muir exemplified such period champions of the natural world. Muir's worldview is articulated well in his influential *Our National Parks*:

> Thousands of tired, nerve-shaken, over-civilized people are beginning to find out that going to the mountains is going home; that wildness is a necessity; and that mountain parks and reservations are useful not only as fountains of timber and irrigating rivers, but as fountains of life. Awakening from the stupefying effects of the vice of over-industry and the deadly apathy of luxury, they are trying as best they can to mix and enrich their own little ongoings with those of Nature, and to get rid of rust and disease.[33]

Muir would come to be associated most closely with the preservation movement; and according to preservationism's tenets, wilderness should indeed be set aside most importantly as a "superior mass recreational experience" for the public.[34] As Jedediah Purdy summarizes in "The Politics of Nature," the "national parks and wilderness reserves exist in part because their advocates developed arguments that certain kinds of aesthetic and spiritual experience were uniquely available in spectacular natural settings," and "Romantic and Transcendentalist aesthetics formed a backdrop to these ideas."[35]

Women also participated in the preservation and conservation movements, particularly white women. As Dorceta Taylor explains, such women both engaged in outdoors activities and supported the evolving movements, and similar to men, "were influenced by romanticism, transcendentalism, nativism, frontierism, and pioneer life."[36] Taylor adds that "some of these women—wealthy and the first generation of college-educated females in the country—used their wilderness exploits and outdoor experiences to defy stereotypes of white womanhood," such as that women were indeed highly willing and capable of engaging in strenuous outdoor activities.[37] One such prominent example included the Appalachian Mountain Club, through which women participated.[38]

While the conservation and preservation movements at first were viewed as reasonably complimentary—as both focused on a shift towards public control of natural resources—movement divergence became pronounced throughout the first half of the twentieth century.[39] The preservation movement would go on to make significant contributions to environmental law's development. This involved, for instance, continued resistance to massive public works, as based on aesthetics rationales, in that the preservation movement's overarching "objection to dams and other public works projects was that they destroyed natural areas of great beauty." [40] And the preservation movement also furthered the aim of expanding publicly owned wilderness areas and related dimensions. By the 1960s, this policy agenda led to tangible legislative victories, including the National Wild and Scenic Rivers Act and the Wilderness Act, which constitute "two of the strongest preservation laws" still in force today. [41] More broadly speaking, prior to environmental law's ascendancy in the 1970s, Congress passed a range of acts furthering, at least in part, preservation objectives, including the National Park Service Organic Act, the Migratory Bird Treaty Act, and the Taylor Grazing Act; added to this list are other preservation-focused acts passed in the 1960s, such as the Refuge Protection Act and the National Wildlife Refuge Administration Act. [42]

For Appalachia specifically, it should be noted that a primary legacy of the conservation and preservation movements was the designation of vast wilderness tracts as public lands (e.g., through national forests and state parks). As Sara Gregg discusses in *Managing the Mountains*, "millions of acres of the mountains were placed under federal management with farms and private forests converted to public lands." [43] Among other things, such a mass conversion of private to public lands affected regional agricultural trends: "In Appalachia, this change meant that small subsistence farms were targeted for conversion to federally managed forests." [44] And to be sure, such a top-down approach to land reform has engendered regional controversy since its inception, as such policies—as derived from collaboration among the federal government, states, and "experts imported from afar"—were often "at odds with local perceptions of best use." [45] As is discussed in chapter 7, the phenomenon of large public and absentee corporate land ownership continues to have important implications for Appalachia—including the context of potential efforts towards ecofeminist- and ecosocialist-steeped solidarity economy– and subsistence-based modes in the region.

Thus, nascent natural resource management regimes were certainly impactful in both Appalachia and beyond; through at least one dimension, however, such regimes were less influential on environmental law as might be expected. This is because, as subsequent chapters discuss, environmental law includes public regulation of private activities—whereas early resource management regimes involved public regulation of public lands. Therefore, as Lazarus notes, until the coming of environmental law, "the primary, if not exclusive, basis for the government's assertion of authority over natural resources had been its proprietary ownership of the particular resource at issue." [46] Such conditions would change, however, with environmental law's rise in the 1970s, as the "core regulatory premise of much environmental protection law today is the sovereign's police power to regulate private activities that adversely affect public health and welfare"—and this is due to "the impact of those activities on the natural environmental notwithstanding property claims."[47]

CLASSICAL LIBERALISM

Environmental law is wholly embedded within the hegemonic liberal paradigm. Moreover, environmental law's foundations were established throughout the era wherein classical liberalism was dominant. That is, the "values and normative assumptions of liberalism dominate Western industrial societies," and the "classical liberalism of the eighteenth and nineteenth centuries" constitutes their foundational roots.[48] Thus, an overview of classical liberalism in its pure ideological conceptualization will be provided, which demonstrates that the paradigm generally promotes environmental despoliation. However, a materialist-critical analysis of law and classical liberalism will thereafter be detailed, which unveils more insidious dimensions though which hegemonic liberalism has not only proven ecologically unsustainable—but also has produced intersecting economic and social ills along lines of class, race, gender, indigenous status, and so forth. This chapter then discusses how classical liberalism specifically failed the Appalachian environment and citizenry during the era of rapid timber- and coal-based industrial growth.

In "Environmental Law's Liberal Roots," Geoffrey Leane argues that environmental law is fundamentally embedded within the liberal paradigm. Leane notes that classical liberalism is comprised of two intersecting dimensions: economic liberalism and political liberalism.[49] The individual citizen is of central importance under political liberalism. The core notion is that if individuals are free to maximally pursue their "own vision of the good life and to maximize their own personal 'utility,' " this will correspondingly, on the macro scale, benefit society as a whole.[50] Therefore, under political liberalism, "aggregate welfare" simply constitutes the sum of "individual welfares," and the "individual is thus the unit of supreme social welfare."[51] This characteristic liberal fixation is often termed atomistic individualism.

The state's role is severely constrained under the pure ideological conceptualization of classical liberalism (as compared, in many ways, to its actual material-historical embodiment). In accordance with liberal laissez-faire principles, state intervention is eschewed except in those circumstances in which intervention would greatly enhance pursuit of individuals' aims.[52] As M'Gonigle and Takeda argue, per pure notions of liberalism, "the state is limited, refraining from intruding upon these individual strivings except . . . to put in place those conditions that can facilitate the individuals' ability to pursue their self-interest."[53] The concept of individual rights as guaranteed by the state holds primacy of place under political liberalism (e.g., political equality rights and freedom of speech and association).[54]

Under pure notions of economic liberalism, the liberal market economy, as a "system of private ordering," has a central role of "produc[ing] those goods and services which individuals" pursue—in a supposedly rational, self-interested fashion—so as to actualize their personal conceptualization of the "good life."[55] Wholly unencumbered markets are therefore crucial under liberal economic theory, as they optimize conditions for the "realisation of individual (and therefore aggregate) welfare," as steeped in allocative efficiency and the drive towards wealth maximization.[56] Perpetual economic growth also is central to the liberal economic paradigm. For defenders of economic liberalism, the concern is not with equitable wealth distribution; rather, the aim is maximal economic growth—or an "ever-growing economic pie," which ultimately results in absolute growth that benefits all.[57] The overarching liberal aim, then, is not an equal pie distribution: rather, the goal is instead a continuously expanding pie, which—as liberal theory posits—will ultimately benefit society as a whole, including those who are least advantaged.[58] (Note that, as discussed below, the materialist-critical account also identifies the growth imperative as a core feature of economic liberalism—i.e., as capitalism, as historically operationalized, functionally requires perpetual growth as part of the process of ceaseless-capital-accumulation-through-commodification-of-everything.)

Wealth inequality is therefore the natural and intended consequence of economic liberalism. And indeed, under the historical conditions of early industrial capitalism—i.e., during the classical liberalism era—a mere fraction of the citizenry owned the vast majority of the capital required to produce goods.[59] This phenomenon resulted in extreme wealth inequality between such large owners of capital and the mass of wage laborers—which, as will be discussed, was exemplified in the period Appalachian coalfields. And as is examined in subsequent chapters, such extreme wealth inequality has again arisen under contemporary late liberalism.

Such is classical liberalism, or at least the pure theoretical characterization of the paradigm; as will be demonstrated, critical commentators provide an alternate account of core aspects of the framework—and correspondingly, dispute that much of the historical era broadly defined as "classical liberalism" in fact tracked its paradigmatic conception. Additionally, liberalism has not remained static—liberalism has undergone numerous transformations. After classical liberalism's predominance, the liberal welfare model predominated in the 1930s through the 1970s—as ushered in by the struggles leading to

New Deal reforms. And neoliberalism has defined our current era since the 1980s. Each of these latter incarnations of liberalism—and their accompanying profound impacts on U.S. energy and environmental law and policy (and on Appalachia specifically)—are addressed in subsequent chapters.[60]

Despite liberalism's various iterations, many of its central characteristics have largely transcended time and place.[61] Thus, the core of liberalism—in both its economic and political dimensions—has constituted a fundamental through-line in Western society since its very inception.[62] And as will be discussed, liberalism's various period transformations have only served, on a macro scale, to exacerbate the growing global ecological crisis and that in Appalachia specifically.

LAW AND CLASSICAL LIBERALISM

In the context of U.S. political liberalism, individual rights are guaranteed most fundamentally in the national constitution. Significantly, under liberalism, guarantees of individual rights are accomplished in a narrow, largely negative rights fashion. Formal enshrinement of rights and freedoms is intended only "to guarantee those freedoms from state interference"—but, beyond that point, there is less formal protection.[63] In contrast, in many circumstances, private actors can discriminate against other private actors under a liberal regime. Liberal political ideology rationalizes such discrimination as free individuals pursuing their personalized conceptualizations of the good life.[64]

Liberal economics also are made manifest by law—albeit often less directly visibly than is the case with political liberalism. Citizen life under liberalism is, in particular, actualized through individuals engaging in capitalism's system of private ordering. Liberal economics centers on individuals—both human and, significantly, corporations-as-artificial-persons—having maximum freedom to enter into economic relationships and having the guarantee of state protection *of* those relationships (and their agreed on terms).[65] Leane, in examining the role of law in making manifest liberal economics, characterizes crucial dimensions of Western legal regimes as "development law." As Leane argues, the primary aim of liberal economics "is rooted in liberal law," as it is "defined by it, created by it, and legitimised by it."[66] M'Gonigle and Takeda likewise conclude that, under liberalism, one of the few "acceptable [state] intrusions is to put in place those conditions that can facilitate the individuals' ability to pursue their self-interest including, first and foremost, state enforcement of private property and contractional relations."[67]

Property law constitutes the first pillar of development law. In the common law tradition, property law is concerned with ensuring that individuals retain, to the extent possible, exclusive rights to their private property (including further use rights). That is, the "common law defines and protects our right to possess and use those things which are ours, to the exclusion of others, that is to say, of community."[68] Therefore, a core "function of the modern state" involves "protecting property rights."[69] Per the liberal conception of property law, an emphasis on community, social responsibility, and environmental stewardship is explicitly eschewed—in the context of both present and future generations. Individuals, whether human or corporate, are free to exploit such property due to the legal regime's guarantee of the exclusion of all others—with constraints only emanating from potential competing property rights. (Of course, harmed individuals may have certain recourse through other civil or criminal law regimes, such as tort; but as is discussed below in the Appalachian context, tort law as actually operationalized during the period of rapid industrialization largely neutralized such actions against industry.) Liberal notions of private property are therefore, and to a remarkable degree, fundamentally *unconcerned* with effects pertaining to the community, to future generations, or to the broader environment (i.e., including notions of the unowned ecological "commons," which themselves have no cognizable legal rights.)[70]

The influence of Lockean property theory on common law conceptions of property rights—with their focus on economic development—is therefore readily apparent. According to Locke's natural law approach to property, an individual gains rights to property, which formerly existed in the commons, only after adding labor to that property and thereby transforming it into a useful purpose—or "improving" it.[71] As Locke wrote in his 1689 *Two Treatises of Government*, an individual who has improved resources from the commons can claim that the "labour that was mine, removing them out of that common state they were in, hath fixed my property in them."[72] Locke's individualism- and development-based theory is therefore broadly reflected in Western property law (and this despite the essentially positivist turn in contemporary liberalism).

Contract law is the second pillar of development law. Aside from establishing largely exclusive entitlement rights through the property regime, contract doctrine creates a mechanism through which an individual can securely engage in transactions in pursuit of their aims (including, of course, transferring property with the aim of wealth maximization).[73] What is more, to ensure the stability of the overarching liberal regime, the U.S. judicial system is inordinately concerned with ensuring that parties strictly abide by all contractual obligations. Under the common law, courts generally enforce any freely entered into contractual relationship, with the rare exceptions limited to extreme circumstances (e.g., fraud and duress).[74] Thus, significant for the liberal paradigm, courts are not concerned about parity among bargaining parties—nor about the substantive fairness (or justice) of the ultimate contractual terms. Liberalism instead requires the state to view individuals-as-contractual-parties as formal equals only, as under the liberal contract regime, the prime criterion is thus not equity but rather efficiency.[75]

During the era of classical liberalism, courts were also preoccupied with protecting contractual rights from state interference. This era is popularly termed the "Lochner era," based on the 1905 U.S. Supreme Court decision *Lochner v. New York*. In *Lochner*, the court struck down New York state regulations infringing on private contract rights on constitutional grounds—thus broadly upholding economic laissez-faire principles; and such principles were further upheld through related decisions of the era.[76]

Similar to the property regime, contract law also is fundamentally unconcerned with external effects pertaining to third parties—broadly speaking, community interests, both present and future—and to the environment. Common law contract doctrine is instead preoccupied with contractual parties alone. Even a cursory review of the long Western legal tradition reveals that a communal- or environmental stewardship-focused ethos has not sprung spontaneously from contract law's liberal, individualist focus. But this outcome is unsurprising. Under liberalism's strictures, there is absolutely "no reason to think that individuals calculating personal advantage under a system of private ordering will somehow arrive collectively at an environmentally desirable result."[77]

CRITICAL EXPLORATION OF LAW AND CAPITALISM IN CLASSICAL LIBERALISM ERA

As discussed above, in taking liberalism's traditional ideological conceptualization—and corresponding self-justifications—even at face value, it is abundantly clear that the paradigm broadly promotes environmental despoliation. This is due to liberalism's fixation on perpetual economic growth in addition to its eschewment of notions of community, future generations' welfare, or environmental preservation as an end in and of itself. However, in taking a crucial step further, a critically informed approach to economic liberalism reveals yet more insidious forces at work—which is particularly important given *Remaking Appalachia*'s core themes.

Such a critical analysis is ultimately grounded in the foundational Marxian critique of capitalism (i.e., including the intersection of law and capitalism). Most basically, Marx argues that the mode of production generally produces particular legal formations such as the liberal property and contract regimes discussed above—and that, additionally, class conflict constitutes the central feature of the organization of production for both capitalism and all other modes of production.[78] In prior societies, class divisions fell along such lines as slaves, plebeians, and patricians in Rome and peasants, merchants, and lords in the case of feudal times. Under capitalism, Marx—together with his frequent collaborator Friedrich Engels—focuses on struggle between the bourgeoisie, or capitalists who own the means of production, and the proletariat, or the working class who are compelled by economic need to sell their labor to capitalists[79]—who in turn appropriate surplus value produced by workers.[80]

Marx formulated the highly influential distinction between "economic base" and the legal and political "superstructure." That is, Marx posits that "legal relations as well as forms of state [can] neither be understood by themselves, nor explained by the so-called general progress of the human mind" but are instead located in the "the material conditions of life."[81] More specifically, Marx argues that in "the social production which men carry on they enter into definite relations that are indispensable and independent of their will" and that "these relations of production correspond to a definite stage of development of their material powers of production."[82] Marx adds that the "sum total of these relations of production constitute the economic structure of society—the real foundation, on which rise legal and political superstructures and to which correspond definite forms of social consciousness."[83] Thus, the "mode of production in material life determines the general character of the social, political and spiritual processes of life," or stated most plainly, the economic base determines the nature of political and legal formations.[84] (Note that this foundational Marxian analysis deeply informs the contemporary, critical legal theory–informed approach to transformative economic and socio-legal change outlined in chapter 6—i.e., namely that liberal "law reform" itself is insufficient, as what is required is true systemic re-formations of forces operating above or behind the law. This latter discussion, however, is situated in the context of our current era of late capitalism.)

Subsequent critical commentators have noted that the most fruitful interpretation of Marx's framework does not necessarily involve a "crude determinism" wherein an economic base mechanistically produces the superstructure (e.g., law).[85] As Tor Krever notes in "The Rule of Law and the Rise of Capitalism," there does not exist a strict binary between the economic base and superstructure—i.e., with political and legal institutions separated out entirely from economic institutions. Consequently, the economic base is not always the most significant, impactful, or visible societal dimension per se—although the base does determine why differing social formations gain predominance given shifting modes of production.[86]

In the specific context of capitalism, the rise of a private ownership-based mode of production thus involved a "cystallisation coeval with the development of private property and the new legal forms it called forth."[87] Prior to capitalism's rise, early modes of production, for instance, involved communal ownership of the means of production. And even ancient (e.g., Roman) and feudal societies did not wholly involve displacing peasant classes from control over the means of production. But the capitalist mode of production indeed comprehensively displaced workers from control over the means of production, and thus the bourgeoisie formulated private property–steeped law in support of this new economic base.[88] In *Law and the Rise of Capitalism*, Michael Tigar and Madeleine Levy provide a comprehensive treatment of how, over the course of eight centuries in Europe, class conflict drove this historical phenomenon.[89] As Tigar and Levy argue, the merchant class "felt compelled to establish conditions which permitted trade," but in time this "conflict intensified and broadened until the bourgeois gradually discovered the points at which the legal system could no longer be bent to his will, accommodated at an affordable price, or evaded."[90] The merchant class, then, in striving against their disfavored status under feudalism, engaged in intense conflict with hegemonic feudal interests—until eventually merchants seized political and legal power within nations.[91] Thereafter, the bourgeois pursued "lawmaking [that] saw the creation and application of specific rules about contracts, property and procedure," which constituted "legal rules consistent with freer commerce."[92]

But what of the context of the broad, classical liberalism–era conditions in particular? The critical reading correspondingly suggests that classical liberalism's "universalised protection of private economic rights" functioned "to protect and legitimise the interests of those who control disproportionate amounts of wealth," which thus perpetuated "hierarchy, exploitation, and oppression."[93] As Eduardo Bonilla-Silva has noted, when the "bourgeoisies of early modern capitalism . . . applauded 'individualism,' they had in mind the 'bourgeois . . . the middle-class owner of property,' " and that therefore "classical liberalism was the philosophy of a nascent class that as an aspiring ruling class that expressed its needs (political as well as economic) as general societal goals."[94] As discussed below, this critical-steeped analysis of classical liberalism's true character—i.e., a regime based on subordination—is particularly apropos to a discussion on Appalachia's deeply exploitative period of rapid industrialization.

Significant for *Remaking Appalachia*, this critical analysis of classical liberalism extends beyond class subordination singularly to include discrimination along lines of race, sex, and gender, etc. as both explicitly state-implemented subordination and in more insidious forms. As Bonilla-Silva adds:

> The liberal tradition informed the American Revolution, the U.S. Constitution, and the 'the leading American liberal thinker of this period, Thomas Jefferson.' And in the United States . . . the exclusion of the majority of white men and all white women from the rights of citizenship and the classification of Native Americans and African Americans as subpersons accompanied the development of the new liberal nation-state. Specifically, racially based policies such as slavery, the removal of Native Americans from their lands and their banishment to reservations . . . Jim Crow, and many other policies were part of the United States' 'liberal' history from 1776 to the 1960s.[95]

Therefore, in a broad sense, despite classical liberalism's superficial emphasis on political equality and on economic freedom of choice, the reality of the classical liberalism historical era was marked by widespread and multifaceted systems of economic-, social-, and political-based subordination.

The overt injustices stemming from Jim Crow laws, the regime denying women's suffrage, etc. could not directly be reconciled with classical liberalism's core principles. An array of justifications was therefore put forth, often based on false biological or racial notions of superiority and fitness. For instance, as Kate Nash writes, "it was held . . . that women did not need the right to vote" because there existed "natural differences between the sexes which suited women for the private domestic sphere."[96] Nash adds that "the most important features of women's position in classical liberalism" revolved around the proposition that "women are naturally subordinate in the private sphere and that they *must* be subordinate there if there is to be unity and harmony in the home," and that moreover "difference must be excluded from the public sphere in the interests of the common good."[97] The actual conditions of classical liberalism—characterized by multifaceted systems of subordination—were thus irreconcilable with the purely theoretical liberal ideal.

Under historical classical liberalism conditions, such class-, race-, and gender-based subordination also had crucial intersections with environmental devastation. As introduced in chapter 1 (and unpacked more fully in chapter 6) the ecofeminist school holds that all forms of domination under hegemonic liberalism are intrinsically interlinked—i.e., as undergirded by such normative dualisms such as masculine over feminine, white over non-white, society over nature, etc., where women, non-whites, and the environment are "othered" and thus subordinated. For instance, in the specific context of economic liberalism, profit maximization is achieved via exploitation along such "othered" lines, as powerful owners of capital exploit the unpaid reproductive labor of women, minority populations, and natural resources alike (i.e., in addition to other dimensions such as indigenous populations, the Global South-North divide via, for instance, the history of colonialism and imperialism, and so forth.). Thus, during the classical liberalism era and thereafter, the liberal paradigm was wholly dependent on not just exploitation along lines of gender, race, etc.—but also along lines of the environment.

The liberal capitalism-produced destruction of the environment receives significant treatment vis-à-vis the critical-steeped "tragedy of commodity" model, as discussed by Stefano Longo, Rebecca Clausen, and Brett Clark. Garrett Hardin formulated the initial and vastly influential "tragedy of the commons" model—from which the tragedy of the commodity was formulated in response. Per Hardin's model, resources such as land that are held in common inevitably are overexploited, due to unheedful, selfish use by individuals (i.e., as part and parcel of essentialist conceptualizations of supposed "human nature"). Thus, Hardin and subsequent, related commentators argue that rules are required to curb individual use, as implemented, for instance, through arrangements such as top-down state control over resources, typically entailing enclosure of the commons and establishment of resource management regimes. Hardin also favors liberal capitalist-based private property arrangements as a solution to the tragedy of the commons—i.e., carrying with them exclusionary use rules for outside parties (as discussed above) and supposed intrinsic incentives towards protection of such privately owned resources.[98]

In *Tragedy of the Commodity*, Longo, Clausen, and Clark, however, deploy an alternative framework, as steeped in a materialist approach in the Marxian tradition. Per their account, the historical growth of the capitalist mode of production "introduced significant changes in social relations, which influenced the interchanges linking social conditions and natural processes."[99] In *Tragedy of the Commodity*, then, they "offer a careful analysis of the capitalist commodity form as a microcosm of modern social relations and develop a socio-ecological examination of it," which ultimately emphasizes "the growth imperative of capitalism and the role of commodification in producing the institutional rules by which nature and . . . the commons are governed."[100]

Rather than attributing ecological destruction to the supposed universal failings of human nature—that is, the inherent selfishness of humanity, as undergirds Hardin's work—rather, the focal point is on capitalism's drive towards capital accumulation and the "commodification of everything."[101] Most basically, "in a society organized around the logic of capital," ceaseless capital accumulation is achieved through production of commodities—i.e., commodities being products sold for the market (not for direct use by producers), wherein "exchange value" is preeminent.[102] What is more, the "foundation of all products made for human consumption" is comprised of human labor (or that labor which has been accumulated in technology) as applied to natural resources.[103] Capitalism, then, "subordinates labor and nature to its impulse to accumulate" and additionally, "the system is organized around continuous growth, and thus must expand to survive."[104] Perpetual growth—as a constitutive mandate—has thus proven catastrophic, because the "growth imperative of capital systematizes commodity production, accelerating the intensity and scale of the demands placed on ecosystems," and as such dynamics "exceed natural limits, they produce ecological rifts in the cycles and processes that maintain ecosystems."[105]

Prior modes of production were often similarly exploitative of labor and the environment—but capitalism is thus unique (i.e., constitutes the tragedy of the commodity), due to the scale and scope of its devastation.[106] Under the tragedy of the commodity model, then, the core issue is that ceaseless capital accumulation achieved through commodity production—as intertwined with the growth imperative—is incompatible with our bounded universe of resources. Ultimately, then, the "consequence of the historically specific capitalist commodity production is the tragedy of resource degradation"—in addition to follow-up issues including capitalist-steeped "solutions" to such degradation such as through remediation efforts via increased technological efficiencies.[107]

Also from a material-historical perspective, the question of how fossil fuels came to drive liberal capitalism in the first place constitutes an important foundational analysis for *Remaking Appalachia*. In *Fossil Capital*, Andreas Malm argues that the early adoption of coal-fired steam power was not a foregone conclusion during the Industrial Revolution in Britain, but rather an explicit exploitative choice by powerful owners of capital: "steam arose as a form of power exercised by some people against others."[108]

While waterpower existed as a viable alternative, capital interests instead adopted coal-fired steam as a better mechanism through which to subordinate workers. Unlike more static waterpowered sources, coal-fired steam could be operationalized, for instance, where conditions were most ideal for worker discipline—such as dense population centers. As Malm argues, "not only were the inhabitants more numerous in certain locations: they had also . . . acquired an 'industrious character'—in other words, resigned themselves to the discipline of the master inside the mill."[109] As an overarching consequence, coal-fired steam power "had the prime advantage of overcoming the barriers to procurement not of energy, but of *labour*," as the steam engine "was a superior medium for extracting surplus wealth from the working class, because, unlike the waterwheel, it could be put up practically anywhere."[110] So, too, did coal-fired steam provide capitalists with other intertwined benefits, such as freeing production from natural cycles' vagaries and fluctuations: coal-fired steam could therefore be brought to bear at those locations and times in which capital accumulation via worker exploitation was maximized.[111]

Following the inception of the fossil fuel–driven economy, it was subsequently "reproduced and enlarged" to the extent to which the fossil economy is extraordinary entrenched within our late liberalist era (as is discussed in chapter 4).[112] As Malm notes in detailing the permanent establishment of fossil economy dynamics, "for capitalists to burn fossil fuels, there have to be other capitalists specialized in their production, and for the former to burn more, the latter have to deliver it in greater quantities, the two cycles ever intertwined."[113] And so the "primitive accumulation of fossil capital is a *permanent foundation for the fossil economy*."[114] Of course, such dynamics also are "supra-ecological" in being ultimately wholly untethered to the "natural limits of ecosystems."[115]

EXPANSION OF CORPORATE POWER UNDER CLASSICAL LIBERALISM

The legal expansion of corporate power in the United States—and the accompanying rise of large, exploitative corporate entities—was a core feature of the historic era of classical liberalism; moreover, as will be discussed, this phenomenon similarly supports the critical reading of the period liberal paradigm. In the latter half of the nineteenth century, U.S. corporations continued to advance their legal status—which already allowed corporations to "hold property, to sue and be sued, just 'as if' they were natural persons"—and this allowed "large corporations to develop [further] within the framework of classical liberalism."[116] A particularly important Supreme Court decision, *Santa Clara County v. Southern Pacific Railroad*, was handed down in 1886. The Fourteenth Amendment, with its equal protection clause, was passed in 1868; although ratified in the Reconstruction Era—with intent to bolster the rights of recently emancipated African Americans—corporate interests viewed the amendment as an opportunity to expand their own rights vis-à-vis a perversion of the amendment. And corporations emerged victorious with the *Santa Clara County* decision: the court expanded preexisting corporate rights and established modern "corporate personhood" per se, as it recognized such rights under the Fourteenth Amendment.[117] To be sure, *Santa Clara County* constituted a prime power- and wealth-enhancing precedent for corporations, as "corporations held few or none of the limitations placed on individuals but most of the individual's legal protections."[118]

While the *Santa Clara County* decision constituted a crucial legal event, other judicial action of the classical liberalism period expanded corporate power. As Janel Curry and Steven McGuire chronicle in *Community on Land*: "At a time of rapid economic change, corporations pushed the gray areas of their limitations and the courts granted increasing latitude regarding corporations' specified purposes."[119] Curry and McGuire add that "state courts increasingly took on a Lockean cast in that they began to concede that private commercial enterprises held a natural right to accumulate wealth," and what is more, "spokesmen for the 'artificial persons' characterized their institutions by reference to Locke and capitalized on a Supreme Court decision that asserted that corporations should have a natural freedom from political regulation."[120] As Curry and McGuire conclude, "individualism culminated in a triumph at the expense of the individual."[121] During this time period, large corporations therefore wielded mono- or oligopolistic power in the context of natural resource development, transportation, and related sectors[122]—and this era also was marked by "the growing prominence of large companies as sites of employment and production."[123]

Classical liberalism as actually operationalized in the nineteenth century thus resulted in the expansion of large corporations—which exercised exploitative hegemonic power. The corporate entity in the United States "gradually won freedoms from restrictions on its being able to concentrate wealth and power," and it was "able to form factory towns, threaten unemployment, and use its resources to influence newspapers and political figures."[124] And as was demonstrated all too well in the Appalachian context, corporations took "powers heretofore limited to the sovereign [in that it] issued its own scrip, built its own private roads, and could and did hire private detectives and armies for labor control."[125]

CLASSICAL LIBERALISM FAILS APPALACHIA

Exploitative actors wrought profound and irrevocable damage on Appalachia throughout the late nineteenth and early twentieth centuries—i.e., the historical era of late classical liberalism. Even in exploring the paradigm most favorably vis-à-vis its pure ideological conceptualization, classical liberalism's fixation on individuals pursuing personalized versions of the "good"—to the exclusion of competing community or environmental interests—proved disastrous for Appalachia. In taking a step further, however, exploring Appalachian classical liberalism–era conditions via an explicit critical theory standpoint demonstrates the manner in which the regime indeed ultimately functioned to benefit powerful owners of capital at the expense of Appalachian workers in a general sense—and also at the expense of "othered" groups along such lines as gender, race, and the environment. Chapter 1 provides many of the historical details on how extractive industries and allied Appalachian elites wrought extensive social, economic, and environmental devastation on Appalachia during this period; thus, this factual account will not be repeated here. However, certain aspects of this historical period do bear further scrutiny through an explicit classical liberal lens.

To begin with, for turn-of-the-century Appalachia, development law—with its twin pillars of the property and contract regimes—was instrumental in effectuating the long-term ascendancy of the fossil fuel hegemony. It was these legal regimes that accomplished the mass transference of Appalachian property (including mineral and timber rights) from the regional Appalachian citizenry to outside capital interests. What is more, the inequality of bargaining power between the prime negotiating parties was, at least on its face, compatible with pure notions of liberalism. The well-backed mineral buyers had intricate "understanding of litigation procedures and access to the courts," whereas the small Appalachian landowner typically lacked such expertise; thus the "negotiations were hardly between equals."[126] However, since liberalism is not concerned with equal bargaining power, the lack of parity between Appalachian small landowners and large capital interests could be characterized as being part and parcel of the liberal contract regime. (Recall though that, as is unpacked in chapter 1, landownership in classical liberalism–era Appalachia constitutes a much-debated, complex issue—as, many Appalachians, for instance, were squatters.)

Like the inequality of bargaining parties, the ultimate fairness (or substantive justice) of the contractual results regarding the period land transference was wholly irrelevant under the liberal contract regime. For the Appalachian citizenry, the end contractual result of mass land transference was neither fair nor just—land sale rates generally averaged from "twenty-five cents to three dollars per acre," which were low by period standards, and indeed "some mountaineers were reported to have sold entire mountains rich in coal and timber for a mule, a saddle horse, or a hog rifle."[127] Additionally, the fundamental unfairness of the contractual terms would become apparent only in subsequent decades—as in Kentucky, broad form deeds "effectively transferred to the land agents all the mineral wealth and the right to remove it by whatever means necessary, while leaving the farmer and his descendants with the semblance of land ownership."[128] Nevertheless, as contract doctrine under liberalism is unconcerned with notions of substantive justice, this Appalachian land transference was generally characteristic of the paradigm.

The explicit classical liberal lens also adds important detail to the phenomenon of corporations acquiring outsized power in turn-of-the-century Appalachia. The rise of large corporations such as the U.S. Coal and Oil Company and the Clinchfield Coal Corporation are generally illustrative of a core characteristic of the historic period of classical liberalism. Recall that period corporations "gradually won freedoms from restrictions on [their] being able to concentrate wealth and power" and took "powers heretofore limited to the sovereign" such as through establishing comprehensive company town infrastructure and regulating all aspects of coal town life.[129] Thus, enhanced corporate power gained during the classical liberalism era certainly facilitated the fossil fuel hegemony in arising as a preeminent regional actor: in Appalachia, "individualism culminated in a triumph at the expense of the individual."[130]

More specifically, as is chronicled in chapter 1, Appalachian wage earners and their dependents—in addition to the broader environment—were profoundly exploited by these hegemonic corporate conditions. However, it should first be noted that, in many ways, acute Appalachian wealth inequality seemingly was characteristic of pure notions of the classical liberalism paradigm. Recall that economic inequality is not only tolerated but also expected and indeed integral to liberalism's system of private ordering (i.e., pure conceptualizations of liberalism only require formal *political* equality.) Thus, that the mass of the Appalachian citizenry did not share equally in coal-produced wealth potentially is consistent with liberalism—in that rapid economic growth was nevertheless occurring overall. In period Appalachia, the economic pie was expanding, and liberalism's core contention is that general economic welfare—including that of the Appalachian citizenry—would eventually benefit from such growth. And the industry-produced environmental and related public health damage was, in fact, perfectly consistent with liberalism—because under liberalism, the unowned environment itself has no value (in constituting part of the commons) and also because liberalism, with its fixation on private property interests, eschews a community or environmental stewardship approach, which certainly was the case in period Appalachia.

In taking a step further, however, from a critical theory standpoint, that powerful capital interests dominated the period Appalachian political economy is consistent with a "darker reading" of classical liberalism—and thus is inconsistent with liberalism's pure ideological conceptualization. That is, in

Appalachia, "universalised protection of private economic rights" was operationalized in such a manner as to "to protect and legitimise the interests of those who control disproportionate amounts of wealth"—notably, the coal, timber, and railroad interests, and so forth.[131] To be sure, this was not in keeping with liberalism's laissez-faire economic principles. For instance, as chapter 1 details, the coal industry created a veritable vassal system in which Appalachian wage earners, through mechanisms such as the company town and scrip, were deeply subordinated and gained scarce, ultimate economic benefit—as exemplified by courts of the era ruling that the relationship between coal operator and miner was that of "master to servant."[132]

Additionally, that period Appalachia suffered from endemic and pronounced forms of structural subordination—i.e., along lines of coalfield racial oppression, an unjust gendered division of labor, etc.—further supports this critical reading. Recall that, to maximize profits, Appalachian mining operators not only exploited coal miners in a general sense (i.e., along class lines), but also exploited the unpaid reproductive work of coal town women (e.g., domestic work), African American mining communities through multifaceted forms of subordination of (i.e., including disproportionate subordination of African American women through compound oppressions), foreign-born miners, and the Appalachian environment. So, too, did period coal operators deliberately cultivate a "judicious mixture" of "blacks, native whites, and foreign-born whites" to most easily control labor (and therefore maximize capital accumulation) by pitting group against group.[133] Therefore, a critical analysis of this era demonstrates that classical liberalism's supposed universal protection of political and economic rights in fact insidiously veiled "hierarchy, exploitation, and oppression" in Appalachia.[134]

Indeed, additional broad legal transitions that occurred in Appalachia throughout the late nineteenth and early twentieth centuries further support this critical reading of the classical liberalism era—as law was explicitly transformed to support favored industry at the expense of the Appalachian environment and citizenry. That is, in much of Appalachia, "bourgeois elite[s] advanced" legal reforms during this time that much of citizenry resisted—as "new industrial elites . . . seemed to be more intent on looking after themselves than the common good," and thus "far from taking a hands-off approach to the economy, government and the law sided with business to exploit the people."[135] As will be discussed, Appalachian state legislatures accomplished pro-industry measures through such means as tax breaks—and state judiciaries actively transformed common law doctrines to support industry and otherwise favored industry through pertinent doctrine. As Lewis notes in *Transforming the*

Appalachian Countryside, many commentators assert "that nineteenth-century law was deliberately altered to accommodate emerging industrial interests." [136] Thus, widespread legislative and judicial action in Appalachia served to intensify favored industrial development and to concentrate wealth and power in the hands of outside capital interests and local elites—and this phenomenon certainly was not in keeping with classical liberalism's pure ideological precepts (i.e., laissez-faire precepts).

In a broad sense, legal support of extractive industries was the period status quo—as a matter of public policy—within the U.S. legal system. For instance, in the 1882 U.S. Supreme Court decision *Steel v. St. Louis Smelting & Ref. Co.*, the court declared "it is the policy of the country to encourage the development of its mineral resources." [137] Appalachian courts followed this and related precedent, as was demonstrated in the Supreme Court of Pennsylvania decision *Pennsylvania Coal Co. v. Sanderson*. In that case, a plaintiff landowner brought an action against a coal company for damaging a waterway. But the court held: "The plaintiff's grievance is for a mere personal inconvenience," and to "encourage the development of the great natural resources of a country trifling inconveniences to particular persons must sometimes give way to the necessities of a great community." [138] Thus, Appalachian courts generally held that developing natural resources was a matter of overriding public policy— despite the harm inflicted on the small landowner (i.e., as often engaged in agricultural activities) and, of course, on the environment.

What is more, many of the common law regimes at issue in Appalachia constituted prime "proto-environmental law" of the era. As Wood details in *Nature's Trust*, prior to the enactment of environmental law in the late 1960s and 1970s, "the courts played a fairly key role in environmental disputes" in that courts "borrowed doctrines of property law from England and applied them, with logic and reason, to the environmental circumstances of the new nation," thereby creating "bodies of water law, wildlife law, and mining law." [139] For instance, the period judiciary developed the public trust doctrine, as exemplified by the influential U.S. Supreme Court decision *Illinois Central Railroad v. Illinois*. The public trust doctrine "recognizes inalienable public property rights in crucial natural resources," and, as will be discussed, occupies an important role in the latter chapters of *Remaking Appalachia*. [140] Also, judges utilized common law doctrine to resolve environmental disputes between states, such as in the Supreme Court decision *Georgia v. Tennessee Copper Co.*, wherein the court held that one state could be liable to another for air pollution under nuisance doctrine. [141] Nuisance occupied primacy of place in the context of environmental disputes between private actors as well, as prior to the enactment of environmental law per se, "judges resolved most environmental conflicts through nuisance law," which required judges to "balance private property rights with the economic interests of society." [142] Therefore, as the era of rapid industrialization intensified in Appalachia and in the broader United States, nuisance and related doctrines constituted key law governing environmental disputes; however, as will be discussed, such doctrines failed utterly to protect the regional environment and citizenry.

WEST VIRGINIA'S "LEGAL REVOLUTION"

In the context of Appalachian state support of industry, West Virginia constitutes a period exemplar, as it engaged in numerous state legal transformations (both common law and otherwise) that explicitly supported favored industry. West Virginia gained statehood in 1863. Although a first state constitution was ratified in that founding year, it was superseded by a second constitution in 1872. This second constitution—known as the "lawyers' constitution," due to the large number of attorney-delegates at the convention—was criticized by many for complicating tax and land policies in the state; moreover, as Lewis chronicles in *Transforming the Appalachian Countryside*, critics claimed this second constitution would also serve to facilitate "transfer of land from smallholders to the coal and lumber companies." [143] Such pro-industry constitutional features would ultimately prove indicative of what was to follow in West Virginia—as state legal actors would largely succeed in "transform[ing] the law into a progressive partner in industrial development," to the exclusion of other sectors. [144] In the first place, West Virginia legal support of industry was accomplished through legislative means; like many state legislatures of the era, West Virginia would engage in support of key industrial sectors. For instance, the West Virginia legislature "provide[d] tax favors to railroads." [145]

The West Virginia judiciary also radically transformed doctrine to support industry. West Virginia had initially derived much of its legal system from Virginia; in many respects, this system remained relatively static in the 1870s and 1880s, in that the West Virginia Supreme Court continued to follow "precedents inherited from a Virginia tradition" that specifically "favored agricultural over industrial interests," and which was correspondingly steeped in natural rights principles. [146] However, West Virginia common law shifted precipitously towards industry from the last portion of the nineteenth century onwards, as the West Virginia judiciary underwent a veritable "legal revolution" through which common law doctrines such as nuisance were explicitly modified to support favored industrial development. [147] In the broader context of *Remaking Appalachia*, such pro-industry common law transformations indeed reflected the failure of "proto-environmental law" in the region—which, in time, would only be mirrored by environmental law's failure in the latter twentieth century and beyond.

The West Virginia legal revolution was attributed to the New Court that was represented, most notably, by Justice Henry Brannon, who was first elected in 1889. Brannon was a former railroad lawyer, owner, and businessperson. Brannon and like-minded justices on the New Court eschewed the Virginia natural rights– and agrarian-based common law tradition, instead adopting the more "modern" legal positivistic (pro-industry) trend.[148] Most basically, the positivistic trend was concerned with the "economic effect a decision would have on business," and thus "focused on the public benefits generated by railroads in opening West Virginia for economic development."[149] Through this dramatic positivistic shift, the "New Court of the 1889–90 finally made a complete break with Virginia legal tradition and reinterpreted the law to favor, rather than hinder, industrial development."[150]

The relaxation of West Virginia nuisance doctrine constitutes a primary example of the New Court's pro-industry transition—and the broader failure of "proto-environmental law" to protect the region. As Jeff Lewin chronicles in "The Silent Revolution in West Virginia's Law of Nuisance," prior to the New Court's rise, the West Virginia Supreme Court had "viewed nuisance law as a protection of a landowner's 'natural right' to the use and enjoyment of property."[151] This stringent nuisance doctrine was embodied by the legal principle of *sic utere tuo ut alienum non laedas* ("to use your own as not to injure that of another").[152] This rule, as derived from Virginia's natural rights common law tradition, favored agricultural interests, as it focused "on maintaining the rights of agricultural plaintiffs in disputes with industrial defendants."[153] The rule thus upheld the agricultural "plaintiffs' right to be free of interference in the enjoyment of their property."[154]

Early West Virginia Supreme Court precedent held with the Virginia common law tradition; however, the modern positivistic trend gained sway under the New Court. That is, earlier West Virginia precedent "protected a status quo dominated by agricultural interests, which represented the overwhelming majority of Americans in the early nineteenth century."[155] But by the end of the nineteenth century, "industrial growth forced judges to shift away from natural rights and to adopt a more dynamic approach to nuisances such as smoke, noise, pollution, and other damages created by industry."[156] Thus, in adopting this modern view after 1890, the West Virginia Supreme Court "abandoned the static view of their Virginia-trained forebears and, to the great relief of business and government leaders, adopted a dynamic theory that recognized the economic use of property for commercial and industrial enterprise as well as for agriculture." [157] Thereafter, the implications of this shift became clear to the mass of the West Virginia citizenry—two-thirds of whom constituted farmers in 1890—because undoubtedly the "strategic support provided by the West Virginia Supreme Court constituted a subsidy for industry in the state." [158]

Another dimension of the New Court's legal revolution pertained to overturning strict liability principles under negligence doctrine. An important example includes actions brought against railroads for destruction of livestock or for property damage caused by fires (often produced by locomotive sparks). Broadly speaking, West Virginia Supreme Court precedent evolved towards "protecting the railroads from suits brought by farmers." [159] For instance, in the 1911 decision *Jacobs v. Baltimore & O.R. Co.*, the court held that a railroad is not guilty of negligence "when it shows that its engines were equipped with approved apparatus for preventing the escaping of sparks, and that such apparatus was in good repair, and as effective as any in general use on well-conducted railroads." [160] As the court adds: "What more can be required of a railroad company? From a perfect arrester a spark might escape. Human effort sometimes is inadequate. The Legislature has authorized it to run its trains, and in doing so it must use fire." [161] Ultimately, the West Virginia "New Court was so bold in reversing the strict liability standard in nuisance and negligence cases that its decisions can only be interpreted as the judicial subsidization of industry to the disadvantage of other segments in society"—which clearly was not in keeping with purely ideological formulations of classical liberalism favoring laissez-faire economic principles. [162]

West Virginia's New Court, in supporting industrial development, also modified doctrine pertaining to riparian rights, particularly in the context of streams. For instance, timber companies aimed to use all waterways—including non-navigable streams, typically unavailable for industry use—to transport logs. [163] In the 1889 decision *Gaston v. Mace*, the court ruled in favor of timber interests in holding that "the rights of the public and riparian property owners in such a stream was governed by 'reasonable use.'" [164] Reasonable use dictates that the "true test to be applied in such cases was not whether a stream was navigable but whether it was capable of floating vessels, rafts, or logs for purposes of commerce." [165] As the court held: "Reasonable use is the touchstone for determining the rights of the respective parties." [166] The effect of this adoption of reasonable use was that the court implemented a "more dynamic theory of the law's role in shaping society," which specifically was one that "directly benefitted industry over agriculture." [167]

The West Virginia Supreme Court established similar pro–coal industry precedent during this era—which squarely reflects the failure of period legal regimes to protect Appalachia. In the 1924 decision *Squires v. Lafferty*, small surface landowners sought to prevent a coal corporation from using a multi-acre tract of land as a public highway to transport mining machinery. However, the court held that "as incident to this ownership," the coal operator retains "the right to use the 'surface' of the land in such manner and with such means as would be fairly necessary for the enjoyment of the mineral estate."[168] The court adds that "when a thing is granted, all the means to obtain it and all the fruits and effects of it are also granted," and that the "use of the surface here involved is not only a reasonable burden to the surface owner, but is fairly necessary in the development and operation of the coal."[169]

Ultimately, while West Virginia's legal transitions stand out as a period exemplar, other Appalachia legal regimes certainly developed explicitly pro-industry precedent. For instance, in the common law context, period Appalachian judiciaries, like the West Virginia judiciary, not only shaped doctrine to provide "economic advantages to the industrialists," but also "to immunize the corporations from damages arising out of civil cases."[170] Consequently, the emerging Appalachian industrial sector was insulated from liability, which facilitated it in "overwhelm[ing] the weak and relatively powerless segments of the American economy."[171]

Wendy Davis discusses this region-wide phenomenon in the coal industry context in "Out of the Black Hole." As Davis chronicles, "courts in the coal mining regions of Appalachia have a long history of favoring coal companies," as Appalachian "courts have been adamant in their support of the mining industry, at the expense of any individual rights."[172] What is more, not only has this judicial support of the mining industry degraded the rights of the citizenry, but in the environmental context, the "judicial presumption that the rights to mine coal are superior to all other rights . . . contributed to the devastation of the surface lands in Appalachia."[173] The West Virginia *Squires* decision above reflects this regional trend; as another period example, the Virginia Supreme Court handed down a foundational decision in 1916, *Colliery v. Hamilton*, in which the court strengthened the rights of coal operators at the expense of small surface landowners. In *Colliery*, the "owner sought damages for subsidence, when cracks, fissures and holes appeared in the surface, making the land unsafe and unsuitable for agriculture."[174] The coal operator also rendered streams and springs on that land unusable. However, because the severance deed at issue in the case reserved for the coal operators "all the usual mining privileges,"[175] the court ruled against the plaintiff landowners—and this decision "paved the way for future courts to validate waivers of liability or to deny responsibility for the loss of subterranean streams or springs."[176]

Kentucky precedent developed during this era similarly favored coal operators at the expense of small surface landowners. In the context of coal operators' "necessary" use of surface lands, the 1921 Supreme Court of Kentucky decision *McIntire v. Marian Coal Co.* set significant foundational precedent. In *McIntire*, the deed at issue granted the coal operator the right "to use and operate the said land and the surface thereof" including using the surface as "deemed necessary and convenient for the full and free exercise and enjoyment of any and all the property."[177] Additionally, the deed contained a reservation for the grantor to retain "the free use of said land for agricultural purposes so far as such use is consistent with the rights hereby bargained [and] sold."[178] The question presented in *McIntire* thus turned on what rights the coal operator (or mineral grantee) had to the surface lands—i.e., given the agricultural reservation.

McIntire was decided in the interests of the mineral grantee. The court argued that the deed gives "sweeping and complete conveyance of all the coal and other minerals and certain specified rights and privileges to the company, to be by it exercised at will; that is, when it or its successors shall 'deem it necessary or convenient' to do so."[179] The court also notes that a "fundamental rule of construction governing in cases like this is that the instrument shall be construed most strongly against the grantors and in favor of the grantee both upon the grant of the property and the rights and privileges specified."[180] The court adds that under the deed the mineral estate constitutes the "dominant estate" and that "the other the surface, or servient estate."[181] Thus, the court ultimately held that "the parties agreed, and by their deed evidenced their purpose, to allow the company to have the full use of the surface for all the above-mentioned purposes, and others mentioned elsewhere in the deed, whenever and where 'deemed necessary or convenient' by the grantee or its successors in title."[182] The mineral grantee was therefore permitted to use as much as the surface as it determined "necessary" to conduct operations despite the agricultural reservation—which indeed could rise to "excluding the plaintiff and taking his house and garden," although per the holding compensatory damages would have to be provided.[183]

The Supreme Court of Kentucky continued to expand such pro-coal industry precedent. For instance, in the 1925 decision *Case v. Elk Horn Coal Corp.* the court upheld the *McIntire* principles while adding a caveat: "Clearly the defendant has the paramount right to the use of the surface in the prosecution of its business for any purpose of necessity or convenience, and of this it is to be the judge, and unless it exercised this power oppressively, arbitrarily, wantonly, or maliciously, plaintiff cannot complain."[184] As the court later would reflect, after *Case*, "restrictions on the previously unlimited, subjectively defined rights of mineral owners to use the surface estate appeared in our case law."[185] However, this caveat produced scant actual benefit for landowners, as "later cases made it clear that this was not a very significant restriction on the mineral owner's use of the surface."[186] As a prime example, in the 1934 decision *Wells v. North East Coal Company*, where the mineral owner constructed a railway across the surface lands after all coal had been mined, the restriction was of little benefit.[187] As the court later reflected, "one wonders why such action was not 'oppressive or arbitrary', at the very least."[188] That Kentucky precedent continued to generally favor coal operators also was illustrated by the 1946 decision *Treadway v. Wilson*, where the court extended the *McIntire* line of precedent to any surface mining practices (except for those conducted oppressively, arbitrarily, etc.).[189] Thus, similar to West Virginia, dimensions of legal regimes across Appalachia, such as those in Kentucky and Virginia, supported favored industry during the era of classical liberalism, which had disastrous effects for the region.

This chapter began by tracing the historical roots of environmental law. It was demonstrated that many societies that have adopted intensive modes of production have experienced pronounced environmental despoliation—such was the case with the Greco-Romans. Moreover, Western society also developed an intertwined socio-cultural ethos marked by the radical modification and heedless exploitation of natural resources. This chapter then explored a critical analysis of hegemonic liberalism, in which environmental law is wholly embedded; but liberal capitalism, as marked by ceaseless capital accumulation through "commodification of everything" and a growth imperative, is incompatible with our bounded universe of resources, which has thus precipitated our global ecological crisis per se. Lastly, this chapter analyzed the disastrous consequences produced by classical liberalism–era industrialization in Appalachia. A critical analysis of classical liberalism revealed that the paradigm—as actually implemented in Appalachia and beyond by exploitative actors—supported favored industrial interests while profoundly subordinating the mass of the citizenry (along lines of class, race, gender, etc.) in addition to the environment. As part and parcel of this phenomenon, elements of Appalachian common law regimes constituting "proto-environmental law" (e.g., tort-related doctrines such as nuisance and negligence) in addition to other legal regimes were explicitly transformed or otherwise developed to support favored industry. Therefore, it is wholly unsurprising that such period legal regimes failed to protect Appalachia.

Unfortunately, the era of classical liberalism was not a historical aberration; rather, it would merely lay the foundations for what was to come economically, socially, and environmentally in the region. Indeed, as subsequent chapters detail, the fundamental through-line in liberal environmental law—in both its proto- and modern manifestations—is such support for favored industrial interests, including the fossil fuel hegemony, at the expense of Appalachia's welfare.

CHAPTER 3

TWENTIETH-CENTURY APPALACHIA: FAILED DEVELOPMENT MODELS AND COAL'S HEGEMONY

This chapter discusses Appalachia's early-to-mid-twentieth century period, beginning with the dramatic transitions the region underwent during the Great Depression and New Deal era. Even prior to the Depression per se, the region already had endured considerable tumult throughout the 1920s. The coal market experienced a substantial, post–World War I bust; so, too, had the timber industry declined rapidly. And the Depression per se indeed wrought disastrous economic and social harms on the region. With the coming of New Deal–era reforms, however, the Appalachia from the era of classical liberalism would give way to an Appalachia increasingly defined by a newer strain of liberalism: welfare state liberalism. But even as New Deal–era reforms, and later the Appalachian-focused War on Poverty, aimed to "uplift" the region, the liberal paradigm, as operationalized by exploitative actors, would continue to wreak social, economic, and environmental devastation on the region. Specifically, such liberal development paradigms failed to challenge the fossil fuel hegemony—which was the true cornerstone of Appalachia's exploitative ecological political economy. Thus, because twentieth-century Appalachian reform paradigms ultimately failed to challenge the liberal status quo, truly transformative change was not achieved.

Next, this chapter discusses the coal industry's continued role in environmental and related social and economic devastation in the region. During the mid-century period, the coal industry engaged in a widespread pivot from underground mining towards mechanization-centric surface mining; also beginning in this era, coal operators effectuated a mass, systemic, and essentially permanent reduction in the mining workforce. Such transitions resulted in the intensification of the destruction of the Appalachian environment and in accompanying multidimensional harms to the citizenry. (This, of course, in addition to Appalachian coal's growing contribution to the global ecological crisis vis-à-vis carbon emissions from coal-fired power plants.) Lastly, this chapter turns to a more positive phenomenon: such mid-century mining upheaval did lead to the eventual development of a robust Appalachian citizen resistance movement. More broadly speaking, environmental and other progressive grassroots activism—i.e., as emanating from War on Poverty organizing activities, continued labor organizing, the nascent Appalachian studies movement, etc.—would persist as central forces for social change in Appalachia (even if not always complementary), leading to the diverse Appalachian grassroots landscape of today, as chronicled in subsequent chapters.

NEW DEAL IN APPALACHIA

The Great Depression was devastating for Appalachia. It can actually be said that the Depression commenced a decade early in the region, when the coal industry declined precipitously in the post–World War I years due to overproduction and greater competition (such as from reinvigorated European markets); also during this time period, the Appalachian timber industry declined rapidly.[1] What is more, the early onset of Appalachian Depression conditions can also be traced to the lack of a diversified Appalachian economy—as explicitly engineered by exploitative actors (e.g., the fossil fuel hegemony)—thus resulting in the initial 1920s coal "bust" period becoming particularly consequential. Even prior to the formal Depression era, then, Appalachia's undiversified regional economy collapsed; thereafter, the period conditions in Appalachia were "marked by the most severe hardships—hunger, homelessness, and starvation."[2]

In the context of labor in the Appalachian coalfields, following their victories in "coal wars" incidents such as the Battle of Blair Mountain, coal operators had largely succeeded in consolidating their power in the 1920s—although labor struggles would persist in the coalfields in subsequent decades. Indeed, critical commentators argue that the New Deal at large was the product of class struggles. That is, as Rhonda Levine notes in *Class Struggle and the New Deal*, at the time "when Roosevelt took office, the industrial working class was becoming increasingly restive," as "capitalists . . . were gradually losing the iron grip that during the 1920s boom period they had enjoyed over the working class."[3] As a consequence, by the mid-1930s, "the industrial working class had actively intervened to determine the future course of industrial production," which "meant that whatever policy was pursued for economic recovery was hindered not only by the structural reality of the accumulation process but also by the activities of the industrial working class that interrupted the capital-accumulation process."[4]

But the coming of labor-focused New Deal legislation would create lasting impacts on the coal industry and on Appalachia as a whole. The tragic irony was that such legislation, despite its progressive underpinnings and its notable short-term victories, would nevertheless produce numerous, long-term negative outcomes for Appalachia. As will be discussed, such was the remarkably consistent through-line in much Appalachian-related reform and "development" efforts of the twentieth century. That is, in those instances in which the fossil fuel hegemony and allied governmental elites failed to outright thwart reform work, it would nevertheless succeed in thereafter limiting that promulgated reform to a mere marginal scope (or a superficial "fix" only). Even worse, the fossil fuel hegemony has often outright perverted implementation of such reform to create lasting pro-industry outcomes—as was the case with New Deal labor legislation.

The Wagner Act constitutes the most significant and far-reaching New Deal–era labor legislation; the act was a watershed moment for both Appalachia and the broader U.S. labor movement. The Wagner Act established basic guarantees for labor, which included the right to self-organize, to collectively bargain, and to engage in concerted activities; passage of the Wagner Act was of particular concern to Appalachia due to the prominence of the UMWA in the region, which, as Drake notes, was the "union in the nation most able to take advantage of the new legislation."[5] But the enactment of the Wagner Act would not in and of itself guarantee a newfound security and prosperity for coalfield residents. The effects of the Depression were long-lasting in the coalfields and were followed by a "declining boom-and-bust rhythm" for the remainder of the century.[6]

What is more, despite the seeming-victories attained by New Deal labor legislation, in a relatively short period of time, the "gains of the 1930s and 1940s were replaced by the uncertainties of the 1950s and 1960s."[7] Highly representative of labor's struggles was the Love-Lewis agreement reached between the UMWA and the Bituminous Coal Operators Association in 1950.[8] The UMWA leadership adopted a policy of maximizing compensation for miners. Unfortunately, however, this bargaining approach produced perversely negative outcomes for miners, as bad-faith coal operators pursued mechanization in the coalfields to explicitly displace more highly paid workers—because while "the agreement provided a high wage and improved health benefits for miners, it prevented the union from opposing any form of mechanization."[9]

Mechanization—in both surface and underground mines—would, in short decades, take a massive toll on mining employment. As Eller details, by "1960 fewer than half of the 475,000 miners in the region at the end of World War II still found work in the deep mines, and by 1970 that number had declined to 107,000."[10] Thus, for coal miners and the UMWA, the long-term implications of mechanization were dire: not only would mining technology displace jobs— but so, too, would the UMWA's influence wane as the UMWA's membership declined in tandem with displaced jobs. Consequently, many of the remaining Appalachian miners were again of nonunion status by the 1970s and 1980s.[11] (Note that chapter 5 discusses this mechanization-based coal worker displacement in the specific context of the treadmill of production explanatory model.)

Aside from the New Deal's effects on labor, the agricultural policies of the era were highly impactful on Appalachia. As chapters 1 and 2 detail, during the period of rapid industrialization, the coal, timber, and railroad industries radically transformed the region—and in the process, further degraded traditional agricultural modes (i.e., that already were under strain due to population growth etc.) in addition to severely despoiling the landbase itself. Nevertheless, subsistence and related agriculture modes retained a relatively robust presence in the region at this time.[12] And due to the market collapse (and consequent phenomenon of widespread displaced labor), small Appalachian farming was revitalized in Appalachia during the Depression: "subsistence agriculture . . . had to support people who were returning to Appalachia's farms from residence elsewhere."[13]

New Deal–era agricultural legislation would create highly controversial outcomes in Appalachia. The most important legislation of the era—the Agricultural Adjustments Acts (AAAs)—involved, among other things, the government guaranteeing prices for crops and regulating the amount of crops produced.[14] But as Salstrom chronicles in *Appalachia's Path to Dependency*, AAA-associated payments allowed larger operations to mechanize (and to otherwise gain more efficiencies, such as through fertilizer techniques), which increased productivity and profits—and thus facilitated the buy-out of smaller Appalachian farms.[15] Similarly, as Jerry Thomas notes in *An Appalachian New Deal*, the 1933 AAA "gave little attention to the lower end of the scale—the sharecroppers, tenants, and subsistence farmers," which ultimately "promoted the expansion of agribusiness."[16]

On the other hand, New Deal agricultural efforts did provide some measure of assistance for small Appalachian farmers, including through introducing more ecologically sustainable practices.[17] And period policies, as associated with the Subsistence Homestead Division (and later, the Resettlement Administration), also produced worthwhile experiments in planned resettlement communities such as in Arthurdale and Tygart Valley, West Virginia, that had industrial modes combined with a subsistence-agricultural undergirding (i.e., and which are thus of interest to *Remaking Appalachia*).[18] While many residents would "regard subsistence homesteading as a success," ultimately the program did not engender lasting results.[19] Such an outcome likely was inevitable, however, due to both its essential top-down nature and the fact that broader, more radical transformations of the Appalachian political economy were not effectuated. Stoll, for instance, notes that such planning "was no experiment in agrarian autonomy," as the "garden would be wedded to the factory."[20] (Chapters 6 and 7, in contrast, discuss mass mobilization–steeped bottom-up transformations towards truly radically conceived solidarity- and subsistence-based modes in Appalachia, including in the context of community-based agriculture.)

Dimensions of the New Deal pertaining to nascent welfare systems also were highly consequential in the region. Programs such as Social Security were established during this era—but so, too, did New Deal innovations geared towards providing public work–based income to disadvantaged citizens constitute welfare programs, such as the Civilian Conservation Corps (CCC).[21] Also, the creation of the Tennessee Valley Authority (TVA) had substantial impacts on the region. The TVA was initially created to "coordinate flood control, reforestation, and economic development," but by the WWII era, the TVA transitioned towards low-cost electricity generation as driven by Appalachian coal produced by surface mining; consequently, the TVA contributed greatly "to the further desolation of the mountains."[22]

Appalachia would come to intensively utilize welfare programming from the New Deal–era onwards. Although conservative commentators incorrectly trace Appalachia's widespread use of welfare programs to deficient cultural characteristics of the region—as part and parcel of the "myth of Appalachia" phenomenon—the foundational cause emanates from the structural conditions discussed thus far in *Remaking Appalachia*. Most directly, Drake argues that it was "maladjustments in Appalachia's major industries, particularly coal mining and agriculture," that produced intensive welfare state use—as exacerbated by the mono-economy conditions and boom-and-bust cycles engineered by fossil fuel hegemony and complicit governmental elites.[23]

What is more, liberal welfare state programming, as operationalized in the region, largely served to reinforce the exploitive status quo. This is due to the fact that local Appalachian elites utilized the administration of such programs—in the New Deal era and thereafter—as a control mechanism over the greater citizenry. As Eller chronicles in *Uneven Ground*, as the twentieth century progressed, coal operators exercised less direct control over the day-to-day governance of Appalachia—as previously exemplified by the company town model discussed in chapter 1.[24] However, local Appalachian elites soon occupied this power vacuum. So long as corporate absentee interests were maintained (largely through guaranteeing low tax rates on resources such as land and minerals), local elites were afforded a relatively free hand. And the "local leaders had little incentive to change existing economic and political relationships."[25] Consequently, New Deal–era welfare programs constituted a "boon to the local elite," as political power was maintained, for instance, by exchanging public jobs for votes.[26] Welfare expansions in the 1950s would only serve to further enhance the local elite power structure, thus producing a deeply entrenched, systemic barrier to any future attempts at transformative Appalachian change—in that the "mountain political structure fed on the poverty and dependent relationships that had emerged in the region and choked efforts at long-range planning and community development."[27]

This is not to say that New Deal–era policies were wholly detrimental. Surely, the class struggles that resulted in the Roosevelt administration adopting policies associated with expanded public programs and the social safety net—and the corresponding rejection of the prior era of classical liberalism—resulted in a more just and humane strain of liberalism. Therefore, there is much to admire in the New Deal, and such progressive policies no doubt improved the quality of life for many Appalachian citizens—at least in specific circumstances. But as the arguments put forth above demonstrate, one central flaw of the New Deal was that, as actually operationalized, such policies constituted a "miscarriage of development strategies" in the region—as illustrated by policies generally favoring large agricultural interests and by local elites corrupting nascent welfare programs.[28]

The New Deal, then, as actually implemented, furthered the degradation of select positive Appalachian dimensions while simultaneously failing to catalyze egalitarian and strongly sustainable alternative economic and sociolegal modes. Salstrom, for instance, has argued that New Deal policies further turned "subsistence farmers away from their traditional noncash systems toward cash."[29] Salstrom adds that the "vast scale of money's penetration into Appalachian farming areas, during and since the New Deal, has weakened . . . the region's subsistence-barter-and-borrow systems."[30] While Salstrom also argues that the earlier period of rapid industrialization helped degrade Appalachian agrarianism—as did even earlier phenomena such as pre–Civil War era population growth as accompanied by both "lowered per capita farm output" and reliance on more marginal lands for farming[31]—the New Deal–era agricultural policies (and their progeny) indeed would help further such trends (as would the treadmill of production–associated material phenomena discussed in chapter 5). And as discussed in chapter 2, period Appalachian agrarianism was further degraded through the mass conversion of private to public lands (e.g., in creating national forest lands in Appalachia).

More broadly speaking, period policies—like all liberal development programs that would follow in Appalachia—failed to challenge the fossil fuel hegemony and liberal capitalism at large. The exploitative coal industry remained the cornerstone of the region's ecological political economy. To be sure, New Deal–era policy transitions did not challenge this fundamental reality—nor did the New Deal radically alter liberal capitalism's broader exploitative conditions. For instance, in the environmental context, the New Deal did not fundamentally challenge liberalism's ceaseless-capital-accumulation-through-commodification-of-everything paradigm; period policies would thus only perpetuate and expedite widespread ecological destruction in Appalachia, the United States, and globally—as twentieth century perpetual economic growth was primarily fossil fuel–driven.

WAR ON POVERTY IN APPALACHIA

The 1960s War on Poverty was a second key twentieth-century policy initiative aimed at Appalachian development. Similar to New Deal–era policies, the War on Poverty was certainly grounded in good faith motives on the part of the federal government and collected actors. The War on Poverty has indeed been described as "a high point in the realization of the welfare state in the United States."[32] However, the War on Poverty would constitute, in large part, a New Deal–like "miscarriage of development strategies" in Appalachia—and thus its legacy is that of another failed liberal model. Like the New Deal, the War on Poverty's failures stem from the fact that it was merely part and parcel of the overarching liberal paradigm—systemic change was not effectuated, and so the exploitative status quo remained entrenched in the region. An additional (and interrelated) flaw of the War on Poverty was the inability to secure local citizen participation within the initiative—as the local Appalachian elite quashed such participatory democracy-steeped efforts. There were, however, some legitimate (and unexpected) victories derived from the War on Poverty. An exceedingly positive consequence was the catalyzation of a more robust grassroots landscape in the region—which would come to have a profound and lasting effect on the Appalachian social change landscape.

The War on Poverty is often traced, in considerable part, to a series of studies and outreach work conducted at the mid-century point. Regional studies

and related work were carried out that linked Appalachia's issues, most fundamentally, to "educational and economic deficiencies" in the region—and which
thus primed policymakers for a liberal development-steeped initiative.[33] Also
during this time period, Michael Harrington published the influential *The
Other America*—in which Appalachia, along with other subordinated U.S. regions, constituted one such "other America" that had failed to develop.[34]

The theoretical foundations for the War on Poverty can be discerned from
many such collected mid-century works. Specifically, the policymakers responsible for constructing the War on Poverty were heavily influenced by a combination of "economic growth theory" and "human capital theory."[35] In the
economic growth dimension, a central notion of the War on Poverty was that
by better incorporating Appalachia into the liberal capitalist mainstream—
vis-à-vis stimulating and supporting economic development and growth—the
"War on Poverty" could be won. Appalachia could, in other words, join in the
economic boom that much of the rest of the nation had enjoyed since the post–
World War II years.[36] The War on Poverty's economic growth underpinnings
were dependent on the human capital theory—which held that "deficiencies"
among impoverished peoples could be remedied through workforce training
and, on the broader scale, cultural rehabilitation; per this school, supposed
Appalachian deficiencies were traced to individual and broader regional-
cultural failings—i.e., that the "roots of poverty" emanate from "the culture
and social psychology of the poor themselves."[37] By the 1960s, the myth of
Appalachia—that of the "land that time forgot"—had wholly embedded itself
in the national consciousness. Due to the Appalachian myth's ascendancy, it is
therefore unsurprising that War on Poverty architects simply aimed to "uplift"
the region through "development and assimilation."[38]

Of course, Appalachia did not require cultural uplift or assimilation—but
rather transformative change beyond the fossil fuel hegemony and broader
liberal capitalist paradigm. Such systemic change, however, was not envisioned
by War on Poverty policymakers. As Eller notes, when formulating and implementing the War on Poverty, few "questioned the benefits of growth or associated poverty with systemic inequalities in political or economic structures."[39]
Fewer still advocated for such systemic inequalities to be remedied via "the redistribution of wealth or political re-structuring" in Appalachia.[40] Thus, Great
Society policymakers eschewed the prospect of transformative change, instead
relying on the liberal-steeped paradigms of economic growth and human capital theory.[41]

Beyond these conceptual foundations—and their apparent liberal failings—the immediate political causes for the War on Poverty arose from John F.

Kennedy's 1960 campaign. West Virginia emerged as a primaries battleground state for then-candidate Kennedy; after touring the beleaguered state he promised that he would "inaugurate a War on Poverty" if successfully elected.[42] But it was the Johnson administration that carried out the War on Poverty as such. For Appalachia, the core statutes of the War on Poverty ushered in under Johnson included the 1964 Economic Opportunity Act (EOA) and the statute establishing the Appalachian Regional Commission (ARC) in 1965, the latter of which was the outcome of a President's Appalachian Research Commission report written on Appalachia.

ARC was established as an Appalachian economic development agency: specifically, as a federal-state partnership spanning thirteen states that was characterized, at the time, as a new federalism mode. Originally, ARC had a central focus on physical infrastructure development in the context of transportation (e.g., roads) but also healthcare facilities and the like.[43] ARC developed the influential division of Appalachia into three geographic regions: Northern, Southern, and Central Appalachia; the current ARC sub-regions include Northern, North Central, Central, South Central, and Southern.[44] The relative merits of the ARC-designated boundaries along with other traditional geographic definitions of the region are currently a source of robust debate among scholars who challenge traditional Appalachian geographic conceptualizations. As William Schumann helpfully explains, "Appalachia's boundaries can be defined in numerous ways, and these ways reflect the research objectives, worldviews, and/or power positions of the individuals, groups, and institutions making claims about what constitutes the region."[45]

The EOA's programs constituted those War on Poverty programs aimed predominantly at enhancing human capital development in Appalachia. To implement these programs, the EOA established the Office of Economic Opportunity (OEO). An important aspect of the OEO—an aspect that was, in many ways, groundbreaking, and which is of central importance to *Remaking Appalachia*—pertained to local-based participation in development strategies. The OEO created Community Action Programs (CAPs), through which organizers engaged with impacted citizens themselves, such as through forming groups that "consist[ed] of low-income citizens organized together to identify their problems and work toward possible solutions."[46] In crucial language in the EOA, Congress required that these programs be implemented with the "maximum feasible participation of the poor."[47] As will be discussed below, the inclusion of ordinary citizens in War on Poverty development efforts—vis-à-vis the "maximum feasible participation of the poor" precepts—would directly challenge the local Appalachian elite power structure.

Huey Perry was one such community developer in West Virginia, and he detailed his experience in *They'll Cut Off Your Project*. As Perry reflects on his period ethos, "I feel it is necessary that we take our time and build an organization that involves the poor in the decisions as to what types of programs they want, rather than to sit down and write up what we think they want."[48] However, as Billings and Blee note, during the nascent "War on Poverty . . . the intent of allowing poor people a significant role" ultimately constituted "direct challenges to the local political machine and its control over patronage" in West Virginia.[49]

Specifically, the conflict involved Appalachian community developers and the related citizenry as allied against the local political and economic elites; while local Appalachian elites responded favorably to the War on Poverty at its inception, by the late 1960s, resistance emerged against the "potentially revolutionary notion of 'participatory democracy.'"[50] Douglas Arnett described this conflict as follows: "the local elite was willing to tolerate the work of the development association as long as the innovations involved were merely 'functioning innovations' and not 're-structuring innovations' which would threaten the social structure."[51] Indeed, as Perry argues, challenging both exploitative corporations and complicit local elites—while organizing the greater, subordinated Appalachian citizenry at the grassroots level—ought to have been a central aim of the War on Poverty. Perry had initially thought that if "we can change the conditions of Mingo County, perhaps the whole state of West Virginia can be changed," and that "we should work to make this a model for the rest of Appalachia to follow."[52] Moreover, he felt that "any progress for empowerment had to come at the expense of the powerful."[53] As Perry reflected:

> The people were powerless to counteract the avalanche of individual and community problems inflicted upon them by the selfish economic system that had been organized to remove the coal and timber, leaving the area devoid of wealth. They had also fallen prey to a vicious welfare system that tended to frustrate them with its rules and regulations—imposed by middle class investigators and case workers with less compassion than commitment to the political *status quo*. Adding to the problem was the fact that Mingo's middle class went to great lengths to hide the injustices inflicted on the poor.[54]

Therefore, as Perry articulates, the central struggle for genuine Appalachian transformative change ought to have involved challenging the fossil fuel hegemony and complicit local elites—but this did not occur.

Unfortunately, not least of all because the local elites had strong, preexisting ties to the centralized D.C. administrators, the struggle between the community developers and the local Appalachian elites proved to be "no contest."[55] Such a local elite victory was solidified via a 1967 amendment to OEO appropriations legislation, known as the "Green Amendment," that required that local officials approve all funded OEO programs.[56]

Although the formal War on Poverty faltered by the late 1960s, the initiative would have some lasting positive legacies. In the first place, War on Poverty and related subsequent programming would play a role in the reduction of Appalachian poverty in the decades that would follow (albeit unevenly and only to a relative degree).[57] The War on Poverty also produced an unexpected outcome in the region: it catalyzed the development of a more rich and diverse web of Appalachian grassroots organizations and activists that persist—in robust form—in the present era.[58] This grassroots Appalachian renaissance would be far-reaching: "An unlikely coalition of ages, classes, and cultural backgrounds came together in the poverty wars to challenge popular ideas about the region and confront economic and political injustice," and "their collective experiences would test the limits of the social services model and shift the focus of the antipoverty campaign from individual uplift and local action to regional collaboration and structural change."[59] Relatedly, Jessica Wilkerson argues that despite the formal conclusion of the "top-down" War of Poverty in the late 1960s, nevertheless, a "grassroots war on poverty reverberated for over a decade" and "its legacies continue into the present."[60]

One such example of the burgeoning Appalachian grassroots movement includes the late 1960s campaign for miners' black lung benefits and enhanced safety laws. Black lung disease, or coal miners' pneumoconiosis, is a consequence of miners' exposure to coal dust; black lung and related issues, however, were (and continue to be) severely underregulated. But particularly after a fatal mining blast in Farmington, West Virginia, large numbers of miners were joined by other activists and allies, and this coalition was successful in securing passage of black lung and coal safety-related laws; reforms included state-based legislation followed by the Federal Coal Mine Health and Safety Act of 1969.[61]

In *To Live Here, You Have to Fight*, Wilkerson also chronicles the crucial grassroots activist and leadership role that Appalachian women occupied in the War on Poverty. Wilkerson draws on notions of a "grassroots war on poverty" in finding that when "antipoverty programs emerged in mountain communities, local women joined and shaped them to respond to the daily and entrenched problems that they observed," and that women also played a key role in implementing War on Poverty policies on the ground.[62] Moreover, in centralizing the import of notions of caregiving and reproductive labor in this analysis, Wilkerson argues that Appalachian women activists, even as often engaging in paid work, labor actions, etc., "drew on their social positions as caregivers as they articulated the goals of a multitude of grassroots campaigns," as "they infused social and political movements with those experiences of taking care of parents, husbands, children, and neighbors in the hostile environment created by coalfield capitalism."[63]

Wilkerson also unpacks the complex, material race- and class-based issues at work during this period, in first broadly noting that white Appalachian women activists generally benefited from white privilege–steeped social structures. However, class and gender issues inform this analysis, as poor and working-class white women often were "committed to relationships of economic dependence, in which they would trade reproductive labor for largely male-controlled property and wealth," and also, for instance, were disadvantaged in seeking paid jobs in industries dominated by men (i.e., even as white women enjoyed a structural advantage over African American women job-seekers).[64] Married white Appalachian women also received greater liberal welfare state support than both single white women and people of color.[65] What is more, while Wilkerson emphasizes that "Appalachia was not a place of white racial innocence" and that it correspondingly exhibited a wide range of patterns on race and interracial alliances, she nevertheless notes that many Appalachian activists "went on to identify common class goals and join interracial alliances in poor people's campaigns and the welfare rights movement."[66] Wilkerson concludes that many activists, who were both "black and white, countered images of Appalachia as a mythic white space" by "casting regional campaigns as part of broader, national struggles that saw racism, poverty, and oppression as interwoven."[67]

The anti–strip mining movement also was a significant contributor to solidifying Appalachian grassroots activism as a significant, lasting regional force. As Eller details, mining-related activism would create a potent alliance among small Appalachian landowners, War on Poverty organizers, regional academics, environmentalists, and the like. In an overarching sense, the movement coalesced due to such unifying factors as shared concerns over environmental harms (in addition to related issues, like under-taxation of industry) and also emerging conceptions of a shared Appalachian identity.[68]

The seeds of this mid-century grassroots movement can be traced to a small cohort of environmentalists who sought, at the beginning of the 1960s, to halt mining-produced harms; however, the movement arose in full force when small landowners and allied activists combated the growing encroachment of surface mining through formation of grassroots organizations and the like.[69] What is more, the mining-produced destruction of Appalachia became popularized nationwide during this era through works such as Henry Caudill's *Night Comes to the Cumberlands*. As Caudill writes, the "present crisis is compounded of many elements, human and material. They have produced what is probably the most seriously depressed region in the nation . . . The essential element of the plateau's economic malaise lies in the fact that for a hundred and thirty years it has exported its resources, all of which—timber, coal, and even crops—have had to be wrested violently from the earth."[70]

MID-CENTURY TRANSITION TO SURFACE MINING

The widespread pivot from underground to surface mining was primarily responsible for the intensification of the Appalachian environmental disaster. As discussed above, the transition to mechanized surface mining was due in part to changes in the labor landscape brought about by New Deal–era labor legislation—and as chapter 5 discusses, the treadmill of production explanatory model also sheds key light on coal-related mechanization. Consequently, as Chad Montrie details in *To Save the Land and People*, operators developed exceedingly "efficient," mechanized surface mining techniques as the twentieth century progressed.[71] In the early days of Appalachian coal, crude methods of non-mechanized surface mining were utilized: miners used horse- or mule-driven "steel scrapers, drills, and black powder to expose coal beds," and the coal was thereafter transported via wagon to waterways and floated downriver.[72] The eventual introduction of steam-powered machinery resulted in an early mechanized form of surface mining, and by the 1950s, steam power was displaced by diesel and electric equipment such as shovels.[73]

The "contour" mechanized mining approach, in particular, would make inroads in Appalachia. Contour mining involved creating a "bench" on mountainsides, thereby exposing coal seams. Contour operators removed overburden to create both a vertical surface, known as the "highwall," and a horizontal surface, which was constructed "at the level of the coal seam . . . and met the highwall at its base."[74] The overburden materials were then deposited down the mountainside creating massive "spoil" piles. West Virginia was an illustrative example of strip mining's rapid growth. As Montrie chronicles, in West Virginia, strip mining production "increased tenfold between 1939 and 1943."[75] And mechanized mining continued to expand in subsequent decades; by 1963, strip mining accounted for a third of all U.S.-produced bituminous coal.[76] Underground mining, too, was prominent in the region—but by this time, surface operators increasingly took "market share from deep mines."[77]

In the 1960s and 1970s, mechanized surface mining underwent additional transformations. First, in the 1960s, a variety of contour mining emerged in West Virginia and Kentucky that would eventually be termed mountaintop removal mining (MTR). MTR, which involves removing upper portions of mountains to reach coal, initially was adopted for ridgetops; rather than continuing to follow the contour, operators simply removed ridges to reach the coal seams beneath.[78] MTR was limited in scope during this period, though, for reasons such as easier-to-reach coal still being widely available (and due to other complex factors discussed in chapter 5).[79] Also in the 1960s, the mechanized practice of auger mining increasingly was utilized in Appalachia. With this variety of surface mining, operators utilized large drills to bore directly into exposed coal outcroppings.[80]

Due to the rapid increase of mechanized surface mining (and, of course, the continued destruction wrought by underground mining), Appalachia was beset by severe environmental damage by the mid-century point. As Mary Beth Bingman relates: "Tens of thousands of acres were stripped. Streams were polluted with sediment and acid mine runoff. Millions of dollars worth of timber was left to rot. Strip mining damaged all the Appalachian coalfield states and was resisted in all."[81] The environmental destruction wrought by mid-century mining practices was therefore extraordinary—and caused cascading ecological harms. For instance, not only did surface mining obliterate forest vegetation, but this also resulted in erosion and thus "stream sedimentation and siltation, accompanied by negative impacts" on both the environment and human communities.[82] Period mining also caused other negative environmental impacts. For instance, the noise, dust, and debris produced by blasting caused substantial harms; and spoil-related landslides also were negatively impactful, as both lives and property were lost due to "indiscriminate dumping of mine spoil" on upper slopes.[83] Extensive water supply issues also arose in this era, as both underground and surface mining contaminated the aquifers (and other waters) small Appalachian landowners depended on. As a consequence of such collective practices, "vast tracts of Appalachia lay denuded by mid-20th century."[84]

Aside from general, long-term environmental destruction in Appalachia, there also were severe isolated events. One such event includes the extensive flooding of 1957. By that point in time, both the timber industry and surface mining had denuded much of the landscape, resulting in sedimentation, for instance, inhibiting streamflow and a lack of absorptive vegetation on hillslopes. Consequently, the Central Appalachian coalfields were beset by severe flooding in 1957, resulting in mass property damage and over a dozen fatalities.[85] Another isolated incident was the 1972 disaster at Buffalo Creek, where 125 people in Logan County, West Virginia, were killed. The incident occurred when a coal waste dam from a Pittston Coal Company subsidiary collapsed, thus inundating communities with the wastewater and refuse. Although the Pittston Coal Company had a record of poor safety—and, in fact, Buffalo Creek–like coal impoundments had been banned by a federal statute—the Pittston company characterized the disaster as an "act of God."[86] Such is merely a sampling of the environmental and public health disasters wrought by the period mining industry.

APPALACHIAN ENVIRONMENTAL GRASSROOTS MOVEMENT

The rise of the historic 1960s environmental grassroots movement in Appalachia emanated most directly from surface mining's negative effects on human communities and the environment.[87] In Kentucky, surface owners were particularly vulnerable to surface mining–produced harms due to the broad form deed phenomenon. Broad form deeds, many of which were executed during the earlier period of rapid industrial growth, tragically emerged as a prime factor weighing against surface owners. Recall that, through broad form deeds, operators obtained mineral rights only—as the mineral rights were severed from surface rights.[88] What is more, recall that broad form deeds generally permitted operators the right to access those mineral rights as required—i.e., via provisions entitling operators to obtain coal "by any means convenient or necessary."[89] The small landowner, then, retained surface rights to the land (including tax responsibilities). Unfortunately, as mechanized surface mining increased, coal operators sought yet greater access, and through such "by any means convenient or necessary" provisions, engaged in destructive development activities on surface lands against the will of surface owners.[90] For small landowners affected by surface mining, much of their land—which, in many instances, was in small-scale agricultural use—was severely degraded. (Note that while the broad form deed phenomenon in Kentucky was particularly egregious, more broadly speaking, "in much of Appalachia, mineral rights has been severed from surface rights by the actions of mineral buyers at the turn of the century.")[91]

As discussed in chapter 2, the Supreme Court of Kentucky developed radically pro-industry precedent in this legal area—e.g., the 1934 decision *Wells v. North East Coal Company*.[92] But such precedent trends continued; for instance, in the 1968 decision *Martin v. Kentucky Oak Min. Co.*, the court held that "whether or not the parties actually contemplated or envisioned strip or auger mining is not important—the question is whether they intended that the mineral owner's rights to use the surface in removal of the minerals would be superior to any competing right of the surface owner." [93] Eventually, a Kentucky constitutional amendment, as approved by 82 percent of voters, was ratified in 1988 abrogating the broad form deed—and the 1993 Kentucky Supreme Court decision *Ward v. Harding* upheld this amendment.[94] However, a great many Appalachians were displaced in Kentucky and beyond;[95] and indeed it was during this era that the so-called "Great Migration" out of Appalachia occurred, wherein millions of Appalachians—facing poverty and displacement—emigrated to Midwest industrial cities such as Cincinnati, Detroit, and Chicago.[96]

Also detailed in chapter 2, elements of the larger legal regime were transformed to support the mining industry, and this similarly catalyzed the development of a robust grassroots movement. Recall that tort actions against mining operators (e.g., nuisance and negligence) were a prime form of period law governing environmental disputes. Recall also that such tort actions against industry were not only unsuccessful—but that pertinent doctrines were, in fact, modified to support industry (as was exemplified by the West Virginia judiciary's "legal revolution"). However, in response to the growing recognition of surface mining's multitudinous harms, additional, state-level legislation was enacted in this era. Following sustained public outcry pertaining to surface mining's ravages, "several states responded by passing laws regulating the practice." [97] In 1939, West Virginia was the first state to pass such legislation, and it enacted numerous follow-up acts, with 1969 legislation including criminal liability for failure to reclaim mining sites.[98] Other states followed suit, but such statutes were underfunded and marked by noncompliance (on the part of operators) and non-enforcement (on the part of the states). As Patrick McGinley summarizes, rather than "placing limits on the worst of strip mining abuses, legislators chose to protect their own domestic industry." [99] McGinley adds that surface mining–produced environmental devastation reached "catastrophic levels" during this time period, as "coal mining was essentially unregulated." [100] Therefore, like the common law regime, state-based legislation enacted during this period was wholly ineffectual.

A grassroots Appalachian movement arose to seek relief via legal-institutional channels, but also to pursue robust direct-action practices against mining operators including civil disobedience. Montrie has referred to this grassroots movement as "environmentalism of the common people," in that the "campaign to abolish stripping was primarily a movement of farmers and working people of various sorts, originating at the local level." [101] (This compared to the more explicitly Romanticism-steeped mainstream environmentalism, which was often based on middle- and upper-middle-class values steeped in aesthetic appreciation for nature—rather than in protection of individual homes or property.) Such a bottom-up, grassroots approach to Appalachian environmentalism was, in many ways, historically groundbreaking: in the mid-century period and thereafter in Appalachia—up to and including the present era—ordinary citizens would occupy a central role in the regional environmental movement.

Numerous grassroots environmental organizations formed during this period. Prominent examples include the Appalachian Group to Save the Land and People (AGSLP) formed in 1965; Save Our Cumberland Mountains (SOCM) formed in 1972 in Tennessee; the Citizens Coal Council, which constituted "an umbrella group to bring grassroots groups together," [102] and, similarly; the Appalachian Coalition, which was formed by "leaders of anti-strip mining organizations from Kentucky, Ohio, West Virginia, and Virginia . . . to coordinate a regional movement for a federal ban" of surface mining. [103]

While legal efforts were important during this era, so too did direct action and civil disobedience occur, especially as citizens "became disillusioned while seeking change through political and judicial channels." [104] Thus, as a result, "the 1960s witnessed some of the most militant direct resistance to strip mining." [105] Resistance practices included nonviolent actions but also more violent occurrences (e.g., property damage and gunfire). In terms of more violent practices, Appalachia resisters sabotaged mining property with explosives; for instance, at the Round Mountain Coal Company in Kentucky, resisters used explosives to cause $750,000 in damage to equipment. [106] Gunfire exchanges between opponents and operators also occurred during this period, such as a 1967 incident at the Tarr Heel Coal Company. [107]

Civil disobedience of this era typically involved the illegal occupation of mining sites, blocking coal road traffic, and so forth. As one example, an anti–surface mining civil disobedience action occurred in 1967, when Kentucky residents Carl West and Don Branham halted operations by standing in the path of bulldozers. [108] However, Kentucky resident Ollie Combs—known popularly as "The Widow Combs"—carried out the most prominent act of civil disobedience of the era. As Joyce Barry writes in *Standing Our Grand*: "Combs climbed upon the ridge by her house and stood in front of bulldozers to stop their operations. She was subsequently arrested, and local newspapers carried dramatic pictures of this older woman being carried away in handcuffs . . . [thus] garnering a lot of attention for the anti-strip-mining campaigns." [109] Combs' act of civil disobedience therefore assisted in galvanizing public support—in both Appalachia and the broader United States—for the anti-mining movement.

Combs' act also underscores the extent to which women were involved in the period anti-mining movement (which, as will be discussed, constitutes an important and much-discussed through-line in modern Appalachian activism). As Barry notes, women were highly active in this campaign, with resistance work including lobbying for state and national law reform.[110] So, too, were women involved in direct action and disobedience actions against strip mining operations. For instance, in 1972, women halted operations on a strip mine in Knott County, Kentucky. As Bingman, one of the participants, reflects in *Fighting Back in Appalachia*, "we did shut down the mining operation . . . [and] it helped increase state and national awareness about strip mining and probably contributed to the passage of reform legislation."[111]

As Robert Perdue and Christopher McCarty write in "Unearthing a Network of Resistance," the broader grassroots movement indeed had a profound national impact: "By the early 1970s images of denuded landscapes and heartbreaking stories of personal loss due to strip mining hoisted the issue into the American collective consciousness."[112] Additionally, by this time, the broader U.S. "environmental revolution"—and the accompanying transition towards environmental law—were in full force, as is detailed in chapter 4. Therefore, such collective socio-legal conditions provided the opportunity for meaningful mining legislation. While it was readily apparent that such regulation was required, however, "the specifics of the intervention were hotly debated."[113] As noted above, many Appalachian grassroots organizations (and, of course, individual citizens) favored outright abolition of surface mining, or a "ban" bill. In contrast, national environmental organizations—namely, the so-called "Big Greens," including the Sierra Club and the Environmental Policy Center—were more open to legislative compromise.

The outcome of this conflict was compromise: the Big Greens eventually co-opted legislative stakeholder discussions and accepted regulation over abolition. As Perdue and McCarty chronicle, "the influence of these groups quickly became evident, as their large lobbying capabilities and credibility in the eyes of politicians resulted in their commandeering of negotiations over strip mining legislation."[114] What is more, during the stakeholder negotiation process, the Big Greens "ill-served local activists"[115] as they "convinced many strip mining opponents with deeper roots in Appalachia to lend their influence and resources to passage of regulatory legislation rather than an abolition bill"— which would take the form of the Surface Mining Control and Reclamation Act of 1977 (SMCRA).[116]

While the specific mechanics of SMCRA are discussed in chapter 5, here it can emphasized that SMCRA received substantial criticism following its enactment. President Carter, for instance, characterized SMCRA as a "watered down" act.[117] And the Appalachian Coalition labeled SMCRA a "blatant travesty" and "betrayal."[118] The Appalachian Coalition also accurately predicted the cascading failures of SMCRA, due to the fact that it helped legitimate MTR, relied on conservative Appalachian state governments for implementation (as a cooperative federalism scheme), and otherwise did not protect surface owners.[119] Likewise, J. W. Bradley of SOCM characterized SMCRA as "shortsighted, unrealistic, and a waste of time."[120]

SMCRA's passage likely had a permanent impact on grassroots organizing in Appalachia. The controversy over regulation versus abolition of surface mining created a long-lasting "divide between the Big Greens and grassroots groups."[121] As Eller writes, "the fight for a national abolition bill dramatized the gap between middle-class conservationists who saw surface mining essentially as an aesthetic and moral assault against the environment and Appalachian activists who perceived the practice as part of a larger system of regional exploitation."[122] Ultimately, the national conservationists "were more willing to compromise in favor of government regulation," while the "former poverty warriors and poor people who led the mountain resistance organizations distrusted the ability of institutions to protect their lives and homesteads."[123] Of course, fears of the Appalachian citizenry were borne out. As is detailed in chapter 5, SMCRA-as-operationalized only marginally regulated industry—and what is more, due to SMCRA's ultimate inability to halt mountaintop removal, SMCRA could be said to perversely help *accelerate* regional devastation through crucial dimensions.[124] (As discussed in chapter 4, this dovetails with the central critical argument that, once enacted, liberal law reform very often veils and indeed exacerbates the harms supposedly being newly regulated—as such formal legal enshrinements lead the public to believe that the legal system now is "taking care" of matters—and so the public thus disengages in concern and advocacy on those issues.) SMCRA, then, constituted a watershed event for Appalachia: the opportunity to outright ban surface mining had passed—to the profound determinant of the region.

As this chapter has demonstrated, early-to-mid-century Appalachia was marked by both the rise of welfare state liberalism and the continued hegemony of the coal industry. In the context of coal, the rise of mechanization-intensive surface mining (and the continuation of underground mining) produced truly catastrophic results in the region. Additionally, period legal regimes offered no recourse from such regional destruction, as tort doctrines and nascent state-based environmental regimes were ineffective. Lastly, the circumstances surrounding passage of SMCRA ultimately proved tragic, as an outright ban of surface mining was not achieved. The rise of welfare liberalism also occurred during this era, and at first blush, this development produced positive and far-reaching outcomes for the region. That is, the struggles that produced the New Deal and later the Appalachian-focused War on Poverty certainly constituted well-intentioned policies and a more just alternative to the prior classical liberalism period. However, the overarching failure of these initiatives in Appalachia can be traced to intertwined flaws including, among other things, first, their failure to challenge the local Appalachian elite power structure via a genuine bottom-up grassroots approach, and second, such reforms failed due to their mere incremental scope—that is, transformative change beyond hegemonic liberal capitalism was not accomplished in the region and beyond. Despite such failures to achieve transformative change, there was, however, an exceedingly significant regional development that occurred: an emergence of an Appalachian "renaissance" made up of ordinary citizens, grassroots activists, allied academics, and the like.[125]

CHAPTER 4

ENVIRONMENTAL LAW: A CRITICALLY FLAWED PARADIGM

Environmental law's rise, in many ways, was a remarkable phenomenon: through the 1960s environmental revolution leading up to the first historic 1970 Earth Day, millions of good-faith activists and reformers swiftly catalyzed passage of the nascent regime. Tragically, however, despite the best intentions of these citizens and of many policymakers, environmental law has proven a comprehensive failure. This chapter chronicles environmental law's critical flaws. First, the immediate factors leading to the regime's rise are discussed: namely, the 1962 publication of Rachel Carson's *Silent Spring*, acute environmental disasters, and the broad 1960s environmental revolution per se. This chapter then discusses the core elements of environmental law as rapidly enacted in the late 1960s and 1970s and subsequently developed further.

Next, this chapter unpacks the multitudinous, intersecting dimensions through which environmental law has failed. Such failures emanate from the fact that environmental law was enacted in an ad hoc and therefore disjointed manner; that industry and complicit lawmakers succeeded in embedding nascent environmental law with legislative "outs" through which industry could continue polluting vis-à-vis permitting regimes (thus thwarting the very intent of the acts); that administrative agencies lack direct democratic accountability, and so are largely unresponsive to public pressure; relatedly, that agencies are susceptible to endemic "industry capture," which occurs when industry co-opts the very administrative bodies charged with their regulation; and, more broadly, that environmental law, as ultimately relying on all branches of government and at differing levels, constitutes a massively intricate and slow-moving governance scheme. However, beyond these considerable flaws, environmental law has fundamentally failed due to its embeddedness within the hegemonic liberal paradigm. That is, environmental law was designed to merely support energy law's productionist orientation and, more broadly, the ecologically unsustainable liberal capitalist paradigm. Consequently, despite incremental "successes" achieved by environmental law, the global ecological crisis has only intensified since the regime's enactment due its essential liberal character.

ENVIRONMENTAL LAW'S RISE

The historical undergirding for contemporary environmental law and its early legal foundations are discussed in chapter 2; however, there were also more immediate social, political, and ecological causes for environmental law's rise. In fact, the basic environmental law framework was constructed on an exceedingly swift timeline: largely in the late 1960s and 1970s. Unfortunately, as is discussed below, environmental law's failure can at least partially be traced to the quasi-revolutionary manner in which it was enacted. That is, because environmental law was based on a legitimate ecological awakening among the public—as combined with the good-faith efforts of many reformers and policymakers—the environmental regime was largely hailed as an overwhelming victory and enjoyed an exceedingly positive reputation thereafter. But such widespread goodwill towards the environmental law regime long served to *veil* its critical flaws (i.e., although, as discussed in subsequent chapters, increasing public alarm over the climate crisis has in very recent years countered this long-standing trend).

The environmental revolution arose in the United States and internationally in the 1960s and was, on a macro scale, the immediate socio-political cause for environmental law's enactment. The birth of the environmental movement is commonly traced to the 1962 publication of Rachel Carson's *Silent Spring*, which argues that pesticides pose a severe ecological threat.[1] As Carson writes, through modern "approaches to the problem of sharing our earth with other creatures there runs a constant theme, the awareness that we are dealing with life—with living populations and all their pressures and counter-pressures, their surges and recessions," and that the "current vogue for poisons has failed utterly to take into account these most fundamental considerations."[2] *Silent Spring* was informed by a much longer tradition of essentially environmental-related thought as introduced in chapter 2—i.e., dating back to the Romantic and Enlightenment traditions—as combined with conservation- and preservation-centered developments. *Silent Spring* also was largely responsible for the rapid growth of an explicitly ecology-steeped epistemology in the broad public; thus, *Silent Spring* ultimately "resonated with the public and elites throughout the world," and played a key role in shaping the popular environmental movement.[3]

The environmental revolution of the 1960s was, in essence, an organic, bottom-up movement. As Tarlock details in "History of Environmental Law," the decade's nascent environmentalism "started as guerila protests against public and private actions that threatened continued air, water, and soil pollution or the destruction of the 'natural' areas of scenic beauty."[4] Additionally, such popular environmental concerns involved contestations over continued development projects perceived as either harmful or too radical in scope. Thus, the birth of the environmental movement was organic and often at the grassroots level, having "developed from a series of decentralized protests against specific public works and other forms of unwanted development and was initially entirely negative, seeking to prohibit environmentally undesirable activities by political means."[5] As is detailed in chapter 3, the Appalachian anti–surface mining movement of the 1960s at least partially constitutes a niche microcosm of this broad phenomenon, as small landowners were preoccupied with protecting their health, welfare, and property from the mining industry onslaught—and as small landowners and allied activists shared related concerns over broader environmental protection and aesthetics.

During the environmental revolution era, there also were specific, high-profile ecological events that galvanized public support in the U.S. and internationally. One such event was the 1966 coal spoil collapse in Aberfan, South Wales, that killed 144 people—the great majority of whom tragically were children—and which "prepared the way for a greater understanding of the implications of pollution."[6] (The previously discussed 1972 Buffalo Creek disaster in West Virginia resembled and indeed followed a similar pattern of corporate recklessness as Aberfan.)[7] Another high-profile environmental incident was the 1967 *Torrey Canyon* tanker wreck, wherein 117,000 tons of crude oil spilled off the English coast.[8] Ultimately, specific environmental disasters such as Aberfan and *Torrey Canyon*—and numerous subsequent incidents, such as the 1969 oil spill off the Santa Barbara coast—"brought home to a great many Americans a feeling that protection of their environment would not simply happen, but required their active support and involvement."[9]

The environmental movement of the 1960s, then, was animated by a combination of longer-term socio-historical trends and more specific watershed moments such as the publication of Carson's *Silent Spring* and high-profile ecological disasters. However, it should also be noted that the environment movement intersected—i.e., was both informed and was informed by—other grassroots social movements of the era. In the United States and internationally, this generally was a period of great grassroots tumult, in that the civil rights, feminist, environmental, and anti-war movements arose in quick succession.[10]

The historic 1970 Earth Day was the most immediate political precursor to the enactment of environmental law. In April of that year, twenty million protestors participated in the first Earth Day, rallying around such issues as air and water pollution and toxic waste. The event coalesced around the explicit aim of limiting environmental harms through transformation of both the state and industry; as an essentially direct result of these historic protests, the federal legislature commenced the process of constructing environmental law.[11] Although environmental law would continue to evolve over the decades, the framework established during this period constitutes the nascent core of the regime.

OVERARCHING FEATURES OF ENVIRONMENTAL LAW

The nascent heart of environmental law was enacted in the late 1960s and 1970s. The Surface Mining Control and Reclamation Act of 1977, as introduced in chapter 3 (and as is discussed at length in chapter 5), was one such act; however, it was merely one act among an emerging constellation of environmental law. The National Environmental Policy Act of 1969 (NEPA) is considered the progressive landmark environmental law in the United States; NEPA is a procedural-based act that requires federal agencies to formally incorporate environmental values into their decision-making. For instance, under NEPA, "environmental impact statements" are used to determine the ecological impacts of development activities. NEPA, though, was only the beginning—or the "big legislative step that led to the cornucopia of 1970s legislation."[12] Many of the most notable federal pollution-control acts that followed include the Clean Water Act (CWA), the Clean Air Act (CAA), the Comprehensive Environmental Response, Compensation, and Liability Act (CERCLA), the Resource Conservation and Recovery Act (RCRA), the Safe Drinking Water Act (SWDA), the Toxic Substances Control Act (TSCA), and the Marine Protection, Research, and Sanctuaries Act (MPRSA).[13]

However, these acts only constitute a representative sample of environmental law. For instance, to NEPA we can add additional procedural-based acts that were highly consequential for environmental law, including the Administrative Procedure Act (APA)—actually promulgated well before the environmental revolution—establishing rules for agency-promulgated law (e.g., "notice and comment" rulemaking) and the Freedom of Information Act (FOIA) creating a formal mechanism through which citizens request government information. And aside from pollution-control and procedural-related acts, numerous other acts govern land and water resources, such as SMCRA, the National Forest Management Act (NFMA), the Wilderness Act, and the Federal Land Policy and

Management Act (FLPMA).[14] What is more, as Wood notes, not only do such acts constitute a mere sampling of federal environmental law—but so, too, did state and local environmental law proliferate from this period onwards, as by design, each state was required to implement pollution-control laws; and at the local level, a similar phenomenon occurred vis-à-vis land use ordinances and the like.[15] As Lazarus similarly concludes, new environmental "federal law contemplated a substantial role for state implementation, albeit subject to federal oversight," and "most states had begun to develop their own environmental programs and agencies by the end of the 1970s."[16]

ENVIRONMENTAL LAW'S DEFICIENT TECHNICAL DESIGN

As many commentators have noted, the overwhelming majority of these legislative acts were passed to address specific environmental problems piecemeal; consequently, the environmental regime is marked by needless complexity and inefficiency. (So, too, is the essential piecemeal nature of environmental law one major factor—among a great many that will be discussed—that contributes to the environmental law regime's sheer, overarching ineffectiveness.) Tarlock has described environmental law as "a series of *ad hoc* . . . legislative reactions to perceived problems."[17] Likewise, Wood has characterized environmental law as suffering from "extreme fragmentation" vis-à-vis a "splintered statutory scheme."[18] And Lazarus writes that such "fragmentation also makes it difficult to address issues in a comprehensive, holistic fashion."[19]

Due to a complex and intersecting range of factors—aside from the broader critique of environmental law's liberal character, which will be discussed below—environmental law failed to achieve its intended ends. As already noted, one central flaw of environmental law relates to its disjointed nature: rather than enacting a harmonious and mutually supporting set of environmental statutes, the legislative strategy was instead largely ad hoc. But another key factor contributing to environmental law's failure is its fundamental reliance on administrative agencies in implementing the regime—which is tantamount to a non-democratic delegation of environmental regulatory authority.

A vast cohort of administrative agencies, under the general authority of the executive branch, was required to commence implementation of the environmental regime as conceived of in the United States.[20] Recall that, previously, the judiciary primarily governed environmental disputes, but environmental-related power was in large part transferred to the executive branch: "today's environmentalism entrusts major action to expert bureaucracies," and there exists a widespread "belief in the good intensions of these agencies as the norm" and in a corresponding high level of agency competency and professionalism.[21] However, such environmental agencies often are marked by overlapping missions and mismanagement.[22]

More broadly speaking, Lazarus notes that such issues are compounded by environmental law's ultimate reliance on "authority among branches of government," as substantial efforts are required to "garner majority votes in both chambers; obtain presidential signature; achieve agency implementation and enforcement; and, if necessary, defeat challenges in court to the law's validity."[23] On this latter point, as will be discussed in chapter 5, reliance on the courts in a general sense has been an important dimension to Appalachian-related environmental legal efforts—as federal litigation often has been pursued in attempts to redress governmental failures to enforce environmental statutes and regulations; but such efforts have too rarely succeeded in the region. Lazarus thus concludes that the "natural and deliberate effect of fragmenting authority among branches of government and between sovereign authorities is to make it more difficult to enact" and to enforce laws in the environmental context.[24]

Widespread institutional capture—which occurs when the private industry supposedly being regulated co-opts the regulatory process and shapes it towards its own ends—was one immediate and long-lasting result of the environmental law regime's delegation of decision-making to administrative agencies.[25] The fact is, "enforcement agencies are securely captured by the industries they regulate."[26] Most basically, from the 1970s onwards, the constellation of environmental agencies largely became a technocratic-steeped bureaucracy charged with organizing and coordinating the destruction of ecological systems.[27] But how did such widespread agency capture come about—especially given the good-faith intentions of many period environmental law architects?

Environmental agencies were wholly susceptible to such capture, in the first place, due to their built-in structural flaws. Unlike lawmakers from the legislative branch who are, at least in theory, beholden to the voting populace, executive branch administrative officials are simply appointees and often careerist professionals.[28] For instance, Craig Collins argues in *Toxic Loopholes* that many EPA employees "know that maintaining a tranquil, nonconfrontational relationship with the polluting industries they regulate is the key to pleasing their superiors and advancing their careers," and that such a "polluter-friendly orientation helps many EPA regulators land lucrative industry jobs when they leave the agency."[29] Of course, policy oscillation—or changes in presidential administrations causing corresponding political shifts in agency missions—results in some marginal and indirect accountability to the electorate. But by and large, agencies are shielded from direct democratic accountability.[30] A central flaw in agency-promulgated environmental law, then, is its fundamentally non-democratic nature—creating issues of transparency and accountability while simultaneously making agencies vulnerable to institutional capture.[31]

An additional, interrelated structural flaw in environmental agency design—which also implicates the capture phenomenon—pertains to the legislative "outs" built into the environmental regime from its very inception. As Wood argues, legislative history studies demonstrate that fossil fuel industries successfully pursued "outs" during the legislative process (i.e., via allied anti-environmental interests in Congress), wherein industry acquiesced to regulation on its face—but nevertheless secured mechanisms through which agencies would largely permit the very environmental harms the legislation was intended to curtail; the CWA is an exemplar of industry securing such "outs" during the legislative process, as it explicitly affords the U.S. Army Corps of Engineers great leeway to permit destruction of waterways.[32] As is discussed in chapter 5, such CWA language would, in time, create disastrous conditions in Appalachia, as it "provides a legal lever that the Corps uses to allow obliteration of streams resulting from mountaintop removal."[33]

Beyond the fact that such permitting regimes harm—rather than protect—the environment, the highly technocratic nature of environmental agency work produces an additional negative effect: it discourages citizen participation in environmental regulatory matters. In a broad sense, the environmental regime seemingly provides legitimate channels for citizen participation. For instance, NEPA- and APA-related mechanisms such as the APA "notice and comment" rule-making requirements are explicitly intended to generate citizen input within the administrative process.[34] However, a sad irony of those supposedly democratic procedural mechanisms is that industry interests—which, of course, are tantamount to anti-environmental interests—have largely co-opted and perverted these channels. Unlike the general public, which often lacks the technical expertise required for negotiating complex administrative processes, industry interests possess subject matter expertise—and, ultimately, of course, *capital*, which is crucial for co-opting regulatory channels. Consequently, industry often is able to "dictate the law" for "private advantage."[35] Specifically, industry interests "pay lobbyists, consultants, and lawyers to game the process at every turn."[36]

Large, professionalized environmental groups can, in theory, advocate for the environment and greater citizenry (as a de facto replacement for direct citizen participation in APA processes and the like). However, there are profound and fatal issues with large environmental groups constituting such "middlemen of democracy."[37] The most obvious issue is that direct citizen engagement—which, from a participatory democracy standpoint, should always be maximized—does not occur.[38] What is more, as the chapter 3 example of Big Greens co-opting the SMCRA legislative stakeholder discussions illustrates, broad-based environment groups do not represent the diverse needs of communities or regions. Indeed, from the 1970s and 1980s onwards—and in the entirety of the United States—there often emerged a stark divide between grassroots activists and large environmental organizations—as the "national organizations seemed too little interested in the plight of local communities, too seduced by their fund-raising efforts, and too willing to compromise local concerns for the pragmatic fashioning of national compromises."[39] (It is for this reason, among others, that explicitly mass mobilization–steeped systemic stepping stone environmental measures are put forth in chapters 6 and 7 as a radical alternative to modern technocratic environmental law—which has indeed engendered reliance on such large, "expert" environmental organizations as "middlemen.") From the explicit critical perspective, an additional issue with environmental-organizations-as-middlemen is that such organizations become dedicated to incremental, intra-systemic reform only—instead of pursuing wholesale systemic re-formations targeting the liberal capitalist paradigm at large. Consequently, contemporary mainstream environmental organizations typically are characterized as being captured by neoliberal forces, and therefore wholly complicit in the paradigm.

As a logical counter-argument to this critique of environmental law, many commentators might pose a seemingly pertinent question: has the U.S. environmental law regime not mitigated substantial negative environmental impacts? At least—and this is the critical point—on an incremental scale, this undoubtedly has been the case. As M'Gonigle and Takeda acknowledge: "These laws have had an enormous practical impact, from removing lead additives in gasoline to protect brain development in children, to making many previously polluted streams and rivers drinkable, and protecting large swaths of wilderness to facilitate biodiversity conservation."[40] As Wood adds, we would "probably . . . be worse off without any environmental law," because while "environmental law may be a failure," it is at least a " 'mitigated' failure" as it likely "slowed the pace of ecological demise."[41]

The considered response to this counter-argument is that while many incremental gains have been achieved vis-à-vis a critically flawed environmental law regime, nevertheless, on the macro scale, the United States and the world at large are beset by a severe environmental crisis that generally only *accelerated*—such was the case with climate change—since the enactment of the regime. And the consensus of the scientific community is that these combined catastrophes pose a truly existential threat—in that they already are degrading ecological systems worldwide and that, through further exacerbation, could result in the exhaustion—and corresponding collapse—of both human and broader global ecological systems (i.e., as discussed at length in chapter 5).[42]

What is more, the critical perspective illuminates the fact that the very enactment of the U.S. environmental law regime has, paradoxically, contributed to this catastrophic state of affairs—as the enactment of a seemingly comprehensive suite of environmental laws served to obscure the accelerating ecological degradation that nevertheless followed. Prior to the environmental regime's enactment, it had become readily apparent to the general citizenry that massive environmental harm was occurring in the United States and that legal measures were therefore required to alleviate this harm. However, after such environmental issues were formally addressed through law, the environmental problem seemed, to a great many, to be resolved—as highly regarded agencies such as the EPA were presumably monitoring ecological issues and redressing any substantial harms. And this phenomenon dovetails with the issue raised above regarding lack of citizen participation in environmental law—as there long existed a widely held notion that environmental law constituted a benign, largely self-sufficient regime, citizens often believed that environmental agencies were essentially "taking care" of matters (i.e., although again, as will be discussed, the increasing public alarm raised over the climate crisis stands as a very recent counter-trend).[43] Collins thus notes that in the decades following environmental law's enactment, there existed a "relatively low level of public knowledge, concern, and activism around the environment."[44]

The 1970s enactment of environmental law therefore facilitated the obscurement of a half century's worth of global environmental degradation because, once granted, formalized protections typically provide a false impression that an issue has been effectively resolved—and the issue thus fades from the collective public consciousness. Indeed, beyond environmental law alone, critical commentators have often unpacked comparable "obscurement" patterns in the context of new rights created via good-faith legal enshrinement. The case of the formal legal enshrinement of environmental protection principles is certainly in keeping with this broader pattern of well-intentioned—but failed—liberal law reform efforts.

HEGEMONIC LIBERALISM UNDERGIRDING OF ENVIRONMENTAL LAW

For additional reasons, the critical legal theory–steeped critique of the liberal paradigm demonstrates why U.S. environmental law—as actually enacted in the 1970s and thereafter—was destined for failure. Chapter 2 explains that during the historical era roughly classified as classical liberalism, powerful capital interests secured changes to prime "proto-environmental law" such as negligence and nuisance doctrine in addition to other key legal regimes. Thus, in Appalachian states such as West Virginia and Kentucky, powerful capital interests as aided by complicit governmental elites operationalized widespread legal support for favored industrial sectors (e.g., the coal, timber, and railroad interests) at the direct expense of the citizenry and environment. As chapter 3 discusses, the struggles leading to the ushering in of the liberal welfare state did not fundamentally disrupt the overarching liberal capitalist paradigm. Although the historic liberal welfare period did, through many dimensions, create a more just and humane strain of liberalism (e.g., a more robust social safety net), the essential through-line of liberal capitalism—ceaseless capital accumulation through multidimensional subordination of labor and the environment—persisted. Thus, from the New Deal era forward, the liberal paradigm (as supported by prime legal regimes) remained fundamentally in full force.

The environmental law regime, as enacted in the 1970s, was also merely supportive of the liberal capitalist paradigm. Thus, for this core, structural reason—even aside from environmental law's additional flaws discussed above, environmental law was wholly incapable of stemming the global ecological crisis. More specifically, as M'Gonigle and Takeda argue, both U.S. energy law and (supportive) environmental law are "framed by the overriding commitment to economic development and growth based on access to cheap energy resources," and more broadly, by ceaseless capital accumulation among elites.[45] Therefore, while the environmental law enacted in the 1970s and thereafter did serve to mitigate at least some environmental impacts, on the balance, the legal regime did not challenge liberal capitalism's (ecologically unsustainable) exploitative paradigm.

U.S. PRODUCTIONIST ORIENTATION OF ENERGY LAW AND POLICY

The liberal capitalist-steeped productionist orientation of energy law and policy spans back more than a century in the United States. As is detailed in chapter 2, the pro-industry development of the common law in Appalachian states was highly indicative of this phenomenon, as state courts explicitly transformed doctrines like nuisance and negligence to support railroads, the coal industry etc.—and relied on the public policy goal of industrial development to support such doctrinal transformations. So, too, did Appalachian states like West Virginia offer legislative-based tax breaks to favored industrial sectors (e.g., the railroads) during the period of rapid industrial growth.

Numerous other U.S. historical examples, however, illustrate how law transformed to support development during this period. One early example includes the common law "rule of capture" which "gives a mineral rights owner
title to the oil and gas produced from a lawful well bottomed on the property, even if the oil and gas flowed to the well from beneath another owner's
tract."[46] Such a rule produced a logical effect of landowners rapidly developing
oil beneath their tracts—so as to forestall adjacent landowners from exploiting that same common oil source.[47] Also in the oil and gas context, in the
early twentieth century, federal-level legislative "tax breaks reduced effective
tax rates and ultimately the costs of production, thereby increasing exploitation."[48] For more than a century, then, energy and related policy has been
geared towards increased production—and thus, ultimately, towards capital
accumulation among elites. As Tracey Roberts concludes, there exists a "long
history of federal support for fossil fuels," as the United States has been "picking winners and losers among energy providers for over 100 years," and what
is more, "today, the federal government provides continuing support for fossil
fuels."[49]

In the United States, fossil fuel subsidies to coal and oil and gas producers total an estimated $20 billion annually.[50] And the "largest subsidies for
fossil fuel sources" include "the foreign tax credit, tax credits for production
of nonconventional fuels, oil and gas exploration, and development deduc-
tions."[51] Coal accounts for an estimated 20 percent of all U.S. fossil fuel subsidies, with coal extraction (as compared to electricity production etc.) receiving
the majority of those subsidies.[52] There also exist implicit subsidies for fossil
fuels, as emanating from ecological, infrastructure-related, and public health
harms produced by the industry. One way to quantitatively account for these
more implicit subsidies is the social cost of carbon, which quantifies, in a dollar
amount, the societal harms caused by an extra ton of carbon dioxide emissions. As Amir Jina argues, the "U.S. emitted 5.4 billion tons of carbon dioxide
in 2015, with a cost per ton of $36," the then-social cost of carbon.[53] In 2015,
then, the U.S. was spending "$200 billion to cover the costs of all the emissions
being burned," which is "in effect . . . a $200 billion hidden subsidy to the fossil
fuel industry."[54] This annual expenditure is not abstract: rather, it constitutes
a "cost in real money—in lost labor productivity, healthcare costs, increased
energy expenditures, coastal damages—that is paid somewhere in the world
for each ton of carbon dioxide that is emitted."[55]

While fossil fuel interests have traditionally benefited from government
subsidies, numerous other polluting industries also receive significant government support. The U.S. agriculture industry is one such example—and

important for *Remaking Appalachia* (as community-based Appalachian food systems constitute an important dimension of the prescriptive recommendations put forth in chapter 7). From the New Deal–era AAAs forward, crop commodity subsidies have had the effect of favoring large agricultural interests (i.e., as introduced in chapter 3 in the Appalachian context), but also have incentivized specialization in those commodity crops that maximize agribusiness profits—namely corn, wheat, soybeans, and other monocultures.[56] As a result of these perverse government incentives—i.e., in addition to other material forces, such as those implicated by the treadmill of production model discussed in the agricultural context in chapter 7—small U.S. farms were largely eliminated and large, agribusiness-based industrialized farms have wrought extensive environmental damage. As Jason Czarnezki argues in "Food, Law and The Environment," the "existing industrial food model, heavy on chemicals, fossil fuels, and industrial processing, has been created, in part, by laws that have also impeded" alternative—and more ecologically sustainable and just—agricultural modes.[57]

As M'Gonigle and Takeda contend, in addition to industry interests, the productionist orientation of energy law has created, for the past century, another prime beneficiary: the state itself. In the period between the early 1980s and the late 2000s, oil producers annually provided over fourteen billion dollars of income taxes to states and the federal government—and over a trillion dollars in sales taxes and excise taxes.[58] The state then uses such funds for highway systems (i.e., that require oil-powered cars on the part of the citizenry). Consequently, in the "never-ending circle that is the modern capitalist economy," for the state, "the promise of incoming investments, taxes, and/or export dollars drives all governments to support the outgoing costs of developing the energy industry with incentives and subsidies."[59] This example aptly demonstrates what has long been an egregious status quo: fossil fuel industries and the state have engaged in a mutually beneficial, symbiotic relationship.

U.S. environmental law exists entirely within this ecologically unsustainable liberal paradigm. Environmental law, which arose long after the inception of energy law's intrinsic fixation on fossil fuel–driven growth—and of course, long after the capitalist mode of production at large emerged—simply mitigates (at best) the impacts of the energy sector and others. And as discussed above, environmental law very often, at worst, perversely veils unmitigated environmental destruction. As a consequence, the dilemma of "practical" intra-systemic law reform versus "impractical-but-needed" systemic reformations has long beset would-be environmental change agents.[60] As Keith Hirokawa argues in "Some Pragmatic Observations about Radical Critique in

Environmental Law," an "environmentalist must choose between two strategies. She can persist in the hope that courts will determine that the current environmental regime is inherently faulty, which will lead to the destruction of environmental law and property rights as we know them," or else, in the alternative, "she can recognize that the perceived barriers to integrating environmental ethics and environmental law are themselves a result of the rhetoric and persuasion from those opposing radical change."[61] *Remaking Appalachia* more specifically focuses on pursuing transformative economic and sociolegal change vis-à-vis bottom-up, grassroots mass mobilization, but Hirokawa's comments on the long-standing dilemma of would-be environmental change agents aptly characterize the perennial debate.

Significant current developments, in part, involve the fact that energy policy and practices have shifted "toward making new, and risky, forms of supply workable," including in the context of fossil fuels.[62] To be sure, the continued reliance on fossil fuels constitutes a profound civilizational error in the age of the Capitalocene (i.e., as discussed at length in chapter 5). For Appalachia specifically, the development of the Marcellus shale gas region and continued talk of "clean coal" technologies—among other examples (including MTR, as also discussed in chapter 5)—constitute such contemporary "new, and risky" forms of fossil fuel development. The much-derided notion of "clean coal" typically involves discussions on capturing carbon dioxide emissions from coal-fired power plants and burying them through the technology of "carbon capture and storage." Clean coal, however, has proven cost-prohibitive, and it fails to account for massive ecological damage caused by the coal extraction process.[63] And the massive development of Marcellus shale natural gas has resulted in re-investment in fossil fuels at the very time in which climate change risks have become existential indeed. Natural gas, as an "alternative" energy source, is thus not a viable option. More specifically, studies are demonstrating that natural gas's contribution to climate change is considerably higher than early accounts suggested. For instance, as has been argued in *The Human and Environmental Impact of Fracking*, important studies indicate that "methane escaping during shale gas extraction and the release of CO_2 during gas end use mean that the carbon footprint ($CO_2 + CH_4$) of shale gas is significantly greater than that of conventional gas and is actually very similar to coal when compared over the long term (e.g., 100 years)," although some debate still exists on these and related studies.[64]

Less intuitively—but equally alarming—the apparent redemptive potential of energy alternatives to fossil fuels is a false promise, at least in the liberal capitalist context, despite the recent breakthroughs in pertinent technology (and in the corresponding energy market penetration of these alternatives). This is largely because, to date, the "renewables revolution" has largely been conceptualized from within the liberal capitalist paradigm. This is not to say that the redemptive potential for clean energy sources does not exist—indeed, as is discussed at length in chapter 7, an ecofeminist- and ecosocialist-steeped transition towards clean energy systems is a viable path forward for Appalachia and beyond. However, clean energy as merely incorporated within the current paradigm is an unsustainable and unjust approach, as perpetual economic growth and other ecological harms produced by the capitalist mode of production (e.g., mineral mining practices for clean energy technology that exploit global indigenous communities)[65] will continuously offset such incrementalist clean energy gains.

James Speth also discusses the futility of mere incrementalist clean energy transitions in *The Bridge at the Edge of the World*. As Speth broadly notes, there is insufficient movement on the part of governments towards "systematically, adequately promoting the universal, rapid, and sustained penetration of green technology, at home and abroad, on the scale required," but that nations "are, however, profoundly committed to promoting growth."[66] Speth adds that "all we have to do to destroy the planet's climate and biota and leave a ruined world to our children and grandchildren is to keep doing exactly what we are doing today, with no growth in the human population or the world economy" as involving "release [of] greenhouses gases at current rates," but in fact, such activities are "accelerating, dramatically."[67] Thus, per such projections, a mere incremental transition to clean energy over time will not reduce the global greenhouse gas output sufficient to avert catastrophic climate change. Currently, the core benchmark to avert such disaster is set at a 2 degrees Celsius rise above preindustrial levels, which is articulated most notably in the Paris Agreement.[68] To reach this (increasingly unlikely) goal, what is required is an extraordinarily rapid decrease in greenhouse gas emissions; however, this is not occurring under the current incrementalist transition.[69]

Additionally, in our current era of late liberalism, Malm emphasizes that eliminating the fossil fuel–driven economy is exceedingly difficult due to the entrenched power structure. Climate science indeed dictates that we ought to eliminate fossil fuel use immediately, but for "the involved capital, that would be tantamount to an asteroid impact obliterating a whole planet of value, still awaiting its first harvest or ripe for a second or third."[70] As a specific example, a preexisting coal-fired power plant cannot be powered via renewable energy, it would simply have to be eliminated, thus constituting a loss for fixed capital. Also, the more emissions reduction is postponed, the more such "fixed capital operating as a block against them amasses more weight," and what has thus transpired long-term is that "inertia builds inertia, each generation in the fossil economy passing on a heavier nightmare to the next." [71] As Malm concludes, a "dark cloud of 'committed emissions' is hung over the future," despite recent and historic transitions towards renewable energy. [72]

NEOLIBERAL TURN IN ENVIRONMENTAL LAW

The failure of environmental law has been exacerbated by the rise of neoliberalism—or the specific incarnation of liberalism that arose (and has persisted as a dominant global hegemonic force) soon after the environmental law regime was enacted. Following the historic periods of classical liberalism (1700s–1900s) and welfare state liberalism (1930s–1970s), neoliberalism has defined our contemporary historical epoch. [73] Neoliberal-associated actors have, most basically, succeeded in dismantling welfare liberalism's more humane paradigm—thus creating, in effect, a quasi-revival of classical liberalism conditions and a resulting series of social, cultural, economic, and environmental ills. As will be discussed, in the explicit environmental law context, neoliberal actors have produced profoundly negative impacts through such dimensions as market-based solutions, deregulation, and the degradation of democratic forces—and thus have achieved more intensive structural support for powerful capital interests at the expense of the environment and citizenry. Consequently, the neoliberal paradigm has only exacerbated environmental law's interlocking failures discussed above.

As a starting place, neoliberalism can be thought of as a quasi-revival of classical liberalism—as steeped in laissez-faire, supposedly free market principles. While, as David Singh Grewal and Purdy discuss in "Introduction: Law and Neoliberalism," the "neo" denotes the fact that the neoliberal paradigm constitutes a novel form of liberalism, nevertheless, both classical liberalism and neoliberalism generally promote free markets and unjust concentrations of power—as compared to modes of governmental intervention. Grewal and Purdy add the following: "Neoliberalism refers to a set of recurring claims made by policymakers, advocates, and scholars in the ongoing contest between the imperatives of market economies and nonmarket values grounded in the requirements of democratic legitimacy." [74] Under the neoliberalism paradigm, the former, rather than the latter, reigns dominant: "Neoliberal claims advance the market side of this contest in capitalist democracies between capitalist imperatives and democratic demands." [75]

Grewal and Purdy investigate the fundamental linkages between neoliberalism and law. Neoliberal-associated conditions have insidiously seeped into most dimensions of "public and private life," including the law—as law has been utilized to help make manifest the neoliberal agenda by large capital interests and complicit policymakers.[76] As is discussed in chapter 2, during the historical era of classical liberalism, the law also was utilized to further classical liberal—and thus essentially pro-industrial—ends: "From the prohibition of labor unions through the shackling of government regulations, the ideology of classical liberalism secured the structures and fundamental relations of early industrial capitalism from collective interventions that threatened its ideal of 'free contract.' "[77] But a central feature of classical liberalism was that, "throughout, courts and other actors were fairly transparent about what they were doing and why they thought these actions were justified."[78] Similarly, in the contemporary landscape, law is one mechanism through which neoliberal-associated ends are furthered. Neoliberal-associated actors, however, make use of more diverse (and insidious) governance mechanisms; this is due to the fact that, among other things, the complexity of modern industrial states is not compatible with the mere laissez-faire posture of classical liberalism.[79]

More specifically, as conceptualized by Grewal and Purdy, neoliberal-associated conditions are operationalized through three core dimensions: deregulation, affirmative implementation of market-based approaches, and more purely ideological justifications for political and state action. In this way, neoliberal policy can justify deregulatory "roll-back[s]," as accomplished through a restoration of (quasi-classically liberal) laissez-faire conditions, such as through dismantling public welfare programs, efforts towards privatization, and so forth. But so, too, can neoliberalism involve the affirmative "roll-out" of market-styled governance, which, as will be discussed, has become an important dimension of the neoliberal turn in environmental law (e.g., cap-and-trade frameworks).[80]

Neoliberalism, then, is not a variety of pure "market fundamentalism."[81] Neoliberalism encompasses the highly normative questions of how "market discipline [is] being distributed—on whom is it imposed, who is exempted from it, and on what grounds?"[82] As Grewal and Purdy argue, "neoliberal policies are always distributive decisions," but are "ones in which distributive choices get couched in the neutral-sounding language of efficiency, liberty, and responsibility, or the pragmatic language of 'what works.' "[83] Neoliberal policies have followed a relatively straightforward pattern since their inception: they benefit elite capital interests at the expense of the greater citizenry and the environment—even if this entails a blatant "betrayal" of basic market principles. Perhaps the most easily identifiable exemplar of this neoliberal status quo is the outcome of the 2008 financial crisis; bailout funds were allocated towards banks (i.e., as not in keeping with laissez-faire precepts)—whereas homeowners did not receive such government support (i.e., and who thus suffered greatly vis-à-vis targeted imposition of market discipline).[84]

Relatedly, David Harvey explores neoliberalism as a fundamentally political project in *A Brief History of Neoliberalism*. Harvey argues that neoliberalism was operationalized by elite interests aiming to restore class power—i.e., in direct response to the redistributive effects of the liberal welfare state era—through such means as eliminating laws that limit elite capital accumulation and the social safety net, and that furthermore "it has succeeded remarkably well in restoring, or in some instances (as in Russia and China) creating, the power of an economic elite."[85] Harvey adds that neoliberal-associated actors generally have been unsuccessful in generating wealth across the board, because neoliberalism's primary achievement has been to "redistribute, rather than to generate, wealth and income"—i.e., as achieved through the phenomena of "accumulation by dispossession" of subordinated classes, populations, and natural resources.[86] Similar to Grewal and Purdy, Harvey also notes that "when neoliberal principles clash with the need to restore or sustain elite power then the principles are either abandoned or become so twisted as to be unrecognizable."[87]

Commentators also have explored the significance of neoliberalism vis-à-vis feminist and ecological feminist thought. Nancy Fraser puts forth one such exploration in *Fortunes of Feminism* in arguing that feminism at large was essentially co-opted by neoliberal forces over the course of several decades. Per Fraser's account, the "most advanced currents" of second-wave feminism were steeped in a radical, multidimensional aim to end to sexism, racism, classism, and imperialism—and which explicitly entailed a "transformation of the deep structures of capitalist society."[88] However, under neoliberalism's influence, feminism generally underwent a transition from "redistribution" to "recognition"—i.e., as feminism increasingly focused on cultural politics singularly rather than the intertwined project of transforming liberal capitalism.[89] As chapter 5 discusses, the Democratic Party's comprehensive failure during the 2016 presidential election reflects the broader, disastrous neoliberal-left consensus that has driven the party since the Clinton administration (and of which the neoliberalization of mainstream feminism was only one constituent dimension).

Feminism, in fact, expanded dramatically throughout the neoliberal era both in the United States and abroad, as "feminist ideas found their way into every nook and cranny of social life."[90] As compared to prior historical eras, women, of course, increasingly engaged in productive work; however, women had to contend with labor market segmentation by gender, depressed wages and reduced job security (i.e., as associated with neoliberalism across the board), an increase in sole female-headed households, continued disproportionate performance of (socially devalued) reproductive work (both paid and unpaid), and other related injustices, such as subordination in private life (as synergistically interlinked with wider structural injustices).[91] Consequently, Fraser indeed notes that capitalist forces favored recognition over redistribution, and constructed "a new regime of accumulation on the cornerstone of women's waged labor" while simultaneously disembedding "markets from democratic political regulation in order to operate all the more freely on a global scale."[92]

Such commentators naturally provide a strong critique of the neoliberal turn. Grewal and Purdy argue that "decent societies in which markets play a subordinate role to other decisionmaking processes are not utopian fantasies, however unsustainable any particular accommodation between capitalism and democracy may have become in recent decades."[93] Likewise, Harvey argues that the "more neoliberalism is recognized as a failed utopian rhetoric masking a successful project for the restoration of ruling class power, the more the basis is laid for a resurgence of mass movements voicing egalitarian political demands."[94] And Fraser argues that while, in an overarching sense, neoliberal forces succeeded in "defusing the more radical currents of second-wave feminism," hopefully a "new insurrectionary upsurge" can "reanimate them," and we can thus "reconnect feminist critique to the critique of capitalism—and thereby reposition feminism squarely on the Left."[95] Of course, *Remaking Appalachia* also is critical of the neoliberal capitalist project in its entirety—and is thus concerned with both an overarching critique of neoliberalism and accompanying prescriptive recommendations on how this hegemonic paradigm can be transcended vis-à-vis ecofeminist- and ecosocialist-steeped systemic re-formations.

Remaking Appalachia is particularly concerned with how neoliberal-associated conditions, as operationalized by elite capital interests and complicit policymakers, have wrought pervasive ecological and related social damage in Appalachia (but also in the United States and globally); thus, this chapter concludes with a discussion of the neoliberal turn in environmental law and policy. As noted above, the enactment of environmental law in the 1970s occurred just prior to neoliberalism's rise; environmental law was then, in short order, deeply influenced by the neoliberal paradigm. In the first place, through the neoliberal dimension of deregulation, the environmental law regime—deeply flawed as it was to begin with—has been strategically weakened to the direct benefit of large capital interests. As Benjamin Richardson writes in *Time and Environmental Law*, since the 1980s, "many reforms to environmental law [have both] left existing resource users relatively unscathed" and have "benefitted them through deregulation programs."[96] Similarly, as Daniel Faber writes in *Capitalizing on Environmental Injustice*, one strategy "utilized by neoliberal politicians in the rollback of environmental law" includes "a *wholesale rollback* of existing environmental laws, regulations, and programs considered to be detrimental to business" based on the justification that the "costs of regulations to American business, taxpayers and workers are excessive."[97]

Aside from deregulation, many aspects of the neoliberal turn in environmental law involve affirmative, market-based approaches to environmental regulation. While such market-based approaches are allegedly "efficient" within narrowly proscribed parameters, they have proven wholly inadequate in stemming ecological destruction on the macro scale. In the 1980s, the notion of "sustainable development" emerged as the dominant neoliberal paradigm in environmental law and policy. The aim of sustainable development involves relying on economic growth to simultaneously produce both development and higher environmental quality, including in both the Global South and in the Global North.[98] By the 1990s, however, sustainable development would be further refined vis-à-vis the related neoliberal paradigm of "ecological modernization." As Chukwumerije Okereke argues, the " 'neoliberal consensus' " has dominated "discourses of environmental governance of which the notion of ecological modernization is the core narrative."[99]

Ecological modernization is fundamentally concerned with maximization of efficiencies. That is, ecological modernization sees "sustainable development being achieved even for Western countries by engaging in environmentally beneficial growth through enhanced resource efficiencies—doing more with less—so that the negative consequences of growth would not arise in the first place."[100] Ecological modernization is therefore best conceptualized as attempting to "square the circle" of achieving greater environmental protections *through* continued growth—as it centers on the notion that government can "enhance the competitiveness of industry by unilaterally increasing rather than decreasing the stringency of environmental regulation."[101] This is because, supposedly, under appropriate technological and economic conditions, competition among private market actors can be redirected towards creating greater eco-efficiencies. Thus, ultimately, by creating incentives by which market actors can internalize pollution costs, increased economic growth need not result in a corresponding increase in environmental harm. Ecological modernization, then, "promise[s] to simultaneously deliver on both economic growth and environmental protection," and consequently the "ecological modernization discourse represents a very powerful handmaiden to the neoliberal project."[102]

Through the paradigm of ecological modernization, law occupies a central role in supposedly eliminating negative environmental externalities through market-based mechanisms. (Note that such a market-based approach to environmental governance is in keeping with the broader and truly disastrous "law and economics" tradition.) This market orientation relies in large part on Pareto optimality, which involves creating market outcomes that are maximally efficient. Specifically, optimality is reached when "no reallocation of resources through changes in consumption, exchange, or production could *unambiguously* augment the value of the commodities being produced and exchanged."[103] Allocative efficiency requires the market receiving accurate price signals—but, traditionally, markets did not account for negative environmental externalities wrought by polluting market actors (i.e., creating market failures). It is the state, then, that corrects environmental-related market failures, in providing subsidies, enacting taxes, etc. in order to ensure that all true prices are then accounted for. Robyn Eckersley thus broadly contends that "ecological modernization still succumbs to the alluring momentum of material progress and the belief in the rational, technological mastery of nature in ways that uphold economic freedoms while ruling out more critical deliberation over the ultimate purpose and character of the modernization process," and it thus "reinforces rather than questions the liberal dogmas."[104] As operationalized via policy, ecological modernization, then, supposedly resolves structural problems produced by liberalism—namely, those engendered by ceaseless capital accumulation and perpetual economic growth—not with systemic re-formations, but instead with greater (technology-driven) eco-efficiencies as derived from market forces.

A prominent example of ecological modernization includes cap-and-trade systems. Cap-and-trade systems involve the state setting a nationwide limit (or cap) on a pollutant and issuing permits—but then allowing the market participants (or the polluters) to work towards the "market ideal" distribution through permit trading. For instance, in the CAA context, "emissions trading" involves placing a nationwide cap on all air emissions of a certain type—for instance, acid rain-causing sulfur dioxide—and on issuing tradable permits to market participants: industrial participants must then collectively emit within the scheme's limitations.[105] What is more, in strategically reducing the cap's size, new "improvements will always be needed, the continuing pressure continuously driving up the value of the credits, thus keeping the momentum going."[106] This supposedly incentivizes the development of eco-efficient technologies, the achievement of Pareto optimality among the market participants, and the reduction of negative environmental externalities overall.

Ecological modernization, at its core, is therefore concerned with market-based approaches that increase technology-driven eco-efficiencies while simultaneously operating within liberalism's paradigm. However, after decades of operationalization, ecological modernization had indeed proven a comprehensive failure, as it is merely operates within the liberal capitalist paradigm—and thus only exacerbates environmental law's failure. To be sure, with its market- and technology-reform-based approach, ecological modernization has been unsuccessful in altering the trajectory of the global ecological crisis. As Richard Smith argues, under the capitalist system, "cheaper inputs only give producers greater incentive to 'grow the market' by selling more product at lower prices to more consumers and thus to push sales and profits still higher," and so "ironically, the very capitalist efficiency and market organization of production" engenders "growth and further environmental destruction." [107] The "Jevons paradox" is thus often invoked in discussions on ecological modernization;[108] as developed by William Stanley Jevons in *The Coal Question*, the Jevons paradox involves that proposition that increases in efficiency of the coal industry in Great Britain in the mid-nineteenth century "facilitated the production of more goods per unit of coal, thus increasing the consumption of this resource," and so "production and consumption actually expanded because of the decreased price for the resource, despite the perceived benefits of better efficiency." [109] Similarly, in the explicit neoliberal context, Brian Elliott notes that "incorporated into the economic growth paradigm, the guiding question of sustainability becomes how quickly we can devise technologies to maximise resource extraction, distribution and usage," but that "the neoliberal ruling passion for unlimited economic growth in effect denies . . . a limited material foundation." [110]

Environmental law, then, as embedded within hegemonic liberalism, has constituted a critically flawed paradigm. Environmental law's failings emanate from multitudinous, intersecting sources, including a fragmented legislative scheme, legislative "outs" embedded by industry, the non-democratic nature of administrative agencies, and the related and pervasive phenomenon of industry capture of environmental agencies. However, the core structural flaw in environmental law is that it is merely designed to support—not to disrupt—liberal capitalism's paradigm of ceaseless capital accumulation through subordination of nature and labor and perpetual economic growth. Energy law and supportive environmental law and policy therefore have a wholly productionist orientation to the benefit of elite capital interests. Lastly, since the 1980s, the neoliberal turn in environmental law, which centers on deregulation and market-based policy, has only exacerbated this overarching state of affairs—thus worsening the global ecological crisis. Chapter 5 next examines how environmental law has failed Appalachia specifically through intersecting ecological, social, cultural, and economic dimensions.

MODERN APPALACHIA: ENVIRONMENTAL LAW'S FAILURE AND THE BROADER REGIONAL LANDSCAPE

The U.S. environmental law regime, as enacted in the 1970s and further refined over the decades, has proven a wholly inadequate paradigm. Chapter 5 details the profound ecological damage Appalachia has experienced since environmental law was enacted—and also the specific manner in which the environmental regime has failed the region. As discussed in prior chapters, the coal extraction industry, in particular, has wrought extensive devastation in Appalachia since the late nineteenth century. And the transition to mechanization-intensive surface mining at the mid-century point rapidly accelerated such ecological destruction. As chapter 5 discusses, following the environmental revolution that swept through the United States in the 1960s and the subsequent enactment of the environmental regime, there was legitimate hope that statutes such as the CWA and SMCRA would provide new and substantial environmental protections for the region. Unfortunately, the opposite transpired. Similar to prior Appalachian eras, the fossil fuel hegemony and allied governmental elites succeeded in thwarting the (already critically flawed) environmental law regime and in further degrading the region. In fact, industry-based damage reached disastrous new heights with the dramatic rise of mountaintop removal mining in the 1990s—which, for three decades, has wrought extensive harms in Central Appalachia. This chapter next chronicles additional ecological issues—that environmental law has similarly failed to curtail—both in Appalachia and at the broader national and global scales. In the Appalachian context, the natural gas industry and related chemical industry resurgence are producing a new onslaught. And the broader global ecological crisis, as associated with notions of the Capitalocene, poses a true threat to the world at large.

Chapter 5 then pivots in providing a broad overview of crucial dimensions of modern Appalachia's social, political, and economic landscape, as shaped by the rapid decline of the coal industry and longer-term decline of coal mining employment (i.e., the latter trend as associated with the "treadmill of production" explanatory model)—and the corresponding rise of coal industry–produced cultural manipulation tactics. Significantly, Donald Trump's 2016 presidential campaign at least implicitly leveraged such long-standing coal industry–produced cultural messaging—as operationalized within a broader Appalachian landscape beset by neoliberal-associated ills—to garner support in the region. What is more, the rising natural gas industry has likely also benefited from such cultural manipulation, as the Marcellus shale gas boom is merely the latest manifestation of the fossil fuel hegemony in Appalachia. Consequently, such cultural manipulation tactics must be combated and comprehensively countered in efforts to achieve true transformative change in Appalachia and beyond. In detailing preexisting networks that could be radically expanded to drive such change, this chapter concludes by chronicling modern, select Appalachian grassroots resistance practices.

MOUNTAINTOP REMOVAL MINING IN APPALACHIA

Appalachia was marked by intensive coal extraction practices throughout the entirety of the twentieth century. Underground mining continued in Appalachia through increasingly mechanized forms. But as discussed in chapter 3, from the mid-century point onwards, mechanization-intensive surface mining arose in the region as a uniquely destructive force. What is more, as the resource curse and sacrifice zone explanatory models illustrate, the fossil fuel hegemony at large also was a fundamental structural cause of the long-standing social, economic, and political ills in Appalachia—as not just the environment, but also the citizenry has been profoundly and multidimensionally exploited in order to facilitate the extraction of Appalachia's natural resources to the benefit of elite capital interests.

MTR's rapid rise in the early 1990s was one of the most consequential Appalachian developments in the prior three decades; an extended treatment of MTR will therefore follow. MTR arose in Appalachia due to a combination of interrelated factors. During this era, as in keeping with global neoliberal capitalist trends generally, "corporate mergers, consolidations, and bankruptcies accompanied intense competition between eastern and western coal mining operations," and thus the "coal industry's competition-driven movement to new mining methods in central Appalachia," such as through MTR, proved catastrophic.[1] Also, the treadmill of production model (as explained more fully below) helps illustrate how the industry sought technological advances required for MTR—making "workers obsolete"—in endless pursuit of ever-greater productivity and profits.[2] In the MTR context, such "mega-technologies" included oversized draglines, dump trucks, drilling machinery, and bulldozers.[3]

The CAA amendments of 1990 also incentivized power plants to favor low-sulfur Central Appalachian coal. The CAA amendments required reduction of sulfur dioxide emissions; to comply with these new standards, coal-fired power plants could rely on technology fixes (e.g., scrubbers that reduced sulfur emissions) or else obtain coal with lower sulfur content.[4] Most plants would take the "easy course" in burning low-sulfur coal.[5] What transpired, then, was an industry transition towards the low-sulfur coal endemic to western mining areas and Central Appalachia. Thus, the role of the CAA amendments in catalyzing MTR's rise was a "cruel irony"[6]—and the phenomenon exemplifies a core critical critique of environmental law. That is, supposedly beneficial liberal law reform very often tends to, in the end, exacerbate overarching negative environmental conditions through unintended consequences, ill-design, or perverse implementation—and due to ultimately, of course, its embeddedness within the liberal capitalist paradigm.

Also of significance, SMCRA provided an exemption that was later latched onto and perverted by operators and complicit governmental officials. SMCRA generally requires operators to restore mining sites to their approximate original contour (AOC). However, during SMCRA's legislative debates, "central Appalachian coal operators and coal-state congressional representatives sought an exemption from the AOC requirement for mountaintop removal mining."[7] This was because MTR, "they argued, could produce flat land for development—a commodity in very short supply in the mountainous coalfields of West Virginia, Kentucky, Virginia, and Tennessee."[8] MTR apologists have thus "viewed this [AOC exemption] provision as encouraging economic development in the struggling coalfields," but in fact, the exemption, intended for narrow circumstances, became a mere "giveaway to mine companies that effectively negated the mandate for restoration."[9] Specifically, groundbreaking *Charleston Gazette* reporting by Ken Ward Jr. in the late 1990s demonstrated "a systemic failure on the part of state regulators to apply SMCRA's AOC requirements to mountaintop removal mines."[10] Such reporting revealed that at one time three-fourths of all MTR sites active in West Virginia were "being operated in violation of state and federal law," as required AOC exemptions had not been obtained by MTR operators.[11] As will be discussed, these MTR AOC-related issues were not an isolated incidence of what might be characterized as the outright failure of the rule of law in the environmental governance context (i.e., as even conceived under liberalism's own strictures): a long-term, pervasive such pattern can be discerned.

Since MTR's rapid rise in the 1990s, environmental harms caused by the practice have been among the most egregious in the nation's history, and, in many instances, are irrevocable. To conduct MTR operations, mining operators clear-cut forests and then "[chop] off mountaintops"; "underlying coal seams . . . lie sandwiched in layers of rock," and each "layer of the rock above a coal seam is blasted and removed, the coal is extracted, and then the next layer is removed until the removal of rock and coal layers is no longer cost-effective." [12] Operators then use massive equipment to deposit some of the blasted refuse material back on the mountain—but such "spoil," which enlarges after blasting, also is deposited down the valleys adjacent to MTR sites. [13] These valley deposits are termed "valley fills," which rise "hundreds of feet high on top of headwater streams." [14] MTR causes severe ecological damage. MTR has, to date, destroyed five hundred mountains in Appalachia extending over 1.2 million acres. [15] MTR's extensive deforestation obliterates native ecosystems—resulting in widespread loss of diverse plant and animal life. After mining is completed, the sites are often replanted with non-native grass species (insofar as revegetation occurs)—which limit the return of native wildlife and the broader re-establishment of pre-mining ecosystems. [16]

MTR has also wrought extensive waterway damage in Appalachia. In an overarching sense, the destruction of streams likely constitutes the "most pronounced and significant environmental impact of MTR." [17] Valley fills from MTR sites have destroyed more than two thousand miles of ecologically crucial headwater streams; thus, in the first place, MTR often eliminates streams altogether. However, in terms of broader effects, toxic pollutants released during mining operations—e.g., selenium, mercury, and arsenic—also degrade Appalachian waterways. [18] The sulfuric acid released by acid mine drainage also is severely harmful. Water pollution is therefore an extreme negative consequence of MTR.

A study on MTR demonstrates that the practice is, in fact, geologic in scope. As Matthew Ross and related researchers found in *Deep Impact*:

> Mountaintop mining has little physically in common with deforestation, where the dominant effects from disturbance are mediated through ecological factors, and ecosystems return to similar predisturbance hydrologic and biogeochemical regimes over decadal time scales. The physical effects from mountaintop mining are much more similar to volcanic

eruptions, where the entire landscape is fractured, deepened, and decoupled from prior landscape evolution trajectories, effectively resetting the clock on landscape and ecosystem coevolution.[19]

Thus, the "severity and the longevity of the resulting environmental impacts" of MTR are extraordinary.[20] This is logical, however, due to the mega-technology-produced invasive nature of the practice. Tragically, then, no amount of "reclamation" or "remediation" will ever restore MTR-scoured regions to their former state.

Aside from environmental impacts per se, MTR also has produced substantial negative harms on Appalachian human communities. MTR mining became pervasive throughout Central Appalachia, thus affecting citizens through such mechanisms as blasting (which produces dust and debris), flooding, and polluted water sources. Flooding, for instance, frequently follows MTR operations as deforestation removes absorption functions within ecosystems and because streams (which provide natural drainage) are buried. Moreover, extensive coal waste is housed in ponds—but such "mine ponds are frequently constructed inadequately," thus "causing run-off during heavy rain."[21]

The public health impacts of MTR have become increasingly well-documented. Ill-health effects linked to MTR include asthma, skin issues, headaches, and nausea; so, too, does MTR potentially produce long-term health conditions, such as digestive tract cancer, organ failure, and birth defects.[22] Many of these health studies on MTR have been led by researcher Michael Hendryx.[23] Additional work is required to further study the health effects of MTR (including abandoned MTR sites); however, the Trump administration stymied important contemporary efforts. The Trump administration canceled funding for a significant MTR study entitled *Potential Human Health Effects of Surface Coal Mining Operations in Central Appalachia*.[24] As one legislator noted shortly thereafter: "It increasingly appears as if DOI ended the study because of fears that it would conclusively show that mountaintop removal (MTR) coal mining is a serious threat to the health of people living in Appalachia," and thus "cutting off funding for a scientific study because it will likely produce uncomfortable results for powerful Administration allies is unconscionable."[25]

ENVIRONMENTAL JUSTICE

MTR concerns implicate the crucial discourse of environmental justice (EJ). EJ was one of the first movements that explicitly applied the insights of critical theory to environmental law and policy. Initially, "environmental law took root as a reformist project" that largely "avoided the critical concerns of 'race, class, and gender' and the postmodern insights of late twentieth-century social thinking and practice."[26] In more recent decades, however, critically informed environmental commentators have linked ecological issues with the broader ills of late liberalism, in correctly positing that "the exploitation of the environment with which environmental law is concerned props up the unjust modernism with which critical theory is concerned."[27] To be sure, *Remaking Appalachia* is firmly embedded within this vein of critical environmental thinking.

One dimension of EJ involves distributive justice—namely, that the ill-effects caused by polluting industries such as coal tend not to be distributed equally in society.[28] Rather, subordinated groups in society—along lines of race, class, educational attainment, gender, age, ability, indigenous status, etc.—suffer disproportionate negative environmental impacts. Therefore, the "general thrust of environmental justice is a proportionate share issue regarding environmental burdens," and overall, "the concept is that when living in an industrialized society, there are both benefits and burdens associated with environmental issues, and when environmental injustice occurs, those burdens are disproportionately thrust" on subordinated groups.[29] It should also be noted that newer waves of EJ are explicitly materialist and non-essentialist, in expanding "environmental justice to recognize that each racial group is differently situated according to its specific socio-economic needs, political power, cultural values, and group goals."[30] This then enables "scholars and activists to better grapple with varying forms of subordination and to tailor specific remedies for the harms that are specific to each racial community."[31]

Appalachia's MTR-related EJ issues are certainly multidimensional; many commentators have specifically focused on gender- and sex-related MTR issues in addition to those pertaining to (and intersecting with) class. For instance, class is a core MTR-related EJ issue in Central Appalachia, as has been noted in such studies as "Poverty and Mortality Disparities in Central Appalachia."[32] Moreover, recent studies on class-related EJ concerns demonstrate that persistent, long-term issues involve inadequately reclaimed MTR sites. This phenomenon has been explored in "Disparate Impacts of Coal Mining and Reclamation Concerns for West Virginia and Central Appalachia," where it was noted that negative environmental impacts from unreclaimed mining sites affect "vulnerable populations within these mining communities afflicted by poor health and low socioeconomic status."[33] The authors emphasize that there exists scant funding to improve such conditions, which perpetuates "further cycles of environmental injustice."[34] Thus, not only have class-related EJ issues long existed in the MTR context—but the toxic vestiges of the coal industry guarantee their long-term impact.

Gender- and sex-related EJ issues also are implicated by MTR, as has been explored in such works as Barry's *Standing Our Ground* and Bell's *Our Roots Run Deep as Ironwood*. Barry, for instance, broadly notes that "women in central Appalachia, particularly in the coalfields . . . lack social, political, and economic equality with men,"[35] and so "women, with their productive or social reproductive work, suffer the harshest effects of all social ills, whether those ills are poverty, unemployment, or environmental destruction."[36] In the specific MTR context, compound oppressions are thus at work, because not only are low-income Appalachians disproportionately impacted by MTR—but women in such low-income areas are further disproportionately affected, for instance, due to the traditional gender regime's reliance on women performing reproductive labor such as childcare and elderly and sick care.[37]

As an example of a public health-related disproportionate harm, Barry notes that "women are particularly vulnerable to the accumulation of chemicals" potentially associated with activities like MTR and may also "potentially pass these toxins on to their fetuses and/or children."[38] Barry thus examines "the ways in which the body, and biological differences between men and women and their susceptibility to environmental toxins, [are] linked to material realities."[39] And reproductive labor disparities are again implicated by such material phenomena, as women are primarily responsible for childcare (i.e., as compounded by sickness or disability produced by the coal industry).

While MTR has largely impacted white poor and working-class populations in the Central Appalachian coalfields, other dimensions of distributive EJ, such as race-based concerns, are implicated in the broader region. Indeed, the EJ movement at large was formulated when minority communities organized around disproportionate race-based environmental harms (e.g., toxic waste sites), as chronicled by a 1983 U.S. Government Accounting Office study and the groundbreaking book *Toxic Waste and Race in the United States*.[40] Such race-related EJ harms were, in fact, exacerbated by earlier middle-class-white-led environmental movements to safeguard their own communities—and thus industry, in seeking the "path of least resistance," targeted working-class white communities, and after resistance also was met there, communities of color were then selected as repositories for harmful substances.[41] As Taylor summarizes, *Toxic Waste and Race in the United States*, in particular, "did for people of color and the environmental justice movement what 'Silent Spring' did for middle class Whites in the 1960s" in helping to widely reveal such distributive injustices.[42] Thereafter, the EJ movement continued to expand, as informed by race-based concerns as intertwined with critiques of the traditional environmental reform agenda (i.e., as embedded in middle- and upper-middle-class white hegemonic value systems).[43]

In the context of Appalachia, a core example of race-related EJ concerns emanated from the chemical industry in the West Virginia Kanawha River Valley area—as discussed below. Additionally, yet more compound oppressions are implicated by race-related EJ issues in Appalachia and beyond. As an example, for Appalachians of color, disproportionate race-based harms can further be compounded by class dimensions, and yet further compound oppressions can subordinate low-income Appalachian women of color and low-income indigenous women. As Taylor explores in "Women of Color, Environmental Justice, and Ecofeminism," "while both white women and women of color have some commonality in the fact that both groups are oppressed by men, women of color have to deal with oppression from women, too."[44] Taylor adds that "women of color will agree that they are fighting gender issues," however, "they will also argue that they are fighting much more than that," as their "fight is also about racial and sexual discrimination, inequality, civil rights, and labor rights."[45]

In dovetailing with Taylor's final point, beyond distributive justice, another important EJ dimension pertains to an exploration of who constitutes activists and activist-leaders in EJ movements. Historically, women have constituted large percentages of EJ activists both in the United States and globally: particularly, women of color and poor and working-class women.[46] And as is discussed at length below, such trends certainly hold true in Appalachia—as Appalachian women often have been at the forefront of EJ and related activism.[47]

LEGAL EFFORTS TO HALT MOUNTAINTOP REMOVAL MINING

Legal efforts to halt MTR-produced environmental destruction in Appalachia bear close scrutiny; broadly speaking, such efforts have been met with overarching failure, despite the crucial work of would-be environmental reformers in the region and beyond. In this way, attempts at MTR reform are merely a continuation of the wholesale failures of the liberal legal paradigm at large to protect Appalachia. What follows, then, is an intensive discussion of the environmental framework governing MTR and of its specific failures to protect Appalachia in the prior three decades. Thereafter, subsequent industry-based environmental issues in Appalachia (e.g., emanating from the natural gas industry) will be discussed—in addition to comparable failures of their legal-institutional governance. Lastly, core elements of the broader global ecological crisis are then detailed.[48]

Efforts to halt MTR—or in the very least, to mitigate its worst effects—have involved both environmental law and common law actions. In the environmental law context, MTR is governed by a complex federal and state legal regime (i.e., typically involving modes of cooperative federalism), including components of SMCRA, CWA, and NEPA. SMCRA is one such cooperative federalism-steeped act: broad standards are set at the federal level, and then states promulgate comprehensive plans to meet those standards.[49] As discussed above, SMCRA contains such important provisions as the MTR AOC exemption; SMCRA also has a savings clause, indicating that the act does not supersede the CWA; and the CWA is implicated, for instance, by MTR-produced valley fills.[50]

The CWA contains a permitting scheme—of the very sort discussed at length in chapter 4 (i.e., as a crucial element of environmental law's failure)—for MTR-produced valley fills. Two permits required for MTR operations often are at issue in MTR legal constestations. The first is a National Pollutant Discharge Elimination Systems (NPDES) permit, issued by the EPA or an EPA-approved state agency under CWA § 402;[51] and the second emanates from the dredge-and-fill permitting program administered by the Army Corps of Engineers (Corps) under CWA § 404.[52] Corps-issued permits under CWA § 404, however, are required to be issued in accordance with standards produced by the EPA, termed the § 404(b)(1) Guidelines.[53] The EPA also provides other, extra-statutory guidance to Corps.[54] Lastly, NEPA, as a procedural act, requires agencies that propose "major federal actions 'significantly affecting' the human environment" to first complete an environmental impact statement (EIS).[55]

A public interest review also is required prior to permit issuances.[56] This provision states in pertinent part: "The decision whether to issue a permit will be based on an evaluation of the probable impacts, including cumulative impacts, of the proposed activity and its intended use on the public interest," and that "the benefits which reasonably may be expected to accrue from the proposal must be balanced against its reasonably foreseeable detriments."[57] Also at issue, the Clinton administration issued Executive Order 12898 in 1994 ("E.O. 12898"), known as the "Environmental Justice Executive Order," which requires that "each Federal agency shall make achieving environmental justice part of its mission by identifying and addressing, as appropriate, disproportionately high and adverse human health or environmental effects of its programs, policies, and activities on minority populations and low-income populations in the United States and its territories and possessions."[58] Generally speaking, E.O. 12898 "formalizes the principles of environmental justice and obligates federal agencies to adhere to them"[59] and is reviewed in MTR permitting.[60]

Over a period of three decades, the general MTR governance trend has involved pertinent federal and state regulators failing to properly implement these statutes. Environmental plaintiffs have attempted to secure federal court enforcement of these acts, principally in the federal Fourth Circuit (which includes West Virginia and Virginia) and the Sixth Circuit (which includes Kentucky). However, environmental plaintiffs have been unsuccessful in most federal actions pursued—which has been characterized as a "history of adverse outcomes for environmental plaintiffs."[61] Such negative outcomes are especially egregious given that the plain statutory language and legislative history of pertinent statutes have often unambiguously supported environmental plaintiff arguments.

A number of federal decisions from the prior three decades illustrate this long-standing pro-industry trend. Many MTR-related decisions were handed down by the Southern District of West Virginia (i.e., at the federal trial court level)—which, in fact, often held that mining operators violated the federal environmental statutes at issue. However, on appeal, the Fourth Circuit—widely considered the most conservative Circuit in the nation during the MTR era[62]— would repeatedly reverse the district court in pro-industry rulings. Thus, the "Fourth Circuit's inclination to defer to permitting agencies, and the Court's unwillingness to enforce the application of federal law by state officials," resulted in a clear pattern of decisions supporting disastrous MTR practices.[63] The court generally "resolved the diverging government interests . . . in favor of Corps decisions that promote energy extraction," despite the fact that the "Corps has granted permits in a manner that directly contradicts the statutory and regulatory commands of NEPA and the CWA."[64]

The Fourth Circuit's deep conservative disposition during the MTR era was due largely to political factors regarding judge appointments. Although the Fourth Circuit constituted a more liberal jurisdiction prior to the 1980s (and indeed shifted towards the center during the Obama administration), conservative appointments by Presidents Reagan and George H. W. Bush transformed the court.[65] Such appointments were facilitated by the home-state senator ideologues of Strom Thurmond of South Carolina and Jesse Helms of North Carolina, who exercised substantial sway over Fourth Circuit appointments.[66] Consequently, on environmental matters and beyond, the Fourth Circuit issued far-right opinions, which had dire effects on Appalachia.

Bragg v. Robertson was one such decision; in *Bragg*, environmental plaintiffs brought claims against the Corps and the West Virginia Department of Environmental Protection (WVDEP) alleging MTR-related violations of SMCRA, the CWA, and NEPA. In its 1999 decision, the Southern District of West Virginia "enjoined the WVDEP from issuing mining permits without enforcing SMCRA's requirement that land within one hundred feet of streams remain undisturbed by surface mining operations" in accordance with SMCRA's buffer zone rule.[67] This rule was designed to ensure that mining operators did not unduly impact water quality, and the court found that the WVDEP director failed to complete the appropriate impact findings.[68] As the court stated: "The Court has determined the Director's legal rationales for failure to make the required buffer zone findings were inconsistent with the controlling statutes and regulations and relied on clearly erroneous interpretations of those laws," and thus held that "the Director has a nondiscretionary duty to make the findings required under the buffer zone rule before authorizing any incursions, including valley fills, within one hundred feet of an intermittent or perennial stream."[69] The court also held that "the Director has a nondiscretionary duty under the buffer zone rule to deny variances for valley fills in intermittent and perennial streams because they necessarily adversely affect stream flow, stream gradient, fish migration, related environmental values, water quality and quantity, and violate state and federal water quality standards."[70]

The Fourth Circuit, however, reversed this decision by citing to sovereign immunity grounds under the Eleventh Amendment. Specifically, the court reasoned that because the WVDEP director was a state official, the director was immune from federal court challenges in these circumstances.[71] As the court noted in pertinent part: "We conclude that the injunctive relief sought against the State Director in this case" is "barred by the Eleventh Amendment."[72] The Fourth Circuit thus eschewed addressing the substantive issues of the case.

Another prominent example includes *Kentuckians for the Commonwealth, Inc. v. Rivenburgh*. In its decision, the Southern District of West Virginia ruled in favor of environmental plaintiffs, in holding that the Corps violated the CWA in issuing a mining permit for valley fill practices. Specifically, the court enjoined the Corps from issuing overburden fill material permits "solely for the purpose of waste disposal" under CWA § 404.[73] As the court argues, "for the past twenty years, particularly in the Huntington Corps District, § 404 permits have been issued for mountaintop removal overburden disposal in valley fills that have obliterated and destroyed almost a thousand miles of streams, by the Corps' own account."[74] However, such CWA "§ 404 permit approvals were issued in express disregard of the Corps' own regulations and the CWA . . . As such, they were illegal."[75] As the court adds, the regulators belatedly changed their rules to account for this illegality, but "the agencies' attempt to legalize their longstanding illegal regulatory practice must fail. The practice is contrary to law, not because the agencies said so, although their longstanding regulations correctly forbade it. The regulators' practice is illegal because it is contrary to the spirit and the letter of the Clean Water Act" and moreover "the rule change was designed simply for the benefit of the mining industry and its employees."[76]

Unfortunately, on appeal, the Fourth Circuit overturned this decision. The court held that the district court's injunction was overbroad and that there existed statutory ambiguity in CWA § 404—which thus allowed the Corps' interpretation of its regulatory definition of "fill material."[77] In support of its decision, the court deployed the "*Chevron* deference" doctrine in a different manner than the district court; this doctrine dictates that, if statutory language is deemed ambiguous, courts must defer to agency expertise so long as the agency interpretation is reasonable.[78] Thus, on appeal, the "Fourth Circuit reversed, reviewing the Army Corps' interpretation of the CWA regulations under [a] deferential standard."[79]

Yet another example includes the *Ohio Valley Environmental Coalition v. Aracoma Coal Co.* decision. In the Southern District of West Virginia, environmental plaintiffs again brought a MTR-related claim against the Corps under the CWA and NEPA, in challenging four permits the Corps issued for nearly two dozen MTR valley fills.[80] As the court argues, the CWA § "404(b)(1) Guidelines require the Corps to assess the effects of the discharge on the 'structure and function' of the aquatic ecosystem" and that the "Corps may rely upon the best professional judgment of its staff" in completing its assessment.[81] Nevertheless, the "the Corps still must take a 'hard look' at the evidence and explain its decision on an objective or scientific basis sufficient to provide a reasoned basis for its conclusions," and through this assessment "the Corps has failed," as "the Corps has not assessed the full impacts of destroying headwater streams within a watershed."[82] For the NEPA claims, plaintiffs alleged that the Corps failed to produce an EIS that adequately accounted for the water quality impacts of the operations.[83] The court agreed, in noting that "the Corps abused its discretion by limiting its scope of analysis to just the stream and immediately adjacent riparian areas."[84] The court adds that "under NEPA the Corps failed to consider significant impact from the proposed activity in relation to past, present and future activity," and that while "the proposed activity is in a heavily mined area and the Corps is requiring mitigation, the Corps is not relieved of its duty to provide an analysis of cumulative impacts when making its conclusion."[85]

The Fourth Circuit reversed on appeal, arguing that the "district court failed to heed" the standard that "in reviewing agency action, 'the court is not empowered to substitute its judgment for that of the agency.' " [86] The court added that "viewing the Corps' findings through the lens of arbitrary and capricious review, we cannot say that its findings regarding stream structure and function, mitigation, or cumulative impacts were an 'abuse of discretion' or 'not in accordance with law.' " [87] And the court also noted that "having found that the Corps was not obligated to engage in a full functional assessment, it is not our place to dictate how the Corps should go about assessing stream functions and losses. In matters involving complex predictions based on special expertise, 'a reviewing court must generally be at its most deferential.' " [88] Thus, the Fourth Circuit's decision in *Ohio Valley Environmental Coalition* was wholly in keeping with its pattern of supporting the coal extraction industry—and its blatant disregard for a plain reading of the environmental law at issue. Indeed, as one judge noted in a dissent (as a part of a broader dissent in part and concurrence in part): "Today's decision will have far-reaching consequences for the environment of Appalachia," as "it is not disputed that the impact of filling valleys and headwater streams is irreversible or that headwater streams provide crucial ecosystem functions" and that the "cumulative effects of the permitted fill activities on local streams and watersheds are considerable." [89] As a consequence, "we should rescind the four permits at issue in this case until the Corps complies with the clear mandates of the regulations." [90]

A final example includes a Kentucky-based decision handed down by the Sixth Circuit, *Kentuckians for the Commonwealth v. U.S. Army Corps of Engineers*. Environmental plaintiffs in this case again brought a federal claim against the Corps, alleging that in issuing an MTR-related valley fill permit under CWA § 404, the Corps violated CWA, NEPA, and the federal regulation mandating the public interest review of actions that could negatively impact citizen welfare. Specifically, plaintiffs alleged that the Corps "failed to consider the needs and welfare of the people" in the public interest review "by refusing to consider or address any potential human health impacts of the Permit." [91] Plaintiffs also alleged that the Corps failed to take a "hard look" at environmental impacts under NEPA and also that the "Corps did not consider or prevent adverse effects on human health and welfare as required by the CWA's Section 404(b)(1) Guidelines." [92] While environmental plaintiffs alleged that the Corps did not adequately address the "overall mining operations," the District Court for the Western District of Kentucky disagreed, arguing that "the Corps' decision to evaluate only the impacts of the specific permitted activities, and not the overall mining project, is entitled to deference." [93] Likewise, the court held that the Corps' public interest review was not arbitrary and capricious, in arguing that "plaintiffs' argument, however, again rests on the premise that the Corps was required to examine the impacts of overall mining operations, which this Court has rejected."[94] As a final point, the court argued that the "remainder of the proposed project fell exclusively under the purview of the Kentucky Division of Mine Permits," as an appropriate state-authorized agency in accordance with SMCRA.[95]

The Sixth Circuit affirmed on appeal, agreeing that the Corps' decision to limit its scope of review to the impacts of the specific permitted activities was reasonable. In fact, the court went even further than the district court in noting that "it is clear that Congress intended SMCRA to create a centralized regulatory program for surface coal mining, and that the Corps's role in the overlapping permitting scheme is secondary, affecting only a small albeit necessary part of the particular surface coal mining operation."[96] Thus, the Sixth Circuit's reasoning in this decision illustrates a problematic state of affairs for MTR governance—even when only analyzing such governance in the context of environmental law's given parameters (i.e., and not within the broader critique of the liberal paradigm put forth in Remaking Appalachia). In effect, this holding suggests that both the CWA and NEPA should be construed as in secondary importance to SMCRA's cooperative federalism scheme. However, as decisions from both the Sixth Circuit and Fourth Circuits have demonstrated, state agency-based MTR governance is extraordinarily ineffectual. Thus, so long as this regime remains unchanged, the courts will "defer . . . heavily to agency judgment" and "it will be entirely possible for SMCRA-approved state agencies to be the only bodies that could fill the regulatory void" on MTR while the mining practice persists.[97]

Aside from the cooperative federal-state environmental law regime governing MTR (involving SMCRA, the CWA, NEPA, etc.), anti-MTR advocates have explored additional legal approaches to combat the practice. For instance, as Sara Gersen chronicles, proposals for state-based legislation targeting MTR were put forth: "Facing underenforcement by regulatory agencies and a string of litigation reversals, some MTR activists" went "directly to state legislatures for a solution."[98] A notable example includes state legislation that would have prohibited utilities from purchasing MTR-produced coal. North Carolina legislators introduced one such bill that read in pertinent part: "no investor-owned public utility that operates a coal-fired generating unit located in North Carolina to generate electricity shall purchase or use coal extracted by MTR coal mining."[99] Such state-legislative efforts, however, proved ineffectual.

Appalachian citizens also have pursued common law actions—similar to nascent efforts to combat the industry during the era of rapid coal-based industrial growth and thereafter in Appalachia.[100] Specifically, tort actions potentially implicated by MTR could include negligence, private nuisance, and public nuisance, among others. Modern private nuisance claims are generally defined as a "nontrespassory invasion of another's interest in the private use and enjoyment of land."[101] Private nuisance is applicable for MTR due to increased risk of flooding, toxic dust particles, vibrations caused by blasting, and so forth.[102] A public nuisance, on the other hand, involves "an unreasonable interference with a right common to the general public,"[103] and such an action could be brought due to the "myriad public health consequences stem[ming] from aspects of the practice that current mining regulations do not specifically authorize."[104] Widespread groundwater contamination by unreasonable, MTR-produced activities not expressly authorized in a permit constitutes one example of a potential public nuisance claim, and negligence claims against MTR operations could be based on such harms as drinking water contamination.[105]

In keeping with more than a century's worth of pro-industry tort trends, plaintiffs have not enjoyed widespread success in pursuing such tort actions against MTR operators. Regardless of the substantive merits of MTR-related tort claims, Appalachian "state court judges may be predisposed to rule for coal companies for political reasons."[106] Unlike federal judges who are appointed, many Appalachian state judges have historically relied on coal-based campaign contributions: "Elected state judges are more likely to be partial and sympathetic to the coal mining industry," and indeed "some state judges have received substantial campaign contributions and support from the coal industry in order to get elected" to their terms.[107] The problematic influence of coal contributions to state judges is illustrated in part by the extraordinary U.S. Supreme Court decision *Caperton v. A.T. Massey Coal Co.* In this case, the court held that a West Virginia State Supreme Court justice, Brent Benjamin, who received millions of dollars' worth of coal contributions, was, under the due process clause of the Fourteenth Amendment, constitutionally required to recuse himself in a coal industry–related matter.[108] Note, however, that more technical litigation concerns are also implicated in discussions on tort action limitations; for instance, it can be difficult to establish causation in contexts such as MTR negligence suits given the complexities of mining-related health effects (i.e., which, as noted below, also are an issue in the natural gas context).[109]

The coal industry—including MTR—has experienced a historic decline in the prior decade. As the Energy Information Administration (EIA) has reported, MTR declined by an astounding 62 percent between 2008 and 2015.[110] Enhanced Obama-era regulations, such as stricter power plant regulations, played a marginal role in this decline. However, sheer market forces constituted the overriding factor, as coal faced steep market competition from low-priced natural gas particularly—but also from an increasingly competitive renewables sector.[111] Coal's precipitous decline is perhaps best illustrated by a series of high-profile bankruptcies filed throughout the 2010s, including by Peabody Energy, Arch Coal, and Alpha Natural Resources.[112] However, the coal industry nevertheless persists in Appalachia through MTR and other mining practices, and addressing the vestiges of the mining industry will constitute a long-term issue for the region, especially as mining corporations potentially can abandon reclamation duties in bankruptcy. Consequently, coal-related concerns will long constitute central environmental issues for Appalachia. A significant example of coal's continued potency is the 2019 reintroduction of the Appalachian Community Health Emergency Act in Congress—which would "prevent all new mountaintop coal removal mining permits from being issued until federal officials examine health consequences in surrounding communities,"[113] which, as noted above, the Trump administration has halted in its efforts to revitalize the industry. As such potential Congressional action indicates, coal clearly persists as a prime negative actor in the region.

NEW INDUSTRY-BASED HARMS IN APPALACHIA

Beyond MTR and the broader coal industry, contemporary Appalachia is also beset by other industry-related ecological issues that environmental law has similarly failed to address. As broached above, aside from active mining sites, numerous vestiges of a declining coal industry will create long-term environmental and EJ issues. For instance, Appalachia is beset by hundreds of coal waste impoundments located throughout the region. Such impoundments can rupture; such was the case in 2008, when a Tennessee pond spilled over a billion gallons of slurry—that contained contaminants (e.g., heavy metals)—into the surrounding environment.[114] The Tennessee incident constitutes the "largest of it type in U.S. history"—but "for residents of rural Appalachia, it was not an unusual event."[115] Another such incident occurred in Kentucky in 2000, when a sludge impoundment housed within an underground mine ruptured, spilling over three hundred million gallons of sludge. Waterways for hundreds of miles were polluted, which affected twenty-seven thousand citizens; this Kentucky incident has been characterized as "one of the worst environmental disasters to take place east of the Mississippi River."[116] Aside from dramatic ruptures, coal impoundments also pose persistent risks due to small (often unreported) spills and chronic leaks. That is, for "every major incident that has taken place over the past four decades, dozens of minor ones have occurred but have not been reported."[117] A number of such on-going incidents involve either marginal spills or slow leaks that pollute sur-rounding waterways, including drinking water. However, for "residents of Appalachia's coalfields, it is the price they pay for living in an 'energy sacrifice zone.'"[118] Class-related EJ concerns also are implicated by impoundments. As Pierce Greenberg concludes in "Disproportionality and Resource-Based Environmental Inequality," there exists a "significant, but weak, correlation between measures of neighborhood-level socioeconomic disadvantage and proximity to coal waste impoundments," and additionally, "descriptive sta-tistics reveal an unequal balance between the economic benefits and environ-mental and social costs of coal waste disposal."[119]

Although coal has historically constituted Appalachia's prime negative actor, the chemical industry has similarly produced long-term negative conse-quences for the region. For instance, as is discussed in the influential *Dumping in Dixie*, the West Virginia Kanawha River Valley area long constituted a chem-ical industry hub that created both ecological and EJ-related concerns.[120] A prominent example includes the 1980s events surrounding the Union Carbide plant located in Institute, a majority African American community. The Union Carbide Institute plant produced methyl isocyanate (or "MIC")—which was the same chemical released at Union Carbide's Bhopal, India, disaster in 1984, resulting in over three thousand fatalities and tens of thousands of injuries.[121] Following this disaster, Institute residents' concern about the local plant in-creased, and in 1985, there was a leak that "sent a poisonous plume of gas over Institute and sent 135 people to the hospital."[122] What is more, the EPA ruled that "Union Carbide's emergency notification took too long" and subse-quent agency investigations "revealed that this incident was not the only time the deadly MIC had leaked from this plant."[123] For these reasons, the Union Carbine experience has become notorious and much remarked-on in subse-quent decades from an Appalachian EJ standpoint.

More recently, the 2014 West Virginia Elk River chemical spill was a dra-matic example of Appalachia's persistent—and diverse—chemical industry-related environmental issues. The Elk River spill involved the coal-washing agent 4-methylcyclohexane methanol (MCHM). Thousands of gallons of the compound leaked into the river, and following the spill, an estimated three hundred thousand West Virginia citizens—constituting a significant percent-age of the entire state's population—were left without potable water for up-wards of ten days.[124] It was later determined that officials with the company responsible for the spill, Freedom Industries, had knowledge of the site's de-graded containment structure, but nevertheless failed to make the required improvements; six former officials would eventually receive criminal sentences for their conduct.[125]

The chemical industry is, in fact, in the midst of a potential "renaissance" in the Appalachian region, due primarily to the Marcellus shale natural gas boom.[126] As the twentieth century drew to a close, many domestic chemical plants shuttered (or were subsumed by larger conglomerates) due to neoliberal era–associated consolidation and market competition from an increasingly globalized chemical industry, and similar to coal, technological advances resulted in a decreasing chemical sector workforce.[127] Ultimately, however, the industry remains a significant cornerstone of West Virginia's economy. What is more, in recent times, the Marcellus shale and Utica shale formations in the region have made natural gas byproducts, such as ethane, widely available—which has led to an invigoration of the petrochemical sector (i.e., and a movement towards a true chemical industry "renaissance").[128] For instance, in 2017, it was announced that a memorandum of understanding had been signed between West Virginia officials and China Energy Investment Corporation regarding "plans to invest $83.7 billion in shale gas development and chemical manufacturing projects in the state over two decades."[129] Thus, due to such developments, chemical industry–related issues will likely constitute a long-term issue for Appalachia.

The dramatic Appalachian natural gas boom has indeed produced vast current and future-projected negative environmental impacts on the region. The Marcellus shale natural gas deposit extends throughout West Virginia and into Ohio, Pennsylvania, and New York; the Utica shale formation covers a substantial portion of the northeastern United States and is located thousands of feet beneath the Marcellus shale and also adjacent to that formation.[130] In the early 2000s, the hydraulic fracturing of horizontally drilled wells, following vertical drilling, rapidly emerged as a profitable means of gas extraction;[131] and by the end of that decade, the natural gas boom was in full force. Shale gas accounted for nearly a third of all U.S. gas production in 2013—and by 2035, this figure is project to rise to 45 percent.[132]

The current and future-projected transition to natural gas—as a leading Appalachian fossil fuel industry—is deeply problematic; like coal, natural gas produces dire environmental- and public health–related harms. As discussed in chapter 4, although natural gas has been characterized as " 'environmentally friendly' by the oil and gas industry as well as by governments that continue to support fossil fuel use," this is inaccurate, as studies indicate that natural gas likely is producing higher greenhouse gas emissions than previously reported.[133] The natural gas industry also constitutes a major indirect contributor to climate change. Despite industry claims that gas is "cleaner" than coal—and thus can constitute a bridge towards an ecologically sustainable future—developing a comprehensive infrastructure for natural gas will "significantly increase the cost of mitigation actions required to maintain a livable climate and will significantly increase the cost of adaptation actions required to support human societies in a less hospitable climate." [134] Consequently, rather than natural gas, clean energy transformations should be vigorously pursued in Appalachia and beyond; indeed, a transition to comprehensive clean energy systems is one core focal point of the prescriptive recommendations put forth in chapter 7.

Nevertheless, West Virginia, in particular, is furthering an energy policy that explicitly eschews (or otherwise limits) clean energy system development. As Jamie Van Nostrand notes, West Virginia has "nothing as a matter of state policy, unlike the vast majority of states in the country, that encourages development of renewable energy resources." [135] Continued coal reliance and natural gas development has instead been prioritized, as has been demonstrated by the expansion of the natural gas industry infrastructure. For instance, several pending interstate pipeline projects—most notably, the Atlantic Coast Pipeline and Mountain Valley Pipeline—will transport natural gas from West Virginia to Virginia (with the Atlantic Coast Pipeline also extending to North Carolina). Additionally, Appalachian utility companies "plan to invest billions of dollars in several new gas-burning power plants" in the region; as a consequence, "every dollar invested in this outdated and destructive infrastructure could be invested in clean, renewable energy instead." [136]

Similar to MTR, legal-institutional efforts to halt the development of the natural gas industry in Appalachia have largely been met with failure. For instance, common law actions for negligence (as emanating from harms caused by injection wells, etc.) have typically failed due to the difficulty in establishing causation,[137] and successful private nuisance claims also constitute a "difficult" cause of action.[138] And, of course, the broader structural issues of Appalachian courts long favoring the fossil fuel industry persists. Also, comprehensive federal regulation is nonexistent for fracking, thus leaving the practice largely to state governance—and many conservative Appalachian state governments such as West Virginia have profoundly underregulated the industry. In fracking-intensive states, many municipalities attempted to regulate the practice— but state governments have generally preempted such actions.[139] Recently, much of the most significant legal action regarding the natural gas industry has involved efforts to stymie development of regional natural gas infrastructure, including gas-fired power plants and the pending Atlantic Coast Pipeline and Mountain Valley Pipeline in particular. Environmental groups such as the

Appalachian Mountain Advocates have contested numerous phases of pipeline-related development—such as when, in 2017, the organization filed a motion for a dredge-and-fill permit issued under the CWA to be suspended (as it was unlawfully issued by the Corps).[140] Such infrastructure development largely persists, however, despite such admirable legal efforts and occasional victories; thus, the natural gas era has largely echoed the MTR-related failures to secure legal-institutional protections from industry.

Climate change itself constitutes an increasingly potent threat to the Appalachian region. Interestingly, a study conducted by the Nature Conservancy demonstrates that some sub-regions of Appalachia constitute unusually resilient "strongholds" for climate change, including West Virginia highland forest areas. The study sought "landscapes that are best-equipped to handle global warming" and "places with diverse topography, geology and elevation scored highest," as "varied environments give plants and animals more opportunities to adapt."[141] However, the study cautions that while "Appalachia still has vast wilderness areas that give it a leg up as temperatures rise," nevertheless, such strongholds can become degraded due to destructive human activities, and "even in resilient habitats that stay intact, things could still turn out badly if too many people and wildlife immigrate from harder-hit areas."[142] Thus, while these research findings are heartening, such Appalachian strongholds are both limited in geographic area and ultimately vulnerable to degradation.

More broadly, researchers are identifying current and future-projected climate change impacts in Appalachia. Wildfires constitute one important example, with increased risks present in West Virginia, southern Ohio, and western Pennsylvania.[143] The historic 2016 wildfires in Tennessee likely demonstrate this newfound threat.[144] So, too, is increased precipitation—and correspondingly, flooding—in Appalachia likely linked to climate change. As the EPA has noted, in West Virginia, "rising temperatures and shifting rainfall patterns are likely to increase the intensity of both floods and droughts," particularly during the winter and spring months, and as discussed in prior chapters, strip-mined areas in Appalachia exacerbate such flooding conditions. Additionally, climate change will cause cascading ecosystem stress in Appalachia, through disruption of "existing relationships between species."[145]

Climate change also will negatively impact Appalachian human communities through a range of (likely intersecting) factors. Higher annual temperatures and increased droughts could create problematic conditions for regional farms (e.g., reduced crop yields due to drought). Higher annual temperatures also demonstrably produce negative human health effects, as "high air temperatures can cause heat stroke and dehydration, and affect people's cardiovascular and nervous systems."[146] Climate change also reduces air quality through release of increased allergens and ground-level ozone. And warming temperatures in the Appalachian region will increase the prevalence of vector-borne diseases, including tick-transmitted Lyme disease and potential mosquito-transmitted diseases.[147] From an EJ standpoint, it should also be noted that vulnerable populations in Appalachia—based on age (both elderly and young), class, race, gender, poor preexisting health status, and so forth—will be disproportionately affected by many potential climate change impacts, including those extending beyond direct environmental impacts to profound (and intersecting) social, political, and economic dimensions.[148]

TRUMP ADMINISTRATION'S ROLLBACK OF ENVIRONMENTAL LAW

The Trump administration effectuated tangible shifts in U.S. environmental and energy policy, which are wreaking substantial negative outcomes not just for the United States and world at large—but also for Appalachia in particular. In the first place, in what was tantamount to a policy centerpiece during the 2016 presidential campaign, Trump pledged that, if elected, he would restore the U.S. coal industry—and coal mining jobs, specifically—in Appalachia. And post-election, the Trump administration implemented numerous policy shifts with the explicit aim of Appalachian coal industry restoration.

The first of these measures involved signaling a withdrawal of the United States from the Paris Climate Agreement, which Trump announced in 2017. The Paris Agreement is an international accord—achieved through a United Nations Framework Convention on Climate Change (UNFCCC) conference—whereby 195 countries pledged to combat climate change by reducing greenhouse gas emissions; the overarching Paris Agreement goal is to ensure that global temperatures do not rise above 2 degrees Celsius above preindustrial levels (and to strive for a 1.5 degree limit if possible).[149] In signaling the withdrawal from the Paris Agreement, Trump specifically cited, as a rationale, the harm the agreement would cause on the U.S. coal industry. As Trump stated, "the current agreement effectively blocks the development of clean coal in America," and "the agreement doesn't eliminate coal jobs; it just transfers those jobs out of America and the United States, and ships them to foreign countries."[150] Then, in late 2017, Trump moved to dismantle the EPA's nascent Clean Power Plan (CPP), which was a prime regulatory mechanism through which the United States was to comply with the Paris Agreement.[151]

While potential legal challenges and standard regulatory roadblocks will likely result in a prolonged struggle over the CPP, it is clear the Trump administration's policy shifts surrounding the Paris Agreement are impacting the energy landscape. Indeed, the U.S. signaling a withdrawal from the Paris Agreement and the move towards eliminating the CPP is problematic for at least three reasons (which affect Appalachia both directly and indirectly). First, the United States is currently the second highest carbon emitter after China (and is the largest emitter in history), and thus the withdrawal could stymie transitions to renewable energy.[152] Second, the withdrawal may weaken international resolve on climate change, as it will "shock international governance and cooperation systems for climate change."[153] And third, Trump's actions can prolong the coal-induced environmental- and public health–related devastation in Appalachia.

Commentators, however, almost universally agree that eliminating regulations alone (e.g., the CPP) will fail to restore the coal industry in Appalachia in the long-term; this is due to both low-priced natural gas and the rising energy-marketplace dominance of renewables. Nevertheless, Trump's comprehensive deregulation efforts might provide a marginal lifeline, as it were, to the coal industry; for instance, in the "Central Appalachia region . . . the number of coal mining jobs grew from slightly below 15,000 to slightly above that number from January to March" of 2017.[154] What is more, in 2018, the Trump administration announced its intentions to provide potential regulatory bailouts for the coal industry—through support of coal-fired power plants—which, if effectuated, would further buoy the industry.[155] (Such a potential bailout exemplifies a key characteristic of neoliberalism outlined in chapter 4—namely, that despite claims to "market fundamentalism," the state *does* intervene to support favored capital interests. And in the context of energy and environmental policy, in particular, Trump certainly has perpetuated and indeed magnified neoliberal-style governance.)

The Trump administration also effectuated other policy shifts in energy and environmental law that are, broadly speaking, tantamount to a comprehensive anti-environmental agenda. The fact that Scott Pruitt—often characterized as questioning human activity–produced climate change—was appointed as the EPA chief administrator underscores this essential fact.[156] However, additional specific changes in environmental law and policy include Trump's action to rescind the OSMRE's Stream Protection Rule.[157] This rule was the result of the Obama administration's efforts to overhaul a prior version of the rule from 1983 (i.e., the buffer zone rule discussed in chapter 5), which would have required operators to engage in enhanced monitoring of streams throughout the mining process; also, the rule would have "detailed environmental impacts that were prohibited . . . to streams and groundwater outside a mine area."[158]

While the rule would not have banned MTR-produced valley fills outright, it would have provided some enhanced measure of protection for Appalachian waterways. To be sure, the Trump administration's rollback of the Stream Protection Rule is a classic illustration of the neoliberal turn in environmental governance—in which deregulation is of central importance.

Aside from the Stream Protection Rule, the Trump administration has overturned or commenced rollback procedures on dozens of additional environmental rules—many of which directly affect Appalachia. Rules that have been outright overturned include rules on coal ash–related waste; public land fracking regulations; the Obama-era moratorium on new coal mining leases on public lands; a rule on "royalties for oil, gas and coal leases on federal lands;" and agency use of the social cost of carbon calculation discussed in chapter 4.[159] Environmental regulatory rollbacks that are currently in progress include the coal dust rule (i.e., designed to protect miners from black lung disease); "standards for carbon dioxide emissions from new, modified and reconstructed power plants"; and "review of regulations on oil and gas drilling in national parks where mineral rights are privately owned."[160] The guiding principle, of course, is that the Trump administration "with help from Republicans in Congress, has targeted environmental rules it sees as overly burdensome to the fossil fuel industry," including, as the Paris Climate Agreement withdrawal and CPP rollback illustrate, those "major Obama-era policies aimed at fighting climate change."[161]

The Trump administration's impact on U.S. environmental and energy policy therefore has been remarkably far-reaching. In the explicit Appalachian context, the impacts are dire. Trump's emphasis on restoring the coal industry has been largely achieved through targeting environmental regulations designed to protect Appalachia's environment and citizenry—with rollback examples including the Stream Protection Rule, coal ash regulations, and the proposed rollback of the coal dust rule—and the Trump administration will likely secure additional environmental rollbacks. It should also be noted that, as discussed above, Appalachian environmental advocacy groups have often utilized federal litigation tactics to combat regulatory failures on the part of state and federal agencies. However, Trump has succeeded in appointing a record number of deeply conservative—and, at times, questionably qualified—federal judges. Therefore, this long-term weakening of an important site of environmental legal action could produce further issues during and long after the Trump administration.[162]

Ultimately, then, environmental law has failed Appalachia, as has been demonstrated by the MTR phenomenon and, more recently, the unchecked rise of natural gas and a potentially reinvigorated chemical sector, and the Trump administration's vigorous deregulatory campaign only perpetuates this phenomenon. At the same time, however, it must be emphasized that the failures of environmental law in Appalachia are merely a continuation of the wholesale failures of the liberal paradigm at large to protect the region. That is, the Appalachian destruction that has occurred since the 1990s is intrinsically interlinked with that same capitalist-produced devastation that occurred from the period of the Euro-American conquest onwards in the region. Of course, as early chapters of *Remaking Appalachia* chronicle, from the late nineteenth-century period of rapid coal-based industrial growth onwards, Appalachia indeed was uniquely and disproportionately devastated vis-à-vis fossil fuel hegemony–engendered sacrifice zone conditions. But as these chapters also demonstrate, such Appalachian devastation ultimately was operationalized within the broader, exploitative strictures of the liberal capitalist paradigm— i.e., as driven by ceaseless capital accumulation through commodification of everything and perpetual economic growth.

BEYOND APPALACHIA: GLOBAL ECOLOGICAL CRISIS OR "CAPITALOCENE"

In looking beyond Appalachia exclusively, it must indeed be recognized that the region's persistent, multifaceted forms of subordination—while certainly pronounced, as an energy sacrifice zone—are merely part and parcel of the greater set of intertwined global ecological crises. Speth details these crises in *The Bridge at the End of the World*, noting that, in an overarching sense, "global environmental problems have gone from bad to worse," and that "governments are not yet prepared to deal with them."[163] A foremost global crisis, of course, is climate change. Climate change has been primarily caused by human industrial activities—namely, the release of greenhouse gases like carbon dioxide into the atmosphere (known as anthropogenic emissions). Such emissions have exacerbated the "greenhouse effect," whereby heat radiating from the earth's surface is unduly trapped by these atmospheric gases.[164] The scientific community has also reached a high degree of consensus that climate change is human-caused: "Natural variation on their own are simply insufficient to describe the current warming trends, and it is only when the effects of greenhouse gas emissions are taken into consideration that we can account for global warming."[165]

There also exists a scientific consensus that climate change poses a severe threat to the planet. Recall that the specific aim of the Paris Agreement is to ensure that global temperatures do not rise 2 degrees Celsius above preindustrial levels—and to strive for 1.5 degree limit if possible.[166] This is for good reason: the impacts of climate change are projected to grow substantially past the 2 degrees limit.[167] As NASA reports, while even a 1.5 degree increase would create substantial negative impacts, past the 2 degree threshold, there would be increases in "heat-wave duration, rainstorm intensity and sea-level rise," a "disproportionately greater impact on certain basic crops," and "tropical coral reefs would be wiped out."[168] What is more, recent U.N. projections indicate that the world is, in fact, poised to experience a 3-to-5 degree increase by 2100—which would only greatly exacerbate the catastrophic effects of climate change.[169] And the 2018 U.N. Intergovernmental Panel on Climate Change report constitutes a watershed scientific and political moment for the climate crisis. The predictions are so dire—and the report's language and recommendations are so radical—that the document has since been popularized as the "Doomsday" report.[170] This report ultimately calls for "rapid, far-reaching, and unprecedented changes in all aspects of society,"[171] and that the "geographical and economic scales at which the required rates of change in the energy, land, urban, infrastructure, and industrial systems would need to take place . . . have no documented historic precedent."[172]

It is consequently no longer alarmism to note that human societies certainly are imperiled by climate change—along with all other species on the planet. As Wood details in *Nature's Trust*, "climate upheaval will hurl new threats to society on a scale unimaginable to those sitting in government office today," due to "rising sea levels, forest loss, species extinctions, searing heat waves, diminished waters, superstorms, raging wildfires, desertification, spread of disease, massive flooding, and many other disasters that will test humanity's ability to survive."[173] Climate change thus poses a very real "civilizational issue."[174] Cascading negative impacts would also result worldwide, as those displaced by climate change (i.e., climate refugees), for instance, engage in mass migrations—likely leading to phenomena such as mass social unrest and war. As Wood thus concludes: "Warnings of tipping points, irreversible losses, and unpredictable cataclysmic planetary change now pour from the scientific community in growing torrents of alarm. Increasingly, the science makes clear that this moment can be revolutionary, or it can be suicidal."[175] Climate change therefore likely constitutes the pivotal issue—ecological or otherwise—that the world currently faces, and this threat is certainly existential in scope.

However, there exist other dimensions to the global ecological crisis. Speth divides these issues into two broad categories in *The Bridge at the End of the World*: pollution-based issues (under which climate change, too, is categorized) and issues resulting from the overuse of renewable resources. Global pollution-based issues include widespread toxic chemical inundation in addition to nitrogen excess and acid rain (creating ecosystem-related chemical imbalances).[176] For instance, chemical imbalances resulting from phenomena like nitrogen excess are a substantial pollution-based global harm. Currently, through a combination of fertilizer utilization and combustion of fossil fuels, "fixed" nitrogen—or nitrogen of a "biologically active form" that plants can process—is rapidly altering ecosystems. Nitrogen introduced into waterways has led "to overfertilization and, when heavy, to algal blooms and eutrophication—aquatic life simply dies from lack of oxygen."[177] There are now hundreds of ocean "dead zones" due to such human-produced nitrogen excesses.[178]

Issues emanating from the overuse of renewable resources are numerous. Deforestation constitutes a significant example; to date, World Resources Institute research indicates that 30 percent of forests have been outright cleared, 20 percent degraded, and as much as 35 percent have been fragmented.[179] Deforestation results in such ills as increased climate change, loss of biodiversity, flooding, and soil degradation.[180] A global freshwater crisis is also intensifying worldwide. This crisis emanates from a range of factors: human activities, like dams and wetland fills, have reduced freshwater systems. Industrial society has also made great demands on freshwater for agriculture purposes specifically. So, too, have human-produced pollutants been introduced into freshwater supplies, thus "reducing the capacities of bodies of water to support life in the water and to support human communities."[181]

Rapid biodiversity loss, too, is technically a "renewable resource overuse" issue—but is indeed better characterized as an unparalleled world-historical tragedy. Biodiversity includes the following dimensions: a specific species' genetic variety, all species of plants and animals (i.e., which number in the millions), and differing ecosystems' diversity—such as forests, deserts, marine ecosystems, and so forth.[182] Extreme global degradation of all three levels of biodiversity is currently underway. Habitat loss has been the principal cause of this phenomenon. Other causes include the introduction of invasive species; the overharvesting of select species; toxic chemicals; acid rain; ultraviolet radiation; and climate change (which increasingly is exacerbating biodiversity loss).[183]

The global loss of marine fish populations stands out as a particularly egregious example of biodiversity loss. Overfishing is the core issue, which has been driven by large fishing-industry interests aided by government subsidies.[184] To date, a third of global fisheries have been "pushed beyond their biological limits,"[185] and the cumulative "negative impact that human societies are having on the health of marine fisheries and on the world's oceans and estuaries generally is difficult to exaggerate."[186] From an explicit critical perspective, capitalist-steeped fishing and aquaculture systems are, in fact, the primary study of *Tragedy of the Commodity* introduced in chapter 2. As the authors note, numerous "modern systems of fish production are organized around producing global commodities that offer the best opportunity for economic growth, supplying—in large part—the Global North with particularly desirable species."[187]

Indeed, in the context of both terrestrial and aquatic life, Speth notes that it is projected that half of all species will functionally disappear within the next century, and scientists project that "nothing—not national or international laws, global bioreseves, local sustainability schemes or even 'wildlands' fantasies—can change the current course."[188] Therefore, the "broad path for biological evolution is now set for the next several million years," and the "extinction crisis—the race to save the composition, structure, and organization of biodiversity as it exists today—is over, and we have lost."[189] (The perspective of *Remaking Appalachia*, of course, is that despite such dire projections, we nevertheless should mass mobilize to make those radical economic and socio-legal transformations that will allow us to save what we can.)

These global ecological crises are ultimately interlinked. They generally operate in tandem with one another, which largely serves to worsen environmental conditions across the board. The reduction in forests, for example, "contributes to biodiversity loss, climate change, and desertification."[190] Climate change, in turn, contributes to exacerbation of essentially all global ecological crises discussed above—as climate change will produce "additional flooding and increased droughts, reduce freshwater supplies, adversely affect biodiversity and forests and further degrade aquatic ecosystems."[191] Johan Rockström and related researchers put forth significant work in exploring such collected impacts—particularly on nonlinear relationships and tipping points—in "Planetary Boundaries." The researchers identify nine global boundaries that cannot be transgressed for "humanity [to] operate safely," and further estimate that three of the boundaries already have been transgressed: climate change, biodiversity loss, and global nitrogen cycle changes.[192] What is more, the researchers argue the following: "Transgressing one or more planetary boundaries may be deleterious or even catastrophic due to the risk of crossing thresholds that will trigger non-linear, abrupt environmental change within continental- to planetary-scale systems."[193] The researchers thus conclude that "planetary boundaries define, as it were, the boundaries of the 'planetary playing field' for humanity if we want to be sure of avoiding major human-induced environmental change on a global scale."[194]

Collectively, these intertwined ecological crises are now commonly recognized as being part and parcel of the Anthropocene, after "*anthropo*, for 'man,' and *cene*, for 'new.'"[195] Although in use for decades, the term *Anthropocene* was popularized in 2000 by Paul Crutzen; it is an explanatory device for how "human-kind has caused mass extinctions of plant and animal species, polluted the oceans and altered the atmosphere, among other lasting impacts."[196] What is more, the term "Capitalocene" has been put forth as a more apt critical alternative to Anthropocene. Jason Moore argues that "the Capitalocene signifies capitalism as a way of organizing nature—as a multispecies, situated, capitalist world-ecology."[197] Consequently, per general notions of Capitalocene, humans as an essentialized species are not most directly responsible for the global ecological crisis, but rather the historically specific capitalist mode of production is the true root cause for the global crisis.[198] "Capitalocene," and not "Anthropocene," is therefore the overarching term for situating the true scope of the global ecological crisis used throughout *Remaking Appalachia*. Many commentators also assert that global destruction of species constitutes an "ongoing sixth mass extinction" event.[199] Lastly, the "Doomsday Clock," as produced by the Bulletin of the Atomic Scientists, now lists climate change as a key existential threat to humanity—alongside more traditional existential threats such as nuclear weapons.[200] Therefore, the risks posed by the global ecological crisis are extraordinarily dire.

MODERN APPALACHIA'S ECONOMIC, CULTURAL, AND POLITICAL LANDSCAPE

The coal industry, in increasingly adopting mechanization, systematically reduced Appalachian mining employment throughout the latter twentieth century—and, as noted above, the industry itself has declined precipitously in the most recent decade. Nevertheless, the coal industry persists in exercising outsized political and cultural influence in Appalachia. As compared to prior eras, however, the coal industry has relied on not the traditional employment relationship for regional support—but rather on cultural manipulation tactics.

In the first place, the transition to mechanized mining in the twentieth century resulted in a remarkable decrease in Appalachian mining employment, which produced obvious negative impacts in the form of unemployment and broader economic decline. The "treadmill of production" is a particularly apt model through which to conceptualize this coalfield phenomenon in Appalachia. Bell and York explore the treadmill of production model extensively—and its intersection with gender—in "Community Economic Identity."

The treadmill of production model posits that both environmental destruction and worker displacement are "intrinsic to capitalist (as well as some other) modes of production."[201] Essentially, following the post-WWII economic boom, "increased production and profits . . . were invested in the development of new production technologies."[202] Such technologies required higher operation costs, and so this incentivized industry to increase production in order to gain the additional profits required to cover those costs. But increased production required more natural resources, resulting in greater resource extraction and more radical environmental degradation. Consequently, this phenomenon of "increasing extraction and degradation in order to generate greater and greater profits has become the central operating framework of the global market," and "it is widely held that the treadmill of production, along with the ecological degradation it generates, is unavoidable unless the relations of production under corporate capitalism are changed."[203]

Displacement of workers is a direct consequence of the treadmill of production. Technology improvements lead to increased productivity among workers, which inevitably "accelerates the treadmill," thus allowing smaller numbers of workers to generate increased productivity—and thus profits for industry.[204] This phenomenon certainly is at work in the context of extractive industries such as coal and timber, as "consistent with treadmill of production theorizing, even when production increases in these industries, employment levels decrease."[205] National-level data on coal production in the United States supports this negative association, and in the specific context of the Appalachian coalfields, "job losses between the late 1940s and the early 2000s clearly were due to the ongoing process of the treadmill of production" through which "workers are replaced by machines."[206] West Virginia constitutes a representative exemplar: the state employed roughly 130,000 miners in 1948, but by 2010, this number dropped to roughly 22,500.[207] By 2017, there were only 50,000 coal industry employees remaining in all of the United States.[208]

The coal industry adopted ideological strategies to account for the treadmill of production–produced displacement of workers. Whereas previously the coal industry could rely on the employment relationship for support in the region, following mass worker displacement, the industry faced a potential "legitimation crisis."[209] The coal industry's "response to this challenge has been to engage in cultural manipulation, attempting to construct a pro-coal ideology that shapes community economic identity."[210] Analyzing West Virginia specifically, Bell and York argue that prime strategies the coal industry has adopted include "appropriation of West Virginia cultural icons and the infusion of coal-industry ideology into a variety of social arenas," thus resulting in an overarching strategy to "(re)construct the identity of West Virginia as both economically dependent on coal and culturally defined by coal."[211]

Bell and York specifically investigate, as an important example, the Friends of Coal organization formed by the West Virginia Coal Association in 2002; Friends of Coal was indeed a response not just to worker displacement but also to the rising environmental justice movement in the region.[212] Through an intensive public relations campaign, Friends of Coal aimed to "reconstruct a bond between the coal industry and West Virginia communities."[213]

There are important gender dimensions to such cultural manipulation (in addition to, as discussed below, race- and nationalist-based dimensions). Friends of Coal, in reconstructing a community bond, relied extensively on the traditional gender ideology outlined at length in chapter 1—i.e., that of men engaging in the (socially valued) productive work of coal mining, and women engaging in the (socially devalued yet crucial) reproductive work such as domestic labor. However, as Bell and York argue, the ideology put forth by the coal industry adds a new dimension to this gender regime. As actual coal miners were displaced from employment, the coal industry itself took on the hegemonic masculine role through messaging relating to such dimensions as "winner," "provider and defender," and "outdoorsman."[214] This ideology was effectuated, for instance, by selecting male spokespersons who reflected this masculine role—e.g., prominent sports coaches (winner), a military officer (defender), and a professional fisherman (outdoorsman).[215] Friends of Coal also deployed images of working-class male coal miners in its advertisements to highlight hegemonic masculinity, which "works within the historical gender structure of Appalachia," as it "reinforce[es] mainstream images of a working-class male provider as the true face of the coal industry."[216] Friends of Coal also established "a visible presence in the social landscape of West Virginia through stickers, yard signs, and sponsorships."[217] Bell and York thus conclude "that public acquiescence to the wishes of industry is in part achieved by industries' calculated efforts to reconstruct a bond with the communities they degrade, attempting to replace the employment connection between industry and community with a constructed ideology of dependency and economic identity."[218]

The traditional gendered division of labor in Appalachia—as previously embodied in turn-of-the-century company towns—had, of course, undergone significant transformations in the twentieth century as women increasingly entered the paid workforce. In the specific context of coal mining, women were granted the right to enter the workforce in the late 1970s; that said, women miners were among the first laid off as mechanization continued to decimate the workforce.[219] Furthermore, Lewis notes that while some African American women joined these ranks, they were among the vastly reduced number of *all* African American miners "in an industry which had provided employment to countless thousands" of African American miners "over the last two centuries."[220]

Beyond coal specifically, however, material changes in the economic, social, and political structures of Central Appalachia significantly impacted the gendered division of labor. Perhaps most notably, some degree of economic diversification led to (fundamentally exploitative) service sector jobs displacing mining as a major employment source, and women increasingly entered such service sector jobs among others forms of waged labor.[221] Broadly speaking, this reflects Fraser's analysis that contemporary capitalist forces have constructed "a new regime of accumulation on the cornerstone of women's waged labor."[222]

Furthermore, in Appalachia (and indeed in the broader nation and world) despite the fact that women increasingly have entered the paid workforce, they continue to disproportionally engage in unpaid reproductive labor as well (i.e., along traditional gender lines).[223] And so, too, do women disproportionately engage in paid reproductive labor, such as waged-based household labor or childcare—which receives relatively low compensation rates and is socially devalued.[224] And from an intersectional perspective, there exists a profound "racial-ethnic division of paid reproductive labor in the contemporary service sector," as white women disproportionately occupy supervisory positions and those with "some degree of moral authority" (e.g., nurses).[225] Lastly, despite greater rates of waged labor participation, women experience higher poverty rates than men. For instance, in West Virginia, 20.9 percent of women were impoverished in 2017, as compared to 17.2 percent of men. And so, too, are African American West Virginians impoverished at disproportionately higher rates (i.e., in 2017, 31.7 percent versus the 19.1 percent total poverty rate for the state). African American West Virginian women, then, experience disproportionate economic marginalization across these intersecting dimensions.[226] And so, too, are high poverty rates among female-headed households an issue in West Virginia.[227]

Complex gender forces have therefore been at work in modern Appalachia. On the one hand, the strict gendered division of labor declined, but on the other, the traditional "gender ideology 'is still felt' " in the coalfields—as has been leveraged by Friends of Coal.[228] For Appalachian men, such a "disconnect between ideology and economic reality has meant that many men are no longer able to live up to their traditional definition of masculinity," which has contributed, at least in part, to domestic strife at home, including domestic violence, suicide, and so forth.[229] It is a great irony, then, that "the very industry that created the hegemonic masculinity of the region in the first place is also responsible for preventing most coalfield men from achieving it," and thus, in the end, "it is necessary for the coal industry to convince residents that men are still the breadwinners of the family if it is to convince them that coal is still the backbone of the economy."[230]

The interlinking of hegemonic masculinity with whiteness also adds crucial dimensions to coal industry cultural manipulation tactics. That is, in reconstructing a bond with Appalachian coal communities based on ideology rather employment, not only is the coal industry reliant on hegemonic masculinity—but so, too, can the industry rely on white supremacy, as relying on the long tradition of encoding Appalachians and coal miners, in particular, with whiteness (i.e., as is unpacked more fully below). Thus, the coal industry can leverage whiteness as a crucial dimension through which a bond with Appalachian communities can be reconstructed based on (white) cultural identity.[231]

The natural gas industry likely has benefited from such coal industry–produced cultural manipulation. As discussed above, the Marcellus shale gas boom constitutes the latest manifestation of the fossil fuel hegemony in Appalachia. And so the natural gas industry likely at least implicitly leverages such core coal industry messaging to similarly advance its cultural influence in the region. Similar to coal, the natural gas industry essentially is coded as white and masculine, as the industry is associated with blue-collar, natural resource extractive-related employment: natural gas cultural messaging thus works within historic gender regimes in Appalachia. When natural gas is assailed along environmental and employment lines, then—i.e., on the latter point, the total number of jobs generated by the natural gas industry is somewhat unclear—pro-natural gas arguments carry great cultural weight regardless.[232] That is, due to the extensive ideological groundwork laid by the coal industry (as aided by the long-term structural momentum of coal), the natural gas industry likely can encourage Appalachians to culturally self-identify, at least in part, with the natural gas industry—i.e., as a regional extractive industry encoded with white hegemonic masculinity. And it should additionally be noted that similar to the coal industry, complicit Appalachian elites have long supported the rise of natural gas as a supposed economic driver for the region—when in actuality, the Appalachian shale gas boom is merely the latest iteration of exploitative fossil fuel hegemony in the region.

CONTINUED FAILURES OF APPALACHIAN GOVERNMENTAL ELITES

The core of West Virginia's institutional elites indeed has been complicit in continuing to support the coal industry and the greater fossil fuel hegemony.

Such support has been effectuated, for instance, by continued low severance tax rates and continued degradation of workplace safety and environmental regulations.[233] In achieving such policy support, West Virginia politicians also have perpetuated the coal industry's cultural manipulation messaging. As a now-infamous example, West Virginia Senate candidate Joe Manchin used a rifle to shoot cap-and-trade legislation in a campaign ad, stating "I'll take on Washington and this administration to get the federal government off of our back and out of our pockets . . . I sued EPA and I'll take dead aim at the cap-and-trade bill." [234] That Manchin similarly adopts a white hegemonic male affect in the ad (i.e., a male "outdoorsman") illustrates the extent to which Appalachian politicians' messaging explicitly dovetails with that of the coal industry.

Such governmental support, however, is hardly surprising, as Central Appalachian elites (and those of West Virginia, particularly) have long been economically and politically beholden to the fossil fuel hegemony. As McGinley notes, "the coal industry and those who directly profit from mining," such as "state and local politicians," have "led the coalfields to its present condition" and, moreover, "those same players continue to exert enormous influence, which promises to extend the economic status quo." [235] The coal industry has, in fact, managed to largely retain its political influence in West Virginia despite the fact that not just have coal mining jobs been systematically reduced— but coal has also produced a lesser economic impact overall in recent decades and this decline is projected to continue (as discussed above).[236] That the coal industry nevertheless commands an outsized political influence in Central Appalachian regions and in West Virginia specifically is therefore a testament to such factors as the long-term structural momentum of coal, the comprehensive failure of regional elites to pursue a post–fossil fuel future in good faith, and also to explicit cultural manipulation tactics outlined above.

Appalachian elites have indeed, for decades, failed the regional citizenry and environment not just by continuing to fixate on coal- and other fossil fuel–related development (e.g., natural gas)—but have, more broadly, focused on market-based approaches to growth and development that are detrimental to the region. As Eller notes, Appalachian policymakers have long "diverted millions of dollars to the creation of jobs that were disappearing in the rest of the nation," such as manufacturing, and such policies have thus "encouraged short-term growth at the expense of more sustainable development." [237] The choice development of other sectors in the region, such as the nascent petrochemical sector resurgence—and, in the retail context, the cultivation of transnational superstore conglomerates, has similarly "facilitated the transfer of wealth out of the region, contributing to the decline of smaller, community-based businesses," while also draining public resources that might have better supported "innovative, sustainable alternatives to the delivery of good and services."[238] As Eller thus concludes, Appalachian elites in recent decades have "continued to look to external models of development that perpetuated old dependences on outside markets and absentee capital."[239]

THE TRUMP PHENOMENON'S INTERTWINEMENTS WITH APPALACHIA

It was within this embattled Appalachian landscape that the 2016 presidential election transpired, in which Appalachia's coalfields featured prominently in Donald Trump's campaign; as introduced above, Trump promised that, if elected, he would reverse the decline of coal, and that he would, more specifically, restore the systemic loss of coal mining jobs. During campaign rallies, Trump made such claims as follows: "We're going to get those miners back to work . . . the miners of West Virginia and Pennsylvania, which was so great to me last week, Ohio and all over are going to start to work again, believe me. They are going to be proud again to be miners."[240] Indeed, in one of the signature moments of his campaign, Trump made similar remarks at a rally in West Virginia and also donned a hardhat and mimicked shoveling coal.[241] Likely based at least in part on such rhetoric, swaths of Appalachia voted relatively heavily for Trump (although the discussion below unpacks many more nuanced forces at work in the region). In Appalachia, Trump won 95 percent of the 420 ARC-designated counties—and in West Virginia specifically, a higher percentage of voters supported Trump than in any other state.[242]

Trump's campaign fixation on the revitalization of coal was significant for a number of reasons important to *Remaking Appalachia*. In the first place, as the treadmill of production model so starkly illustrates, whatever the fate of the industry itself, revitalizing coal mining jobs is largely an impossibility—as mechanization has permanently displaced jobs. What is more, as unpacked above, coal's decline is due primarily to sheer market forces in the form of low-priced natural gas (and to a growing extent, renewables). A revitalization of both coal mining jobs and the industry itself, then, is a near-impossibility, especially when viewed on a longer-term timeframe, and thus it should come as no surprise that Trump largely has failed to deliver on this campaign promise. That Trump's coal-related rhetoric nevertheless resonated in some swaths of Appalachia partially can be attributed to coal's long-term structural importance in the region (as buttressed by Appalachian elite support)—but also to the continued potency of industry-produced cultural manipulation tactics, as are dependent on white hegemonic masculinity.

Trump's campaign rhetoric, in essence, perpetuated and indeed magnified the coal industry's core messaging—namely, that coalfield communities should ideologically self-identify with the coal industry, and should thus be both "economically dependent on coal and culturally defined by coal."[243] As discussed above, the coal industry has very successfully encoded itself with masculine characteristics: Trump's pledge to revitalize coal therefore carried with it an implicit promise to restore Appalachian men to mining jobs, or their historically dominant form of productive labor, which would constitute, at least in part, a restoration of white hegemonic masculinity in Appalachia. In taking a step further, Trump also symbolically equated himself with coal miners—e.g., one of the most indelible images of the campaign was indeed Trump "performing" mining with his shoveling mimicry. Trump's self-identification with the coal industry thus further imbued the contemporary coal industry with hegemonic masculinity—as Trump personally embodies a much-analyzed variety of toxic hyper-masculinity. This is illustrated by Trump's overt, well-documented sexism and misogyny, as well as his more insidious fixation on restoring traditionally male-centered blue-collar jobs (i.e., not just coal but, for instance, manufacturing in the Midwest).[244] Thus, the Trump campaign at least implicitly leveraged the coal industry's legacy of cultural manipulation in Appalachia, in suggesting that not just jobs but also white hegemonic masculinity could be revitalized through a Trump victory.

Trump's emphasis on self-identifying with the coal industry can be contrasted with Hilary Clinton's campaign experience. Clinton was characterized essentially as coal's primary antagonist following this Ohio town hall comment: "We're going to put a lot of coal miners and coal companies out of business."[245] Just as the coal revitalization rhetoric was a central pillar of Trump's messaging, Clinton's coal-related statement became a defining moment of her campaign. As Clinton reflected in *What Happened*: "I wish more than anything that I could have done a better job speaking to their fears and frustrations."[246] Of course, Clinton's comment was taken out of context—Clinton was, in fact, attempting to make a good-faith argument for economic revitalization in Appalachia (albeit as ultimately steeped in neoliberal-centrist policies).[247] Nevertheless, Clinton's rhetoric and the accompanying conservative media backlash that followed was likely a contributor (or was highly representative of) her campaign's steep losses in Appalachia.

Significantly, pro-coal media commentators were no doubt cognizant of the fact that in equating Clinton with an anti–coal miner (and pro–environmental protection) position, such efforts, by extension, equated Clinton with an anti-hegemonic white masculinity position—which also intersects with Clinton's identity as the first female presidential nominee of a major party. In Clinton's particular case, such a gender-steeped analysis is indeed complicated by her class-based status as a neoliberal elite (i.e., as Trump's campaign targeted both the left and right wings of the neoliberal establishment). Nevertheless, this analysis at least partially accounts for the intensive antipathy directed towards her campaign. In short, Clinton constituted a female candidate in favor of at least some degree of environmental protection in addition to neoliberal identity politics generally (along lines of race, nationality, etc.)—and thus in representing such "othered" standpoints poised to potentially exert considerable control over the region, the Clinton campaign was insidiously characterized by conservative media commentators as threatening coal-as-white-hegemonic-masculinity in Appalachia.

Also important for *Remaking Appalachia*, issues of race, racism, and xenophobia were fundamentally intertwined with Trump's campaign coalfield rhetoric. Similar to his sexism and misogyny, it is well documented that Trump constructed his nationalist campaign (and subsequent presidency) through direct appeals towards subordination of marginalized groups along lines of race and nationality; Trump has also frequently denigrated indigenous groups.[248] As a candidate explicitly steeped in xenophobia and white supremacy, then, Trump's fixation on revitalizing coal mining jobs is significant because the coal industry (and Appalachia at large) is encoded not just as working class and masculine but also as white. As Rebecca Scott notes, in addition to working-class status, "Appalachians are symbolically coded white in U.S. racial formations."[249] Numerous commentators have further unpacked the fixation on Appalachians-as-whites—particularly the notion that all Appalachians constitute whites of a "pure" Scots-Irish heritage (as introduced in chapter 1 as part of the myth of Appalachia).[250] Allen Batteau's concept of "Holy Appalachia" also is pertinent. According to Batteau's account, historic characterizations of Appalachia involved the proposition that because the region supposedly constituted a homogenized white mountain culture, Appalachians somehow were untainted by systemic prejudices found elsewhere in the United States.[251] Appalachians were therefore uniquely devoid of racial and ethnic prejudices—i.e., "Holy Appalachia"[252]—and possess a variety of intrinsic "racial innocence."[253] To be sure, such phenomena are demonstrably false, and furthermore, the perpetuation of such narratives can occur both inside and outside of the region.

Notions of Appalachian whiteness certainly apply to Appalachian coal miners specifically—as exploited by the Trump campaign. Scott notes that miners are indeed "symbolically white," as "the racially segmented labor market has historically reserved the family wage as a privilege of white men."[254] Thus, in the context of Trump's campaign, as contemporary Appalachian coal miners are associated with working-class white men, it has been observed that, for "Trump, the fixation on coal is less about energy than about white masculinity," because "if a West Virginia coal miner could fall on hard times, what chance did the rest of the nation's men have?"[255] Consequently, for Trump, the "coal industry and its workers [occupy] an outsized place" due to "the simple fact that it has long been coded as white and masculine."[256] Similar to his amplification of coal industry–produced hegemonic masculinity in the region, Trump's fixation on the coal industry also served to amplify insidious white supremacy–related messaging.

Trump's messaging largely promoted the reification of a white cultural Appalachian identity wholly dependent on coal; correspondingly, Trump's messaging foreclosed explorations of a post–fossil fuel future for Appalachia (as often discussed in the context of a progressive or radical "just transition")[257]— and thus by extension, of a post-white hegemonic masculine future. On the latter point, such race, gender, etc. elements were ultimately intertwined— in Appalachia and beyond—as Trump is best characterized as a "invok[ing] a masculine, class-based reactionary white identity politics," wherein these differing forms of subordination and oppression intrinsically work in tandem (i.e., as again invoking the central tenets of the ecofeminist discourse).[258] This phenomenon is illustrated, for instance, by Trump's proclivity for disproportionately targeting women along lines of immigrant, minority, and indigenous status in particular.[259] What is more, Trump also intertwined environmental issues with such messaging, both explicitly and implicitly. As noted above, Trump argued for, and later actually effectuated, a historic rollback of environmental regulations in order to supposedly revitalize coal—and again, by extension, white male patriarchy—in Appalachia. Trump's 2016 campaign had the ultimate effect, then, of perpetuating intersecting forms of marginalization and oppression in the broader United States, and through unique formations, in Appalachia specifically.

TRANSFORMATIVE ALTERNATIVE VISIONS CRUCIAL TO COMBAT TRUMP PHENOMENON

Such a white male supremacy-steeped fixation on the coal industry, as exploited by Trump during the election and thereafter, is a profoundly alarming phenomenon. As numerous commentators have explored, however, subordinated regions such as Appalachia were particularly vulnerable to the Trump phenomenon in the first place due to the ascendancy of neoliberal-associated conditions (i.e., of which treadmill of production–related coal job displacement is merely a cornerstone condition).[260] Deteriorating material conditions in Central Appalachia broadly characterized as neoliberal in nature—i.e., vast wealth inequality, the degradation of unions (e.g., the UMWA), and the overarching displacement of relatively high-paying (and culturally valued) jobs for precarious, devalued employment (e.g., the service sector)—led to an Appalachian citizenry desperate for alternative visions. Unfortunately, the Clinton campaign merely proffered more of the neoliberal status quo, as compared to a more radical vision for a transformative path forward; devoid of meaningful alternatives, it is therefore unsurprising that Trump's coal reinvigoration messaging resonated with a considerable swath of the Appalachian citizenry.[261]

Of crucial importance, however, is that Trump's rhetoric—and that of any right-wing reactionaries who follow—need not influence Appalachia nor similarly vulnerable regions in the United States and beyond (i.e., as the rise of reactionary right-wing politics is a truly global phenomenon). West Virginia, for instance, historically constituted a Democratic Party stronghold (due to, among other factors, strong union affiliation), and only in recent decades has the state transitioned towards conservative governance.[262] On the one hand, even prior to Trump's presidential campaign, the Republican Party and allied conservative forces (e.g., right-wing news outlets) have long deployed often-coded rhetoric steeped in racism, misogyny, and xenophobia geared towards bolstering white working-class support—which, of course, was directly in service to "deflect[ing] potential anger and criticism away from the failings of neoliberal capitalism."[263] Trump, with his more overt rhetoric, can thus in some ways be conceived of as a perverse logical endpoint (with his "revitalization of the 'Southern strategy' "),[264] not as an aberration, within the Republican Party's now-decades' long trajectory.[265] (Although again, this analysis is complicated by Trump's targeted attacks on the neoliberal establishment.) This phenomenon more broadly illustrates the extent to which conservative forces have successfully capitalized on coal's decline and broader deteriorating material conditions in Appalachia and beyond—in addition to the wholesale failure of the Democrat's neoliberal-centrist messaging—in order to exert considerable influence through such cultural manipulation based on racism, misogyny, nationalism, etc.[266]

On the other hand, the Republican Party ascendancy in West Virginia is a relatively recent historical trend, which thus belies more complex, nuanced forces at work in the region. To begin, in the specific context of the 2016 presidential election, elite media commentators incorrectly fixated on Appalachia as a wholly homogenized exemplar of "Trump country"—essentially blaming

Appalachia in large part for the Trump victory. However, such a homogeniza-tion of Appalachia-as-Trump-country merely constitutes yet another dimen-sion of the Appalachian myth—i.e., the material-historical roots of which are discussed in chapter 1. As commentators such as Catte argue, such homogeni-zation is problematic, in the first place, due to numerous complicating factors. Voter turnout was low in southern West Virginia and in the greater region; and so the Trump victory hardly reflects the will of all Appalachian citizens.[267] It has been similarly noted that "the white working class did not strike back," as "they mostly refused to participate."[268] Furthermore, in the Democratic pri-mary, West Virginia voted heavily for Bernie Sanders—a democratic social-ist candidate—over the neoliberal-centrist Clinton. While Clinton's gender, energy and environmental politics, and broader neoliberal-steeped identity politics were contributing factors, Sanders' victory in West Virginia neverthe-less greatly complicates the narrative of Appalachia-as-homogenized-Trump-county—as Sanders' class-focused, redistributive economic policies likely resonated with the populace.[269]

Beyond such complicating factors, the homogenization of Appalachia-as-Trump-country is also problematic for additional reasons that impact the nation at large. As Catte argues, "we need to examine why journalists from elite and prestige publications are invested in presenting Appalachians" as being "representative of all Trump supporters."[270] Catte adds that, "histori-cally, cultural elites . . . have used flawed representations of Appalachia" to both "enhance the cultural difference between progressive white individuals and those thought to be 'yesterday's people' " and to "absolve cultural elites from the responsibility of thinking critically about race and racism."[271] On this latter point, Appalachia, for instance, did not solely deliver Trump the presi-dency: millions of voters from outside Appalachia—the majority of whom were not from the working class—contributed to the Trump victory.[272] That media elites nevertheless fixated on Appalachia is thus alarming, because the struc-tural racism, sexism, xenophobia, etc., that are endemic to all of the United States (i.e., under liberal capitalism)—not just to Appalachia—are veiled, as are the neoliberal-specific material conditions that made Trump's nationalist campaign so successful in the first place. Recognizing such essential facts is a crucial step in mobilizing for transformative change in the entirety of the United States. Rather than "othering" entire regions such as Appalachia as homogenized "Trump country," radically conceived, intersectional-steeped al-liances (along lines of class, race, gender, etc.) instead should be cultivated across geographic lines—i.e., as is explored in subsequent chapters of *Remaking Appalachia*.[273]

Another core, related issue in homogenizing Appalachia as Trump country is that this elite media narrative veils the very real racial, cultural, and political diversity in Appalachia—which further forestalls efforts towards intersectional-steeped transformative change beyond liberal capitalism. In the political context, Sanders' democratic primary victory in West Virginia indeed constitutes one exemplar of such diversity in the region—but more broadly speaking, Appalachia has long been marked by robust pockets of progressive and indeed radical politics and activism. Prior chapters identify important examples of such dimensions; namely, the labor organizing and the "coal wars" of the early twentieth century, surface mining–related environmental activism of the 1960s, and so forth. And the final portion of this chapter unpacks contemporary manifestations of this grassroots activism tradition, as have involved the anti-MTR and anti–natural gas movements, among others. Moreover, much contemporary Appalachian activism is marked by both intersectional precepts (along lines of race, gender, etc.) and also multi-coalitional interlinking (involving intertwinements of environmental advocacy, labor organizing, etc.). Appalachia-as-homogenized-Trump-country, therefore, veils this vitally important historical and contemporary grassroots tradition.

In the context of racial and ethnic diversity, the false narrative of Appalachia as a homogenized white population also serves to, as Catte observes, "[exclude] people of color from our shared regional heritage."[274] As discussed in chapter 1, Appalachia has always been marked by racial diversity, illustrated by indigenous populations, African American populations, and so forth. While such levels have fluctuated (i.e., due in no small part to white supremacy–steeped social structures), nevertheless, the region continues to exhibit crucial diversity. As ARC reports on Appalachia's contemporary demographics, racial minorities constitute 18.6 percent of the region's population, which is up from 16.4 percent in 2010—and which constitutes millions of citizens. African Americans are the largest population (9.7 percent), with Latinos constituting the fastest-growing population.[275] On this latter statistic, as Schumann notes in *Appalachia Revisited*, "Latina/o in-migration into southern Appalachia is responsible for nearly half of all the region's population growth since 1990, which contrasts with greater levels of white out-migration and lower cultural diversity in the North."[276]

Appalachia does not have precise statistical parity with the broader United States. For instance, Appalachia's minority population is smaller than the U.S. national average (39.3 percent). Contemporary Appalachia also differs in other demographic categories, as compared to the broader nation. For instance, Appalachia's population is growing more slowly than the U.S. average—since

2010, Appalachia's population has grown at 1.4 percent compared to the 5.3 percent average.[277] (And indeed, West Virginia has had a declining population in the past decade—its population has fallen 0.10 percent per year.)[278] Appalachia's population is older than the U.S. average, with a median age of 40.5 as compared to the national average of 37.6. The region also is more rural, as 42 percent of Appalachia is rural compared to the 20 percent national average.[279]

Despite such notable variations, the overarching myth of Appalachia—as operationalized by exploitative actors during and after the 2016 presidential election ultimately serves to mask the fact that diversity *does* exist in the region. In summary, not only does this phenomenon serve to veil (and to thus further subordinate) marginalized populations, but the myth of Appalachia-as-homogenized-whites also directly forestalls efforts towards intersectional-steeped organizing in the region (i.e., true solidarity building along lines of race, gender, class, etc.)—as interlinked with the geographic-political homogenization of Appalachia-as-Trump-country-conservative that further hinders Appalachian alliance building across regional, national, and global levels.

MODERN APPALACHIAN GRASSROOTS MOVEMENTS

Appalachia has experienced a deeply robust and, in many ways, revitalized grassroots tradition throughout the entirety of the MTR era. As has been detailed in prior chapters, Appalachia's modern resistance tradition is a long and storied one—as it reaches back, at least, to the "coal wars" that arose over labor issues. (And, of course, an analysis of even earlier resistance traditions in the region would implicate indigenous peoples' resistance to the Euro-American conquest and colonization and African American resistance to slavery—among many other dimensions.) Thereafter, in the 1960s, a rich grassroots environmental movement emerged in Appalachia in response to the rise of mechanized surface mining. This movement, which was largely comprised of ordinary Appalachian citizens whose health and property were imperiled by mining practices (in addition to allied activists) eventually entered the national consciousness and helped catalyze passage of SMCRA. In subsequent decades, both the environmental and labor movements, among many others, would persist as significant forces in the region. However, by the late twentieth century, the formal labor movement in Appalachia would be marked by general decline—i.e., as exacerbated by neoliberal forces across the board—as powerful interests indeed would continue to succeed in rolling back progressive gains from the liberal welfare state era.[280]

At the same time, the rise of MTR in the 1990s resulted in reinvigorated environmental grassroots activism, and the contemporary Appalachian grass-roots environmental movement extends beyond the mining industry in targeting the natural gas industry, the chemical industry, broader issues (e.g., climate change), and intersectional concerns (along lines of class, race, gender, indigenous status, etc.). So, too, are the Appalachian environmental and labor movements—which often came into conflict in the past over such issues as "jobs vs. environment" (i.e., as aided by the industry's cultural manipulation tactics)—increasingly finding common ground. The historic 2018 West Virginia teacher's strike, which explicitly targeted dimensions of the fossil fuel hegemony, is a notable exemplar of such Appalachian grassroots coalitional intertwinements. And such bottom-up, organic movements certainly reflect Bryan McNeil's general observations that, in Appalachia, "the emergence of community-based activist networks represents a trend to recreate social solidarities that the neoliberal tide attempted to wash away."[281]

Recent work has chronicled the decades' long resurgence of Appalachia's environmental movement. Perdue and McCarty's "Unearthing a Network of Resistance" discusses this grassroots activism in the context of ongoing Appalachian law reform efforts. As Perdue and McCarty note, in examining the anti–strip mining movement since the 1960s, there was, first, a "period of abeyance following the passage of SMCRCA in 1977."[282] However, the authors then "observe a reinvigoration of the movement" from the 1990s forward.[283] In chronicling the Appalachian anti–strip mining movement in the prior three decades, their analysis traces "the steady growth of this movement as connections among anti-stripping groups have culminated in a dense network of resistance today."[284]

Beginning in the 1990s and especially by the 2000s, anti-MTR efforts constituted a focal point for the Appalachian environmental grassroots movement. MTR increased dramatically during this time and was a prime negative actor in the region; thus, correspondingly, MTR "catalyzed resistance in the region."[285] Appalachian resistance to MTR covered a full spectrum of actions, including litigation and policy advocacy, diverse protests, and for some organizations and individuals, intensive forms of civil disobedience.[286]

Generally speaking, some older grassroots organizations in Appalachia, such as SOCM which arose in 1972 (and was renamed in 2008 as Statewide Organizing for Community eMpowerment), remain vital grassroots organizations today.[287] To this list can be added the famed Tennessee-based Highlander Research and Education Center, which was founded as the Highlander Folk School in 1932, and which provides grassroots leadership training in Appalachia and the South. Moreover, numerous new state- and regional-based organizations emerged during the 1980s and 1990s and are still in force. These include the Ohio Valley Environmental Coalition (OVEC), Appalachian Voices, and Kentuckians for the Commonwealth (KFTC), the latter of which "formed in 1981 as the Kentucky Fair Tax Coalition with the goals of ending the abuses of broad-form deeds and forcing coal and land companies to pay [fair] tax rates."[288] While mining practices and related EJ concerns often constituted focal points for these organizations in the last decades (and more recently, natural gas), many are, in fact, "well-established . . . multi-issue organizations with large memberships" that hold "relatively large amounts of resources."[289]

Many Appalachian grassroots organizations are marked by both close collaboration efforts and a focus on legal channels for achieving environmental-related change. Social mobilization scholars have concluded that, for grassroots organizations, "success, in the form of affecting legislation and public awareness, is often more attainable in highly connected and dense networks"—and the Appalachian "network has become [increasingly so] over the last thirty years."[290] Moreover, for Appalachian grassroots organizations, joint litigation participation has often constituted the main driver of such collaboration. Many of the federal environmental plaintiff-based decisions discussed above demonstrate this phenomenon. For instance, in the *Bragg v. Robertson* case, the West Virginia Highlands Conservancy (WVHC) and coalfield residents were on the environmental plaintiffs' side.[291] Another example includes the *Ohio Valley Environmental Coalition v. Bulen* decision, handed down by the Southern District of West Virginia in 2004. In this case—which again involved a claim against the Corps in an MTR-related issue—environment plaintiffs included OVEC and the Coal River Mountain Watch (CRMW), who were joined by the Natural Resources Defense Council (NRDC).[292] So, too, have KFTC and Southern Appalchian Mountain Stewards (SAMS) often been involved in joint litigation efforts, and Appalachian groups have generally benefited from assistance from such public interest law and policy organizations as the Appalachian Mountain Advocates.[293]

Appalachian law and policy organizations faced extreme challenges during this era. For instance, Joe Lovett, the founder and executive director of the Appalachian Mountain Advocates, has said, "When we first brought [*Bragg*], I thought that it would be as simple as pointing out to the government that the law wasn't being enforced."[294] However, for Lovett, it "turned out to be far from simple. The government instead of enforcing the law has done everything it can to contort the law and to misconstrue it to allow practices that continue to devastate and I was surprised by that."[295] Despite such structural challenges, however, the efforts of attorneys like Lovett have further "spurred the formation of local grassroots organizations and sparked regional and national public interest in the harms of mountaintop removal."[296] And law and policy focused Appalachian organizations, such as the Appalachian Mountain Advocates, the Southern Environmental Law Center, and the Appalachian Citizens' Law Center indeed have broad, diverse scopes of action that variously include coal impacts, the rising natural gas industry, EJ issues, and other dire issues in the region (i.e., which can include issues beyond the environment or public health per se).

MTR-focused grassroots activism emerged as a particularly vital force in the mid-2000s. A 2004 tragedy in Virginia is often cited as a core, contributing factor for this resurgence: a boulder from an A & G Coal strip mine tragically killed a three-year-old child when it crashed into his bedroom.[297] This event "placed a human face on the cost of coal extraction and reinvigorated the movement."[298] Soon after the accident, "many in the nearby town of Appalachia decided to march in protest, and were soon joined by others across the region."[299] In seeking to build on this momentum, "Mountain Justice Summer" was held in 2005; organizers of Mountain Justice Summer were keenly aware of "earlier direct action movements," and sought to tap into this tradition: "The name 'Mountain Justice Summer' was chosen specifically to reference both Freedom Summer, the 1964 voter registration drive through southern states during the struggle for civil rights, and Redwood Summer, a series of Earth First!-sponsored protests against deforestation throughout the Pacific Northwest in 1990."[300] While Mountain Justice did not coalesce into a formal, membership-based group, participants would continue to engage in organizing, education, and college student-focused retreats in subsequent years.[301]

Also during this era, a number of groups and individuals emerged in Appalachia that engaged in civil disobedience. These included Radical Action for Mountains' and Peoples' Survival (RAMPS), United Mountain Defense (UMD), and Climate Ground Zero.[302] The general tactics involved occupy-type actions, such as lockdowns, aimed at halting mining activities and garnering media attention—and thus public and institutional sympathy—for the movement.[303] For instance, MTR-related sites were illegally occupied by disobedients, such as in West Virginia in 2009, when activists locked themselves to equipment on a Kayford Mountain site while others floated a banner on a coal slurry impoundment at another location.[304] Another example of occupy-type anti-MTR disobedience occurred in 2012 when activists locked themselves to a coal barge.[305] Ricki Draper, one of coal barge disobedients, would state: "I have broken the law because the legal system is broken. I have broken the law because MTR is destroying our health, our mountains, and our futures. I have broken the law because the destruction of our landbase, which is our endowment, is illegal."[306] Also, the "Appalachia Rising" rally occurred in Washington, D.C., in 2010, which involved more than two thousand protestors (over a hundred of whom were arrested outside of the White House for disobedience).[307]

The scope of MTR-related civil disobedient actions in Appalachia has been, in many ways, remarkable. Prior to the emergence of these dissent practices, there had been somewhat of an abeyance of radical grassroots resistance in both Appalachia and the United States at large; this is because a "green scare" occurred in the early 2000s, in which "many radical environmental activists were labeled as 'domestic terrorists,'" resulting in a decline of disobedient tactics.[308] With the rise of MTR-related civil disobedience in Appalachia, however, the campaign "represented a reemergence of environmental activism in North America."[309]

In more recent years, MTR-related disobedient practices have declined in Appalachia[310]—while natural gas–related disobedience has increased (and appears poised to expand). As the Atlantic Coast Pipeline and Mountain Valley Pipeline have progressed—and as legal-institutional efforts to halt the pipelines and other natural gas infrastructure have seen uneven success—disobedient practices have emerged along the Mountain Valley Pipeline route. Specifically, over half a dozen protestors have, to date, engaged in tree-sitting activities and other occupy-type actions, which already have received regional, national, and international media attention.[311] Women constitute many such protestors—as illustrated by Theresa "Red" Terry and her daughter, Minor, both of whom were "trespassing on their own property" by engaging in a tree-sit in Roanoke County, Virginia (as the property had been seized by eminent domain for the Mountain Valley Pipeline).[312] Red and Minor expressed concern about a lack of local benefit from the pipeline, in addition to environmental harms, such as water pollution.[313] Another woman protestor, nicknamed "Nutty," similarly engaged in a tree-sit for fifty-seven days—which constituted the "longest monopod protest sit in US history."[314] So, too, did Appalachian studies professor and protestor Emily Satterwhite engage in anti-pipeline disobedience by locking herself to construction equipment from the Mountain Valley Pipeline.[315]

The core role of Appalachian women activists in the MTR and natural gas era is one of the most notable characteristics of the movement. This phenomenon has been explored intensively in such works as Barry's *Standing Our Ground* and Bell's *Our Roots Run Deep as Ironweed*. For instance, Barry centralizes gender in her analysis of the anti-MTR movement in Appalachia. Barry finds that "women activists are a vital part of the movement—representing in large numbers and in some cases shaping the nature" of anti-MTR campaigns.[316] Environmental justice has often been a focal point, with motivations including "a desire to keep their families, community, and natural environment safe and healthy for present and future generations."[317] Concerns regarding family health and welfare are often discussed (i.e., particularly for children); so, too, do women activists recognize "links between both cultural and environmental annihilation," and thus in "their efforts to end MTR, women environmental justice activists link local culture to the natural environment, particularly its mountains."[318] Barry ultimately concludes that "gender is at the heart of the anti-MTR movement in Appalachia."[319]

Bell similarly examines the role of women EJ activists in Central Appalachia. Specifically, in *Our Roots Run Deep as Ironweed*, Bell demonstrates that working-class women occupy activist and activist-leadership roles, and that a prime motivating factor emanates from notions of motherhood—namely, women activists protecting their immediate children and grandchildren in addition to other children in the community. In defense of EJ activism, many women also express that a deep-seated "mothering instinct" drives their efforts, as compared to a more conscious political choice. Further, Bell argues that such a self-justification for "activism as a result of mothering 'instincts,' rather than a conscious decision, affords women a level of cultural protection and legitimation for their protest activities."[320] From a materialist perspective, such self-justifications are significant, as they demonstrate the extent to which activism always occurs within real-world conditions—such as those informed by gender regimes in Central Appalachia. Relatedly, Bell argues that a broader "protector identity" also appears to be part and parcel of such activist articulations, as some activists explain that the " 'the drive to protect' is something inherent in most women, especially Appalachian women."[321] Such a protector role, however, extends beyond children and grandchildren alone to encompass the broader community, the Appalachian mountains and environment, and "their heritage, their family homeplaces, and their way of life"—and thus seemingly extends beyond motherhood per se to include broader protection notions.[322]

Such an expansive "protector identity" articulated by women activists also is significant because, as Bell notes, it could "open up a wider space for Appalachian men to find a connection to the movement."[323] Appalachian men historically have been less present in EJ activism and activist-leadership roles— but such an all-encompassing protector identity, extending beyond motherhood per se, better comports with masculine values embedded in traditional Central Appalachian gender regimes. Consequently, as Bell concludes, "while the coal-related hegemonic masculinity of the Central Appalachian region may pose a barrier to local men's entry into the environmental justice movement, those men who *are* able to escape its influence may connect with identities that are closely aligned with the protector identities of local women activists."[324] This certainly is a crucial concept for *Remaking Appalachia*. As chapter 7 discusses, systemic re-formations in the region and beyond will require reconstructed gender regimes requiring change on the part of Appalachian men specifically (i.e., in addition, of course, to dovetailed transformations of broader institutions and structures fundamentally encoded with hegemonic white masculinity).

Turning to the Appalachian anti–natural gas movement, in a study on women activists, Anna Willow and Samantha Keefer conclude that motivations behind such activism are complex.[325] Overarching concerns pertaining to power, control, and justice often catalyze anti–natural gas activism, "with women working to restructure political systems and using political methods to control local realities (usually seen as masculine domains)."[326] However, the women interviewed also express EJ-related natural gas concerns, which constitutes "a classic feminist point of entry into the political field."[327] And so, too, were concerns expressed over children's health and community well-being demonstrative of many "interviewees proclaiming their own maternal role as an initial inspiration for more politically-engaged efforts that followed."[328] Thus, Willow and Keefer find that women activists who "oppose shale energy are called to action by a constellation of concerns encompassing home and away, personal and political," and that the "coexistence of established and innovative femininities indicates that women's motives for grassroots environmental engagement—and, by extension, their dynamic relationships to personal and political in other arenas—cannot be reduced to any single agenda or any simple expression or refutation of traditionally gendered expectations and identities."[329]

Important work also has examined the contemporary role of women in the Appalachian labor context. The Pittston Coal strike of 1989–1990 was one such significant event. This strike—characterized as "perhaps the last of the great industry and labor battles in the Appalachian coalfields"—was a UMWA labor action.[330] It occurred due to Pittston's decision to cut retired miners' health benefits and nonunion miners use by Pittston, among other factors.[331] During this strike, women were organized within a UMWA Family Auxiliary and "under the name Daughters of Mother Jones," which was a "nod to past women coalfield activists" (as detailed in chapter 1).[332] Numerous commentators have unpacked the complex forces at work in the Pittston strike, including how gender differences impacted strike conditions and how gender also intersected multidimensionally with class.[333] As an important example, women recalled forming an outward barrier in order to minimize police violence against the men—i.e., as police were less likely to harm women given the gender regime (although women eventually were arrested).[334]

Women additionally engaged in a nonviolent all-women sit-in of the Pittston headquarters.[335] During the headquarters occupation, the women only identified themselves as "Daughters of Mother Jones" when questioned by Pittston officials.[336] As Karen Beckwith explains, through this action, the "activist women embraced an identity as women, collectively claiming themselves to be daughters of the most famous and revered woman in UMWA history . . . and suggesting thereby a sisterhood of daughters, bound together in struggle."[337] At the same time, Beckwith notes that "activist women were not positioned to imbue their actions with complete political meaning or to offer the sole definitive interpretation of the event."[338] Many women viewed the sit-in as a core, direct contribution to the strike. However, UMWA field staff, for instance, reinterpreted the act as more "limited and exemplary," and activists alleged that such actors reinterpreted the sit-in as an opportunity to encourage men to engage in more radical activities.[339] UMWA leadership, then, "used assumptions about women's nature and gender roles to their advantage,"[340] and more broadly, undermined the emergence of an "autonomous female collective identity" among women—in service of presenting a "unified, homogeneous community in solidarity" along working-class lines, as generally steeped in broad conceptions of family and community.[341]

More recently, the wave of teachers' strikes sweeping through many U.S. states had its genesis in the historic 2018 West Virginia teachers' strike.[342] West Virginian women occupied a key role in this movement, and it has been widely recognized that the "strike is part of a larger trend of women's activism in West Virginia."[343] And so, too, did women occupy a central role in the follow-up 2019 West Virginia teacher's strike.[344] As previously discussed, large capital interests and complicit governmental elites have long successfully degraded labor forces in Appalachia and beyond as part and parcel of broader efforts to roll back progressive liberal welfare era gains (i.e., and to thus reconcentrate wealth and power). However, a revitalized and deeply radicalized Appalachian labor movement—and one which explicitly dovetails with the regional environmental movement (and is otherwise based on intersectional and broader multi-coalitional precepts)—constitutes a vital path forward for Appalachia, as is discussed in chapter 7 vis-à-vis modes of bottom-up, ecofeminist- and ecosocialist-steeped systemic re-formations.

As this chapter has demonstrated, environmental law, as embedded in the hegemonic liberal paradigm, has failed to protect the Appalachian region. Despite the enactment of SMCRA, the CWA, and NEPA—and the broader environmental law regime—ecological and related social and economic devastation persists in the region. This was illustrated by the disastrous rise of MTR in the 1990s followed by, more recently, the Marcellus shale gas boom and a reinvigorated chemical sector; to be sure, the environmental law regime has failed to halt (or indeed to meaningfully mitigate) the negative impacts wrought by these industries. What is more, while Appalachia indeed constitutes an energy sacrifice zone, Appalachia's issues are merely part and parcel of the collective global ecological crises of the Capitalocene: namely, climate change, other pollution-based issues, and the overuse of renewable resources. Thus, the environmental crisis extends well beyond subordinated regions such as Appalachia, and is global in scale. This chapter has, however, chronicled a continued positive phenomenon in the prior half century: the continued potency—and broadening scope—of Appalachian grassroots activism, which can indeed be leveraged and dramatically expanded in pursuing truly radical social and economic change beyond liberal capitalism.

CHAPTER 6

SYSTEMIC ECONOMIC AND SOCIO-LEGAL CHANGE: THEORY, PRACTICE, AND PRAXIS

Remaking Appalachia will now pivot towards potential modes of critical reconstructions for the Appalachian region and beyond. This exploration of new economic and socio-legal futures in Appalachia is steeped in a critical legal theory–informed approach that ultimately looks beyond environmental "law reform" towards truly transformative "systemic re-formations." The core notion is that merely reforming the environmental law regime is a futile approach. Instead, we must collectively explore wholly novel frameworks beyond the liberal capitalist paradigm. This chapter outlines pertinent theory and praxis regarding such systemic re-formations; chapter 7 thereafter explores applications of this theory in Appalachia.

This chapter deeply relies on the theoretical school of ecofeminism as entwined with ecosocialism to inform such explorations. Prominent strains of ecofeminism explicitly challenge the modern late liberalism paradigm (i.e., globalized neoliberalism) and its continued fixation on ceaseless capital accumulation and perpetual economic growth. Such strains of ecofeminism, in the alternative, advocate for degrowth-steeped formations that are based on strongly ecologically sustainable systems, such as solidarity economy– and subsistence-based modes, that are focused on production for use value rather than exchange value in the market. This approach also demands interlinking such local- and regional-centered re-formations with broader national and global efforts (i.e., as involves an ecosocialist-steeped approach). What is more, ecofeminism has traditionally constituted a supremely intersectional-steeped school, in positing that the same hegemonic liberal capitalist forces driving ecological destruction are ultimately responsible for structural subordination along lines of gender, race, class, indigenous status, the Global South-North divide, etc., while recognizing the fact that such forces are not wholly identical and are uniquely operationalized in different regions, localities, etc.

Chapter 6 then puts forth systemic stepping stone measures that, through considered design, could help effectuate, expedite, and deeply inform the transformative pivot beyond the current liberal paradigm. The furtherance of environmental human rights and the public trust doctrines in Appalachia and beyond—as informed by contemporary critical legal theory (and therefore as radically conceived)—will constitute the most notable Appalachian systemic stepping stone measures explored. Such doctrines, as pursued through the mechanisms of community lawyering and radical cause lawyering, are particularly useful as stepping stones towards transformative change as they can greatly facilitate and indeed catalyze mass political mobilization while also exhibiting a truly radical critique of patriarchal capitalism.

BEYOND LAW REFORM—SYSTEMIC RE-FORMATIONS

As the preceding chapters demonstrate, the liberal regime has failed Appalachia because of its critical, cascading flaws. We must therefore, as an overarching collective project, look beyond "classic" liberal law reform towards true systemic re-formations of the hegemonic liberal regime at large. Chapter 2 introduces critical work constituting the deep foundations for such a systemic re-formation approach. Recall that, ultimately, this approach is grounded in the initial Marxian analysis of law, wherein the "economic base" generally produces particular political and legal formations, or the "superstructure," in support of that base. Recall, though, that as commentators such as Krever note, the most useful interpretation of Marx does not involve a "crude determinism" of the economic base mechanistically producing the political and legal superstructure, in the case of capitalism or otherwise.[1]

Modern critical legal theory approaches to law and social change draw both explicitly and implicitly on the Marxian analysis—while expanding on such foundational theory through multiple, significant dimensions. M'Gonigle and Takeda articulate one such critical-steeped framework in "The Liberal Limits of Environmental Law"—i.e., discussing this critical approach in the context of environmental and energy law and policy specifically—which will inform much of *Remaking Appalachia*'s core analysis. As they argue, due to the "limitations of environmental law's capacity for prospective action, a corollary need exists to open a new, critical, and theoretically-informed landscape beyond intra-systemic 'reform' and toward larger 're-forms.' "[2] This involves eschewing traditional environmental law practice in favor of robust praxis—which is "a practice that is theoretically-informed and committed to manifesting where that theory leads."[3] Thus, beyond liberal law reform, this praxis focuses on truly foundational "constitutive re-formations" that "address the underlying logics of dominating systems" and "underlying system dynamics."[4] These are the "constitutive social systems and dynamics that exist as law even though they exist above or behind the 'legal law' as it has been narrowly conceived."[5] Ultimately, this involves a "shift in 'legal' understanding" that entails "the embrace of a new set of knowledges, discourses, processes, alliances, and strategies."[6]

Critical legal theorists have been exploring a broader, more open-ended conception of law for decades. Duncan Kennedy, for instance, "contends that the pervasive distributional effects of law are not just felt in economic relations, but in all relations of power."[7] Therefore, one core "critique offered by the realists and further developed by critical legal theorists is that virtually all human action, from going to bed to going to work, is either implicitly or explicitly defined and structured by law."[8] Under such conditions, this broader conceptualization and operationalization of "law" in fact "operates all the more effectively for appearing not to be law."[9] Per this critical approach, then, "the power exerted by a legal regime consists less in the force that it can bring to bear against violators of its rules than in its capacity to persuade people that the world described in its images and categories is the only attainable world in which a sane person would want to live."[10]

Critical environmental law commentators, however, have added crucial new contours to a critically informed theory of law. Commentators such as M'Gonigle and Takeda, in examining how non-state actors essentially create "law," have taken "this expansion further by looking at the effectively legal (i.e., socially structuring) impacts inherent in the dynamics of meta-systems such as capitalism and the sovereign state."[11] Under this expanded framework, legal laws are "not the true (or at least not the most important) sources of social regulation," as "they are themselves products of 'higher' level systems, the needs and dynamics of which provide the truly authoritative momentum and direction of social evolution."[12] Thus, achieving transformative systemic re-formations requires "a diverse set of new understandings about, and approaches to, the dynamics of constitutive material and cultural forces—from the internal needs of capital, to the spatial compulsions of the state, to the hegemonic effects of dominant discourses."[13] In short, the true "need is, in several ways, for a new theoretically-based critique and theoretically-informed understanding of 'law' itself."[14]

BOTTOM-UP, GRASSROOTS APPROACH TO DEGROWTH

Remaking Appalachia draws on this general line of critique—as informed by ecofeminism and ecosocialism specifically. More specifically, *Remaking Appalachia* advocates for transformations of the ecological political economy that entail democratically coordinated degrowth-centered transitions that ultimately focus on production for use value rather than exchange value in the market. *Remaking Appalachia* further argues that such degrowth-centered transformations must be conceived of and furthered beyond the hegemonic liberalism paradigm. As M'Gonigle and Takeda point out, many commentators who "challenge the economics of growth often still do so within the bounds of capitalism," and indeed even explicit degrowth proponents often make such arguments within careful parameters, thus failing to recognize "the impossibility of implementing degrowth under the current configuration of power."[15] Likewise, Diego Andreucci and Terrence McDonough argue that "most degrowth advocates would concede that there is a fundamental incompatibility between capitalism and degrowth," as "capitalism is compelled to grow," but many commentators feel compelled to veil the full implications of this line of critique.[16] However, due to the fundamental incompatibility of capitalism and degrowth, if degrowth measures were attempted, for instance, vis-à-vis top-down policy implementation from within the liberal capitalist paradigm, the potential for economic and social breakdown is exceedingly great. As Smith argues, "under capitalism," society "can't stop consuming more and more because if we stop racing, the system collapses into crisis."[17] Smith adds that "it's time to abandon the fantasy of a steady-state capitalism, go back to the drawing boards and come up with . . . a practical, workable post-capitalist ecological economy—an economy by the people, for the people, that is geared to production for need, not for profit."[18]

As a consequence, *Remaking Appalachia* argues that any genuinely successful degrowth efforts must be conceived of beyond the hegemonic liberalism paradigm—and that a bottom-up, grassroots approach to such transformations is imperative. Generally speaking, numerous commentators have argued that degrowth must be "driven from the grassroots."[19] For instance, Samuel Alexander has examined the "role social movements may have to play" in catalyzing the forces "needed for a degrowth or steady-state economy to materialise," and broadly concludes that such grassroots mobilization efforts are "necessary *preconditions* for such structural change."[20] This is because the general citizenry—long conditioned to hegemonic liberalism—would need to know, in the first place, why degrowth tenets are both desirable and necessary, and just what such transformations potentially would entail. As Alexander thus notes, "it seems highly unlikely that a degrowth or steady-state economy would arise voluntarily unless people had some idea of what needed to be done at the personal and community levels to bring about such an economy."[21] This similarly holds true in the explicit post-capitalist degrowth approach. Relatedly, per a materialist approach (i.e., as unpacked more fully below), such grassroots transformations ought not to be wholly homogenized, but should rather be tailored to best meet the needs of specific localities, sub-regions, regions, etc.

A grassroots approach to post-capitalist degrowth transformations catalyzed through widespread mass political mobilization also substantially redresses the core economic breakdown concerns addressed above. As compared to a top-down degrowth approach attempted within the liberal capitalist system, instead, the citizenry would collectively construct, from the bottom up, explicitly post-capitalist systems removed from growth dictates as democratically coordinated nationally and globally. And indeed, as is discussed in the remainder of this chapter, ecofeminism as entwined with ecosocialism has been recognized as a particularly apt school through which to explore such bottom-up radical transformations. As Devon Peña writes, "according to ecofeminists, the development of steady-state economies is possible only with a complete conversion of human production systems" away from "mass production and consumption norms and objectives"—and towards local- and regional-steeped systems.[22]

Nevertheless, commentators have noted that *any* variety of truly widespread degrowth-centered transformations—as democratically coordinated nationally and globally—are, of course, wholly novel as concrete concepts and are thus highly speculative at this point in time. Questions as to stability both during and after such radical transformations of the ecological political economy therefore persist. What is certain, however, is that late liberalism's accelerating and intertwined economic, social, and ecological crises are propelling the world towards utter collapse. Consequently, exploring radical alternative visions to hegemonic liberalism—such as the bottom-up, ecofeminist- and ecosocialist-steeped systemic re-formations discussed below—are of the utmost importance in the age of the Capitalocene.

ECOFEMINIST-MODELED SYSTEMIC RE-FORMATIONS

As is discussed in chapter 7, systemic re-formations of the ecological political economy are required in Appalachia and beyond. However, in exploring the substance of potential modes of systemic re-formations, ecofeminism constitutes an exceedingly useful school. Since the 1980s, ecofeminism has gone through numerous permutations, and indeed has divided into numerous sub-schools (including what might be deemed post- or "new ecofeminist" discourses altogether). However, prominent strains of contemporary, materialist, and non-essentialist ecofeminism advocate for radical economic and socio-legal change that transcends the global neoliberal paradigm. And in recent years, ecofeminism has been deeply revitalized as the global ecological crisis has intensified.

As Mary Phillips and Nick Rumens discuss in *Contemporary Perspectives on Ecofeminism*, ecofeminism, as such, can be traced to feminist-related social movements of the 1980s, where feminist activists engaged in such contestations as environmental and peace protests and broadly sought to embed ecological concerns into a more inclusive feminism.[23] At the same time, feminists also developed a strong critique of issues pertaining to the environmental movement's lack of concern on gender.[24] By the late 1980s and early 1990s, a more explicit ecofeminist theory emerged—with activist-theoreticians often at the forefront—that increasingly evolved into a robust praxis. It has been recognized that ecofeminism "has always been an activist and an academic movement."[25]

To be sure, ecofeminism lacks a universal definition, as there has always existed much diversity in the discourse. In an overarching sense, however, ecofeminism can be said to have several broad characteristics. As Phillips and Rumens note, in the first place, ecofeminism holds that there is a fundamental interconnectedness—or interlocking nature—of systems of subordination under liberal capitalism. That is, there exists a core interconnectedness of subordination along lines of gender, race and ethnic minority status, indigenous status, ability, LGBTQ+ status, age, and so forth—and also along lines of environmental subordination.[26] And while such phenomena are endemic to the Global North, so, too, is the Global South uniquely and complexly beset by related issues and by additional structural dimensions pertaining to Global North-based exploitation (i.e., often discussed in the context of neocolonialism or neo-imperialism). Ecofeminism holds that such interlocking systems of subordination emanate from a complex logic of domination characteristic of patriarchal capitalist forces.[27] The logic undergirding liberal capitalism is marked, most notably, by normative dualisms such as men vs. women, society vs. nature, white vs. non-white, and reason vs. emotion. Unfortunately, under liberalism, the second component of such dualisms (women, nature, non-white) are disfavored and have thus long been "othered" in order to facilitate, most fundamentally, maximum capital accumulation among elite interests (as discussed in more depth below).[28]

In terms of prescriptive recommendations, Phillips and Rumens note that ecofeminists generally advocate for transformative shifts towards a more just (along lines of gender, race, class, etc.) and sustainable future, often based on notions of care and interconnectivity. Under the ecofeminist view, human societies, then, do not position themselves above or beyond nature—but rather as one constituent part within broader ecological systems. Notably, however, the ecofeminist view does not marginalize the role of human communities within nature, and in fact "holds that a focus on the larger social, political, and historical contexts in which nature *and* humanity are situated is essential to address the full range of issues at stake in meeting real environmental challenges." [29]

As a consequence of these core insights, ecofeminism generally advocates for a holistic approach. In working towards positive modes of change, ecofeminism deploys a multi-layered, intersectional-steeped analysis that accounts for both environmental destruction and interconnected forms of economic, social, and political subordination. Through this approach, ecofeminism focuses on the paramount importance of compound forms of oppression and further holds that individual subordination dimensions (e.g., gender-based subordination) cannot be addressed piecemeal: "to take the 'eco' or the 'feminism' out of ecofeminism would, after all, negate the whole idea." [30] Ecofeminism, then, through a holistic approach, "simultaneously us[es] the common goals of saving nature and ending oppression" to pursue transformative change. [31]

Ecofeminism, however, is indeed a diverse theoretical school—and has in fact been vigorously (and at times, contentiously) debated within feminist, critical, and ecological discourses. In particular, commentators allege that certain strains of early wave ecofeminism are problematic due to their essentializing nature; that is, third wave, poststructuralist-steeped critiques characterized ecofeminism as equating women with nature, conflating gender and sex, and homogenizing women in a general sense. [32] One such prominent—and useful—critique of ecofeminism emanates from Bina Agarwal, who, as Greta Gaard notes, has proffered an influential criticism of the essentialism inherent in homogenizing "woman" as a singular category. [33] Agarwal writes that the widespread degradation of the environment creates niche, localized concerns that further have "specific class-gender" dimensions. [34] Agarwal therefore argues that women "cannot be posited . . . as a unitary category, even within a country, let alone across the Third World or globally." [35] Instead, in a materialist account, Agarwal suggests that any analysis must ultimately be based on actual social and environmental realities; this material approach is in stark contrast to examining the subordination of the environment and women through the lens of universal theorizing alone. In emphasizing these elements, Agarwal adopted the term "feminist environmentalism." [36] As Gaard argues, "Agarwal's distinctions remain critical for an effective ecofeminism and feminist environmentalism alike." [37]

Subsequent refinements and diversified approaches to ecofeminism—in addition to external critiques—continued in later decades. In the context of external critiques, many commentators incorrectly characterized the whole of ecofeminism as essentialist in nature. However, Gaard notes that such broad critiques discredited "ecofeminism's diversity of arguments and standpoints," many of which, from the very outset of the movement, eschewed essentialism. [38] For instance, in addition to Agarwal's work, materialist accounts of ecofeminism were put forth—in both the 1980s and 1990s—by such scholars as Carolyn Merchant, Ariel Salleh, Ynestra King, Karen Warren, and Val Plumwood; such accounts "described a socially constructed association among women (sex), femininity (gender), and nature that was contextual and fluid, not ahistorical and static." [39] Such works made important contributions in, for instance, cautioning against women's workshares increasing (e.g., in unpaid labor)—without securing equal participation by men, [40] and by cautioning, from a materialist perspective, that issues of class, race, etc. specific to particular locations can result in "some elite women [being] oppressors of other women and the natural world alike." [41] Therefore, many ecological feminist works, like *Ecofeminism as Politics* by Salleh, "all use a materialist feminist approach to explore the oppression of women and nature—thereby taking postmodern and poststructuralist thought seriously." [42]

Eventually, such diverse approaches to ecofeminism would result in further divisions within the discourse. There would emerge theoretical schools that similarly explored the intersection of feminism and environmental issues, such as those deemed "ecological feminism," put forth by Warren; "feminist environmentalism," put forth by Agarwal; and "critical feminist eco-socialism," put forth by Plumwood. [43] Therefore, towards the end of the 1990s, "the term 'ecofeminism' had already developed a following, with the terms 'ecological feminism' and 'feminist environmentalism' seeming more like intra-disciplinary distinctions, rather than entirely different approaches." [44] Ecofeminism, then, in its various manifestations and sub-schools, both explicit and implicit, persists as a vital discourse today. [45]

ECOFEMINISM: RADICAL SOLIDARITY ECONOMY AND SUBSISTENCE MODES

Ecofeminism and related ecological feminist schools have adopted niche and vital approaches to the ecological political economy that are of paramount importance to modes of systemic re-formations in Appalachia and beyond.

As noted above, ecofeminism constitutes a leading school advocating for radical transformations beyond hegemonic liberalism. Thus, ecofeminist-related work has examined paradigms that challenge neoliberal global capitalism's ceaseless capital accumulation and perpetual growth paradigm in its entirety. Also as broached above, *Remaking Appalachia* argues for a bottom-up, grassroots approach to pursuing such degrowth-centered transformations, and ecofeminist-steeped solidarity economy– and subsistence-based modes constitute core dimensions of such transformative change.

As a starting point, as Christine Bauhardt notes, "ecofeminist economics can contribute to a more comprehensive understanding of the growth economy, and encourage the development of fresh perspectives on alternatives to capitalist growth."[46] In particular, there exists important synergies between an ecofeminist economics focus on nonmarket work (as traditionally performed by women via the gendered division of labor)—and on broad, degrowth perspectives that challenge hegemonic liberalism. Mary Mellor adds more to this account from an explicit political economy standpoint; as Mellor argues, the ecofeminist political economy identifies a direct link between unpaid work largely performed by women and global environmental exploitation—as the formal economy unjustly is dependent on both "as a 'free,' exploitable resource."[47] Consequently, a materialist ecofeminist perspective examines the real-world practices of what constitutes women's "work" in differing varieties and places—and of how such labor-based exploitation intersects with ecological concerns. Thus, from the broad perspective of ecofeminist economics, "women and the environment are both marginalized in their positions within the formal economy."[48] And so, too is materialist- and intersectionalist-steeped ecofeminism concerned, of course, with how class, race, indigenous status, neocolonialism, speciesism, and other forms of subordination function exploitatively under liberal capitalism.[49]

There are, however, a multiplicity of intersecting (and sometimes, conflicting) feminist economics accounts; that is, all ecofeminist economic approaches do not result in the same prescriptive recommendations. This chapter therefore focuses on—and adopts, as potentially useful for Appalachia and beyond—only particular strains of this broad theoretical discourse. One such strain includes radical approaches to the solidarity economy. Solidarity economy development has arisen most prominently in "parts of western Europe, Latin America, and Africa," and is often classified as constituting a range of alternative, bottom-up modes.[50] *Remaking Appalachia*, however, focuses on the more radical articulations of the solidarity economy—i.e., as explicitly being part and parcel of the broader, multidimensional project of transcending liberal capitalism. Such a radical solidarity economy approach involves a bottom-up mode that "rejects most traditional economic patterns and postulates a 'systemic change' " beyond ceaseless capital accumulation and perpetual growth.[51] Such a radical approach to the solidarity economy is thus at the "core of a post-capitalist politics." [52]

While not necessarily wholly removed from markets, the central structural characteristics of radical solidarity economies involve maximizing the utility of the productive activities for the specific peoples at issue. Consequently, strong local- and regional-based autonomy and egalitarian self-provisioning are crucial, as often steeped in community-based, co-owned production and consumption systems. Radically conceived solidarity economies thus demand a highly "democratic and emancipatory reorganization of the economy," which, by necessity, requires community-wide decision-making regarding property governance.[53] Important for *Remaking Appalachia*, the solidarity economy also "attaches vital importance to debates surrounding commons, including their use and management beyond the state and private property regulations." [54] Such a community-based approach also is a core principle of global-wide development, as niche, local-based approaches are most like to satisfy needs of diverse communities—as compared to top-down approaches involving homogenized liberal development aid.[55]

As Bauhardt notes, the "subsistence approach which has been developed within ecofeminism is a feminist economic current that most strongly accommodates" the radical solidarity economy perspective.[56] Vandana Shiva and Maria Mies put forth one of the most influential articulations of the ecofeminist-based subsistence perspective in *Ecofeminism*. As Mies and Shiva argue, the conditions under which ecofeminist "praxis and theory are respected and preserved can be found only in the survival struggles of grassroots movements" that "radically reject the industrialized countries' prevailing model of capitalist-patriarchal development," and their analysis focuses strongly on such modes within the Global South.[57] Mies and Shiva also, however, explore such subsistence modes in the Global North; as they note, in the North, the "search for an ecologically sound, non-exploitative, just, non-patriarchal, self-sustaining society" ultimately involves not only better-off citizens "disenchanted and despairing about the end-result of the modernization process," but also those citizens who are worst-off in society.[58] The through-line in such investigations is the "need for a qualitative, not simply a quantitative change in what we are accustomed to call the economy." [59]

Mies and Shiva also outline a series of more specific characteristics of their work, as summarized in the Mies-authored chapter "The Need for a New

Vision: The Subsistence Perspective." First, the purpose of economic activity is not to pursue endless capital accumulation through commodity production. The aim is to, instead, accomplish "satisfaction of fundamental needs mainly by the production of use-values and not by the purchase of commodities," with a particular emphasis on "food and other basic needs"; thus, per this economic view, market considerations obviously occupy a subordinate role.[60] Relatedly, decentralization is a focal point, which involves less state oversight and more local- and regional-based autonomy.[61] Also, all economic activities must be steeped in the notion that human communities are interlinked with the broader environment—and must correspondingly have a central aim of reversing global capitalism's extensive ecological harms.[62]

At the same time, as liberal capitalism's domination of the environment is fundamentally interlinked with the subordination of marginalized groups (such as through the gender regime), Mies and Shiva argue that a paradigm of strong environmental sustainability must work in tandem with new and just relationships established between women and men. This involves, among other things, reconstructed notions of gender and the gendered division of labor, in which "men must start a movement to redefine their identity," which will involve "eliminating their involvement in destructive commodity production for the sake of accumulation and begin to share women's work for the preservation of life."[63] Men must therefore "share unpaid subsistence work: in the household, with children, with the old and sick," and men must also share equally in ecological remediation work.[64] Ultimately, then, this "subsistence perspective can be realized only within such a network of reliable, stable human relations, it cannot be based on the atomized, self-centered individuality of the market economy."[65]

Participatory democracy is also a focal point of their framework; that is, the ecofeminist subsistence perspective is steeped in grassroots-centered democracy, both in the context of political decision-making per se but also in regard to broader social, economic, and environmental issues.[66] Mies and Shiva's ecofeminist-steeped subsistence model also does not constitute an anti-science or anti-technology perspective. Rather, it demands a new paradigm in which ecologically sustainable uses of technology are explored and adopted through ecofeminism's preferred channels of communal decision-making.[67] And lastly, their subsistence perspective focuses on commons expansions "and demands their preservation and regeneration."[68]

ECOSOCIALISM AND ECOFEMINISM: FUNDAMENTALLY INTERTWINED

Significant for *Remaking Appalachia*, ecofeminist-steeped discussions on solidarity economy, subsistence, and related modes often are discussed as dovetailing directly with ecosocialist approaches. Ecosocialism arose in the 1980s and 1990s and fundamentally involves a synthesis of neo-Marxian and radical ecological thought.[69] Although, like ecofeminism, ecosocialism constitutes a diverse and varied school, at its core ecosocialism posits that capitalism is unjust and unsustainable; consequently, under ecosocialism, revolutionary rather than reform strategies are required, as typically involving discussions on degrowth precepts, strong ecological sustainability, meeting basic needs only (or again, the "predominance of use value over exchange value"), democratic control, and a corresponding emancipatory transformation of the ecological political economy.[70] John Bellamy Foster, for instance, explores "the creation of a society of associated producers rationally regulating their metabolic relation to nature, and doing so not only in accordance with their own needs but also those of future generations and life as a whole," and concludes that the "transition to socialism and transition to an ecological society are one."[71]

Importantly, the ecosocialist influence on such re-formations also requires broader collective ownership modes and multi-scale democratic economic planning at not just local and regional levels—but also at national and global scales (i.e., which, as discussed at the end of chapter 7, a fully radicalized Green New Deal could help effectuate).[72] Of course, widespread, bottom-up mass mobilization also is a prerequisite for such broader ecosocialist-steeped re-formations. And such planning modes could indeed dovetail with the bottom-up, essentially decentralized recommendations thus far explored in *Remaking Appalachia*. As Michael Löwy notes in *Ecosocialism*, much debate has occurred on the " 'centralized' or 'decentralized' character of planning, but it could be argued that the real issue is democratic control of the plan at all levels"—with a prime example including the fact that, on broader national and global planning, "ecological issues such as global warming are planetary and can be dealt with only a global scale."[73] Löwy adds that "even at this level, it would be quite opposite of what is usually described as 'central planning,' since the economic and social decisions are not made by any 'center' but democratically decided by the populations concerned."[74]

Kali Akuno also has discussed how bottom-up transformations involving radical solidarity economies can dovetail with ecosocialist-steeped democratic planning modes.[75] And ecosocialist commentators likewise have explored how multi-level democratic planning can dovetail with radical recommoning approaches specifically (i.e., of the sort explored in chapter 7 in the Appalachian context vis-à-vis a radically re-envisioned public trust doctrine). As Tero Toivanen argues in "Commons against Capitalism," we can explore "eco-socialist transformation through commons," and indeed "the research of successfully organized commons indicates that planning and collective democratic participation are integral parts of sustainable commons-based economies."[76] As a consequence, "combining the best aspects of eco-socialism with the powerful practice of commoning and the commons, might let us enter a world where the use of natural resources is commonified rather than commodified," but such "commons need to be collectively protected, planned and regulated."[77] Toivanen adds that there is "no need to too sharply distinguish theoretically between commons and public," as this might "distort the perception of the transformative potential of the public and welfare state," and that instead, the "public and the commons are seen as two complementary sites of active political struggle."[78] Ultimately, then, such an ecosocialist approach involves "inverting the neoliberal usage of the state for enhancing the process of commodification into enhancing the practices of 'commonification' instead."[79]

Numerous commentators have noted that core strains of ecosocialism intersect with crucial ecofeminist thought. Ariel Salleh and Martin O'Connor have noted generally that "the eco-feminist project parallels that of eco-socialism."[80] And as Leigh Brownhill and Terisa Turner discuss in "Ecofeminism at the Heart of Ecosocialism," many "social movements seek to actively *replace* capitalism with an alternative political economy," and "this alternative, being creatively pursued by alliances among the exploited (with women at the fore), can be characterized as a global, horizontal, subsistence-oriented, decolonized commoning political economy, or what we call 'ecofeminist ecosocialism.'"[81] Brownhill also has argued that Shiva's approach to ecofeminism is inseparable from ecosocialism, as Shiva's approach outlined in *Earth Democracy* "expresses ecosocialists' commitments to overcome exploitation and re-invent the commons," and that "not only are ecosocialism and Earth Democracy consistent, they are, to me, one and the same struggle."[82] In "The Ecofeminist Ground of Ecosocialism," Joel Kovel similarly argues that one "foundational line of ecosocialism is its gendered ground in human existence and is comprised under the name of ecofeminism," and the most "vital eco-political movements arise spontaneously as collectives of women, often in the South and often working and living under conditions of subsistence. Now we can declare these ventures as prefiguring and announcing a new society."[83]

Salleh cautions, however, that despite such apparent intersections, ecosocialist theorists often fail to incorporate ecofeminist insights and praxis—but that such a synthesis through materialist-steeped theory and praxis is required. More specifically, Salleh argues that while the "subsistence or eco-sufficiency model of economics does not exacerbate" the global ecological crisis as it "proceeds by internalizing responsibility for resource use," nevertheless, many ecosocialists "do not yet acknowledge the unique contribution of women's labours across diverse cultures internationally, nor the radical significance of the ecofeminist-literature which highlights it."[84] Salleh thus concludes that "as housewives, peasants, or indigenes, women are well qualified to design ecosocialist theory and well qualified for practical leadership in the alter-globalisation movement," and that they indeed "know best how to achieve social justice and cultural autonomy with ecological sustainability."[85] Thus, while ecosocialist thought often fails to best incorporate ecofeminism, the two schools are fundamentally inseparable—and, as such, constitute an intertwined undergirding for *Remaking Appalachia*.

SYSTEMIC STEPPING STONE MEASURES

While ecofeminist- and ecosocialist-steeped systemic re-formations are no doubt required in the Capitalocene, such re-formations will likely require a longer-term timeframe (due to, among other factors, a current mass of political will). However, a central argument of *Remaking Appalachia* is that critically informed expansions of niche doctrines can help effectuate, expedite, and deeply inform such re-formations. Because this critical approach constitutes a potential bridge towards systemic re-formations, this niche approach will be termed "systemic stepping stone measures." Therefore, as is discussed in more detail below, *Remaking Appalachia* proposes that a novel reliance on such systemic stepping stone measures can help catalyze (and otherwise deeply support) true transformative change. Critically informed approaches to environmental human rights and the public trust doctrine, as furthered through such mechanisms as radical cause lawyering and allied organizing, are the two systemic stepping stone measures detailed below.

The notion of pursuing intra-systemic legal change, in and of itself, is generally anathema to contemporary critical thought. This is because under hegemonic liberalism, such law reform that is permitted only serves—through such mechanisms as perverse implementation—to ultimately *reinforce* the current neoliberal paradigm.[86] Generally speaking, this critical perspective constitutes an invaluable guiding principle: as the last five decades have demonstrated, environmental law has proven a colossal failure, and so we should be skeptical of any additional "classic" law reform projects. Thus, if pursued negligently, such efforts would very likely produce more negative than positive effects—as has been the long tradition of environmental law reform in the United States and globally.

However, *Remaking Appalachia* posits that relying on radically conceived systemic stepping stone measures is a worthwhile exploratory approach for numerous reasons. To begin with, in the short-term, we seemingly lack the critical mass of political will required to achieve a complete paradigm shift towards a strongly ecologically sustainable (and critically just) future beyond hegemonic liberal capitalism (although, as discussed in chapter 7, rising public alarm over climate change has shifted the public debate towards more radical currents). Therefore, while *Remaking Appalachia* advocates for systemic re-formations, a core issue is the apparently longer-term timeframe required for such re-formations. Also—and of crucial importance—such systemic stepping stone measures could be explicitly designed as such vis-à-vis an infusion of critical legal theory. As the critical analysis outlined above demonstrates, explicit "legal laws" are not the sources of true social regulation, as they are simply the products of "higher-level" economic, social, cultural, and political systems. In recognizing this reality, the systemic stepping stone measures discussed must be critically conceived: that is, they must not be discrete ends in themselves (which implicitly "accept" the current boundaries of the liberal paradigm). Instead, they should have an explicit aim of transcending the existing liberal paradigm—and what is more, they must constitute merely one component in the broader, multidimensional project to transform those higher-level forces operating above or behind the law.

Therefore, as will be discussed, if an ultimate end aim is to pursue transformations towards ecofeminist- and ecosocialist-inspired re-formations in Appalachia and beyond, such systemic stepping stone measures must, through a critically informed approach, be both specifically designed to help achieve those systemic re-formations, and, by necessity, be only one component in the broader struggle for such ecofeminist- and ecosocialist-steeped re-formations. In short, intra-systemic reform as an end in itself is certainly insufficient; however, systemic stepping stone measures explicitly designed as a bridge towards transformative ends—as embedded in broader, collective re-formation efforts—will likely constitute an effective mechanism to help achieve and support that ecofeminist- and ecosocialist-inspired future.

Environmental human rights and the public trust doctrine are selected as the systemic stepping stone measures for *Remaking Appalachia*. These two doctrines, in particular, have been characterized as constituting important outliers to hyper-technical environmental law that are well-suited for reconceptualizations in a general sense.[87] Wood, for instance, has concluded that environmental law has failed and advocates for a radically expanded conception of the public trust doctrine as an alternative environmental paradigm. And David Boyd has put forth a vigorous environmental rights paradigm as a vital path forward.[88] In response to the "system-wide dysfunction" of modern hyper-technical environmental law, then, expansions of the public trust doctrine and environmental human rights are currently among the most notable and far-reaching alternatives yet formulated, and as is discussed below (and as is explored in chapter 7 particularly), each doctrine also can synergistically enhance the other through an intertwined approach.[89]

Additionally, as compared to hyper-technical environmental law, the basic precepts of these outlier doctrines are relatively straightforward, which therefore can facilitate their use in mass mobilizing the broad citizenry vis-à-vis a critically informed, bottom-up approach. (This is in contrast to the failures of, for instance, APA-related "notice and comment" procedures discussed in chapter 4 that rarely engender widespread public participation in the hyper-technical environmental regulatory rulemaking process.) Moreover, that these outlier doctrines also are already globally prominent among many scholars, practitioners, and grassroots activists can further facilitate both their radicalization and their use in mass political mobilization (and indeed, leveraging such a preexisting knowledge base is a core dimension of the radical reframing process of "collective action frames" discussed in more detail below).

Remaking Appalachia, then, ultimately argues that the public trust doctrine and environmental human rights paradigms should be radically re-envisioned as systemic stepping stone measures, rather than as ends in themselves that fail to challenge the higher-level systems of the existing hegemonic liberal capitalist paradigm. This necessitates a critically informed approach to these doctrines that, first, explicitly embeds transformative change of higher-level systems as the ultimate "end aim" of their establishment and furtherance. In support of this first aim, second, a critically informed approach to the public trust doctrine and environmental human rights paradigms incorporates such elements as the following: a bottom-up, grassroots-based approach, which has been explored most fruitfully through the "community lawyering" and "radical cause lawyering" discourses that aim to help drive mass political mobilization towards transformative change (and not issue-specific law reform); built-in distinctions that account for niche issues based on locality or sub-region (as imperative via materialist thought); an intersectional approach (along lines of race, gender, sexuality, class, the environment, indigenous communities, etc.); and an emphasis on linking local and regional efforts with broader national and international re-formation struggles. In this way, such systemic stepping stone measures would be imbued with many of the core characteristics of radical ecological paradigms—namely, of contemporary ecofeminism and ecosocialism. This solidifies the role of these measures as explicit systemic stepping stones towards transformative reform that are merely one component in broader systemic re-formations of higher-level systems.

ENVIRONMENTAL HUMAN RIGHTS

As a first systemic stepping stone measure, environmental human rights constitute a potentially transformative paradigm. Environmental human rights are relatively new manifestations within the broad human rights landscape. The first "generation" of human rights, as they are often classified, "refer to traditional civil and political liberties of the western liberal democracies," including freedom of religion, speech, and so forth, and such rights "presuppose a duty of non-interference on the part of governments towards the individuals."[90] Second generation rights, often referred to as "collective rights," focus on society at large through their emphasis on "affirmative government action for their realization."[91] Included are the rights to self-determination, food, work, and a reasonable standard of living.[92] Environmental human rights only became recognized as part and parcel of the third generation of rights. This third generation of rights, termed " 'solidarity' rights," includes the "right to health, to peace, and to a healthy environment, among others," and the "right to health, which also falls under the right to an adequate standard of living, is now linked with maintaining environmental quality."[93]

Environmental human rights are generally divided into two categories: substantive and procedural. Substantive environmental rights typically guarantee a healthy, safe, or ecologically sound environment. Generally speaking, the older environmental rights formulations tend to reference a healthy or clean environment, whereas newer conceptions often include language relating to ecology and biodiversity.[94] Procedural environmental rights, on the other hand, involve such issues as citizens having the right to access pertinent environmental information (e.g., government reports on pollution), to collaboratively engage in environmental decision-making, and to have meaningful access to legal channels to redress environmental harm.[95]

In the legal context, environmental human rights have been established, to varying degrees of success, in the United States, other nations, and through international instruments and decisions. Core international instruments of global application have historically "accorded minimal attention to environmental issues."[96] Tribunals, though, have held that violations of human rights emanating from failures of environmental protection in the context of the right to life, water, food, and indigenous peoples' collective rights to lands, among other dimensions, have infringed on such instruments as the International Covenant on Economic, Social and Cultural Rights, the International Covenant on Civil and Political Rights, and the American Convention on Human Rights; additionally, a handful of regional instruments have explicitly incorporated environmental human rights provisions, including the San Salvador Protocol to the American Convention on Human Rights, the Arab Charter on Human Rights, and the African Charter on Human and Peoples' Rights.[97] For instance, the latter reads in pertinent part at Article 24: "All peoples shall have the right to a general satisfactory environment favourable to their development."[98] Thus, generally speaking, the "scope and contours of substantive as well as procedural rights are sometimes detailed in legislation, but they are also given content through litigation. . . . International human rights tribunals, in particular, elaborate on the often generally-stated rights whose implementation they monitor."[99]

There has been considerable movement on environmental human rights at the global level in recent years. Notably, the 2015 Paris Agreement links environmental issues (and climate change, specifically) with human rights, in acknowledging in the preamble that because "climate change is a common concern of humankind," parties "should, when taking action to address climate change, respect, promote and consider their respective obligations on human rights, the right to health, the rights of indigenous peoples [etc.]."[100] While such acknowledgments are largely aspirational, Boyd notes that "declarations and resolutions can influence both state behaviour and the evolution of binding law."[101] What is more, in 2018, the U.N. Special Rapporteur on human rights and the environment released a groundbreaking report containing sixteen framework principles on human rights and the environment.[102] The rapporteur also recommends that the United Nations adopt a binding instrument of global application (e.g., a general assembly resolution) recognizing environmental human rights. Such global-level environmental human right principles may thus be established in the near future.

Significantly, at the nation-state level, most countries have explicitly incorporated environmental rights into their constitutions.[103] Similar to international law, this trend commenced in the 1970s, and by the early 1990s, most provisions were in place.[104] As Boyd notes in *The Environmental Rights Revolution*, there are well over a hundred national constitutions that "incorporate some form of environmental protection provisions, including government's duty to protect the environment, the individual right to a healthy environment, procedural environmental rights, the individual responsibility to protect the environment, and diverse other provisions."[105] Boyd adds that "no other human right has achieved such a broad level of constitutional recognition in such a short period of time."[106] Moreover, the majority of these provisions appear to be prima facie enforceable across the spectrum of sub-stantive and procedural rights.[107] And new environmental rights incorpora-tions have occurred at the nation-state level, such as Jamaica's 2011 Charter of Fundamental Rights and Freedoms and Kenya's environmental constitutional provisions added in 2010.[108]

The United States is a notable global exception to environmental human rights–related legal expansions. Some early efforts were, in fact, made to pursue environmental rights; for instance, Senator Gaylord Nelson proposed an amendment to the U.S. constitution in 1970, similar to what other nations were adopting at that time. Nelson proposed recognizing that each person has an "inalienable right to a decent environment" that further required that the federal and state governments "shall guarantee" that environmental right.[109] Such an amendment and others, however, did not materialize—and currently, "the United States appears to be the only nation that expressly denies the exis-tence of the right to a healthy environment in both domestic and international law." [110] Even to the extent that the United States acknowledges that environ-mental human rights have emerged as a form of customary international law, it nevertheless "does not apply to Americans because the US government has persistently objected to its recognition." [111]

At the U.S. state level, however, there was limited adoption of environmen-tal rights in legal regimes (particularly in state-level constitutions) during the 1970s heyday of environmental rights enshrinement. For instance, Article II, Section 3 of Montana's 1972 constitution includes the "right to a clean and healthful environment" as an "inalienable right." [112] However, due in large part to the rise of hyper-technical environmental law, a "surprisingly small number of environmental lawsuits have invoked the state constitutional provisions," and "even in those lawsuits, the constitutional arguments often have been sec-ondary to the plaintiffs' statutory claims." [113] Therefore, the movement to in-clude environmental rights provisions in state constitutions declined with the first environmental wave in the United States—and those provisions that were established have seen relatively scant enforcement and judicial furtherance.

A notable exception, however—and one deeply significant for *Remaking Appalachia*—includes Pennsylvania's environmental amendment. In 1971, Pennsylvania adopted a constitutional amendment, termed the Environmental Rights Amendment, that reads in pertinent part: "The people have a right to clean air, pure water, and to the preservation of the natural, scenic, historic and esthetic values of the environment." [114] Moreover, Pennsylvania embed-ded the public trust doctrine in this same provision (the importance of which will be discussed): "Pennsylvania's public natural resources are the common property of all the people, including generations yet to come. As trustee of these resources, the Commonwealth shall conserve and maintain them for the benefit of all the people."[115] For decades, in keeping with the U.S. general trend, this amendment went largely unenforced and was not furthered through the courts. As is discussed below, though, in just recent years, there has been a reinvigoration of this amendment through a series of remarkable opinions handed down by the Supreme Court of Pennsylvania. And recently, the Hawaii Supreme Court also affirmed its constitutional right to clean environment—which has led some commenters to assert that a nascent trend now exists in U.S. state-based environmental rights furtherance.[116]

Significant for *Remaking Appalachia*—and as entwined with explicit legal furtherance—environmental human rights also constitute a core organizing principle for EJ grassroots activists globally. David Naguib Pellow discusses this phenomenon in *Resisting Global Toxics*, in noting that human rights development has held special significance for environmental justice activists—as core EJ aims appear intrinsic in human rights discourses, and therefore can be furthered through expansions of human rights–specific cultural norms and legal frameworks.[117] Pellow thus argues that "connecting environmental justice and human rights elevates and deepens the discourse, the struggle, and the framework within which activists' claims can be made and resolved."[118] What is more, a central strategic benefit of embedding EJ concerns in human rights is that transnational environmental organizing is greatly facilitated, because a "human rights framework internationalizes the movement's concerns in ways that have rarely been articulated, which can connect local activists and campaigns to a much broader group of actors, discourses, policies and possibilities."[119] As discussed below, that environmental rights constitute a core organizing principle for EJ activists around the world—and furthermore are crucial components of transnational EJ organizing—is vitally important in the context of pursuing environmental rights as explicit systemic stepping stone measures (i.e., which depend on both a bottom-up, grassroots approach and also local-to-global connections).

ENVIRONMENTAL HUMAN RIGHTS—SYSTEMIC STEPPING STONE MEASURES

Radically reconceived environmental human rights constitute one systemic stepping stone measure that could help effectuate and expedite systemic reformations beyond hegemonic liberalism. Significantly, however, to truly serve as a bridge towards transformative ends, a critical legal theory–informed approach to environmental human rights formulations and furtherance is required. Environmental human rights in and of themselves constitute potentially potent alternatives to hyper-technical environmental law; nevertheless, environmental rights have typically been conceptualized from within the existing legal system (as part and parcel of the hegemonic liberal paradigm).[120]

To ensure that such systemic stepping stone measures actually accomplish their bridge-towards-transformative-change ends, in contrast to a traditional liberal approach, a critically informed approach to their formulation is therefore required. The notion of incorporating critical approaches into preexisting legal reform sites—and thereby transforming such reform towards true systemic re formations—has been fruitfully explored through radical strains of the "cause lawyering" discourse. As many commentators have noted, "the pervasive influence of critical theory" on law practice is "most obvious in the 'cause lawyering'" and in the "more recent emergence of community lawyering."[121] In a general sense, "cause lawyering" is a broad umbrella discourse that encompasses a continuum of progressive law practice: more conventional cause lawyering simply involves enhanced service of unmet legal needs, whereas more transgressive cause lawyering involves transcending traditional law practice hierarchies and aims—including towards truly transformative objectives.[122]

Community lawyering constitutes one of the more transgressive approaches to cause lawyering. Community lawyering focuses on the "lawyers' failure to understand or acknowledge the limitations of litigation as a means of social change, with its concomitant diversion of resources away from more promising strategies."[123] Also, community lawyering criticizes the manner in which "lawyers related to their clients, in particular the problem of lawyer domination over client autonomy."[124] Therefore a "unifying theme emerged from the application of critical theory to both scholarship and practice—a call to community."[125]

Focal points of community lawyering thus include non-hierarchical relationships between attorneys and clients and also a turn away from litigation (or "law reform," entirely) as the primary means through achieving social change. Specifically, then, community lawyering "advocates are encouraged to explore and to engage collaboratively with client groups in non-traditional legal fora to advance the clients' objectives, such as organizing for political action," and such lawyers are encouraged "to step outside law and put their faith . . . in community," which can involve "building community resources and mobilizing community action."[126] Community lawyers therefore "act not as saviors or champions, but rather as partners in collective ventures to change the world."[127] Community lawyers "increasingly measure their success in terms of client empowerment, community integration, advances in public awareness and social attitudes," and in their efforts "not to over-rely on litigation as the sole or even primary means to effect change, instead employing multiple approaches."[128] What is more, "collaboration with grassroots organizations is 'widely perceived as critical in securing sustainable social change,'" which typically involves "working in partnership with community groups or coalitions to provide services to secure legal and policy reforms."[129]

It should be noted, however, that other varieties of transgressive cause lawyering have been explored: such approaches often are similar but use different terminology. For instance, "radical cause lawyering" has been that which "endeavors to make changes in the basic structures of society and join forces with the social movements and their transformative interests and values."[130] And the "prototypes for radical lawyering are the Marxist, socialist, and self-styled movement lawyers of the US in the 1960s."[131] Radical cause lawyering thus is a supremely important approach, given *Remaking Appalachia*'s core objectives. And "critical cause lawyering" has been described as that which "focuses less on large-scale transformative politics than on rejecting hierarchy at micro-sites of power, e.g., the workplace, family, community, lawyer-client relationship."[132] Certainly, both radical and critical lawyering exist at the more transgressive end of the continuum; but so, too, do these approaches have deep intersections with the more radical conceptions of community lawyering.

Aside from non-traditional critically informed lawyering in a general sense, radical approaches have been adopted in the context of human rights lawyering. Critical theorists have assailed traditional human rights approaches as "thoughtless, shortsighted, Anglo/Eurocentric, Western Imperialists, perpetuating colonialist stereotypes, and glorifying autonomy" as a "Western construct" over collective action.[133] What is more, as influenced by "critical theories, many U.S. human rights attorneys are circumspect about their roles as elites within the legal system," because, all too often, prior human rights lawyering involved a "top-down approach where legal strategies and decisions are determined by elites who deliberate and debate separate and apart from client communities."[134] Thus, critically informed human rights theorists and practitioners have "endeavored to develop a client-centered, non-hierarchical approach in their work in order to accomplish a 'redistribution of power' within their own relationships as they simultaneously seek such a goal for their clients."[135] Therefore, as Berta Esperanza Hernández-Truyol articulates, "critical theory offers the concepts of multidimensionality, interconnectivity, multiplicity, intersectionality, and anti-essentialism."[136]

To be sure, critical legal theory–informed explorations of human rights are at the very forefront of contemporary thought. Kathryn McNeilly discusses this potential in *Human Rights and Radical Social Transformation*. McNeilly specifically explores "the possibilities for human rights and radical politics" to "spur on the (diverse) project to utilise human rights as a tool to work towards radical social transformation."[137] McNeilly adds that "the theory and practice of human rights may be re-engaged in way that is more compatible with the political pursuit of radical social transformation and that facilitates a challenge to power regimes which operate in marginalising or restrictive ways."[138] Such a creative "re-engagement [can offer] much potential for radical thinkers, activists and groups and the aims they seek to advance."[139] Ratna Kapur reaches related (albeit more measured) conclusions in *Gender, Alterity, and Human Rights*, in arguing that "my argument for 'thinking freedom' outside the fishbowl and within non-liberal spaces is intended to push the dialogues within human rights discourses closer to the fundamental issues that continue to trouble feminists and critical legal scholars."[140] Beyond even critically reconceived human rights, however, Kapur emphasizes that we need true systemic alternatives: "We must therefore not only evolve truly mindful, equitable and inclusive strategies for rights deployment, but also actively direct our attention beyond the fishbowl of familiar liberal hegemonies and seek out alternative registers for their capacity to realize the promise of lasting freedom."[141]

The concept of "framing" and transformative "collective action frames," as discussed in social movement theory, offers further guidance on how radically reconceived environmental human rights can help drive true systemic reformations beyond hegemonic liberalism (i.e., in addition to the public trust doctrine, as discussed below). Taylor discusses the importance of "framing" within social movements in "The Rise of the Environmental Justice Paradigm," providing numerous term definitions to support her argument. To begin, Taylor argues that rhetorics surrounding environmental issues are shaped into "collective action frames" in order to gain supporters within the broad citizenry. Framing constitutes the "process by which individuals and groups identify, interpret, and express social and political grievances."[142] Collective action frames, then, are "emergent, action-oriented sets of beliefs and meanings developed to inspire and legitimate social movement activities and campaigns designed to attract public support."[143]

Significant for *Remaking Appalachia*, such collective action frames also can be transformed, including along truly radical lines. The concept of "frame extension" involves social movements "broaden[ing] the frame of reference to make their messages salient to sympathizers not normally targeted by the movement"—and "frame transformation" entails "new ideas and values about movements and/or issues replac[ing] old ones," and a "general reframing of the issues occurs."[144] Lastly, the concept of "master frames" also is important, which have the same basic character as a collective action frame for a specific movement, but with exaggerated effects. EJ constitutes an example of a master frame, as activists have successfully mass-mobilized around a frame explicitly linking environmental concerns with racism, classism, etc. As has been the case with EJ, Taylor thus notes that "master frames are also potent," due to their magnification function: "They can be viewed as crucial ideological frameworks akin to paradigms."[145]

Environmental human rights thus can be radically reconceived—i.e., beyond hegemonic liberal capitalism—and deployed in mass mobilizing vis-à-vis such transformative reframing approaches. Community and radical cause lawyers, as allied with other organizers, could explicitly drive mass political mobilization not around traditional liberal environmental human rights—but rather a radical "frame transformation" of the environmental rights paradigm. Core rhetorics surrounding this radical frame transformation could be as follows: the realization of environmental rights of clean air, water, biodiversity, etc., is a fundamental impossibility under hegemonic liberalism, as illustrated by the accelerating (capitalist-produced) global ecological crisis. Consequently, in order to actually secure environmental human rights, the citizenry must mobilize around and collectively reconstruct a post-hegemonic liberalism future that is both strongly ecologically sustainable and critically just—i.e., potentially in accordance with ecofeminist- and ecosocialist-steeped re-formations. Such a radical frame transformation of environmental rights' collective action frame, therefore, could radically reconceptualize environmental human rights as a true systemic stepping stone measure aimed at transcending hegemonic liberalism. And an emerging post-liberalism master frame could simply be that systemic re-formations are required in the age of the Capitalocene. Chapter 7 further explores such re-envisioned environmental human rights in the Appalachian context—as potentially entwined with the radically reconceived public trust doctrine. Chapter 7 also emphasizes that the actual citizenry would co-determine the ultimate nature of re-envisioned environmental human rights beyond the basic frame initially introduced by radical cause lawyers, allied organizers, etc.

PUBLIC TRUST DOCTRINE

A critically informed approach to the public trust doctrine constitutes a second potentially potent systemic stepping stone measure in Appalachia and beyond. The modern approach to the public trust doctrine was pioneered by Joseph Sax in his groundbreaking 1970 article "The Public Trust Doctrine in Natural Resource Law."[146] Sax "revived and re-invented" the doctrine by "unhook[ing] it from its traditional moorings on or around water bodies and applied it to dry land as well," and generally speaking, also "added a powerful, if controversial, rhetorical element to the discussion of these resource areas."[147] However, Wood constitutes the leading contemporary commentator advocating for an expansion of the public trust doctrine—and thus it is her foundational work that will be outlined below as a starting place for a more radically conceived approach to the doctrine proposed in *Remaking Appalachia*.

At the definitional level, the public trust doctrine requires that the state hold natural resources in trust for the public (i.e., the public at large being the trust beneficiaries), in the context of both present and future generations; thus, "the governing assumption of the public trust principle is that citizens reserve public ownership of crucial resources as a perpetual trust to sustain society and the nation."[148] The historic foundations of the public trust doctrine are ancient, reaching back to Justinian's Code and the Magna Carta.[149] And in the contemporary global-legal landscape, numerous nations, which are as "far flung as the Philippines, India, and South Africa" have adopted the public trust doctrine as a component of their legal systems.[150] What is more, as Klaus Bosselmann notes in *Earth Governance*, "the rapid embracing of the public trust doctrine in these diverse countries evidences an evolution of the doctrine towards becoming a general principle of international law."[151]

The public trust doctrine is recognized throughout the entirety of the U.S. legal system. For instance, in the 1896 Supreme Court decision *Geer v. Connecticut*, the court held that it is "accurate to say that the ownership of the sovereign authority is in trust for all the people of the state; and hence, by implication, it is the duty of the legislature to enact such laws as will best preserve the subject of the trust, and secure its beneficial use in the future to the people of the state."[152] Likewise, in the Supreme Court's influential 1892 public trust decision *Illinois Central Railroad v. Illinois*, the court considered a case in which the state of Illinois conveyed state lands to a railroad company. In that case, the court held that "the legislature could not give away nor sell the discretion of its successors in respect to matters, the government of which, from the very nature of things, must vary with varying circumstances."[153] The court adds that "every legislature must, at the time of its existence, exercise the power of the State in the execution of the trust devolved upon it."[154] Thus, in an overarching sense, the "most significant advancement in environmental protection made by the public trust doctrine was a reservation of property to the public use that might otherwise be subject to the choices and whims of private parties." [155]

In the more contemporary legal landscape, Sax's pioneering articulation of the modern public trust doctrine resulted in early litigation efforts to further the doctrine in the United States. However, after an early litigation surge in the 1970s, environmental lawyers swiftly turned to the hyper-technical environmental law regime: "as new environmental statutes were enacted, some courts and scholars began to balk and backtrack and hedge," as they "complained that the public trust doctrine should take a backseat to environmental statutes. . . . [o]r that the doctrine should apply only to states. . . . or that it applies only to water and wildlife, and not to other ecological domains." [156] Reliance on the doctrine as a robust path forward for environmental law thus fell dormant.

Similar to environmental rights, some U.S. states, such as Pennsylvania, Hawaii, and Montana, constitutionally established public trust principles in the 1970s. And some states also enacted legislation codifying public trust principles, as was the case with Michigan and Minnesota. [157] Significantly, however, judicial precedent has long indicated that it is the legislatures who constitute prime trustees under U.S. law: "legislatures lead as trustees of the public's natural assets, pursuant to their constitutionally-appointed function of making the law." [158] But then it is the "judicial branch [that] remains the ultimate guardian of the public trust" in ensuring that legislative action is not violative of trust dictates. [159]

In more recent years, and of particular importance to *Remaking Appalachia*, one of the most important state-level developments in terms of the public trust doctrine has occurred in Pennsylvania. As discussed above, recall that Pennsylvania has a constitutional provision containing both environmental rights and public trust doctrine dictates. For decades, this amendment saw relatively scant enforcement. However, in 2013, in the plurality decision *Robinson Township v. Commonwealth*, the Supreme Court of Pennsylvania revitalized this amendment. Specifically, the court held as unconstitutional parts of Act 13, which was "a 2012 oil and gas law designed to facilitate the development of natural gas from Marcellus Shale." [160] As the court notes, the "plain meaning of the terms conserve and maintain [in the Environmental Rights Amendment] implicates a duty to prevent and remedy the degradation, diminution, or depletion of our public natural resources," and "as a fiduciary, the Commonwealth has a duty to act toward the corpus of the trust—the public natural resources—with prudence, loyalty, and impartiality." [161]

In applying such newly reinvigorated principles, the court held, among other things, that dimensions of Act 13 that preempted local governments from regulating oil and gas were unconstitutional, because "the General Assembly can neither offer political subdivisions purported relief from obligations under the Environmental Rights Amendment, nor can it remove necessary and reasonable authority from local governments to carry out these constitutional duties." [162] The court also held that an Act 13 provision that "permits industrial oil and gas operations as a use 'of right' in every zoning district throughout the Commonwealth, including 'in residential, commercial, and agricultural districts," is "incapable of conserving or maintaining the constitutionally-protected aspects of the public environment and of a certain quality of life." [163] While this was a plurality decision only—not a majority decision—*Robinson Township* had the effect of "breath[ing] new life" into the Environmental Rights Amendment. [164]

What is more, in 2017, the Supreme Court of Pennsylvania issued a landmark majority decision in the oil and gas context that definitively broadened the judicial interpretation of the amendment. In this case, *Pennsylvania Environmental Defense Foundation v. Commonwealth*, the Pennsylvania legislature enacted statutes for the purpose of generating funds "from the leasing of state forest and park lands for oil and gas exploration and extraction." [165] However, the court found that these statutory enactments were unconstitutional: as the court stated, "because state parks and forests, including the oil and gas minerals therein, are part of the corpus of Pennsylvania's environmental public trust, we hold that the Commonwealth, as trustee, must manage them according to the plain language of Section 27, which imposes fiduciary duties consistent with Pennsylvania trust law." [166] The court thus concludes that the "Commonwealth (including the Governor and General Assembly) may not approach our public natural resources as a proprietor, and instead must at all times fulfill its role as a trustee" and "because the legislative enactments at issue here do not reflect that the Commonwealth complied with its constitutional duties," the lower court's holding was reversed and vacated. [167] And, of course, what is particularly electrifying about this decision in the context of *Remaking Appalachia* is that it involves an oil-and-gas-related matter in Pennsylvania—and thus challenges the latest iteration of the fossil fuel hegemony.

The public trust doctrine has also been established in U.S. federal law. Indeed, the U.S. Supreme Court has recognized federal trust obligations, such as through the *Light v. United States* decision, wherein the court held that "all the public lands of the nation are held in trust for the people of the whole country." [168] Federal trust obligations are also recognized in federal legislation such as NEPA, which reads in pertinent part that is it a national duty to "fulfill the responsibilities of each generation as trustee of the environment for succeeding generations."[169] As Wood points out, federal-level trust obligations, as compared to state-level obligations, arise in circumstances involving "transboundary interstate assets," such as water, air, and the atmosphere, where "state trustees utterly fail to discharge their fiduciary duties to protect assets within their jurisdiction," and where "national exigencies demand federal involvement," such as the case with "broad ecological or public health threats."[170] Therefore, the global ecological crisis implicates such circumstances "converging at once into a national and planetary emergency that calls forth the federal public trust obligation in no uncertain terms."[171]

In *Nature's Trust* and related work, Wood advocates for a substantial expansion of the public trust doctrine as a vital, alternative path forward. Such an expansion, which by necessity would involve, in the outset, sustained judicial action, would account for environmental law's failures vis-à-vis the political branches (i.e., the legislature and administrative agencies). As Wood writes, "at a time when agencies across the planet use statutory environmental law to eradicate Earth's remaining resources," a transition "back to the trust concept" could curtail the global ecological crisis.[172] Wood adds that the public trust doctrine "neither hinges on, nor plays hostage to, environment statutes and regulations," as it instead "grows from a legally enduring principle having roots in judicially formulated doctrine preceding the modern system of statutory law."[173] As a consequence, a "broad return to trust precepts represents a natural progression in the cycle of legal thought rotating through successive eras of civilization."[174]

Wood argues, however, that a substantial expansion of the doctrine is required: "From an established public trust foundation," a newer "paradigm proposes an organizing framework responsive to the new ecological era" and, "to do so, it must push beyond current limitations associated with the public trust doctrine."[175] This could involve extending beyond the public trust as a judicial tool alone, instead pursuing the doctrine through legislative and executive action; pursuing the doctrine in the context of all natural resources (beyond its traditional scope of water and wildlife protection); pursuing the doctrine not just at the state level, but also the local, federal, and international levels (including oceans and the atmosphere); and moving beyond purely legal formulations of the public trust doctrine to examining it as "a political concept, an ethical mooring, a diplomatic framework, and as economic principle."[176] Ultimately, Wood concludes that a substantial expansion of the public trust doctrine could "create a full paradigm shift in environmental law" as "amid an ecological crisis" expanded public trust principles could "instruct government to protect and restore the Earth endowment."[177]

Indeed, dovetailing with Wood's foundational work, allied attorneys and legal scholars have pursued litigation to further expand the public trust doctrine—as associated most notably with the organization Our Children's Trust. The most significant dimension of such efforts involves atmospheric trust litigation (ATL), which has an explicit aim of curtailing climate change by judicially establishing that the "atmosphere is held in trust for the public" by the state—thus allowing the judiciary to "compel the other branches of the government" to concretely act on the crisis.[178] A remarkable case has developed at the federal level with the ATL suit *Juliana v. U.S.* in the Ninth Circuit. *Juliana* is one such climate lawsuit brought on behalf of youths asserting trust violations pertaining to the atmosphere.[179] The U.S. government—and fossil fuel interests, acting as initial defendant-interveners—previously moved to dismiss the case, but in 2016, a magistrate judge recommended denial of motions to dismiss, which was upheld at the district court level in a historic opinion.[180] Subsequently, however, the Trump administration pursued numerous measures aimed at halting the case, and the Court of Appeals for the Ninth Circuit eventually granted a rare interlocutory (or pretrial) appeal in 2018, which paused the suit pending the higher court's consideration of the government's positions; oral arguments were heard before the Ninth Circuit in July 2019.[181]

Significantly, however, the public trust doctrine as currently conceived—like environmental human rights—has received considerable criticism by commentators concerned about is liberal underpinnings (and thus lack of transformative scope). For instance, in *Our Better Natures*, Richard Delgado argues that the public trust doctrine, as revived in the United States, is intrinsically flawed, as it relies on intra-systemic reform alone. Delgado critiques Sax's approach to the public trust doctrine, in particular, noting that while Sax's reinvigoration of the public trust doctrine constituted a "forward-looking, an imaginative, pragmatic—even gallant—effort to save the environment from further deterioration," it nevertheless only "won wide support" because "it did not promise far-reaching environmental protection" by only offering "exactly what society needs during the middle and late stages of a revolution—a way of confining change to a manageable level."[182] Significant for *Remaking Appalachia*, Delgado adds that by adopting an intra-systemic reform approach vis-à-vis the public trust doctrine, the "ecofeminists and others advocating sweeping change were shut out."[183] Similar to critiques of the environmental human rights paradigm, Delgado and related critical theorists' arguments certainly should be closely accounted for when considering expansions of the public trust doctrine as a potential systemic stepping stone measure. In the first place, however, Wood herself accounts for at least some of these critical concerns in her recent formulation of the doctrine because, as discussed above, Wood's approach explicitly raises the question of how the doctrine might be robustly and creatively expanded in order to meet the demands of the current global ecological crisis.

PUBLIC TRUST DOCTRINE—SYSTEMIC STEPPING STONE MEASURE

In taking a transformative step beyond Wood's formulations, however, we can adopt an explicit critical legal theory–based approach to the public trust doctrine to serve as a systemic stepping stone measure towards true transformative change. As informed by ecofeminism and ecosocialism, the public trust doctrine could be radically reconceived beyond the liberal paradigm, as also involves combating hegemonic liberalism's interlocking subordination systems (along lines of gender, race, class, indigenous status, etc.). Furthermore, in adopting a bottom-up, grassroots approach, expansions of the public trust doctrine could be formulated and furthered vis-à-vis radical cause lawyering and community lawyering. Recall that through such an approach, the traditional hierarchies favoring attorneys is disrupted, thus allowing for the broader community to both formulate and drive transformative change through mass political mobilization surrounding the re-envisioned doctrine. And like the environmental human rights example, this re-envisioning process would entail a radical "frame transformation" of the "collective action frame" surrounding the doctrine. A radically re-envisioned public trust doctrine, then, would be part and parcel of the larger "master frame" through which systemic re-formations are required in the age of the Capitalocene. As discussed at length in chapter 7, a concrete example of a truly radically reconceived public trust doctrine could involve deploying it in the "ecological recommoning" context—i.e., beyond liberal land reform—in Appalachia and beyond.

As a final point, critically informed explorations of environmental human rights and the public trust doctrine, alone, do not constitute an exhaustive list of potential systemic stepping stone measures towards truly transformative futures. Additional paradigms could certainly supplement these doctrines; nevertheless, as discussed above, these two paradigms, of all preexisting options, are ideally suited to effectuate such transformative ends—and thus could be radically furthered through robust theory, practice, and praxis.

Ecofeminism and ecosocialism, then, constitute ideal modes of systemic re-formations beyond hegemonic liberal capitalism. Such ecofeminist- and ecosocialist-steeped re-formations could be strongly ecologically sustainable—as modeled on democratically coordinated degrowth transitions involving solidarity economy and subsistence modes (i.e., that focus on production for use value over exchange value)—and also critically just along lines of gender, race, indigenous status, etc.; and the ecosocialist influence also requires coordinating such bottom-up transformations with broader national and global re-formation efforts. Moreover, systemic stepping stone measures, as infused with critical legal theory, could help effectuate, expedite, and deeply inform these re-formations. Critically informed approaches to environmental human rights and the public trust doctrine constitute two such ideal stepping stone measures, as reconceived vis-à-vis radical frame transformations of the doctrines. Through pursuing such doctrines in a bottom-up, grassroots approach—i.e., as driven by radical cause lawyering-steeped and related mass political mobilization—we could thus more swiftly transition beyond the hegemonic liberal capitalist paradigm.

CHAPTER 7

REMAKING APPALACHIA: STRONGLY ECOLOGICALLY SUSTAINABLE FUTURES

The preceding chapter outlined theory and doctrine regarding potentially potent modes of transformative economic and socio-legal change. Specifically, as undergirded by critical legal theory, chapter 6 advocates for change beyond intra-systemic law reform, which, by necessity, requires systemic re-formations of "higher-level" social, political, and economic systems. Such are the forces that exist above or behind the law—but which essentially function as law in constituting the prime sources of true social regulation. Ecofeminism and ecosocialism were explored as useful models to inform the substance of such systemic re-formations. What is more, systemic stepping stone measures, in the form of critically informed approaches to environmental human rights and the public trust doctrine, were also put forth as crucial components in the multidimensional project to achieve such transformative change.

Chapter 7 will now examine this theoretical framework in the specific context of the Appalachian economic and socio-legal landscape. From the outset, it should be noted that this chapter constitutes an exploratory analysis only; that is, the theoretical framework outlined in chapter 6 is applied to Appalachia, and tentative conclusions are drawn on ideal systemic re-formations. Through praxis—or theory shaping real-world practices—this paired theoretical framework and exploratory Appalachian application can therefore concretely shape paths forward for the region and beyond.

This chapter begins by examining ongoing and future-projected modes of systemic re-formations in Appalachia. In particular, ecofeminist- and ecosocialist-steeped solidarity economy– and subsistence-based systemic re-formations in Appalachia are examined through such modes as community-owned clean energy systems and local food systems—as interlinked with broader systemic re-formations of the neoliberal ecological political economy at the national and international levels. Thereafter, systemic stepping stone measures are examined as one component in achieving such ecofeminist- and ecosocialist-inspired Appalachian systemic re-formations; specifically, critically informed approaches to environmental human rights and the public trust doctrine in Appalachia are discussed, as explored through such modes as community lawyering and radical cause lawyering and as similarly linked with broader re-formation sites. Most notably, rhetorics surrounding a radically re-envisioned public trust doctrine—as entwined with critically informed environmental human rights—are put forth as a model to potentially help effectuate post-liberalism "ecological recommoning" in Appalachia. Chapter 7 concludes by examining *Remaking Appalachia's* prime prescriptive recommendations vis-à-vis the recently revitalized Green New Deal and contends that this proposal will fail if conceived of within hegemonic liberalism—but that a radicalized Green New Deal indeed could help effectuate broader collective ownership and democratic economic planning modes required for multi-scale systemic re-formations beyond liberal capitalism (e.g., a comprehensive, revolutionary elimination of fossil fuel use nationally and globally).

OVERVIEW: ECOFEMINIST- AND ECOSOCIALIST-STEEPED SYSTEMIC RE-FORMATIONS IN APPALACHIA

At the foundational level, what might ecofeminist- and ecosocialist-inspired systemic re-formations entail in Appalachia? To begin, we must target the deeply exploitative, neoliberal-steeped ecological political economy, as has been implemented in Appalachia through liberal capitalist paradigm at large (and through the neoliberal turn in more recent decades). As the critical legal theory–informed approach to law elucidates, law itself is not the prime site of social regulation—rather, it those higher-level forces or "constitutive social systems and dynamics that exist as law even though they exist above or behind the 'legal law' as it has been narrowly conceived."[1] Beyond law reform—for instance, mere intra-systemic corrections to environmental law—we must thus target the " 'constitutive dynamics' of a constructed 'political economy' of industries that inherently generate structural economic (and environmental) consequences that resist correction."[2] For much of Appalachia, and for Central Appalachia, in particular, it is clear that the fossil fuel hegemony—with its complex social, political, and economic intertwinements—constitutes the cornerstone of those constitutive systems and dynamics functioning as higher-level systems. That is, the exploitative industries at work in much of Appalachia—or the coal, oil and gas, and intertwined chemical industries—form an important cornerstone of Appalachia's current, neoliberal-steeped ecological political economy, and thus constitute prime, structural forces existing "as law" in the region.

Consequently, a crucial starting place for ecofeminist- and ecosocialist-inspired Appalachian systemic re-formations requires transcending the fossil fuel hegemony altogether, as necessarily encompassing its broader national and international dimensions within a global-neoliberalized energy landscape (i.e., including the coal industry, as discussed in the MTR context in chapter 5).[3] This necessitates eliminating both the presence and pervasive influence of fossil fuel industries in Appalachia and beyond—including, of course, an Appalachian governmental landscape in which regulatory capture and outright corruption makes that uncontested fossil fuel hegemony possible in the first place. The constitutive dynamics of the fossil fuel hegemony are therefore far-reaching indeed, implicating the full range of economic, legal, cultural, and political dimensions. And as the critical analysis dictates, eliminating this fossil fuel hegemony cannot be achieved through "passing new 'legal laws' promulgated within an accepted political/economic context"—or the unique Appalachian formations of the neoliberal ecological political economy.[4] Rather, through systemic re-formations, these higher-level forces must be comprehensively dismantled—and Appalachian *reconstructions*, as necessarily interlinked with broader national and international efforts, must be collectively and radically conceived. (As discussed at the end of this chapter, a radicalized, ecofeminist- and ecosocialist-steeped Green New Deal potentially could constitute a prime mechanism, among other radical alternatives, for helping to effectuate the collective ownership modes and democratic economic planning required to eliminate the fossil fuel economy in a comprehensive and revolutionary fashion nationally and globally.)

That said, while the fossil fuel hegemony constitutes an important cornerstone of the ecological political economy in vast swaths of Appalachia—and has done so, through various manifestations, for more than a century—the project of effectuating systemic re-formations in the region and beyond does not begin and end with the fossil fuel industry. In the first place, as recent works such as *Appalachia Revisited, Transforming Places, Appalachian Reckoning,* and *What You Are Getting Wrong About Appalachia* illustrate, Appalachia is not a homogenous region with universal economic, social, or cultural characteristics. Powerful capital interests and complicit governmental actors indeed have diversely and complexly operationalized neoliberal-associated conditions in different geographic locations in Appalachia. Thus, as will be discussed, aside from explicit issues emanating from the fossil fuel hegemony, additional neoliberal-associated issues—such as the neoliberal emphasis on global food production, which has left many

Appalachian communities vulnerable to food insecurity—also must be targeted immediately through re-formations. And so, too, are Appalachian-focused trans-formations alone ultimately insufficient to secure a just and ecologically sustainable future; truly global transformations are required, and Appalachian systemic re-formations must work in tandem with these broader struggles if regional transformation efforts are to genuinely succeed.

SELECT LITERATURE ON APPALACHIAN SYSTEMIC RE-FORMATIONS

In terms of modeling systemic re-formations in Appalachia, the neoliberal ecological political economy—as embodied by the fossil fuel hegemony and related dominant forces—must be wholly transcended; moreover, in its place, an ecofeminist- and ecosocialist-inspired future can be collectively constructed. However, it must be emphasized that many activists, scholars, and related commentators, in examining the region's history and in exploring potential modes of re-formations, already have explored radical alternatives to neoliberal capitalism in the region and beyond. (And it must also be emphasized that no single discourse, ecofeminist, ecosocialist, or otherwise, has an absolute monopoly on best transformative paths forward.) For instance, as Ryan Wishart argues in "Coal River's Last Mountain," the "alienated social metabolism of capital accumulation is fundamentally antagonistic to the requirements of a healthy and sustainable ecological metabolism," and thus from a "material vantage point, MTR stands as a symbol of the ultimate destructiveness of capitalism, and of the dire need for a sustainable human alternative."[5]

As an example, Nina Gregg and Doug Gamble discuss the potential of solidarity economies in Appalachia in their *Transforming Places* chapter "This Land Is Your Land: Local Organizing and the Hegemony of Growth." In outlining the contours of solidarity economies as may be operationalized in Appalachia, Gregg and Gamble explain that to "have sustainable communities, we need sustainable businesses and public services," and that "a growing number of economists believe that the hegemony of growth must be challenged directly to meet human needs and avoid environmental disaster; we will need a very different kind of economy" in Appalachia, such as the solidarity economy.[6] Specifically, Gregg and Gamble examine the efforts of community-based organizations in Blount County, Tennessee, that have challenged reckless growth in their area. Although Gregg and Gamble note that the activist community members at issue were not explicitly "motivated by a critique of capitalism," the authors nevertheless argue that further organizing efforts based on positive, community-determined articulations of sustainable alternatives to the growth-centered status quo could help unite this community and others towards concerted social change actions.[7] Gregg and Gamble are, in fact, confident that the Tennessee community members would "endorse the values of the solidarity economy: reciprocity, democracy, sustainability, and equity."[8] Ultimately, Gregg and Gamble conclude that a focus—in Tennessee communities and worldwide—could be on creating systems "focusing on quality of life instead of growth of goods and wealth."[9]

More commonly, Appalachian activists and commentators have explored subsistence-based and closely related Appalachian transformations. For such commentators, subsistence transformations are an especially potent prospect in Appalachia because much of the subordinated population lives in rural settings, and so thus "the mere presence of the resource of land and the tradition of yeomanism can provide the essentials of this self-sufficiency."[10] Stoll, for instance, puts forth a perspective in *Ramp Hollow* focusing on reinvigoration of agrarianism and the commons in Appalachia. After examining Appalachia's century-long exploitation at the hands of the fossil fuel hegemony, Stoll notes that he broadly advocates for "democratic socialism and a reinvention of the nation-state as a conduit for meeting human needs rather than for accumulating capital."[11] However, he adds that he also "favors a realm of democratic autonomy, and that might have more political traction," and that if key federal actors, such as the legislature and the executive branch, supported such initiatives, such semi-autonomous communities could function as part and parcel of the broader United States.[12] Stoll also asserts that initiatives could also be formulated and supported at the U.S. state level (e.g., in West Virginia) and also that, significantly, "people can do it themselves, by squatting on abandoned land and defending their right to the commons."[13]

In support of his recommendations, Stoll discusses the fact that some organizations are currently engaging in concrete discussions with the citizenry on the prospects of regaining control over Appalachian land. Moreover, the RECLAIM Act has been introduced in Congress, which would "distribute funds to states and Indian nations aimed at developing land in communities 'adversely affected by coal mining' "; in examining such citizen and state actions, Stoll would more radically "push this thinking towards creating a reconstituted commons."[14] Stoll therefore speculates, "What if people who wished to do so lived by hunting and gardening as part of a social project that encouraged political participation? What if citizens possessed use-rights over a sustaining landscape?"[15]

To effectuate such recommendations, Stoll then proposes a variety of legislation he entitles the Commons Communities Act, which reads in perti-nent part:

> SECTION 1. The United States shall create a series of commons communi-ties, each designed to include a specified number of households within a larger landscape that will be managed by them, the residents. This land-scape will provide the ecological base for hunting and gathering, cattle grazing, timber harvesting, vegetable gardening, and farming. The eco-logical base will be owned as a conservation easement or land trust under the authority of the states and/or counties where each community resides . . . [16]

Stoll's act and his expanded discussion includes additional dimensions, such as (among other things) that residents may own their homes (with the act thus involving a combination of communal and private property); that edu-cation and social services will be paid for by an Industrial Abandonment Tax and by an income tax on the U.S. households in the top one percent; that such commons communities are not limited to Appalachia alone; and that residents would be free to engage in entrepreneurship or any wage-earning activities.[17]

Stoll, however, indicates that there are important drawbacks with this act—the core of which are addressed directly in *Remaking Appalachia* below. One central drawback is that while localized commons-based transformations would likely enhance justice at the community level, in terms of broader na-tional and global trends, the act itself would not "change or challenge a political economy in which humans and environments serve as inputs in the circulation of capital."[18] For more radical transformations targeting the neoliberal eco-logical political economy itself, Stoll therefore acknowledges that this "would require a government and a set of laws dedicated to human welfare."[19]

Other commentators have, in examining the worldviews of activists in Appalachia, similarly concluded that there exists a preexisting push for truly radical transformations in Appalachia. For instance, in the *Transforming Places* chapter "Mountain Justice," Cassie Robinson Pfleger and collected authors ex-amine the strategies and perspectives of the Mountain Justice organization. They note that many activists and residents have articulated the fact that, "in the face of ecological crises like climate change and the rapacious pressures of global capitalism, we need wholesale reconfiguration of economic produc-tion and consumption in local communities."[20] The residents add that because "absentee land ownership by timber, mining, and land companies is at the heart of regional economic problems . . . agrarian and land reform is necessary for a sustainable Appalachia."[21] Thus, the notion of pursuing transformative social and economic change in Appalachia has already been explored by many residents, activists, and scholars in the region, as has been chronicled by numerous commentators.

Lastly, in *Standing Our Ground*, Barry deploys a comprehensive feminist analysis—including strains of ecofeminism—in exploring subsistence-related transformations in Appalachia. In *Standing Our Ground*, Barry uses the Appalachian anti-MTR movement as a case model to examine issues relating to gender and activism in the region. That is, in her robust, far-reaching analysis, Barry "expands the EJ framework by centralizing gender in this analysis of women's involvement in the movement to end mountaintop removal coal mining in Appalachia."[22] Barry, however, also explores prescriptive recommendations for regional change, as steeped in subsistence-related transformations in Appalachia and, by necessity, worldwide.

Barry first links the location-specific social and environmental destruction caused by the coal industry in Appalachia to broader global struggles—by explicitly using a neoliberal political economy lens.[23] Because the fossil fuel industry creates niche, localized harms in Appalachia and also globalized harms through mechanisms such as climate change—and more broadly speaking, because the neoliberal political economy is destructive, multifaceted force worldwide—Barry therefore adopts a local-to-global approach to Appalachian social change. As Barry writes, while "it is crucial to mitigate the effects of coal consumption on the environment, we must also be aware of the politically transformative possibilities of linking social and environmental conditions in local production areas with the more global sites of consumption."[24] This is because understanding how neoliberal forces at large impact the global society and environment is a prerequisite for addressing niche, localized impacts of neoliberal forces on disenfranchised communities in regions such as Appalachia. As steeped in a materialist approach, such a theoretical framework thus illuminates how "social and environmental differences are produced and sustained across local, regional, national, and international axes."[25]

Barry examines potential transformations beyond the neoliberal political economy in Appalachia—and explicitly discusses subsistence-related approaches currently being cultivated by anti-MTR activists and others (both in Appalachia and worldwide). As Barry writes, many "women environmental justice activists, whether fighting Big Coal in Appalachia or Big Oil in places like Costa Rica, Nigeria, and Ecuador, provide an alternative vision that understands and critiques the current system, offering solutions and alternatives that some feminist social theorists say 'support "commoning" understood as a feminist ecosocialist alternative to capitalist-driven ecocide.' "[26] In the specific context of Appalachia, Barry adds that many women EJ activists emphasize that a transition towards renewable energy is a crucial component in this alternative social, economic, and environmental vision for Appalachia. Barry notes that as compared to neoliberalism's fixation on privatization and exploitation of the world's natural resources, many Appalachian EJ activists "envision the world and its resources as a 'commons,' where the goods and bads of any society are equally and more justly allocated."[27] In this manner Appalachian EJ activists reject neoliberalism in favor of radically conceived alternative visions.

Barry then explicitly links Shiva's subsistence-related thought to women anti-MTR activists in Appalachia. In drawing on Shiva's concept of "living economies" from *Earth Democracy*, Barry explains that "many women in West Virginia promote living economies through sustainable development of the area's renewable natural resources and the global transition from the fossil fuel–based paradigm of energy production to alternative energy development."[28] Through this work, these Appalachian activists aim to not only halt MTR and other destructive practices in their communities—and to create just and strongly sustainable alternatives potentially in line with Shiva's "living economies"—but also to curtail the impacts of climate change worldwide. In examining the material realities of the anti-MTR movement in Appalachia, Barry therefore concludes that bottom-up, grassroots change is already occurring in some regional areas—i.e., ecofeminist-inspired systemic re-formations are currently, in some measure, underway.[29]

Aside from Barry, other Appalachian studies commentators emphasize the importance of local-to-global connections in the era of global neoliberal capitalism. For instance, Fisher has explored such vistas in arguing that while "localism offers a number of advantages, few significant problems can be solved at the local level" alone due to neoliberalism's deleterious effects on local economies and institutions.[30] As a result, Fisher recommends that those "organizing in Appalachia must find ways to make clear the connections that exist between local work and national and international institutions if local citizens are to understand the importance of national and international forces as determinants of what happens locally and to see themselves as actors at the national level."[31] Fisher thus concludes that linking "local fights to national and global struggles is a difficult and slow process, but it is the only approach that has a chance of bringing about fundamental change in Appalachia." [32] And as Fisher and Barbara Ellen Smith add in *Transforming Places*, "place-based organizing in Appalachia is increasingly 'scaling up' in ways that include but are not limited to strategies directed toward attaining a wider geographic reach," and importantly, scaling up "also means 'scaling across' social and geographic space, intentionally creating strategic lateral relationships among peoples, places, and ideas that transcend social, spatial, and ideological barricades (such as between immigrants and labor, peace, environmental, and anti-racist activists, rural and urban, white and black)." [33]

APPALCHIAN SYSTEMIC RE-FORMATIONS: CRITICAL LEGAL THEORY–INFORMED APPROACH

In expanding on such foundational analyses—i.e., in part through a niche, critical legal theory–based lens—*Remaking Appalachia* contends that solidarity- and subsistence-based economies, as based generally along ecofeminist and ecosocialist lines, and as linked with broader de- and re-construction efforts of the neoliberal ecological political economy at the national and international levels (as discussed below), are indeed ideal paths forward in Appalachia and beyond. *Remaking Appalachia* predominantly focuses on the potential for systemic re-formations vis-à-vis radical solidarity economies (i.e., particularly as driven by radical cause lawyers and allied organizers) as one core dimension of such re-formations; however, as has been noted, radical solidarity economies have deep intersections with subsistence-related approaches as well.

Two important examples of preexisting transitions toward the solidarity- and subsistence-based modes—which, through radical expansions, could further contribute to systemic re-formations in Appalachia along ecofeminist- and ecosocialist-related lines—include local-centered, strongly sustainable, and critically just approaches to both community-owned clean energy systems and local food systems. And from a critical legal theory standpoint, such transitions also can be pursued vis-à-vis bottom-up modes such as radical cause lawyering—wherein lawyers help drive radical solidarity economy development through mechanisms such as transactional lawyering support—and otherwise engage in broader educational and organizing efforts geared towards transformative change beyond liberal capitalism. Following such explorations, *Remaking Appalachia* next will turn to the prime, systemic stepping stone measures that can help effectuate, expedite, and deeply inform such transformations of the ecological political economy: critically informed approaches to environmental human rights and the public trust doctrine, as potentially driven by the sort of mass political mobilization that radical cause lawyering could help engender.

Lastly, in recognizing that even radically conceived bottom-up transformations are insufficient in and of themselves, *Remaking Appalachia* turns to ecosocialist-steeped re-formations at the national and global levels, as steeped in broader, collective ownership modes of the means of production and multi-level democratic economic planning. Specifically, a fully radicalized Green New Deal is explored as one potential option of helping to effectuate such truly comprehensive systemic re-formations beyond liberal capitalism—i.e., which, at the same time, could work synergistically with niche bottom-up transformations such as the solidarity economy– and subsistence-based modes.

APPALACHIAN COMMUNITY-OWNED CLEAN ENERGY SYSTEMS

Community clean energy systems constitute one significant instance of emerging modes of potential systemic re-formations in Appalachia. As will be discussed, such community-centered clean energy projects could be diverse indeed, encompassing solar, wind, energy efficiency, and so forth. However, to date, solar energy has made some of the most substantial inroads in the explicit context of local-centered clean energy systems in Appalachia. Therefore, solar energy will be used as the primary case model in terms of both preexisting efforts towards systemic re-formations and potential future-projected re-formations that would involve a radically expanded approach beyond liberal capitalism.

Numerous commentators have identified renewable energy–based cooperatives, in particular, as ideal mechanisms to catalyze solidarity economy development. As is noted in *Social and Solidarity Economy*, "certain sectors of the green economy—renewable energy, green buildings and others—presents an opportunity for SEE [social and solidarity economy] organisations," as the "green economy will often require localised initiatives structured around community needs—demands that are aligned with SSE organisations' underpinning values, processes and goals."[34] The authors point out that community-owned renewable wind power, for instance, has already made substantial inroads in some global regions and is a quickly growing sector. And particularly heartening for Appalachia, solidarity economy–steeped renewable cooperatives have been identified as enticing options for regions that traditionally have suffered from economic, social, and environmental subordination. Community organizing efforts, however, are often required as a first vital step, as building robust "community organisation density" greatly facilitates an explicit citizen-driven approach to revitalization of depressed areas through renewables-based cooperatives and the like.[35]

Renewable-based energy cooperatives are not, as it were, created equal. They exist on a spectrum with more limited, traditional models on one end (e.g., consumer-owned cooperatives), as compared to more radical, multi-stakeholder-steeped models on the other (i.e., among other radical models). For Appalachia, is it these more radical models that hold the most eventual promise in helping to achieve true systemic re-formations in the clean energy systems context. Specifically, in terms of such transformative, multi-stakeholder cooperatives, there can exist comprehensive, community-owned clean energy systems that can be "comprised of worker-owners, consumer-owners, and community-driven funders," which has the strong advantage of integrating such diverse community groups within a single system.[36] Such diverse stakeholders can work to construct community-owned clean energy systems in disenfranchised areas, which would keep resources within communities, create a local cooperative workforce, and which can also involve accompanying training and community educational programs to support broader transformative change along ecofeminist and ecosocialist lines.[37] Thus, broadly speaking, while "traditional cooperatives are often used to enclose a commons" for a select few only, with more radical models such as multi-stakeholder cooperatives, the aim is instead to "share those resources fairly for the benefit of the community."[38] And note that while "community-owned" clean energy systems are an exploratory focal point for *Remaking Appalachia*, from a commoning perspective we also should, at the same time, consider "mov[ing] beyond talking about 'ownership' to looking at our relationships with one another and the natural world"—and indeed some "new energy cooperatives are looking at a more indigenous understanding of our relationship to other people and the Earth."[39] Such an approach also holds great promise for Appalachia and beyond.

Comprehensive, multi-stakeholder solar cooperatives have, in fact, been implemented in U.S. regions such as California—i.e., community-based energy projects have been paired with educational programs in the specific context of low-income communities and communities of color. Such community projects have viewed "renewable energy as the opportunity to build community power—social, political, infrastructure, economic, and generative" and have, correspondingly, been viewed "as being part of the just transition toward solidarity economies."[40] An important caveat, however, is that U.S. states such as California have favorable renewable development policies and an often-strong community organizing infrastructure.

Niche approaches to community and radical cause lawyering could occupy an important role in such multi-stakeholder cooperative development.

Transactional-focused lawyers could adopt approaches that maximize community participation and truly radical objectives—while also linking those efforts with broader struggles towards achieving transformative change beyond liberal capitalism. As Renee Hatcher writes in "Solidarity Economy Lawyering," "an emerging cohort of lawyers are working to transform the dominant economy from one that centers on self-interest, greed, and profit maximization to an economy that centers the needs of people and the planet."[41] More specifically, radical transactional lawyers could spearhead widespread citizenry education efforts on multi-stakeholder cooperatives and could drive organization formations—i.e., such as creating multi-stakeholder solar or wind cooperatives. Radical transactional lawyers would thus occupy a niche supportive role[42]— in addition to interlinking such efforts with broader transformative change (i.e., including "scaling up" efforts). On the latter point, as Gowri Krishna writes in "Worker Cooperative Creation as Progressive Lawyering?," "activists, workers' rights organizations, and progressive lawyers seeking to create cooperatives as vehicles for greater societal change must consciously pursue mechanisms beyond merely choosing the cooperative form to accomplish that end."[43] Krishna adds that "historically, worker cooperatives have shared ties to movements for economic, political, and social change. Opportunities exist for similar connections today. As workers', immigrants', and women's rights movements grow, intersect, and evolve in a way that incorporates alternative institutions, more worker cooperatives can move beyond the individual towards effecting collective action."[44] In this way, such radical transactional lawyering also could conceptualized, at least in part, as stepping stone efforts towards transformative change—and such efforts could indeed be interwoven with the more ecological-focused systemic stepping stones measures discussed at length below.

Such transformative approaches to community-based renewable energy systems are often slower-in-coming in Appalachia; West Virginia, for instance, lacks the comprehensive, pro-renewables policies that some other states enjoy, and there are "inherent difficulties in coordinating new community- or member-owned projects" in localities that lack a robust, progressive-focused organizing infrastructure.[45] Nevertheless, particularly in the case of solar, some community-focused energy projects have developed in Appalachia, and with the requisite organizing activities and structural re-formations, such comprehensive, community-owned clean energy systems—as steeped in the radically conceived, multi-stakeholder approaches and related modes—hold great eventual promise for Appalachian systemic re-formations.

Solar-based cooperatives have indeed established a presence in much of Appalachia. Even in West Virginia—which has one of the least favorable policy landscapes in the nation for renewable energy development—organizations such as Solar United Neighbors of West Virginia exist. Solar United "envision[s] a clean, equitable energy system that directs control and benefits back to local communities" and describes itself as "a community of people building a new energy system" that helps "people go solar, join together, and fight for their energy rights."[46] More broadly in the context of solar development, Solar Holler, a rooftop solar developer and installer, has received considerable attention to recent years, as they broadly note that "solar is new to West Virginia," but that they nevertheless "relentlessly pursue innovative approaches that bring solar within reach of the people and places who have always been left out."[47]

Community solar projects have also made inroads in some Appalachian states. Community projects offer solar-based energy to those who lack rooftop technology, as such projects allow individuals or organizations to lease or purchase a community solar project share or to begin a project within a community.[48] In West Virginia, however, state policies currently forbid community solar altogether.[49] Moreover, not all community solar projects are genuinely emancipatory—as it is often only larger corporate developers or (problematically situated) utilities that are permitted to construct community solar projects.[50] However, as examples in the region, some Appalachian rural electric cooperatives indeed are providing the community solar option, such as, in Tennessee, the Appalachian Electric Cooperative, the Blue Ridge Electric Membership Corporation in North Carolina, and the BARC Electric Cooperative in Virginia.[51]

Aside from solar, wind power also has potential in the context of community-owned clean energy systems in Appalachia. Similar to multi-stakeholder approaches to solar, "wind projects can be locally owned, with the associated revenues remaining within the local area and the jobs employing local residents."[52] This is in stark contrast to large corporate projects, in which revenue often flows outwards and the workforce is imported into the community. Additionally, community wind projects are often located in rural areas to account for both acreage requirements and zoning ordinances—and so rural Appalachian communities are also well suited for wind sites; thus, "wind turbines provide an opportunity for often-impoverished regions to create a new, stable, and diversified income stream."[53]

Community wind projects, however, have not yet achieved the inroads that comparable solar projects have in Appalachia. Like with other renewables, a lack of beneficial state policies in Appalachian states like West Virginia has stymied their development.[54] Another major factor in this delay emanates from both corporate absentee ownership and large public land ownership of many ridgelines in Appalachia that are ideal for community wind development. The geographical remoteness of such ridges also constitutes an issue. And the ecological impacts of wind projects continue to cause controversy: geographical remoteness can increase wilderness damage generally, but large wind turbines also create niche issues, such as negative impacts on bird and bat populations.[55]

Lastly, aside from renewable energy production, community approaches to energy efficiency would constitute an important dimension of radically conceived Appalachian clean energy systems. Energy efficiency involves reducing wasteful consumption modes through energy audits, the installation of energy efficiency measures (e.g., insulation and efficient lighting), and so forth. Like with renewables, energy efficiency modes have often been marked by top-down implementation, as the for-profit utility sector has sought to co-opt "the energy services concept for the benefit of maintaining the present corporate energy structure" and corresponding profit maximization.[56] Of course, a community-owned approach to energy efficiency explicitly rejects corporate, top-town energy efficiency modes. The focus is instead on how energy efficiency projects (together with on-site renewable energy production, as discussed above) can be "effectively developed and implemented at community scales" as steeped in "democratic local governance structures." [57] For Appalachia, then, community energy efficiency projects are a vital component of comprehensive clean energy systems. But also like with renewables, much of the region lacks beneficial state policies—West Virginia, for instance, ranks near-bottom on preexisting policies on energy efficiency.[58] While organizations such as Energy Efficient West Virginia indeed favor "organizing to promote programs and policies to make West Virginia a more energy efficient state," further bottom-up, grassroots organizing will be a foundational imperative to drive the formulation of community clean energy systems steeped in ecofeminist and ecosocialist precepts.[59]

From an ecofeminist standpoint, the question of community clean energy systems also raises issues along lines of gender, race, class, indigenous communities, and so forth. For instance, as Cornelia Fraune has noted in a Germany-based case study—i.e., Germany is a world leader in citizen participation-steeped schemes—hegemonic social, cultural, and political forces can constrain diverse and genuine citizen participation in the renewable energy context. This is because there exist, for instance, gender-based differences in renewable energy co-ownership and governance that "cannot be explained alone by individual preferences and attitudes but have to be traced back to social conditions like gender, wealth gap, occupational segregation, or tax legislation." [60] As unjust gender regimes are also, of course, endemic throughout the United States—including in Appalachia (i.e., albeit uniquely operationalized per a materialist approach)—Fraune's general findings are certainly apropos to any future-projected Appalachian development of community-owned clean energy. In terms of further prescriptive recommendations, Melissa Leach writes that initiatives in clean energy and beyond ought to recognize "women's knowledge, agency and decision-making as fundamental." [61] This approach is required to "build fairer and greener economies" based on truly sustainable and just energy, food, sanitation, and health systems. [62] Likewise, similar issues relating to race, indigenous status, LGBTQ+ status, ability, etc.—or issues of agency, co-ownership, genuine shared governance, and the like—also must be taken into account when constructing critically just clean energy systems.

Such considerations demonstrate aptly why the core insights of ecofeminism are so vital for informing Appalachian systemic re-formations. Recall that, per a broad ecofeminist account, under patriarchal capitalism, the same hegemonic forces driving the destruction of the environment are simultaneously responsible for the systematic subordination of marginalized groups. Therefore, all such forces must be combated holistically in order to truly achieve transformative change. As Mies and Shiva note, different dominance systems of late liberalism are intrinsically intertwined, and thus cannot be addressed separately: the interconnected issues of "patriarchal relations, inequality, alienation, [and] poverty . . . must be solved together with ecological problems." [63]

Therefore, in applying such ecofeminist principles to Appalachia, it is not enough to transition away from the fossil fuel hegemony towards community clean energy systems as part of broader post-liberalism transformations. On the one hand, such transformations would indeed vastly reduce environmental destruction—and such modes also, of course, maximize citizen participation and co-ownership. Nevertheless, such modes, in and of themselves, are insufficient from a holistic ecofeminist perspective. As Fraune's work illustrates, even enhanced citizen-ownership approaches steeped in strong ecological sustainability can fail to account for additional hegemonic ills, such as systemic gender- and race-based subordination. Consequently, as the broad precepts of ecofeminism dictate, community clean energy systems in Appalachia should recognize Appalachian women's shared ownership and governance as fundamental; likewise, systemic concerns relating to race, sexuality, indigenous status, and so forth—or all other dimensions of subordination under late liberalism—also must be holistically accounted for in radically conceiving Appalachian community clean energy systems beyond liberal capitalism.

What is more, a shift in gender-just approaches to community clean energy systems, by necessity, extends beyond mere equality-of-inclusion in ownership and decision-making; rather, deeper changes to the gender regime are required. That is, genuine ecofeminist- and ecosocialist-inspired modes—in the context of radically conceived clean energy systems and beyond—will require comprehensive de- and re-construction of the gender regime, as conceived in the broadest sense. As Gaard writes in "Toward New EcoMasculinities, EcoGenders, and EcoSexualities," for "any egalitarian socioeconomic and eco-political transformation, such as that advocated by ecofeminism to be possible, both individuals and institutions need to shift away from overvaluing exclusively white, male, and masculinized attributes and behaviors, jobs, environments, economic practices, laws and political practices, in order to recognize and enact eco-political sustainability and ecological genders."[64] In the Appalachian context, therefore, such gender regime transitions—particularly in the context of socially constructed concepts of "men" and "masculinity" in addition to reconstructed gendered divisions in labor (i.e., with men performing equal shares of reproductive labor and indeed notions of "labor" itself being reconceptualized)—must occur to achieve truly just, ecofeminist- and ecosocialist-steeped re-formations.

APPALACHIAN COMMUNITY-OWNED FOOD SYSTEMS

A second significant example of preexisting movements towards systemic re-formations in Appalachia—which could be radically expanded via ecofeminist- and ecosocialist-steeped modes—pertain to community food systems. As will be discussed, much has been written about the potential for community food systems in Appalachia in a general sense. However, like clean energy systems, community food systems also could constitute the core of truly radically conceived post-liberalism re-formations. As is the case with renewable energy, not all local food systems are created equal; for instance, there exist some initiatives steeped in a radical approach to foodways, such as solidarity economy–steeped schemes implicating "the mobilization of land, financial capital and other key resources to support the development of local and organic food production in their localities."[65] For some of these initiatives, citizen-consumers are intertwined directly with community food production sites. From a radical solidarity economy standpoint, such initiatives are important as they constitute a fundamental shift in "consumers from passive end-users and mere buyers of food products" towards revitalized citizen-consumers that are wholly integrated into strongly ecologically sustainable food systems.[66]

To be sure, such modes situate food provisioning within a radically and democratically re-envisioned context. Such an approach involves, for instance, citizen-consumers exercising co-ownership and otherwise collaborating with citizen-producers to actively "reshape their relations with different stages of the food system," thus creating community-based, citizen-steeped foodways that eschew a transactional approach—and instead promote a highly democratic system steeped in socially co-determined meanings.[67] Ultimately, such solidarity economy–based transitions reflect the "emergence of new food networks in which citizens play a key role in the operation," and in which "voluntary, associational principles and participatory forms of self-management" are of central importance.[68]

In the context of Appalachia, much has been written about the potential for community-based agriculture and food systems to transform the region. As the ARC report *Assessing the Landscape of Local Food in Appalachia* notes, "perhaps the Region's most vibrant assets, and maybe the most sustainable, are its agricultural and food assets."[69] In fact, in *Place-Based Foods of Appalachia*, the region was characterized as the most diverse North American foodshed—with "nearly 1,500 documented folk and indigenous crop varieties of heirloom vegetables and fruits" cataloged in Appalachia.[70]

ARC further notes that identified assets in Appalachia include the following: a historic tradition of small-scale farming and gardening; a similar tradition of "seed saving" and the cultivation of heirloom crops; a nascent but emerging food infrastructure, including processing facilities and farmers' markets; a cultural tradition celebrating local foodways through custom and the arts; and impressive local and regional leadership, which has been noted within the broader local food movement landscape.[71] The overarching findings of the ARC report reveal "a vigorous and growing regional food economy that has the potential to increase employment opportunities, improve community vitality and quality of life, and become a sustainable and healthy part of Appalachia's future economic and community development."[72]

Presently, consumer points for locally produced food include such sources as farm-based stores, farmers' markets, community-supported agriculture (CSAs), and direct sales to "grocers, restaurants, and [other] institutions."[73] Also, organizations such as Appalachian Sustainable Development have launched initiatives like integrated field-to-table networks, which both train farmers and also provide a centralized facility for produce processing and thereafter transportation to surrounding consumer points; a related initiative has been launched at the Appalachian Staple Food Collaborative in Ohio that "supports regional production of healthy heirloom grains, which it then processes, markets, and ships to regional buyers."[74] There also are ongoing initiatives aimed at addressing niche aspects of the "food desert" phenomenon in Appalachia (i.e., or insufficient community access to healthy whole foods such as fruits and vegetables). For instance, community gardening and the introduction of mobile farmers' markets have occurred in areas of South Carolina and Tennessee.[75]

On this latter trend, such recent Appalachian local food system growth, while heartening, has indeed occurred in conjunction with—and often in direct response to—longer-term forces that have degraded Appalachian foodways. Similar to the neoliberal turn in energy and environmental law negatively impacting Appalachia—i.e., in furthering energy sacrifice zone conditions—neoliberal-steeped agriculture and food policy have produced ill-effects in the region. Of course, the rapid period of coal- and timber-based industrial growth was a prime early force that disrupted traditional Appalachian agriculture (i.e., as were even earlier phenomena, such as pre–Civil War era population growth and unsustainable agricultural practices, as discussed in chapters 1 and 3). But in the twentieth century, ill-conceived liberal development paradigms also have degraded local Appalachian foodways; recall that U.S. agricultural policy has long favored large corporate interests and has thus correspondingly had a deleterious effect on small-scale agriculture in Appalachia and elsewhere. And so, too, have intertwined material forces such as treadmill of production–associated agricultural development modes degraded small-scale agriculture in Appalachia and beyond.[76]

With the coming of global neoliberal forces in the 1980s, Appalachia has been beset by more multifaceted food-related harms. In the first place, global neoliberal agriculture modes have involved a deep "integration of transnational agrifood capital, where global sourcing is the norm, and the national regulation of agriculture is challenged both by corporate-economic strategies and by further international-trade liberalization pressures."[77] More specifically, in terms of Global South and North dynamics, neoliberal food trends have often resulted in the exploitative production of agricultural goods in the Global South for the benefit of consumers in the North; a notable example includes the fresh vegetable and fruit sector. Among many issues caused by these neoliberal food trends, local farming and related subsistence modes have been severely undermined in global regions, including in subordinated Global North regions such as Appalachia.[78] And more broadly, other neoliberal-associated conditions have produced intertwined food-related harms in the region; for instance, numerous local grocery stores have been supplanted by transnational superstore conglomerates—which have, following coal-related economic decline, begun abandoning parts of the region, thus producing greater food insecurity.[79] And in an even broader sense, neoliberal-associated conditions continue to engender economic ills in Appalachia, which further exacerbates the degradation of food system dimensions across the board. Community-based Appalachian food systems thus have reemerged in response to such deleterious conditions while also occurring in tandem with the growth of the local food movement that has occurred both nationally and globally (i.e., as generally aligned against neoliberal forces).

Community-based food systems, then, constitute a vital component of emerging re-formations in Appalachia. As ARC concludes, "growing the local food economy is a major opportunity to create positive, lasting community and economic change based on already existing assets," and what is more, "many communities in the Appalachian region are already utilizing local food and sustainable agriculture as a strategic resource."[80] Numerous other commentators have reached similar conclusions regarding the centrality of local food systems in Appalachian re-formations. For instance, as Sarah Jones writes in "Can Local Food Help Appalachia Build a Post-Coal Future?," "a resurgence in local farming, coupled with renewed interest in traditional Appalachian foodways, could help steer the region toward an environmentally and economically sustainable post-coal future."[81] As Jones adds, "unlike the historical attempts to develop Appalachia—imposed principally by external actors, both public and private—food and farming are located well within the region's own history of political resistance."[82]

It should be noted, however, that similar to issues related to community clean energy systems, there are substantial barriers to further expansions of community-centered Appalachian food systems. One barrier relates to infrastructure, as variously conceived—and as requires niche approaches from the solidarity economy– and subsistence-based perspective. In contemporary Appalachia, there are persistent issues pertaining to food growing, processing, and distribution modes; commentators thus note that additional infrastructure, training, and citizen educational programming are required.[83] For instance, no matter the scale of farming—including solidarity economy– and subsistence-based farming—agriculture is ultimately dependent on "soil and seed," which includes adequate access to such resources and training on best practices for strongly ecologically sustainable utilization.[84] In Appalachia, much is yet to be accomplished on such fronts. However, Appalachian organizations like the Appalachian Sustainable Agriculture Project and West Virginia University's Food Justice Lab are variously examining and promoting strongly sustainable development of food systems in the region and beyond.[85] So, too, have programs such as the Cherokee Nation seed bank emerged, which, in addition to offering "varieties of seeds," also involves the "garden where seeds are grown for distribution every year" emerging as "part of the language program for Cherokee schools."[86]

Of course, *Remaking Appalachia* ultimately advocates for a radical solidarity economy– and subsistence-based approach to community-based food systems, as steeped in ecofeminism and ecosocialism (and thus as conceived of beyond liberal capitalism). Radical solidarity economy modes would favor a highly democratic approach that maximizes community-wide citizen co-ownership and co-governance; for instance, active Appalachian citizen-consumers would exercise co ownership and otherwise be tightly integrated with the production and distribution channels for strongly ecologically sustainable local food-ways; similarly, on the production end, Appalachian farmers could function as citizen-producers who, in conjunction with citizen-consumers and the broader community, adopt highly egalitarian, collaborative models in which "voluntary, associational principles and participatory forms of self-management" are of paramount importance.[87] So, too, could broader training and educational programming maximize the reintroduction of citizenship into local food-ways—and also could involve broader educational programming on broader dimensions of ecofeminist- and ecosocialist-steeped transformations beyond foodways alone.

As a specific example, similar to community clean energy, multi-stake-holder food cooperatives could constitute one dimension of radical solidarity economy–steeped community food systems. As Raquel Ajates Gonzalez argues in "Going Back to Go Forwards?," "multi-stakeholder food cooperatives [present] an opportunity to bridge the common analytical gap that silos food production and consumption activities into two separate categories."[88] Likewise, it has been noted that multi-stakeholder food cooperatives could create "solidarity between local farmers and local buyers," facilitate development of a more "comprehensive community-based food system," and ultimately constitute a concrete "beginning for an anti-capitalist food network."[89] What is more, other solidarity economy–steeped community food system projects have been explored, such as solidarity-driven versions of farmers' markets—termed "citizenship markets"—adopted in the Bergamo area of Italy.[90] Through a screening process, participating farmers must articulate their position and practices regarding "food sovereignty, food democracy, food justice, food responsibility and food quality."[91] And these farmers' markets are accompanied by broader training and educational programming, such as citizen debates on strongly sustainable food systems and solidarity economy fairs.[92]

Like community clean energy systems discussed above, radical transactional lawyers and allied organizers could help drive citizenry educational efforts and the formulation of solidarity economy–steeped Appalachian food system dimensions (e.g., multi-stakeholder food cooperatives). And again, radical transactional lawyers and allies explicitly could interlink such efforts with broader struggles towards true ecofeminist- and ecosocialist-steeped change— i.e., beyond community food and energy systems alone.[93]

Recall also that in core ecofeminist work such as the subsistence perspective put forth in Mies and Shiva's *Ecofeminism*, questions of food systems occupy primacy of place, with examples including ecofeminist-steeped explorations of "permaculture and food production"; and indeed more broadly, Mies and Shiva place "production of food and other basic needs" as constituting the veritable cornerstone of "the satisfaction of fundamental human needs mainly by production for use-values and not by the purchase of commodities."[94] Per the ecofeminist framework, though, simply transitioning to solidarity economy– and subsistence-based food systems is insufficient, because similar to clean energy, such a transition, in and of itself, would fail to account for hegemonic gender- and race-related etc. ills. For instance, in stark contrast to the traditional, unjust gendered division of labor—in which women disproportionally perform unpaid work—under the ecofeminist view, this division of labor must be wholly transcended. That is, men must "share unpaid subsistence work" in the context of "new forms of subsistence production," like subsistence-based Appalachian food production[95]—as part of the transformative process through which "masculinity" is redefined with notions of care and interconnectivity brought to the forefront.[96] Therefore, like with ecofeminist-steeped community clean energy, it is not enough to develop strongly ecologically sustainable community-owned food systems in general sense; so, too, must Appalachian approaches to local food systems be critically just along lines of gender, race, indigenous status, and so forth.

When exploring issues relating to post-liberalism Appalachian food systems that are not just strongly ecologically sustainable, but also critically just, the strengths of adopting a materialist ecofeminist approach become readily apparent. Recall that commentators such as Agarwal—in critiquing essentialist-steeped models—have emphasized that analyses must be steeped in concrete social and environmental realities, and that thus issues relating to gender, race, class, caste, the environment, etc. specific to a particular location often result in uniquely subordinating circumstances that require niche, localized solutions.[97] Like with community clean energy systems and other dimensions of potential systemic re-formations beyond liberal capitalism, differing material realities in Appalachia, then, must be accounted for developing community food systems—which necessarily will vary by locality, region, and so forth.[98]

Many commentators indeed already have begun exploring the explicit, real-world interlinkages between local Appalachian food systems and issues such as gender. For instance, as Roxy Todd and Jessica Lilly chronicle in *Inside Appalachia*, the number of women who run farms is increasing; as the USDA has reported, women now constitute more than 30 percent of farmers and are the fastest-growing farming population.[99] As another example, the Women Farmers of Appalachia Project examines the fact that despite the "number of female farm operators" almost has "tripled in the past three decades," nevertheless, "the male-dominated perception of agriculture pervades."[100] Thus, the project's photography- and narrative-steeped "purpose is to give an honest representation of the daily lives of Appalachian women in agriculture."[101] And specific initiatives such as the North Carolina–based Blue Ridge Women in Agriculture have been formed, which is "a women-led organization that builds an equitable, sustainable High Country local food system by supporting producers and cultivating community connections that educate, inspire, and increase the demand for local food."[102]

Of course, ecofeminism also is concerned with other intertwined critical dimensions (i.e., in holistically combating the interlocking systems of subordination under late liberalism). Thus, in efforts towards establishing ecofeminist-inspired food systems, accounting for additional critical dimensions is of crucial importance. For instance, intersections between LGBTQ+ Appalachians and local foodways constitute one such significant exploration. As Cristina Maza has chronicled in "An Appalachian Haven for LGBTQ People," in one West Virginian town, an intentional community has been created wherein "a small group of young transgender people are working to transform this Appalachian community, with its dwindling population and flailing economy, into a place where LGBTQ people," with a "particular emphasis on people of color," will be able to "rebuild local ecosystems and fight for environmental justice and sustainability."[103] As Maza notes, "much of the region is politically and socially conservative," but the farm's residents "say Appalachia's open spaces and sparse population offer an opportunity for LGBTQ people who feel isolated and alone."[104] As one farm resident adds: "This hollow used to produce so much of its food, and people have gotten away from those ways . . . Community resiliency is about us being in it together and building something sustainable for generations to come. We want to live in a place where we can make connections with our neighbors, where we can grow grains that we know are going to grow in this region."[105]

Additionally, like with clean energy systems, transitions towards eco-feminist- and ecosocialist-steeped community food systems must account for issues of race and racism endemic to both Appalachia and the United States as a whole. As Alison Hope Alkon and Julian Agyeman discuss, in exploring critically just local food systems, we must adopt a materialist perspective in eschewing "essentialist notions of race and racism that ignore the socially constructed and lived dynamics of racial identities and oppressions."[106] Also, and of great importance to Appalachia, Alkon and Agyeman deploy an EJ approach to food-ways and conclude that both "low-income people and people of color have been systematically denied access to the means of food production"—and that the "food movement narrative ignores these injustices, an omission which reflects its adherents' race and class privilege."[107] Consequently, Alkon and Agyeman argue that the "cultivation of a food system that is both environmentally sustainable and socially just will require the creation of alliances between the food movement and the communities most harmed by current conditions."[108] Such a critical approach is of obvious and vital importance in Appalachia. Moreover, in line with ecofeminism's tenets, issues regarding not just race, class, and the environment but also gender, LGBTQ+ status, indigenous status, etc.—which, as has been explored throughout *Remaking Appalachia*, all serve to produce differing forms of compound oppressions given the material realities of specific localities, regions, etc.—must be holistically addressed.

For Appalachia, however, a unique problem in seeking systemic re-formations towards ecofeminist- and ecosocialist-inspired community food systems is the corporate absentee landownership phenomenon. Therefore, to achieve widespread adoption of post-liberalism local food systems—and for that matter, of essentially all other modes of systemic re-formations, such as community-owned clean energy systems—radical, post-liberalism land re-formations are required. As Shiva, Barry, and numerous other commentators have argued, expansions of the ecological commons will be a crucial dimension of this reform. As Eller broadly notes, "land ownership and use has always been at the center of the Appalachian story."[109] Also, Barry, in specifically focusing on the potential for commons expansions in Appalachia—as informed by Shiva's work—notes that many Appalachian activists "support 'commoning'" through establishing "living economies" based on "co-ownership and coproduction, on sharing and participation."[110] Herbert Reid and Betsy Taylor also explore ecological commons and related notions in Appalachia vis-à-vis a material feminist lens in *Recovering the Commons*.[111] And recall that Stoll explores using legislation to effectuate transfer of land back to the Appalachian citizenry for recommoning purposes.[112] As is discussed below, however, effectuating

Appalachian ecological recommoning from beyond the hegemonic liberalism paradigm is a crucial component of broader systemic re-formations—and, to date, mechanisms for achieving such truly radically conceived recommoning (i.e., in both the Appalachian and broader and national and global contexts) are underdeveloped. Consequently, *Remaking Appalachia* puts forth a radically re-envisioned public trust doctrine (as intertwined with radical environmental human rights) as a prime mechanism to help pursue such ecofeminist- and ecosocialist-steeped post-liberalism ecological recommoning efforts vis-à-vis a bottom-up, grassroots approach.

Ultimately, then, solidarity economy– and subsistence-based approaches in Appalachia could constitute one core dimension of ecofeminist- and eco-socialist-steeped re-formations. Moreover, community clean energy and food systems constitute two important examples—both emerging and future-projected—of what such systemic re-formations would actually entail, in a concrete sense, in Appalachia. If such ecofeminist- and ecosocialist-inspired systemic re-formations are to actually succeed in Appalachia, however, they certainly cannot occur in a vacuum. In the first place, these re-formations must be linked with comparable radical transformations at the national and global levels. As Stoll has aptly noted, merely transitioning to a "reconstituted commons" model in Central Appalachia is problematic. This is because such discrete, local-based transformations do not in and of themselves "change or challenge a political economy in which humans and environments serve as inputs in the circulation of capital."[113] Consequently, if systemic re-formations in Appalachia are to achieve long-term viability, a truly global transition away from the neoliberal capitalist paradigm is required. Those seeking systemic re-formations in Appalachia must therefore vigorously interlink their efforts with broader struggles. Moreover, in line with ecosocialist thought, such essentially bottom-up transformations must ultimately occur in conjunction with broader collective ownership modes of the means of production and democratic economic planning at all geographic levels—which a fully radicalized Green New Deal, among other options, could help effectuate (i.e., as discussed at the end of this chapter).

Furthermore, a central argument of *Remaking Appalachia* is that achieving an ecofeminist- and ecosocialist-steeped future in Appalachia and beyond could be in part effectuated and expedited vis-à-vis the systemic stepping stone measures outlined in chapter 6—i.e., environmental human rights and the public trust doctrine. Ultimately, through the infusion of critical theory, these systemic stepping stone approaches can have an explicit aim of transcending the existing hegemonic liberalism paradigm—and thus could constitute merely one component in the broader, multidimensional project of transforming those higher-level constitutive forces towards an ecofeminist- and ecosocialist-inspired future.

ENVIRONMENTAL HUMAN RIGHTS IN APPALACHIA—SYSTEMIC STEPPING STONE MEASURE

The first such systemic stepping stone measure that could be utilized in Appalachia is the critically informed approach to environmental human rights. Recall that environmental human rights are increasingly recognized in the international and domestic context around the world and that many transnational environmental justice movements rely on environmental human rights as an important framing device. However, in a general sense, the United States lags behind in that it has not recognized environmental rights nationally—and less than a dozen U.S. states have recognized such rights via constitutional amendment.[114] Nevertheless, in recent years, there has been some positive movement on environmental rights at the U.S. state level, as illustrated by the Pennsylvania *Robinson Township* line of precedent and a recent Hawaii decision affirming its constitutional right to a clean environment.

Aside from Pennsylvania, however, robust environmental human rights components are largely lacking in the legal frameworks of other Appalachian states. Some states with Appalachian territories, such as Virginia and New York, do have some measure of environmental-related language in their constitutions. For instance, the Virginia constitution, in Article XI § 2, includes non-binding environmental protection language: "The General Assembly may undertake the conservation . . . of lands or natural resources of the Commonwealth . . . and the protection of its atmosphere, lands, and waters from pollution, impairment, or destruction."[115] And the New York constitution, in Article XIV § 4, reads in pertinent part that "the policy of the state shall be to conserve and protect its natural resources and scenic beauty and encourage the development and improvement of its agricultural lands for the production of food and other agricultural products."[116] However, only a handful of U.S. states—namely, Pennsylvania, Hawaii, Montana, and Illinois—both formally establish environmental rights and "call for state action to support those rights."[117] Therefore, most states in Appalachia—including the states with Central Appalachian territories (or West Virginia, Kentucky, Tennessee, and Virginia)—lack formal constitutional recognition of environmental rights principles and supportive state action provisions.

Pursuing environmental rights furtherance in Appalachia, in a general sense, would therefore be a novel path forward for the region; however, as discussed below, radically re-envisioned environmental human rights—i.e., as conceived of beyond hegemonic liberalism—would indeed constitute a true systemic stepping stone measure towards transformative change. Of course, from the outset, it should be reemphasized that many Appalachian states (e.g., West Virginia) are characterized by conservative governmental elites—who have long vilified increased environmental protection as "job killers" for the region (as discussed in chapter 5). Therefore, it is logical that Appalachian states such as West Virginia lack explicit recognition of environmental rights principles—even as conceived of within the hegemonic liberalism paradigm.

Nevertheless, as prior chapters have demonstrated, the Appalachian population at large—through a demographic, cultural, and political heterogeneity rarely acknowledged in popular portrayals of the region—is, in fact, marked by "mixtures of political conservatism and progressive activism."[118] On the particular point of Appalachia's long and storied tradition of progressive and, at times, radical activism, recall that some of the most significant labor activism in U.S. history has occurred in the Appalachian coalfields. Moreover, as chapter 5 details, a rich grassroots movement has long existed in Appalachia and many truly intersectional-steeped organizations have emerged—which, as Schumann details in *Appalachia Revisited*, include "several environmental movements organized around overcoming racial, class, and gender barriers to participation."[119] Therefore, Appalachia "can boast of a long history of inclusive progressive politics," and despite the often conservative trends in Appalachian state governance, this rich Appalachian grassroots tradition can be tapped into in pursuing transformative environmental rights formulations in the region—i.e., in support of broader ecofeminist- and ecosocialist-steeped systemic re-formations.[120]

What is more, because systemic stepping stone approaches to environmental rights explicitly involve a bottom-up, grassroots approach, Appalachia's rich environmental resistance tradition (among other grassroots movements in the region) can serve as a preexisting foundation on which to pursue more radical environmental rights formulations. As outlined in chapter 6, such a critical approach can be achieved in Appalachia through adoption of radical approaches to cause lawyering—namely, community lawyering and radical cause lawyering.[121] With radical cause lawyering—as emanating from strains of 1960s movement lawyering and also Marxist- and socialist-steeped work—recall that transformative-minded lawyers aim "to make changes in the basic structures of society and join forces with the social movements and their transformative interests and values."[122] And with community lawyering, recall that, first, traditional hierarchies in law practice are eliminated, thus accounting for the "problem of lawyer domination over client autonomy."[123] Second, and relatedly, in transcending traditional "law reform" sites such as litigation, "advocates are encouraged to explore and to engage collaboratively with client groups in nontraditional legal fora to advance the clients' objectives, such as organizing for political action," including along radical lines.[124] Therefore, attorneys "act not as saviors or champions, but rather as partners in collective ventures to change the world."[125] In the case of Appalachia, then, the preexisting grassroots tradition can constitute the core focal point in the critically informed expansion of environmental rights principles through community and radical cause lawyering (i.e., as intertwined with allied organizing modes)—which can ultimately support transformations beyond liberal capitalism.

As also outlined in chapter 6, the critical approach rejects traditional, hegemonic liberalism-steeped modes of environmental rights establishment and furtherance—in that the critical approach requires that such efforts do not constitute ends in themselves that implicitly accept the preexisting liberal regime. In this way, a critical approach to environmental human rights furtherance—as a systemic stepping stone measure in Appalachia and beyond—can and should be deeply informed by ecofeminist and ecosocialist principles, thus explicitly linking them with broader systemic re-formation efforts. Consequently, while the Pennsylvania Environmental Rights Amendment and its recent furtherance in the *Robinson Township* line of precedent, for instance, is generally a heartening precedent, such efforts have been conceived of from within the hegemonic liberalism paradigm, and thus ultimately fail to challenge the neoliberal ecological political economy—and should not be emulated.

Rather than establishing environmental human rights vis-à-vis intra-systemic reform from within the hegemonic liberalism paradigm and then working through traditional, liberal-steeped litigation to further such rights—such as was the case with Pennsylvania—instead, through a critically informed approach, the core starting place is a bottom-up, grassroots approach explicitly steeped in systemic re-formations. As introduced in chapter 6, this can entail radical cause lawyers—i.e., radical cause lawyers who are actually *from* the Appalachian localities at issue—and allied organizers deploying a radical "frame transformation" of the "collective action frame" surrounding environmental human rights in helping to drive mass political mobilization towards post-liberalism ends. And of course, such mobilization ultimately would be led by ordinary West Virginian citizens, Appalachian grassroots organizations, etc. (i.e., who also would co-determine the ultimate nature of re-envisioned human rights beyond the basic frame introduced by organizers). For instance, in using

West Virginia as a case model, beyond merely discussing furtherance of intra-systemic substantive and procedural environmental human rights with the state citizenry, radical cause lawyers instead can convey that such rights are ultimately *unattainable* under the current economic, social, political, and environmental conditions of capital accumulation– and perpetual growth–modeled hegemonic liberalism—and that systemic re-formations are thus required to guarantee such rights.

The rhetorics surrounding such a radical "frame transformation" of environmental human rights in the Appalachian context could be relatively straightforward. For instance, in Appalachia, what good would environmental human rights do—as only legally established—if the century-old, colossally destructive fossil fuel hegemony remained in force vis-à-vis the hegemonic status quo? Likewise, many West Virginians lack provision of basic environmental human rights–related services such as clean water, adequate food, and sewerage services—i.e., due not just to the fossil fuel hegemony but also to other neoliberal-associated ills such as deteriorating public infrastructure and the failure of neoliberalized food production for rural areas. Again, in terms of radical cause lawyer–deployed rhetorics, what good would legally established environmental human rights do in and of themselves without a comprehensive transformation of an ecological political economy that fails to provide even the basic necessities of water, food, and sanitation? And so too, in time, could the worsening ecological conditions produced by climate change in Appalachia (e.g., heatwaves, fires, and floods) factor into the rhetoric of the radical "frame transformation" of environmental human rights.

Rhetorics involving clean water, sewerage services, and other basic necessities likely would garner more immediate traction in certain swaths of Appalachia than arguments directly targeting, for instance, the fossil fuel hegemony; a materialist-steeped organizing approach would therefore need to account for such realities. Similarly, some Appalachian communities may be more receptive to essentially positive rhetoric on the ultimate benefits of systemic re-formations—as compared to solely negative rhetoric on the multifaceted ills of liberal capitalism.[126] In the end, however, rhetoric surrounding such a frame transformation must indeed include transcending hegemonic liberal capitalism as a fundamental prerequisite for guaranteeing environmental human rights—as is required in the accelerating catastrophe of the Capitalocene. As compared to Pennsylvania's good-faith (but fundamentally flawed) intra-systemic furtherance of environmental rights from within the liberal paradigm, such radical formulations would therefore truly serve as systemic stepping stone measures in constituting a bridge towards transformative ends in Appalachia and beyond.

As outlined in chapter 6, other dimensions of ecofeminism and ecosocialism can inform such radically re-envisioned environmental human rights. That is, critical concerns relating not just to the environment but also to race, gender, sexuality, class, indigenous status, etc. must be part and parcel of the furtherance of environmental human rights as systemic stepping stone measures in Appalachia. Moreover, an explicit ecofeminist approach to such critical environmental rights concerns also would explore intersectional issues—or the manner in which dominance systems (based on race, gender, etc.) are interlocking under liberal capitalism. Ecofeminism and ecosocialism also dictate that radically reconceived environmental rights must be simultaneously furthered at all levels—namely, the local, regional, national, and global levels. Recall that pursuing systemic re-formations at such differing geographic scales is required to account for both niche, localized concerns (i.e., per a materialist approach)—and also to ensure that truly national and global transformations of the neoliberal political economy transpire. For instance, the United States remains a notable global holdout in recognizing environmental rights at the national level (i.e., even in the intra-systemic hegemonic liberalism context); therefore, even while seeking radically reconceived environmental rights expansions in Appalachia, radical cause lawyers, allied organizers, and the broader citizenry should, at the same time, interlink these efforts with national and international work.

Ultimately, then, radically re-envisioned environmental human rights are potent systemic stepping stone measures in pursuing truly transformative change in Appalachia and beyond. The crux of such a critically informed approach is bottom-up, grassroots efforts in which radical cause lawyers and allied organizers drive mass political mobilization around the radically reframed notion that environmental human rights are unattainable under hegemonic liberal capitalism—and that therefore systemic re-formations along potentially ecofeminist- and ecosocialist-steeped lines are required.

PUBLIC TRUST DOCTRINE IN APPALACHIA—SYSTEMIC STEPPING STONE MEASURE

The public trust doctrine is a second systemic stepping stone measure that could be deployed in Appalachia and beyond. As discussed in chapter 6, the public trust doctrine has ancient roots; in the modern context, the doctrine is well-established worldwide—i.e., in individual nations and is increasingly discussed vis-à-vis international law—and also is well-embedded in U.S. law specifically. Similar to environmental rights, following the environmental revolution of the 1960s, the public trust doctrine was reinvigorated and explored as a potential path forward for enhanced environmental governance. This movement, as pioneered by Joseph Sax, was generally stalled in favor of the hyper-technical environmental regulatory regime that would come to dominate environmental law. But in recent years, Mary Wood (among other commentators) has championed a return to—and the vigorous expansion of—the public trust doctrine, given the comprehensive failures of environmental law and the profound urgency of the global ecological crisis.[127]

As previously discussed, at both the U.S. state and federal levels, there has been recent progress in furthering the public trust doctrine. In a very broad sense, the public trust doctrine is recognized throughout the entirety of the U.S. legal system. And while the doctrine traditionally has relied on courts for furtherance, it is the state and federal legislatures—as primary U.S.-democratic lawmakers—that constitute the central trustees of the public's natural assets. And similar to environmental rights, following the 1960s environmental revolution, there was some movement to constitutionally expand the public trust doctrine at the U.S. state level, as illustrated by the Pennsylvania and Hawaii state constitutional amendments.

In the case of Appalachia, most notably, the Pennsylvania 1971 Environmental Rights Amendment contains intertwined environmental rights and public trust language that has been recently furthered in the *Robinson Township* line of precedent. The Pennsylvania constitutional trust language reads in pertinent part: "As trustee of these resources, the Commonwealth shall conserve and maintain them for the benefit of all the people."[128] As another, less robust Appalachian example, Virginia's constitutional Article XI contains language that implicitly supports the doctrine.[129] Additionally, at the statutory level, Tennessee enacted the state Safe Drinking Water Act recognizing that "that the waters of the state are the property of the state and are held in public trust for the benefit of its citizens" and declares "that the people of the state are beneficiaries of this trust and have a right to both an adequate quantity and quality of drinking water."[130] The state Water Quality Control Act also recognizes "that the waters of Tennessee are the property of the state and are held in public trust for the use of the people of the state."[131] However, Tennessee case law has not, in a general sense, furthered these principles. Therefore, by and large, the public trust doctrine is not expansively conceived in Appalachia (i.e., even within the hegemonic liberalism paradigm)—constitutionally, statutorily, or through case law. What is more, those public trust components that are established throughout Appalachian states certainly have failed, to date, to protect the Appalachian environment and human communities from the comprehensive industry-based devastation outlined in prior chapters.

Similar to environmental human rights, a radical, critically informed approach to the public trust doctrine could therefore constitute a potent systemic stepping stone measure towards systemic re-formations. Recall that Wood, among others, has pioneered novel approaches to the doctrine that aim to account for the urgency posed by the global ecological crisis. As Wood argues, a greatly expanded approach "must push beyond current limitations associated with the public trust doctrine," [132] through which "the whole of our natural assets—air, atmosphere, oceans, rivers, wetlands, aquifers, forests, wildlife, soils, and more—should be regarded as an 'ecological res [thing] that government must protect.' " [133] To secure such an expanded public trust paradigm, Wood recommends not just pursuing enhanced state-level litigation (the traditional mechanism through public trust principles are pursued), but also furtherance through legislative and administrative dimensions; expansions at the local, federal, and international levels; and approaches to the doctrine that extend beyond mere legal furtherance to include "a political concept, an ethical mooring, a diplomatic framework, and an economic principle." [134]

Recall that beyond such theorizing, allied attorneys and academics have also legally pursued such expanded public trust components—such as through the Our Children's Trust organization, which has a mission of "elevat[ing] the voice of youth to secure the legal right to a stable climate and healthy atmosphere for the benefit of all present and future generations." [135] The Ninth Circuit ATL case *Juliana v. U.S.*, as brought by youth plaintiffs, constitutes the most prominent, federal-level example of such action. However, as part and parcel of the ongoing efforts to pursue expanded notions of the public trust at differing legal levels—and throughout the entirely of the United States— Our Children's Trust has also pursued state-level action to further the public trust doctrine throughout Appalachia: the organization has "supported youth around the United States in bringing legal action in the courts and state administrative agencies of their states, to advance science-based climate recovery action at the state level." [136]

In again using West Virginia as a case model, Our Children's Trust utilized state-level administrative channels as the most expedient route to pursue expanded, climate change–related trust principles in the state. That is, Our Children's Trust assisted West Virginia young persons and partners to file a 2011 rulemaking petition, reading in pertinent part: "On behalf of its members, the citizens of the State of West Virginia, and present and future generations of minor children, the petitioner respectfully requests that the West Virginia Department of Environmental Protection and the Air Quality Division promulgate a rule that requires the agency to take the necessary steps in order to protect the integrity of Earth's climate by adequately protecting our atmosphere, a public trust resource upon which all West Virginia residents rely for their health, safety, sustenance, and security." [137] While this petition "was not accepted by state officials," further efforts by Our Children's Trust are on-going. [138] What is more, at a foundational level, the petition "raised awareness in the state about the scientific remedies necessary to address climate change and educated state officials about their duty to protect the atmosphere." [139]

However, like radically reconceived environmental human rights discussed above, re-envisioning the public trust doctrine as a true systemic stepping stone measure would require explicitly transcending the hegemonic liberalism paradigm entirely—which both the Pennsylvania constitutionally established public trust doctrine and ATL fail to encompass. The same general critical principles outlined above in the environmental human rights context also could be applied in furthering the re-envisioned public trust doctrine in Appalachia as an explicit systemic stepping stone measure. In again using West Virginia as a case model, a bottom-up, grassroots approach could be cultivated, in which radical cause lawyers and allied organizers again explicitly frame transcending the hegemonic liberalism paradigm as a core characteristic of a re-envisioned public trust doctrine—and in which, thereafter, the broad West Virginia citizenry, grassroots organizations, etc. would both co-determine the ultimate nature of the re-envisioned doctrine and would actually lead the efforts to further the doctrine as an explicit systemic stepping stone measure. This would again entail a radical "frame transformation" of the doctrine towards post-liberalism ends—i.e., a concrete example of which is outlined below in the Appalachian ecological recommoning context.

So, too, could the radically re-envisioned public trust doctrine simultaneously be furthered at local, regional, national, and international levels. And like radically reframed environmental human rights, critical concerns relating to gender, race, sexuality, etc. (i.e., along ecofeminist lines) could be incorporated into public trust doctrine furtherance. On this point, entwining the doctrine with radically re-envisioned environmental human rights—which, as noted above, greatly lends itself to an intersectional-steeped approach—constitutes a crucial strategy. It indeed has been widely noted that "by linking the . . . Public Trust Doctrine to the modern Environmental Human Rights movement, citizens, scholars, and lawyers can promote a world of deeper equity for individuals, communities, and the natural world." [140] This similarly holds true in the explicit systemic re-formation context—i.e., both systemic stepping stone measures can synergistically enhance the other. Therefore, a radically reframed public trust doctrine, as interlinked with re-envisioned environmental human rights, indeed could constitute a potent bridge towards transformative ends in Appalachia.

EFFECTUATING ECOLOGICAL RECOMMONING: RADICALLY RECONCEIVED PUBLIC TRUST DOCTRINE ENTWINED WITH RADICAL ENVIRONMENTAL HUMAN RIGHTS

In exploring a truly radically conceived approach to the public trust doctrine, a return to the issue of ecological recommoning in Appalachia and beyond— i.e., which simultaneously could help redress mass corporate absentee land-ownership in the region—is one particularly useful dimension through which the doctrine might help transcend hegemonic liberalism. As noted above, commentators such as Barry and Stoll have explored recommoning in Appalachia, but the mechanisms through which this might be achieved remain highly speculative at this point in time. Stoll, for instance, puts forth the federal Commons Communities Act as one potential mechanism, while acknowledging that such hypothetical legislation would prove problematic in failing to challenge the broader neoliberal paradigm.[141]

However, the public trust doctrine, as radically re-envisioned, could help transcend mere liberal land reform approaches, and could potentially help catalyze widespread, grassroots-driven ecological recommoning as conceived of beyond hegemonic liberalism—i.e., in direct support of ecofeminist- and ecosocialist-steeped solidarity economy– and subsistence-based modes. What is more, as facilitated by the recent worldwide advancement of the public trust doctrine (and as intertwined with critically informed environmental human rights), a radically re-envisioned approach to the doctrine could further the broader (and absolutely essential) national and global recommoning efforts as similarly conceived of beyond hegemonic liberalism.

Recall also that chapter 6 explores the notion that "combining the best aspects of eco-socialism with the powerful practice of commoning and the commons" is a deeply worthwhile project.[142] More specifically, such an ecosocialist approach can involve "inverting the neoliberal usage of the state for enhancing the process of commodification into enhancing the practices of 'commonification' instead."[143] The radically re-envisioned public trust doctrine that follows is therefore one dimension through which state action might indeed effectuate such recommoning. And recall that such recommoning modes can dovetail with diverse democratic public ownership approaches and democratic planning precepts as well (i.e., as broached in the radicalized Green New Deal discussion that follows). As Toivanen argues, we need not expend too much energy "distinguish[ing] theoretically between commons and public," as the "public and the commons are seen as two complementary sites of active political struggle,"[144] and what is more, the "commons need to be collectively protected, planned and regulated."[145]

Most fundamentally, the public trust doctrine dictates that the "natural commons should be held in trust as assets to serve the public good," and that "it is the responsibility of the government, as trustee, to protect these assets from harm and ensure their use for the public and future generations."[146] The public trust doctrine thus constitutes "a powerful, venerable legal tool to uphold the principle that the State must act as a conscientious trustee of ecological commons."[147] Of course, in the United States, the public trust doctrine has historically been conceived of within hegemonic liberalism (i.e., as the Pennsylvania constitutional and ATL-related examples illustrate above), and in a relatively limited fashion. In a formalist-legal sense, public trust notions also are traditionally distinguishable from the commons per se—in that commons include a broad range of public benefits or goods that can extend beyond a state regime, whereas the public trust doctrine implicates a state actor's fiduciary duties to citizenry-beneficiaries as involves public natural resources exclusively.[148]

That said, some commentators have called for reexamining the public trust doctrine vis-à-vis furtherance of ecological commons notions specifically. Wood, for instance, notes that "much can be gained by positioning the trust within the broader commons movement," because the "term 'commons' holds galvanizing popular force when used broadly on the less formal and more generic level" and "it strikes a chord for citizens yearning to free their communities from the state's environmental oppression and corruption."[149] Similarly, Burns Weston and David Bollier argue in *Green Governance* that "the public trust doctrine provides a legal framework for the State to define common ownership of natural resources and authorizes State action to protect them," and that "by seeing the State as a trustee of the Commons, we can entertain a more constructive array of State management options."[150] Weston and Bollier thus conclude that the "trust is a familiar legal form that can serve as a template for designing new sorts of commons institutions."[151]

However, a truly radically re-envisioned public trust doctrine could be formulated. Most basically, a bottom-up, grassroots approach to a radically re-envisioned, ecofeminist- and ecosocialist-steeped public trust doctrine could help drive mass political mobilization towards post-liberalism ecological recommoning efforts in Appalachia and beyond. Radical cause lawyering could once again help efforts towards a radical "frame transformation" of the public trust doctrine to help achieve such transformative ends—which, by very design, would be part and parcel of the project to transcend liberal property rights generally and mass corporate absentee ownership of Appalachian land in particular. The central rhetorics surrounding such a radically re-envisioned public trust doctrine could be that, in support of solidarity economy– and subsistence-based transformations, the state must designate land of various localities and sub-regions as the natural commons of Appalachians—including the vast swaths of land currently owned by absentee corporations—and that such commons could thereafter be held in trust for the Appalachian people and future generations vis-à-vis various collective governance modes.[152] On this latter point, "commons trusts" also are relevant and indeed have been discussed as dovetailing specifically with expanded public trust doctrine conceptions;[153] commons trusts allow for a "participatory culture of stewardship" and local-level "commons-based participation," including in the context of land commons.[154] The core idea is that, in the end, "commoners can and should come together to create their own governance mechanisms."[155] And such re-envisioned commons trusts similarly, of course, would be conceived of beyond hegemonic liberalism. Furthermore, such commons should be held in trust along strongly ecologically sustainable lines, as guaranteed by radical environmental human rights principles put forth in *Remaking Appalachia*.

As Weston and Bollier note above, the public trust doctrine already provides the framework for the "State to define common ownership of natural resources and authorizes State action to protect them"[156] and otherwise creates "a duty to manage trust resources for broad public benefit"[157]—rhetorics relating to a re-envisioned public trust doctrine, therefore, transforms such governance actions towards truly radical, redistributive ends. Additionally, as discussed above, commentators already have called for transforming the public trust doctrine beyond its current paradigm, including through all modes of governance and beyond law reform to include broad political mobilization. Thus, while a radical "frame transformation" of the doctrine towards post-liberalism ends is a truly transformative approach, the notion of extending the public trust doctrine to meet the exigencies of the global ecological crisis is, in a general sense, well-established. On the point of radical transformations, it further can be noted that many commentators have linked public trust conceptions with Marx's observations. As Peter Sand argues in "Accountability for the Commons: Reconsiderations," in the "inter-temporal context," public trust "beneficiaries also include future generations, as postulated more than

150 years ago by Karl Marx."[158] Marx's specific comments are as follows: "Even society as a whole, a nation, or all contemporary societies taken together, are not owners of the Earth. They are merely its occupants, its users: and as diligent caretakers, must hand it down improved to subsequent generations."[159]

The public trust doctrine is also well positioned for interlinking regional recommoning work with national and global efforts, as in recent decades, general furtherance of the doctrine has occurred in different nations, has been explored in the international law context, and has catalyzed renewed, vital discussions on global commons resources such as the atmosphere and oceans. And also as noted above, so, too, would entwined radical environmental human rights components facilitate transnational organizing potentially along recommoning lines.

It must be emphasized, however, that ecological recommoning constitutes a particularly contentious dimension of systemic re-formation, given the historic centrality of private real property rights, in particular, under liberalism; thus, the hegemonic status quo would vigorously contest such efforts.[160] As a consequence, again, the only way to achieve such transformative ends— i.e., ecological recommoning as one crucial dimension of true systemic re-formations beyond hegemonic liberalism—is indeed a bottom-up, grassroots approach to such doctrinal-transformation as driven by mass political mobilization that radical cause lawyering (as interlinked with allied organizing) could engender. Also, in the Appalachian context especially, such ecological recommoning efforts as potentially driven by a radically re-envisioned public trust doctrine or related lines would be greatly facilitated by the fact that vast swaths of such targeted lands are, in fact, held by absentee corporate owners. The mass of Appalachian citizenry suffering under neoliberal capitalism's crisis conditions—i.e., a citizenry that actually lives around such recommoning sites—would therefore be less sympathetic (from a collective action frame perspective) to legal-formalistic defenses on the part of far-removed, exploitative corporate entities. And as Reid and Taylor argue, land commons also are part and parcel of historical Appalachian modes, as "regions (such as Appalachia in the United States) that were locked outside the core of the world system have often been able, paradoxically, to nurture civic and ecological commons that provide an alternative (or supplementary) means of subsistence," as was also chronicled in early chapters of Remaking Appalachia.[161] Rhetorics deployed by radical cause lawyers and allied organizers to support this radical "frame transformation," then, could emphasize such crucial points.

Furthermore, to combat a recalcitrant status quo that surely will invoke the formalistic-legal protections of hegemonic liberalism if recommoning (and related transformative modes) are effectuated, a grassroots approach to systemic re-formations can draw on the vital concept of "radical democracy." As Robin Celikates articulates, "institutions and channels themselves" can "become obstacles to democratic action," and therefore radical democracy-steeped action constitutes "a form of struggle in which the vertical form of state authority is confronted with the horizontal power of the association of citizens or the governed."[162] Similarly, a radical democracy-informed approach to civil disobedience "dramatiz[es] . . . the tension between the poles of positive law and existing democratic processes and institutions on the one hand, and the idea of democracy as self-government on the other, which is not exhausted by established law and the institutional status quo."[163] (And indeed, beyond land recommoning, it is now commonly noted that radical democracy precepts and civil disobedience, in particular, likely are required for true systemic re-formations beyond liberal capitalism across *all* dimensions.)[164] Recall also that as Stoll notes on Appalachian recommoning on land: "people can do it themselves, by squatting on abandoned land and defending their right to the commons."[165] And as prior chapters chronicle, Appalachia indeed exhibits an, at times, robust radical democracy tradition that can be drawn on, as illustrated by the early twentieth-century coal wars and subsequent militant labor organizing, a rich grassroots environmental resistance tradition, and so forth. Ultimately, then, notions of radical democracy might fruitfully be explored in the context of a radically reconceived public trust doctrine and other modes of systemic re-formations.

It should be recognized that even radically reconceived rhetorics surrounding the public trust doctrine and related notions (e.g., re-envisioned commons trusts) could be insufficient, in and of themselves, to wholly achieve such postliberalism recommoning efforts. However, as radically re-envisioned, such rhetorics indeed certainly could constitute one cornerstone framing device in achieving such transformative ends.

RADICALIZED GREEN NEW DEAL: REVOLUTIONARY GLOBAL CONVERSION OF FOSSIL FUEL ECONOMY

The Green New Deal has, in recent times, been popularized as an ambitious project to combat both climate change and the intertwined systemic ills of late liberalism—including poverty and other forms of subordination along lines of race, gender, indigenous status, and so forth. *Remaking Appalachia*, therefore, will conclude by examining the Green New Deal proposal vis-à-vis the prescriptive recommendations outlined above. Although notions of a Green New Deal have been relatively long discussed, the concept has been revitalized through a joint resolution spearheaded by the democratic socialist representative Alexandria Ocasio-Cortez. (It should be noted from the outset, however, that the Green New Deal is still in a nascent phase through both this specific proposal and in competing variations.) This particular iteration of the Green New Deal would vastly reduce all U.S. greenhouse gas emissions within a decade through massive national mobilization and investment aimed at "meeting 100 percent of the power demand in the United States through clean, renewable, and zero-emission energy sources."[166] The resolution also aims, through an "economic mobilization on a scale not seen since World War II and the New Deal," to "create millions of good, high-wage jobs in the United States."[167] Such a Green New Deal–based mobilization allegedly would "provide unprecedented levels of prosperity and economic security for all people of the United States."[168]

The Green New Deal resolution has additional dimensions significant for *Remaking Appalachia*. For instance, environmental human rights principles are at least implicitly raised, in stating that it will "secure for all people of the United States for generations to come—(i) clean air and water; (ii) climate and community resiliency; (iii) healthy food; (iv) access to nature; and (v) a sustainable environment."[169] An entwined provision thereafter addresses "systemic injustice" concerns, in stating that the proposal further will "promote justice and equity by stopping current, preventing future, and repairing historic oppression of indigenous peoples, communities of color, migrant communities, deindustrialized communities, depopulated rural communities, the poor, low-income workers, women, the elderly, the unhoused, people with disabilities, and youth."[170] Many such "frontline and vulnerable communities" would, of course, include Appalachian communities—and indeed, an earlier formulation of the Green New Deal had an explicit goal of "diversify[ing] local and regional economies, with a particular focus on communities where the fossil fuel industry holds significant control over the labor market."[171] Lastly, certain Green New Deal sub-provisions, such as those focusing on "building a more sustainable food system that ensures universal access to healthy food" also have important implications for *Remaking Appalachia*, given the systemic re-formation proposals discussed above involving local food systems.[172]

In an overarching sense, then, the Green New Deal is a heartening development. In particular, the elimination of greenhouse gas emissions is of paramount importance. If the mobilization envisioned by the Green New Deal is effectuated, one of the most dire dimensions of the global ecological crisis—i.e., climate change—would be combated directly and on a potentially swift timeline. Additionally, the intertwined aims of reducing poverty, implicitly furthering the environmental human rights of clean air and water, combating environmental injustices (i.e., through the emphasis on "systemic injustice" concerns of race, gender, etc.), and the focus on "frontline and vulnerable communities," such as Central Appalachia, are also positive developments generally.[173] This iteration of the Green New Deal, which has reverberated dramatically throughout the United States and globally, has also beneficially shifted the needle on "political practicality" concerns regarding systemic solutions to the global ecological crisis. (Recall that such "political practicality" concerns are unpacked at length in the introduction.) Thus, beyond the joint resolution's proposals per se, the Green New Deal has succeeded in further popularizing the true implications of the ecological crisis and of potential transformative solutions among the general citizenry.

At the same, however, there are potential structural flaws inherent in the Green New Deal that *Remaking Appalachia* unveils; consequently, to avoid failure, the Green New Deal must be explicitly conceptualized from beyond hegemonic liberalism and driven from the radical grassroots—and additional synergistic, bottom-up approaches are required such as those explored earlier in this chapter and in chapter 6. In the first place, although the Green New Deal is indeed an ambitious proposal (and while it remains at a nascent stage), crucial dimensions of the proposal seemingly fail to challenge the liberal capitalist paradigm at large, or otherwise have the strong potential to be co-opted by hegemonic capitalism.[174] Under the Green New Deal, then, even with zero greenhouse gas emissions, the capitalist mode of production potentially could persist with its "drive for capital accumulation and deliberative progressive commodification of everything" and its perpetual growth imperative.[175] Consequently, with a Green-New-Deal-as-embedded-in-hegemonic-liberalism, other dimensions of the global ecological crisis beyond climate change would continue potentially unabated—such as the global overuse of renewable resources (i.e., exemplified by the biodiversity loss crisis now popularized as the sixth mass extinction, as discussed in chapter 5). Relatedly, the "systemic injustice" concerns outlined in the Green New Deal along lines of race, gender, indigenous status, etc. are a fundamental characteristic of capitalism; thus, as potentially embedded in hegemonic patriarchal capitalism, the Green New Deal would be incapable of genuinely challenging such interlocking subordination systems.[176] (Recall that E.O. 12898, or the Environmental Justice Executive Order, has similar language addressing systemic injustices but has failed utterly due to its liberal character.)

For Appalachia specifically, the Green New Deal also proves to be further problematic due its essential top-down approach to date.[177] In this way, the proposal merely mirrors prior liberal development modes implemented in the region—such as the 1930s New Deal and the 1960s War on Poverty (i.e., as detailed in chapter 3)—which, despite constituting essentially sincere, good-faith efforts on the part of national policymakers, ultimately failed the region due to a top-down approach as embedded in hegemonic liberalism. Therefore, even if a fully operationalized Green New Deal combats crucial dimensions of the global ecological crisis, Appalachia—along with many other similarly situated regions throughout the United States and world—would nevertheless require niche, materialist-steeped bottom-up approaches in order to achieve truly transformative futures. What is more, as chapter 6 also notes, a fully radicalized Green New Deal only could be effectuated, in the first place, vis-à-vis mass, bottom-up political mobilization modes reflecting acute class struggles.

A fully radicalized Green New Deal, however—as steeped in ecofeminism and ecosocialism—could indeed constitute one core dimension of the systemic re-formations outlined in *Remaking Appalachia*. Specifically, a radicalized Green New Deal could exhibit the broader collective ownership modes and the multi-level democratic economic planning required at not just the local and regional levels, but also the national and global scales (i.e., as introduced in chapter 6)—for a complete, revolutionary conversion of energy production and other key sectors (e.g., healthcare).[178] As Löwy has argued, "the whole productive system must be transformed, and this can only be done by ecosocialist methods: i.e., through a democratic planning of the economy" and "public control over the means of production" that as a first step requires the wholesale elimination of fossil fuel sources,[179] and the immediate transition to diverse democratic public ownership– and cooperative-steeped approaches to the new clean energy system at large (e.g., dismantling for-profit utilities).[180] A fully radicalized Green New Deal, among other alternatives, could thus help accomplish such ends on a universal scale.

In contrast to a Green New Deal as potentially conceived of from within hegemonic liberalism, then, *Remaking Appalachia* has argued that liberal capitalism must be transcended in its entirety. Given hegemonic liberalism's multidimensional ecological, economic, social, and political crises—i.e., together, the combined crises of the Capitalocene—the Green New Deal, if furthered from within the hegemonic liberal capitalism paradigm, will fail. However, a fully radicalized Green New Deal could be catalyzed at the grassroots level and effectuated synergistically with such niche, bottom-up modes as outlined in this chapter—while simultaneously exhibiting broader collective ownership and democratic economic planning dimensions required for truly comprehensive systemic re-formations beyond liberal capitalism.

CONCLUSION

The environmental law paradigm, as embedded within hegemonic liberalism, has comprehensively failed Appalachia. Due to such failures, fossil fuel and related industries, such as the coal, oil and gas, and chemical sectors, continue to despoil the Appalachian environment while simultaneously wreaking economic, social, and political devastation on the region—as identified by the resource curse and energy sacrifice zone explanatory models. What is more, in the age of Capitalocene, Appalachia, along with the broader United States and world, faces the truly existential threat posed by the global ecological crisis. The liberal paradigm, in which environmental law merely supports ceaseless capital accumulation through "commodification of everything" and perpetual growth, is therefore a bankrupt model. Environmental "law reform" should therefore be abandoned in favor of true systemic re-formations of "higher-level" systems—i.e., transformations beyond the neoliberal ecological political economy in Appalachia and beyond.

Remaking Appalachia ultimately posits that such systemic re-formations, to be both strongly sustainable and critically just (along lines of class, gender, race, sexuality, indigenous communities, etc.) should be informed by ecofeminism and ecosocialism. As compared to capital accumulation– and perpetual growth–centered neoliberal capitalism, ecofeminist- and ecosocialist-inspired systemic re-formations are based on meeting basic and authentic needs only through a focus primarily on production for use value, as concretely operationalized vis-à-vis such modes as radical solidarity economy and subsistence approaches. Also required is linking Appalachian struggles with broader sites of re-formations, which will by necessity include broader collective ownership modes and democratic planning from local to global levels (i.e., which a fully radicalized Green New Deal could help accomplish). As this chapter detailed, two preexisting sites of nascent Appalachian systemic change include community-based clean energy and local food systems, and through an infusion of ecofeminist and ecosocialist theory and praxis, such nascent sites could be radically expanded in pursuing a truly bottom-up, grassroots approach to post-liberal capitalism re-formations.

While such ecofeminist- and ecosocialist-steeped systemic re-formations are required in Appalachia and beyond—and while failed liberal environmental law indeed should be transcended—a radical, critically informed approach to such paradigms as environmental human rights and the public trust doctrine can serve as systemic stepping stone measures, which could help effectuate, expedite, and deeply inform such systemic re-formations through mobilizing the broad citizenry towards modes of transformative change. As put forth in *Remaking Appalachia*, a concrete example of such systemic stepping stone measures is post-liberalism ecological recommoning that a radically re-envisioned public trust doctrine—as entwined with critically informed environmental human rights—could help engender. For Appalachia and the world at large, such a radical approach to economic and socio-legal transformations is no doubt required to secure a just and ecologically viable future in the age of the Capitalocene.

NOTES

INTRODUCTION

1. Rebecca R. Scott, *Removing Mountains: Extracting Nature and Identity in the Appalachian Coalfields* (Minneapolis: University of Minnesota Press, 2010), 31.
2. Scott, 31.
3. Leigh Brownhill and Terisa E. Turner, "Ecofeminism at the Heart of Ecosocialism," *Capitalism, Nature, Socialism* 30, no. 1 (2019): 5.
4. John R. Burch, *Owsley County, Kentucky, and the Perpetuation of Poverty* (Jefferson: McFarland, 2008), 11–14.
5. William Schumann, "Introduction: Place and Place-Making in Appalachia," in *Appalachia Revisited: New Perspectives on Place, Tradition, and Progress*, ed. William Schumann and Rebecca Adkins Fletcher (Lexington: University Press of Kentucky, 2016), 7.
6. Stefano B. Longo, Rebecca Clausen, and Brett Clark, *The Tragedy of the Commodity: Oceans, Fisheries, and Aquaculture* (New Brunswick, NJ: Rutgers University Press, 2015), 152.
7. Andreas Malm, *Fossil Capital: The Rise of Steam Power and the Roots of Global Warming* (Brooklyn: Verso, 2016), 319.
8. Geoffrey L. Buckley, "History of Coal Mining in Appalachia," in *Concise Encyclopedia of the History of Energy*, ed. Cutler J. Cleveland (San Diego, CA: Elsevier, 2009), 17–18.
9. Ronald L. Lewis, *Transforming the Appalachian Countryside: Railroads, Deforestation, and Social Change in West Virginia 1880–1920* (Chapel Hill: University of North Carolina Press, 1998), 3.
10. Wilma A. Dunaway, "The Incorporation of Mountain Ecosystems into the Capitalist World-System," *Review (Fernand Braudel Center)* 19, no. 4 (1996): 379.
11. Michael M'Gonigle and Louise Takeda, "The Liberal Limits of Environmental Law: A Green Legal Critique," *Pace Environmental Law Review* 30, no. 3 (2013): 1022.
12. M'Gonigle and Louise Takeda, 1022, 1066.
13. Ronald D. Eller, "Foreward," in *Back Talk From Appalachia: Confronting Stereotypes*, ed. Dwight B. Billings, Gurney Norman, and Katherine Ledford (Lexington: University Press of Kentucky, 2000), ix–x; Mary K. Anglin, "Engendering the Struggle: Women's Labor and Traditions of Resistance in Rural Southern Appalachia," in *Fighting Back in Appalachia: Traditions of Resistance and Change*, ed. Stephen L. Fisher (Philadelphia: Temple University Press, 1993), 275.
14. Richard B. Drake, *A History of Appalachia* (Lexington: University Press of Kentucky, 2004), 179.
15. Longo, Clausen, and Clark, *The Tragedy of the Commodity*, 32.
16. M'Gonigle and Takeda, "The Liberal Limits of Environmental Law," 1028–29.
17. Mary Christina Wood, *Nature's Trust: Environmental Law for a New Ecological Age* (New York: Cambridge University Press, 2013), 57–60.

18. M'Gonigle and Takeda, "The Liberal Limits of Environmental Law," 1006.
19. Ellen O'Loughlin, "Questioning Sour Grapes: Ecofeminism and the United Farm Workers Grape Boycott," in *Ecofeminism: Women, Animals, Nature*, ed. Greta Gaard (Philadelphia: Temple University Press, 2010), 148.
20. Maria Mies and Vandana Shiva, *Ecofeminism* (London: Zed Books, 1993), 320.
21. Philip Alston, "Statement on Visit to the USA," United Nations Human Rights Office of the High Commissioner, December 15, 2017, https://www.ohchr.org/EN/NewsEvents /Pages/DisplayNews.aspx?NewsID=22533.
22. Edward N. Wolff, "Household Wealth Trends in the United States, 1962 to 2016: Has Middle Class Wealth Recovered?," Working Paper 24085, National Bureau of Economic Research (2017): 68.
23. Alston, "Statement on Visit to the USA."
24. Alston.
25. Mies and Shiva, *Ecofeminism*, 319.
26. *Oposa v. Factoran*, C.R. No. 101083 (1993), quoted in Wood, *Nature's Trust*, 156.
27. "Summary for Policymakers of IPCC Special Report on Global Warming of 1.5°C Approved by Governments," Intergovernmental Panel on Climate Change, accessed December 5, 2019, https://www.ipcc.ch/2018/10/08/summary-for-policymakers-of -ipcc-special-report-on-global-warming-of-1-5c-approved-by-governments/.
28. Elizabeth Catte, *What You Are Getting Wrong About Appalachia* (Cleveland: Belt Publishing, 2017), 22–26.
29. Nicholas F. Stump and Anne Marie Lofaso, "De-Essentializing Appalachia: Transformative Socio-Legal Change Requires Unmasking Regional Myths," *West Virginia Law Review* 120, no. 3 (2018): 823.
30. "Mission and Methodologies," Highlander Research and Education Center, accessed December 5, 2019, https://www.highlandercenter.org/our-story/mission/.
31. Sarah Jones, "The West Virginia Teachers' Strike Takes Aim at Coal and Gas," *The New Republic*, March 2, 2018, https://newrepublic.com/article/147266/west-virginia -teachers-strike-takes-aim-coal-gas.
32. Valeria Strauss, "This Time, It Wasn't about Pay: West Virginia Teachers Go on Strike over the Privatization of Public Education (And They Won't Be the Last)," *Washington Post*, February 19, 2019, https://www.washingtonpost.com/education/2019/02/20 /this-time-it-wasnt-about-pay-west-virginia-teachers-go-strike-over-privatization -public-education-they-wont-be-last/?utm_term=.7534fb5f0739.
33. Jean Haskell, "Assessing the Landscape of Local Food in Appalachia," Report, Appalachian Regional Commission (2012), https://www.arc.gov/images/programs /entrep/AssessingLandscapeofLocalFoodinAppalachia.pdf.
34. Stephen L. Fisher, "Introduction," in *Fighting Back in Appalachia: Traditions of Resistance and Change*, ed. Stephen L. Fisher (Philadelphia: Temple University Press, 1993), 12.
35. Mies and Shiva, *Ecofeminism*, 297.

CHAPTER 1

1. James Green, *The Devil Is Here in These Hills: West Virginia's Coal Miners and Their Battle for Freedom* (New York: Atlantic Monthly Press, 2015), 14.
2. Buckley, "History of Coal Mining in Appalachia," 17.
3. Lewis, *Transforming the Appalachian Countryside*, 3.
4. "You Would Not Have Recognized Appalachia 150 Years Ago," *Appalachian Magazine*, January 17, 2017, http://appalachianmagazine.com/2017/01/17/you-would-not-have -recognized-appalachia-150-years-ago/.
5. Drake, *A History of Appalachia*, 3.

6. Paul L. Angermeier, "Biodiversity in Appalachia's Future," *Appalachian Voices*, December 15, 2008, http://appvoices.org/2008/12/15/biodiversity-in-appalachias-future/.

7. Drake, *A History of Appalachia*, 4–9.

8. Schumann, "Introduction," 4.

9. Shepard Krech, *The Ecological Indian: Myth and History* (New York: W. W. Norton, 2000), 211–12.

10. Drake, *A History of Appalachia*, 11.

11. Schumann, "Introduction," 4.

12. Wilma A. Dunaway, *The First American Frontier: Transition to Capitalism in Southern Appalachia, 1700–1860* (Chapel Hill: University of North Carolina Press, 1996), 44.

13. J. Angelo Corlett, *Race, Racism, and Reparations* (Ithaca, NY: Cornell University Press, 2003), 182.

14. Andrés Reséndez, *The Other Slavery: The Uncovered Story of Indians Enslavement in America* (Boston: Houghton Mifflin Harcourt, 2016), 8.

15. Ronald L. Lewis, "Beyond Isolation and Homogeneity: Diversity and the History of Appalachia," in *Back Talk from Appalachia: Confronting Stereotypes*, ed., Dwight B. Billings, Gurney Norman, and Katherine Ledford (Lexington: University Press of Kentucky, 2000), 21.

16. Lewis, 21.

17. Lewis, 21.

18. Lewis, 22.

19. Henry D. Shapiro, *Appalachia on Our Mind: The Southern Mountains and Mountaineers in the American Consciousness, 1870–1920* (Chapel Hill: University of North Carolina Press, 1978), 263–64.

20. Dwight B. Billings, Mary Beth Pudup, and Altina L. Waller, "Taking Exception with Exceptionalism: The Emergence and Transformation of Historical Studies of Appalachia," in *Appalachia in the Making: The Mountain South in the Nineteenth Century*, ed. Mary Beth Pudup, Dwight B. Billings, and Altina L. Waller (Chapel Hill: University of North Carolina Press, 1995), 2–3.

21. Catte, *What You Are Getting Wrong About Appalachia*, 19–24.

22. Lewis, "Beyond Isolation and Homogeneity," 22.

23. Lewis, 22.

24. Shannon Elizabeth Bell, *Fighting King Coal: The Challenges to Micromobilization in Central Appalachia* (Cambridge, MA: MIT Press, 2016), 16.

25. Bell, 16–17.

26. Rodger Cunningham, "Reflections on Identify and the Roots of Prejudice," in "Appalachian Identity: Roundtable Discussion," *Appalachian Journal* 38, no. 1 (2010), 75, quoted in Bell, *Fighting King Coal*, 17.

27. Bell, *Fighting King Coal*, 17.

28. Scott, *Removing Mountains*, 63.

29. Lewis, "Beyond Isolation and Homogeneity," 26.

30. Lewis, 25–26.

31. Ronald D. Eller, *Miners, Millhands, and Mountaineers: Industrialization of the Appalachian South, 1880–1930* (Knoxville: University of Tennessee Press, 1982), 18–21.

32. Eller, 29.

33. Eller, 10.

34. Lewis, "Beyond Isolation and Homogeneity," 22.

35. Lewis, 26.

36. Lewis, 26–29.

37. Lewis, 23.

38. Dunaway, *The First American Frontier*, 14.

39. Dunaway, 32.
40. Dunaway, 16.
41. David S. Walls and Dwight Billings, "The Sociology of Southern Appalachia," *Appalachian Journal* 5, no. 1 (1977): 135, quoted in Dunaway, *The First American* Frontier, 16.
42. Dunaway, *The First American Frontier*, 16–17.
43. Steven Stoll, *Ramp Hollow: The Ordeal of Appalachia* (New York: Hill and Wang, 2017), 106–7.
44. Stoll, 106.
45. Stoll, 108.
46. Dunaway, "The Incorporation of Mountain Ecosystems into the Capitalist World-System," 379.
47. Dunaway, 379.
48. Wilma A. Dunaway, "The Legacy of Social Darwinism in Appalachian Scholarship," Online Archives for *Women, Work and Family in the Antebellum Mountain South*, Virginia Tech University Libraries, accessed December 5, 2019, https://scholar.lib.vt.edu /faculty_archives/appalachian_women/legacy.htm.
49. Dunaway, *The First American Frontier*, 257.
50. Dunaway, 109.
51. Dunaway, 111.
52. Kimya Barden, "Neoliberalism and African Americans in Higher Education," in *The Routledge Handbook of Poverty in the United States*, ed. Stephen Haymes, María Vidal de Haymes, and Reuben Miller (New York: Routledge, 2015), 181.
53. Barden, 181.
54. Ronald L. Lewis, "African American Convicts in the Coal Mines of Southern Appalachia," in *Appalachians and Race: The Mountain South from Slavery to Segregation*, ed. John C. Inscoe (Lexington: University Press of Kentucky, 2001), 259.
55. Eller, *Miners, Millhands, and Mountaineers*, 31.
56. Eller, 31.
57. Dunaway, *The First American Frontier*, 118.
58. Dunaway, 117.
59. Dwight B. Billings and Kathleen M. Blee, *The Road to Poverty: The Making of Wealth and Hardship in Appalachia* (Cambridge: Cambridge University Press, 2000), 164.
60. Janet Rifkin, "Toward a Theory of Law and Patriarchy," *Harvard Women's Law Journal* 3 (1980): 93.
61. Rifkin, 93.
62. Sally Ward Maggard, "From Farm to Coal Camp to Back Office and McDonald's: Living in the Midst of Appalachia's Latest Transformation," *Journal of the Appalachian Studies Association* 6 (1994): 17.
63. Rifkin, "Toward a Theory of Law and Patriarchy," 94.
64. Mignon Duffy, *Making Care Count: A Century of Gender, Race, and Paid Care Work* (New Brunswick: Rutgers University Press, 2011), 11.
65. Duffy, 11.
66. Mignon Duffy, "Dirty Work: Gender, Race, and Reproductive Labor in Historical Perspective," *Gender and Society* 21, no. 3 (2007): 315–16.
67. Wilma A. Dunaway, "The Double Register of History: Situating the Forgotten Woman and Her Household in Capitalist Commodity Chains," *Journal of World-Systems Research* 7, no. 1 (2001): 16.
68. Lewis, "Beyond Isolation and Homogeneity," 22–23.
69. Dunaway, *The First American Frontier*, 257.
70. Dunaway, 257.
71. Dunaway, 257.

72. Dunaway, 257.
73. Dunaway, 257.
74. Steve Fisher and Barbara Ellen Smith, "Internal Colony—Are You Sure? Defining, Theorizing, Organizing Appalachia," *The Journal of Appalachian Studies* 22, no. 1 (2016): 45–48.
75. Drake, *A History of Appalachia*, 131, 139.
76. Buckley, "History of Coal Mining in Appalachia," 18.
77. Crandall A. Shifflett, *Coal Towns: Life, Work, and Culture in Company Towns of Southern Appalachia, 1880–1960* (Knoxville: University of Tennessee Press, 1995), 27.
78. Buckley, "History of Coal Mining in Appalachia," 19.
79. Buckley, 19.
80. Eller, *Miners, Millhands, and Mountaineers*, 65, 128.
81. Buckley, "History of Coal Mining in Appalachia," 17.
82. Drake, *A History of Appalachia*, 139.
83. Drake, 60–61.
84. Stoll, *Ramp Hollow*, 156.
85. Stoll, 156.
86. Drake, *A History of Appalachia*, 60–61.
87. Drake, 139.
88. Buckley, "History of Coal Mining in Appalachia," 20.
89. Eller, *Miners, Millhands, and Mountaineers*, 55–56.
90. Eller, 56.
91. Eller, 57.
92. Lewis, *Transforming the Appalachian Countryside*, 4–9.
93. Lewis, 3.
94. Eller, *Miners, Millhands, and Mountaineers*, 92.
95. Eller, 109–10.
96. Lewis, *Transforming the Appalachian Countryside*, 3.
97. Lewis, 132–33, 239.
98. Lewis, 239.
99. Eller, *Miners, Millhands, and Mountaineers*, 126.
100. Lewis, *Transforming the Appalachian Countryside*, 3.
101. Shifflett, *Coal Towns*, 29.
102. Eller, *Miners, Millhands, and Mountaineers*, 128.
103. Eller, 130.
104. Buckley, "History of Coal Mining in Appalachia," 17–18.
105. Shifflett, *Coal Towns*, 35.
106. Eller, *Miners, Millhands, and Mountaineers*, 162.
107. Eller, 167.
108. Eller, 182.
109. "Housing by Employers," U.S. Bureau of Labor Statistics, 21, quoted in Eller, *Miners, Millhands, and Mountaineers*, 192–93.
110. Buckley, "History of Coal Mining in Appalachia," 22.
111. Eller, *Miners, Millhands, and Mountaineers*, 193.
112. Drake, *A History of Appalachia*, 147.
113. Patrick C. McGinley, "Collateral Damage: Turning a Blind Eye to Environmental and Social Injustice in the Coalfields," *Journal of Environmental and Sustainability Law* 19, no. 2 (2013): 357.
114. Eller, *Miners, Millhands, and Mountaineers*, 194.
115. Eller, 183.
116. Eller, 162.

117. Eller, 185.
118. Eller, 186.
119. Wendy B. Davis, "Out of the Black Hole: Reclaiming the Crown of King Coal," *American University Law Review* 51, no. 5 (2002): 917.
120. Eller, *Miners, Millhands, and Mountaineers*, 168.
121. Drake, *A History of Appalachia*, 143.
122. Eller, *Miners, Millhands, and Mountaineers*, 169.
123. Eller, 169.
124. Joe William Trotter, *Coal, Class, and Color: Blacks in Southern West Virginia, 1915–32* (Urbana: University of Illinois Press, 1990), 89–90.
125. Ronald L. Lewis, *Black Coal Miners in America: Race, Class, and Community Conflict 1780–1980* (Lexington: University Press of Kentucky, 1987), 143.
126. Lewis, 143.
127. Eller, *Miners, Millhands, and Mountaineers*, 171.
128. Martin Cherniack, *The Hawk's Nest Incident: America's Worst Industrial Disaster* (New Haven: Yale University Press, 1989).
129. Trotter, *Coal, Class, and Color*, 94.
130. Eller, *Miners, Millhands, and Mountaineers*, 174.
131. Eller, 172, 174.
132. Shifflett, *Coal Towns*, xi.
133. Eller, *Miners, Millhands, and Mountaineers*, 174.
134. Eller, 175.
135. Maggard, "From Farm to Coal Camp," 16.
136. Maggard, 16.
137. Virginia Rinaldo Seitz, "Class, Gender, and Resistance in the Appalachian Coalfields," in *Community Activism and Feminist Politics: Organizing across Race, Class, and Gender*, ed. Nancy A. Naples (New York: Routledge, 1998), 217.
138. Seitz, 217.
139. Dunaway, "The Double Register of History," 22.
140. Stoll, *Ramp Hollow*, 213–22.
141. Shannon Elizabeth Bell and Richard York, "Community Economic Identity: The Coal Industry and Ideology Construction in West Virginia," *Rural Sociology* 75, no. 1 (2010): 120.
142. Maggard, "From Farm to Coal Camp," 17.
143. Bell and York, "Community Economic Identity," 120.
144. Maggard, "From Farm to Coal Camp," 30.
145. Seitz, "Class, Gender, and Resistance in the Appalachian Coalfields," 217.
146. Shelly Romalis, *Pistol Packin' Mama: Aunt Molly Jackson and the Politics of Folksong* (Urbana: University of Illinois Press, 1999), 26.
147. Romalis, 27.
148. Romalis, 26.
149. Trotter, *Coal, Class, and Color*, 91.
150. Shifflett, *Coal Towns*, 82.
151. Trotter, *Coal, Class, and Color*, 52.
152. Trotter, 115.
153. Mary Phillips and Nick Rumens, "Introducing Contemporary Ecofeminism," in *Contemporary Perspectives on Ecofeminism*, ed. Mary Phillips and Nick Rumens (New York: Routledge, 2016), 2.
154. Drake, *A History of Appalachia*, 143.
155. Drake, 148.
156. Drake, 148.

157. Drake, 148.
158. Ronald D. Eller, "The Coal Barons of the Appalachian South, 1880–1930," *Appalachian Journal* 4, no. 3/4 (1977): 201.
159. Eller, 201.
160. Drake, *A History of Appalachia*, 150.
161. Green, *The Devil Is Here in These Hills*, 211.
162. Green, 6.
163. Anne Marie Lofaso, "What We Owe Our Coal Miners," *Harvard Law and Policy Review* 5, no. 1 (2011): 94–95.
164. Drake, *A History of Appalachia*, 152.
165. Lewis, *Black Coal Miners in America*, 101.
166. Trotter, *Coal, Class, and Color*, 52.
167. William H. Turner and Edward J. Cabbell, *Blacks in Appalachia* (Lexington: University Press of Kentucky, 1985), 127.
168. Eller, *Miners, Millhands, and Mountaineers*, 171–72.
169. Trotter, *Coal, Class, and Color*, 17.
170. Trotter, 17.
171. Trotter, 114–15.
172. Seitz, "Class, Gender, and Resistance in the Appalachian Coalfields," 217.
173. John Alexander Williams, *West Virginia: A History* (New York: W. W. Norton, 1984), 132.
174. Seitz, "Class, Gender, and Resistance in the Appalachian Coalfields," 217.
175. Seitz, 217.
176. Seitz, 217.
177. Sally Ward Maggard, "Class and Gender: New Theoretical Priorities in Appalachian Studies," in *The Impact of Institutions in Appalachia*, ed. Jim Llyod and Ann G. Campbell (Boone: Appalachian Consortium Press, 1986), 100, quoted in Seitz, 217–18.
178. Seitz, "Class, Gender, and Resistance in the Appalachian Coalfields," 218.
179. Trotter, *Coal, Class, and Color*, 52.
180. Trotter, 52–53.
181. Eller, *Miners, Millhands, and Mountaineers*, 197.
182. Eller, 198.
183. Ann M. Eisenberg, "Beyond Science and Hysteria: Reality and Perceptions of Environmental Justice Concerns Surrounding Marcellus and Utica Shale Gas Development," *Pittsburgh University Law Review* 77, no. 2 (2015): 195–98.
184. Eller, *Miners, Millhands, and Mountaineers*, 158.
185. Eller, 158.
186. Eller, 157–58.
187. Joyce M. Barry, *Standing Our Ground: Women, Environmental Justice, and the Fight to End Mountain Removal* (Athens: Ohio University Press, 2012), 24.
188. Barry, 23.

CHAPTER 2

1. Gilbert F. LaFreniere, *The Decline of Nature: Environmental History and the Western Worldview* (Corvallis, OR: Oak Savanna Publishing, 2008), 66.
2. G. E. M. de Ste. Croix, *The Class Struggle in the Ancient Greek World: From the Archaic Age to the Arab Conquests* (London: Gerald Duckworth, 1981), 52–53.
3. Dan A. Tarlock, "History of Environmental Law," in *Environmental Laws and Their Enforcement*, vol. 1, ed. Dan. A. Tarlock and John C. Dernback (Oxford: Eolss, 2009), 44–45.

4. Sing C. Chew, *World Ecological Degradation* (Walnut Creek: Rowman & Littlefield, 2001), 109, quoted in, LaFreniere, *The Decline of Nature*, 67.
5. Arran E. Gare, *Postmodernism and the Environmental Crisis* (London and New York: Routledge, 1995), 65.
6. Tarlock, "History of Environmental Law," 44.
7. Tarlock, 44–45.
8. LaFreniere, *The Decline of Nature*, 66.
9. Tarlock, "History of Environmental Law," 46.
10. Tarlock, 47.
11. Joanne Schneider, *The Age of Romanticism* (London: Greenwood Press, 2007), 74.
12. Tarlock, "History of Environmental Law," 46.
13. Theodore Roszak, *Where the Wasteland Ends, Politics and Transcendence in Postindustrial Society* (New York: Doubleday and Company, 1972), 13, quoted in LaFreniere, *The Decline of Nature*, 308.
14. Tarlock, "History of Environmental Law," 46–47.
15. Noël Sturgeon, *Ecofeminist Natures: Race, Gender, Political Theory and Political Action* (New York: Routledge, 1997), 8.
16. Sturgeon, 9.
17. Anne K. Mellor, "Thoughts on *Romanticism and Gender*," *European Romantic Review* 23, no. 3 (2012): 344.
18. Mellor, 345.
19. Mary Mellor, "Eco-feminism and Eco-socialism: Dilemmas of Essentialism and Materialism," *Capitalism, Nature, Socialism* 3, no. 2 (1992): 44, 60.
20. Mellor, 45.
21. Mellor, 46, 57.
22. Tarlock, "History of Environmental Law," 47.
23. Richard J. Lazarus, *The Making of Environmental Law* (Chicago: University of Chicago Press, 2004), 51.
24. Tarlock, "History of Environmental Law," 47.
25. Tarlock, 47.
26. Leslie Paul Thiele, *Environmentalism for a New Millennium: The Challenge of Coevolution* (Oxford: Oxford University Press, 1999), 6.
27. Tarlock, "History of Environmental Law," 48.
28. Tarlock, 48.
29. William E. Shands, "The Lands Nobody Wanted: The Legacy of the Eastern National Forests," in *Origins of the National Forests: A Centennial Symposium*, ed. Harold K. Steen (Durham: Forest Historical Society, 1992), 24–30.
30. Thiele, *Environmentalism for a New Millennium*, 6.
31. Cade A. Jameson, "Radical Conservation and the Politics of Planning: A Historical Study, 1917–1945" (PhD diss., University of Oregon, 2017), iv–v, 5–7.
32. Tarlock, "History of Environmental Law," 48.
33. John Muir, *Our National Parks* (Boston: Houghton Mifflin, 1909), 1.
34. Tarlock, "History of Environmental Law," 48.
35. Jedediah S. Purdy, "The Politics of Nature: Climate Change, Environmental Law, and Democracy," *Yale Law Journal* 119, no. 6 (2010): 1139.
36. Dorceta E. Taylor, "Race, Class, Gender, and American Environmentalism," General Technical Report PNW-GTR-534, Forest Service, U.S. Department of Agriculture (2002): 6.
37. Taylor, 6.
38. Taylor, 7.
39. Tarlock, "History of Environmental Law," 49.
40. Tarlock, 49.

41. Lazarus, *The Making of Environmental Law*, 50.
42. Lazarus, 49–50.
43. Sara M. Gregg, *Managing the Mountains: Land Use Planning, the New Deal, and the Creation of a Federal Landscape in Appalachia* (New Haven, CT: Yale University Press, 2010), xi.
44. Gregg, xii.
45. Gregg, x.
46. Lazarus, *The Making of Environmental Law*, 50.
47. Lazarus, 50.
48. Leane, "Environmental Law's Liberal Roots," in *Green Paradigms and the Law*, ed. Nicole Rogers (Lismore: Southern Cross University Press, 1998), 5–6.
49. Leane, 6–7.
50. M'Gonigle and Takeda, "The Liberal Limits of Environmental Law," 1060.
51. Leane, "Environmental Law's Liberal Roots," 6.
52. Leane, 6.
53. M'Gonigle and Takeda, "The Liberal Limits of Environmental Law," 1060–61.
54. M'Gonigle and Takeda, 1061.
55. Leane, "Environmental Law's Liberal Roots," 7.
56. Leane, 7.
57. Leane, 7.
58. M'Gonigle and Takeda, "The Liberal Limits of Environmental Law," 1064.
59. M'Gonigle and Takeda, 1063–64.
60. Lisa Duggan, *The Twilight of Equality?: Neoliberalism, Cultural Politics, and the Attack on Democracy* (Boston: Beacon Press, 2003), xi.
61. M'Gonigle and Takeda, "The Liberal Limits of Environmental Law," 1059–60.
62. M'Gonigle and Takeda, 1059.
63. Leane, "Environmental Law's Liberal Roots," 12–13.
64. Leane, 13.
65. Leane, 16.
66. Leane, 27.
67. M'Gonigle and Takeda, "The Liberal Limits of Environmental Law," 1060–61.
68. Leane, "Environmental Law's Liberal Roots," 16.
69. M'Gonigle and Takeda, "The Liberal Limits of Environmental Law," 1065.
70. Leane, "Environmental Law's Liberal Roots," 16.
71. Benjamin G. Damstedt, "Limiting Locke: A Natural Law Justification for the Fair Use Doctrine," *Yale Law Journal* 112, no. 5 (2003): 1181.
72. John Locke, *Second Treatise of Government* (New York: Barnes & Noble Books, 2004), 18.
73. Leane, "Environmental Law's Liberal Roots," 18.
74. 3 Corbin on Contracts § 9.19 (2019).
75. Leane, "Environmental Law's Liberal Roots," 18.
76. *Lochner v. New York*, 198 U.S. 45, 53 (1905).
77. Leane, "Environmental Law's Liberal Roots," 17.
78. Karl Marx and Friedrich Engels, *The Communist Manifesto* (Minneapolis: Lerner, 2018), 1.
79. Tor Krever, "The Rule of Law and the Rise of Capitalism," in *Handbook on the Rule of Law*, ed. Christopher May and Adam Winchester (Cheltenham, UK: Edward Elgar, 2018), 195.
80. Karl Marx, *Capital: A Critique of Political Economy*, vol. 1 (Champaign, IL: Modern Barbarian Press, 2018), 167.
81. Karl Marx, *A Contribution to the Critique of Political Economy* (Chicago: Charles H. Kerr, 1904), 11.

82. Marx, 11.
83. Marx, 11.
84. Marx, 11.
85. Krever, "The Rule of Law and the Rise of Capitalism," 193.
86. Krever, 193.
87. Krever, 193.
88. Krever, 193–94.
89. Krever, 195.
90. Michael Tigar and Madeleine R. Levy, *Law and The Rise of Capitalism* (New York: NYU Press, 2000), 20–21.
91. Tigar and Levy, 21.
92. Tigar and Levy, 21.
93. Leane, "Environmental Law's Liberal Roots," 20.
94. Eduardo Bonilla-Silva, *Racism without Racists: Color-Blind Racism and the Persistence of Racial Inequality in America* (Lanham: Rowman & Littlefield, 2018), 55.
95. Bonilla-Silva, 55.
96. Kate Nash, *Universal Difference: Feminism and the Liberal Undecidability of "Women"* (New York: St. Martin's Press, 1998), 100.
97. Nash, 100.
98. Longo, Clausen, and Clark, *The Tragedy of the Commodity*, 9, 29.
99. Longo, Clausen, and Clark, 31.
100. Longo, Clausen, and Clark, 31.
101. Longo, Clausen, and Clark, 32.
102. Longo, Clausen, and Clark, 32.
103. Longo, Clausen, and Clark, 32.
104. Longo, Clausen, and Clark, 33.
105. Longo, Clausen, and Clark, 33, 152.
106. Longo, Clausen, and Clark, 152.
107. Longo, Clausen, and Clark, 37–38.
108. Malm, *Fossil Capital*, 36.
109. Malm, 124.
110. Malm, 124.
111. Malm, 165.
112. Malm, 13.
113. Malm, 326.
114. Malm, 326.
115. Malm, 326.
116. Elisabeth S. Clemens, "The Problem of the Corporation: Liberalism and the Large Organization," in *The Oxford Handbook of Sociology and Organization Studies—Classical Foundations*, ed. Paul S. Adler (Oxford: Oxford University Press, 2009), 537.
117. Adam Winkley, "Corporate Personhood and the Rights of Corporate Speech," *Seattle University Law Review* 30, no. 4 (2007): 865–66.
118. Janel M. Curry and Steven McGuire, *Community on Land: Community, Ecology, and the Public Interest* (New York: Rowman & Littlefield, 2002), 69.
119. Curry and McGuire, 69.
120. Curry and McGuire, 69.
121. Curry and McGuire, 69.
122. Curry and McGuire, 69.
123. Clemens, "The Problem of the Corporation," 537.
124. Curry and McGuire, *Community on Land*, 68–69.
125. Curry and McGuire, 69.

126. Eller, *Miners, Millhands, and Mountaineers*, 56.
127. Eller, 56.
128. Eller, 55.
129. Curry and McGuire, *Community on Land*, 68–69.
130. Curry and McGuire, 69.
131. Leane, "Environmental Law's Liberal Roots," 20.
132. Eller, *Miners, Millhands, and Mountaineers*, 194.
133. Drake, *A History of Appalachia*, 143.
134. Leane, "Environmental Law's Liberal Roots," 20.
135. Lewis, *Transforming the Appalachian Countryside*, 128, 108.
136. Lewis, 109.
137. *Steel v. St. Louis Smelting & Ref. Co.*, 106 U.S. 447, 449 (1882).
138. *Pennsylvania Coal Co. v. Sanderson*, 113 Pa. 126, 149 (1886).
139. Wood, *Nature's Trust*, 53.
140. Wood, 53.
141. Wood, 53; *State of Georgia v. Tennessee Copper Co.*, 237 U.S. 678, 679 (1915).
142. Wood, *Nature's Trust*, 53.
143. Lewis, *Transforming the Appalachian Countryside*, 105.
144. Lewis, 103.
145. Lewis, 106.
146. Lewis, 106.
147. Lewis, 110.
148. Lewis, 110; Jeff L. Lewin, "The Silent Revolution in West Virginia's Law of Nuisance," *West Virginia Law Review* 92, no. 2 (1989): 271.
149. Lewis, *Transforming the Appalachian Countryside*, 123.
150. Lewis, 114.
151. Lewin, "The Silent Revolution in West Virginia's Law of Nuisance," 238.
152. Lewin, 238.
153. Lewis, *Transforming the Appalachian Countryside*, 114.
154. Lewis, 114.
155. Lewis, 114.
156. Lewis, 114.
157. Lewis, 114.
158. Lewis, 115.
159. Lewis, 116.
160. *Jacobs v. Baltimore & O.R. Co.*, 70 S.E. 369, 370 (1911).
161. *Jacobs*, 70 S.E. at 371.
162. Lewis, *Transforming the Appalachian Countryside*, 117.
163. Lewin, "The Silent Revolution in West Virginia's Law of Nuisance," 272.
164. Lewis, *Transforming the Appalachian Countryside*, 119.
165. Lewis, 119.
166. *Gaston v. Mace*, 10 S.E. 60, 63 (1889).
167. Lewis, *Transforming the Appalachian Countryside*, 119.
168. *Squires v. Lafferty*, 121 S.E. 90, 91 (1924).
169. *Squires*, 121 S.E. at 91.
170. Lewis, *Transforming the Appalachian Countryside*, 109.
171. Morton J. Horwitz, *The Transformation of American Law, 1780–1860* (Boston: Harvard University Press, 1977), 99.
172. Davis, "Out of the Black Hole," 916.
173. Davis, 916–17.
174. Davis, 918.

175. *Stonegap Colliery Co. v. Hamilton*, 89 S.E. 305, 309 (1916).
176. Davis, "Out of the Black Hole," 919.
177. *McIntire v. Marian Coal Co.*, 227 S.W. 298, 299 (1921).
178. *McIntire*, 227 S.W. at 299.
179. *McIntire*, 227 S.W. at 299.
180. *McIntire*, 227 S.W. at 299.
181. *McIntire*, 227 S.W. at 299.
182. *McIntire*, 227 S.W. at 299.
183. *McIntire*, 227 S.W. at 300.
184. *Case v. Elk Horn Coal Corp.*, 276 S.W. 573, 574 (1925).
185. *Akers v. Baldwin*, 736 S.W.2d 294, 299 (Ky. 1987).
186. Carolyn S. Bratt and Karen J. Greenwell, "Kentucky's Broad Form Deed Amendment: Constitutional Considerations," *Journal of Mineral Law and Policy* 5, no. 1 (1989): 13.
187. *Wells v. N. E. Coal Co.*, 72 S.W.2d 745, 747 (1934).
188. *Akers v. Baldwin*, 736 S.W.2d 294, 299 (Ky. 1987).
189. *Treadway v. Wilson*, 192 S.W.2d 949, 951 (1946).

CHAPTER 3

1. Richard Straw, "Appalachian History," in *A Handbook to Appalachia: An Introduction to the Region*, ed. Grace Toney Edwards, JoAnn Aust Asbury, and Ricky L. Cox (Knoxville: University of Tennessee Press, 2006), 15.
2. Straw, 15.
3. Rhonda F. Levine, *Class Struggle and the New Deal: Industrial Labor, Industrial Capital, and the State* (Lawrence: University Press of Kansas, 1988), 15–16.
4. Levine, 16.
5. Drake, *A History of Appalachia*, 167.
6. Chris Bolgiano, *The Appalachian Forest: A Search for Roots and Renewal* (Mechanicsburg: Stackpole Books, 1995), 83.
7. Buckley, "History of Coal Mining in Appalachia," 25.
8. Buckley, 26.
9. Buckley, 26.
10. Ronald D. Eller, *Uneven Ground: Appalachia Since 1945 Depression* (Lexington: University Press of Kentucky, 2008), 20.
11. Buckley, "History of Coal Mining in Appalachia," 26.
12. Jerry Bruce Thomas, *An Appalachian New Deal: West Virginia in the Great Depression* (Lexington: University Press of Kentucky, 1998), 160–61.
13. Paul Salstrom, *Appalachia's Path to Dependency: Rethinking a Region's Economic History, 1730–1940* (Lexington: University Press of Kentucky, 1994), 101.
14. Drake, *A History of Appalachia*, 166.
15. Salstrom, *Appalachia's Path to Dependency*, 103.
16. Thomas, *An Appalachian New Deal*, 165.
17. Thomas, 188.
18. Thomas, 172, 188.
19. Thomas, 173.
20. Stoll, *Ramp Hollow*, 228.
21. Drake, *A History of Appalachia*, 166.
22. Eller, *Uneven Ground*, 38–39.
23. Drake, *A History of Appalachia*, 169.
24. Eller, *Uneven Ground*, 34.
25. Eller, 34.

26. Eller, 34.
27. Eller, 34.
28. Drake, *A History of Appalachia*, 265.
29. Thomas, *An Appalachian New Deal*, 2.
30. Salstrom, *Appalachia's Path to Dependency*, 59.
31. Lewis, *Transforming the Appalachian Countryside*, 250–51.
32. Drake, *A History of Appalachia*, 179.
33. Drake, 172.
34. Michael Harrington, *The Other America: Poverty in the United States* (New York: Simon & Schuster, 1997), 42–43.
35. Eller, *Uneven Ground*, 93.
36. Eller, 93.
37. Eller, 92.
38. Eller, 93.
39. Eller, 63.
40. Eller, 100.
41. Eller, 63.
42. Drake, *A History of Appalachia*, 173.
43. Eller, 209.
44. "Geography," Source & Methodology, Appalachian Regional Commission, accessed December 5, 2019, https://www.arc.gov/research/sourceandmethodologygeography .asp.
45. Schumann, "Introduction," 3.
46. Huey Perry, *They'll Cut Off Your Project: A Mingo County Chronicle* (Morgantown: West Virginia University Press, 2011), xv.
47. Perry, 188.
48. Perry, xv.
49. Billings and Blee, *The Road to Poverty*, 330.
50. Drake, *A History of Appalachia*, 177.
51. Billings and Blee, *The Road to Poverty*, 330.
52. Perry, *They'll Cut Off Your Project*, xv.
53. Perry, xviii.
54. Perry, 13–14.
55. Drake, *A History of Appalachia*, 177.
56. Drake, 177.
57. Eller, *Uneven Ground*, 221.
58. Eller, 128.
59. Eller, 132.
60. Jessica Wilkerson, *To Live Here, You Have to Fight: How Women Led Appalachian Movements for Social Justice* (Urbana: Illinois University Press, 2019), 4.
61. Eller, *Uneven Ground*, 158–59.
62. Wilkerson, *To Live Here, You Have to Fight*, 4.
63. Wilkerson, 5–6.
64. Wilkerson, 7.
65. Wilkerson, 7.
66. Wilkerson, 8.
67. Wilkerson, 8–9.
68. Eller, *Uneven Ground*, 161, 170–71.
69. Eller, 161.
70. Henry D. Caudill, *Night Comes to the Cumberlands: A Biography of a Depressed Area* (Boston: Little, Brown, 1963), 325.

71. Chad Montrie, *To Save the Land and People: A History of Opposition to Surface Coal Mining in Appalachia* (Chapel Hill: University of North Carolina Press, 2003), 20–24.
72. Montrie, 18.
73. Montrie, 21, 24.
74. Montrie, 20.
75. Montrie, 21.
76. Montrie, 24.
77. Montrie, 24.
78. Montrie, 23.
79. Mark Baller and Leor J. Pantilat, "Defenders of Appalachia: The Campaign to Eliminate Mountaintop Removal Coal Mining and the Role of Public Justice," *Environmental Law* 37, no. 3 (2007): 631.
80. Montrie, *To Save the Land and People*, 22–23.
81. Mary Beth Bingman, "Stopping the Bulldozers: What Difference Did it Make?," in *Fighting Back in Appalachia: Traditions of Resistance and Change*, ed. Stephen L. Fisher (Philadelphia: Temple University Press, 1993), 21.
82. Patrick C. McGinley, "From Pick and Shovel to Mountaintop Removal: Environmental Injustice in the Appalachian Coalfields," *Environmental Law* 34, no. 1 (2004): 48.
83. McGinley, 49.
84. Robert Todd Perdue and Christopher McCarty, "Unearthing a Network of Resistance: Law and the Anti–Strip Mining Movement in Central Appalachia," in *Studies in Law, Politics, and Society*, ed. Austin Sarat (Bingley: Emerald Books, 2015), 40.
85. Eller, *Uneven Ground*, 39–40.
86. Eller, 164.
87. Eller, 37.
88. Perdue and McCarty, "Unearthing a Network of Resistance," 40.
89. Eller, *Uneven Ground*, 38.
90. Eller, 38.
91. Eller, 37–38.
92. *Wells v. N. E. Coal Co.*, 72 S.W.2d 745, 747 (1934).
93. *Martin v. Kentucky Oak Min. Co.*, 429 S.W.2d 395, 397 (Ky. 1968).
94. Ky. Const. § 19(2); *Ward v. Harding*, 860 S.W.2d 280, 289 (Ky. 1993).
95. Eller, *Uneven Ground*, 38.
96. Drake, *A History of Appalachia*, 190.
97. Perdue and McCarty, "Unearthing a Network of Resistance," 40.
98. Perdue and McCarty, 40.
99. McGinley, "From Pick and Shovel to Mountaintop Removal," 50.
100. McGinley, 54.
101. Montrie, *To Save the Land and People*, 3–4.
102. Perdue and McCarty, "Unearthing a Network of Resistance," 40–41.
103. Eller, *Uneven Ground*, 163.
104. Perdue and McCarty, "Unearthing a Network of Resistance," 40.
105. Perdue and McCarty, 40.
106. Montrie, *To Save the Land and People*, 1.
107. Montrie, 88.
108. Montrie, 91.
109. Barry, *Standing Our Ground*, 76.
110. Barry, 76.
111. Bingman, "Stopping the Bulldozers," 18, 27.
112. Perdue and McCarty, "Unearthing a Network of Resistance," 41.
113. Perdue and McCarty, 41.
114. Perdue and McCarty, 41.

115. Perdue and McCarty, 41.
116. Montrie, *To Save the Land and People*, 156.
117. Perdue and McCarty, "Unearthing a Network of Resistance," 42.
118. Perdue and McCarty, 41.
119. Perdue and McCarty, 42.
120. Montrie, *To Save the Land and People*, 175.
121. Perdue and McCarty, "Unearthing a Network of Resistance," 42.
122. Eller, *Uneven Ground*, 165.
123. Eller, 165.
124. Perdue and McCarty, "Unearthing a Network of Resistance," 42.
125. Eller, *Uneven Ground*, 127–28.

CHAPTER 4

1. Rachel Carson, *Silent Spring* (Boston: Houghton Mifflin Company, 1990), 296–97.
2. Carson, 296–97.
3. Tarlock, "History of Environmental Law," 50.
4. Tarlock, 50.
5. Tarlock, 50.
6. John McCormick, *Reclaiming Paradise: The Global Environmental Movement* (Indianapolis: Indiana University Press, 1989), 57.
7. Gerald M. Stern, *The Buffalo Creek Disaster: How the Survivors of One of the Worst Disasters in Coal-Mining History Brought Suit Against the Coal Company—and Won* (New York: Vintage Books, 2009), 201.
8. McCormick, *Reclaiming Paradise*, 57.
9. Council on Environmental Quality, "Environmental Quality 1979" (Washington, D.C.: U.S. Government Printing Office, 1979), quoted in McCormick, *Reclaiming Paradise*, 58.
10. Tarlock, "History of Environmental Law," 49.
11. Wood, *Nature's Trust*, 51–52.
12. Roger P. Hansen and Theodore A. Wolff, "Environmental Review & Case Study: Reviewing NEPA's Past: Improving NEPA's Future," *Environmental Practice* 13, no. 3 (2011): 236.
13. Robert Esworthy, "Federal Pollution Control Laws: How Are They Enforced?" Congressional Research Service Report 7-5700, Congressional Research Service (2014): 6.
14. Wood, *Nature's Trust*, 55.
15. Wood, 55.
16. Lazarus, *The Making of Environmental Law*, 73–74.
17. Tarlock, "History of Environmental Law," 52.
18. Wood, *Nature's Trust*, 57.
19. Richard J. Lazarus, "Super Wicked Problems and Climate Change: Restraining the Present to Liberate the Future," *Cornell Law Review* 94, no. 5 (2009): 1181.
20. M'Gonigle and Takeda, "The Liberal Limits of Environmental Law," 1056.
21. James Gustave Speth, *Bridge at the End of the World: Capitalism, the Environment, and Crossing from Crisis to Sustainability* (New Haven, CT: Yale University Press, 2008), 70.
22. Wood, *Nature's Trust*, 55.
23. Lazarus, "Super Wicked Problems and Climate Change," 1180.
24. Lazarus, 1180.
25. Craig Collins, *Toxic Loopholes: Failures and Future Prospects of Environmental Law* (Cambridge: Cambridge University Press 2010), 1–3.
26. William Greider, *The Soul of Capitalism: Opening Paths to a Moral Economy* (New York: Simon & Schuster, 2003), 32, quoted in Speth, *Bridge at the End of the World*, 85.

27. M'Gonigle and Takeda, "The Liberal Limits of Environmental Law," 1056.
28. David Schoenbrod, *Power without Responsibility: How Congress Abuses the People through Delegation* (New Haven, CT: Yale University Press, 1993), 55, 105.
29. Collins, *Toxic Loopholes*, 9.
30. Wood, *Nature's Trust*, 69.
31. Wood, 58.
32. Wood, 57–58.
33. Wood, 57.
34. Robert J. Mason, *Collaborative Land Use Management: The Quieter Revolution in Place-Based Planning* (Lanham: Rowman & Littlefield, 2008), 54.
35. Schoenbrod, *Power without Responsibility*, 56.
36. Wood, *Nature's Trust*, 114.
37. Wood, 115.
38. Wood, 116.
39. Lazarus, *The Making of Environmental Law*, 123.
40. M'Gonigle and Takeda, "The Liberal Limits of Environmental Law," 1014–15.
41. Wood, *Nature's Trust*, 63–64.
42. Speth, *The Bridge at the End of the World*, 5–6.
43. Leane, "Environmental Law's Liberal Roots," 13.
44. Craig, *Toxic Loopholes*, 4.
45. M'Gonigle and Takeda, "The Liberal Limits of Environmental Law," 1022.
46. 58 C.J.S. Mines and Minerals § 180.
47. M'Gonigle and Takeda, "The Liberal Limits of Environmental Law," 1023.
48. M'Gonigle and Takeda, 1023.
49. Tracey M. Roberts, "Picking Winners and Losers: A Structural Examination of Tax Subsidies to the Energy Industry," *Columbia Journal Environmental Law* 41, no. 1 (2016): 64, 135.
50. Amir Jina, "The $200 Billion Fossil Fuel Subsidy You've Never Heard Of," *Forbes*, February 1, 2017, https://www.forbes.com/sites/ucenergy/2017/02/01/the-200-billion-fossil-fuel-subsidy-youve-never-heard-of/#bafa652652b7.
51. Robert William Collin, "The Role of Government: Fossil Fuel Energy Sources," in *Energy Choices: How to Power the Future*, ed. Robin Morris and Robert William Collins (Santa Barbara, CA: ABC-CLIO, 2014), 172.
52. David Roberts, "Friendly Policies Keep US Oil and Coal Afloat Far More Than We Thought," Vox, October 7, 2017, https://www.vox.com/energy-and-environment/2017/10/6/16428458/us-energy-subsidies.
53. Jina, "The $200 Billion Fossil Fuel Subsidy You've Never Heard Of."
54. Jina.
55. Jina.
56. M'Gonigle and Takeda, "The Liberal Limits of Environmental Law," 1046.
57. Jason J. Czarnezki, "Food, Law and the Environment: Informational and Structural Changes for a Sustainable Food System," *Utah Environmental Law Review* 31, no. 2 (2011): 266.
58. M'Gonigle and Takeda, 1026.
59. M'Gonigle and Takeda, 1026.
60. Keith Hirokawa, "Some Pragmatic Observations about Radical Critique in Environmental Law," *Stanford Environmental Law Journal* 21, no. 2 (2002): 255.
61. Hirokawa, 255.
62. M'Gonigle and Takeda, "The Liberal Limits of Environmental Law," 1029.
63. Simon Holmes à Court, "It'd be Wonderful If the Claims Made about Carbon Capture Were True," *Guardian*, February 15, 2018, https://www.theguardian.com/comment

isfree/2018/feb/16/itd-be-wonderful-if-the-claims-made-about-carbon-capture-were
-true.

64. Staddon and Depledge, "Implications of Unconventional Gas Extraction on Climate Change," 86.

65. Radhika Shah and Phil Bloomer, "Respecting the Rights of Indigenous Peoples as Renewable Energy Grows," *Stanford Social Innovation Review*, April 23, 2018, https://ssir.org/articles/entry/respecting_the_rights_of_indigenous_peoples_as_renewable_energy_grows.

66. Speth, *Bridge at the End of the World*, 114–15.

67. Speth, x.

68. Ashley Strickland, "Earth to Warm 2 Degrees Celsius by the End of this Century, Studies Say," CNN, July 31, 2017, https://www.cnn.com/2017/07/31/health/climate-change
-two-degrees-studies/index.html.

69. Tim Jackson, *Prosperity without Growth: Economics for a Finite Planet* (London: Earthscan, 2009), 71.

70. Malm, *Fossil Capital*, 359.

71. Malm, 359.

72. Malm, 359.

73. Duggan, *The Twilight of Equality*, xi.

74. David Singh Grewal and Jedediah Purdy, "Introduction: Law and Neoliberalism," *Law and Contemporary Problems* 77, no. 4 (2014): 2–3.

75. Grewal and Purdy, 3.

76. Grewal and Purdy, 1.

77. Grewal and Purdy, 11.

78. Grewal and Purdy, 11.

79. Grewal and Purdy, 14.

80. Grewal and Purdy, 14.

81. Grewal and Purdy, 14.

82. Grewal and Purdy, 16.

83. Grewal and Purdy, 18.

84. Grewal and Purdy, 18; Irma E. Sandoval-Ballesteros, "Rethinking Accountability and Transparency: Breaking the Public Sector Bias in Mexico," *American University International Law Review* 29, no. 2 (2014): 414.

85. David Harvey, *A Brief History of Neoliberalism* (Oxford: Oxford University Press, 2007), 19.

86. Harvey, 159–60.

87. Harvey, 19.

88. Nancy Fraser, *Fortunes of Feminism: From State-Managed Capitalism to Neoliberal Crisis* (Brooklyn: Verso, 2013), 217.

89. Fraser, 219.

90. Fraser, 218.

91. Fraser, 215–20.

92. Fraser, 223.

93. Grewal and Purdy, "Introduction," 9.

94. Harvey, *A Brief History of Neoliberalism*, 203–4.

95. Fraser, *Fortunes of Feminism*, 1, 225.

96. Benjamin J. Richardson, *Time and Environmental Law: Telling Nature's Time* (Cambridge: Cambridge University Press 2017), 148.

97. Daniel Faber, *Capitalizing on Environmental Injustice: The Polluter-Industrial Complex in the Age of Globalization* (Lanham: Rowman & Littlefield, 2008), 127.

98. M'Gonigle and Takeda, "The Liberal Limits of Environmental Law," 1068.

99. Chukwumerije Okereke, *Global Justice and Neoliberal Environmental Governance: Ethics, Sustainable Development and International Co-Operation* (London: Routledge, 2009), 167.

100. M'Gonigle and Takeda, "The Liberal Limits of Environmental Law," 1068.

101. Robyn Eckersley, *The Green State: Rethinking Democracy and Sovereignty* (Cambridge, MA: MIT Press, 2004), 69, quoted in M'Gonigle and Takeda, "The Liberal Limits of Environmental Law," 1071.

102. Okereke, *Global Justice and Neoliberal Environmental Governance*, 186.

103. E. K. Hunt, *History of Economic Thought: A Critical Perspective* (New York: Harper Collins Publishers, 1992), 476, quoted in M'Gonigle and Takeda, "The Liberal Limits of Environmental Law," 1068.

104. Eckersely, *The Green State*, 109.

105. Andries Nentjes and Doede Wiersma, "On Economic Growth, Technology, and The Environment," in *National Income and Nature: Externalities, Growth and Steady State*, ed. J. J. Krabbe and W. J. M. Heijman (Springer Sciences, 1991), 163.

106. M'Gonigle and Takeda, "The Liberal Limits of Environmental Law," 1075.

107. Richard Smith, *Green Capitalism: The God That Failed* (Bristol, UK: World Economics Association, 2015), 45.

108. Eric Bonds and Liam Downey, " 'Green' Technology and Ecologically Unequal Exchange: The Environmental and Social Consequences of Ecological Modernization in the World-System," *Journal of World-Systems Research* 18, no. 2 (2012): 170.

109. Brett A. Miller, "Embracing the Water-Energy Contradiction: The Pebble Mine Conflict and Regulatory Implications Associated with Renewable Energy's Dependence on Non-Renewable Copper," *University of Denver Water Law Review* 19, no. 2 (2016): 220.

110. Brian Elliott, *Natural Catastrophe: Climate Change and Neoliberal Governance* (Edinburgh: Edinburgh University Press, 2016), 144.

CHAPTER 5

1. McGinley, "From Pick and Shovel to Mountaintop Removal," 54–56.

2. Scott, *Removing Mountains*, 148.

3. Donald Edward Davis, *Homeplace Geography: Essays for Appalachia* (Macon, GA: Mercer University Press, 2006), 156.

4. Michael Shnayerson, *Coal River: How a Few Brave Americans Took on a Powerful Company—and the Federal Government—to Save the Land They Love* (New York: Farrar, Straus, and Giroux, 2008), 67.

5. Shnayerson, 67.

6. Shnayerson, 67.

7. McGinley, "From Pick and Shovel to Mountaintop Removal," 58.

8. McGinley, 58.

9. Joseph D. Witt, *Religion and Resistance in Appalachia: Faith and the Fight Against Mountaintop Removal Coal Mining* (Lexington: University Press of Kentucky, 2016), 21.

10. McGinley, "From Pick and Shovel to Mountaintop Removal," 65–66.

11. McGinley, 66–67.

12. McGinley, 57.

13. McGinley, 57.

14. Isaac Forman, "The Uncertain Future of NEPA and Mountaintop Removal," *Columbia Journal of Environmental Law* 36, no. 1 (2011): 164.

15. Richard Martin, *Coal Wars: The Future of Energy and the Fate of the Planet* (New York: St. Martin's Press, 2015), 82.

16. Diana Kaneva, "Let's Face Facts, These Mountains Won't Grow Back: Reducing the Environmental Impact of Mountaintop Removal Coal Mining in Appalachia," *William & Mary Environmental Law & Policy Review* 35, no. 3 (2011): 934.

17. Kaneva, 935.
18. Kaneva, 936.
19. Matthew R. V. Ross, Brian L. McGlynn, and Emily S. Bernhardt, "Deep Impact: Effects of Mountaintop Mining on Surface Topography, Bedrock Structure, and Downstream Waters, Environmental Science & Technology," *Environmental Science & Technology* 50, no. 4 (2016): 2071.
20. Ross, McGlynn, and Bernhardt, 2064.
21. Kaneva, "Let's Face Facts, These Mountains Won't Grow Back," 937.
22. Kaneva, 937; Melissa M. Ahern et al., "The Association Between Mountaintop Mining and Birth Defects Among Live Births in Central Appalachia, 1996–2003," *Environmental Research* 111, no. 6 (2011): 838.
23. Keith J. Zullig and Michael Hendryx, "Health-Related Quality of Life among Central Appalachian Residents in Mountaintop Mining Counties," *American Journal of Public Health* 101, no. 5 (2011): 848.
24. Kate Mishkin, "Without Federal Funding, Study on Health Effects of Mountaintop Removal Ends," *Charleston Gazette-Mail*, March 21, 2018, https://www.wvgazettemail .com/news/health/without-federal-funding-study-on-health-effects-of-mountaintop -removal/article_24a6d16a-faee-59c9-a44b-e1be9494c0ad.html.
25. Jan Pytalski, "We Have Questions: Seeking Explanation for Halted Mining Impact Study in Appalachia," *100 Days in Appalachia*, October 28, 2017, https://www.100daysin appalachia.com/2017/10/28/questions-seeking-explanation-halted-mining-impact -study-appalachia/.
26. M'Gonigle and Takeda, "The Liberal Limits of Environmental Law," 1107.
27. M'Gonigle and Takeda, 1107.
28. Jedediah Purdy, "The Long Environmental Justice Movement," *Ecology Law Quarterly* 44, no. 4 (2018): 810.
29. Jeanne Marie Zokovitch Paben, "Green Power & Environmental Justice—Does Green Discriminate?," *Texas Tech Law Review* 46, no. 4 (2014): 1071.
30. Eric K. Yamamoto and Jen-L W. Lyman, "Racializing Environmental Justice," *Colorado Law Review* 72, no. 2 (2001): 359.
31. Yamamoto and Lyman, 359.
32. Michael Hendryx, "Poverty and Mortality Disparities in Central Appalachia: Mountaintop Mining and Environmental Justice," *Journal of Health Disparities Research and Practice* 4, no. 3 (2011): 50.
33. Sarah J. Surber and D. Scott Simonton, "Disparate Impacts of Coal Mining and Reclamation Concerns for West Virginia and Central Appalachia," *Resources Policy* 54 (2017): 2.
34. Surber and Simonton, 2.
35. Barry, *Standing Our Ground*, 20.
36. Joyce M. Barry, "Mountaineers Are Always Free?: An Examination of the Effects of Mountaintop Removal in West Virginia," *Women's Studies Quarterly* 29, no. 1/2 (2001): 119.
37. Barry, 119.
38. Barry, *Standing Our Ground*, 54.
39. Barry, 54.
40. Taylor, "Race, Class, Gender, and American Environmentalism," 37.
41. Taylor, 37.
42. Talyor, 37.
43. Taylor, 38.
44. Dorceta E. Taylor, "Women of Color, Environmental Justice, and Ecofeminism," in *Ecofeminism: Women, Culture, Nature*, ed. Karen J. Warren (Indianapolis: Indiana University Press, 1997), 63.

45. Talory, 63.
46. Barry, *Standing Our Ground*, 41.
47. Wilkerson, *To Live Here You Have to Fight*, 197–200.
48. Nicholas F. Stump, "Following New Lights: Critical Legal Research Strategies as a Spark for Law Reform in Appalachia," *American University Journal of Gender, Social Policy, and the Law* 23, no. 4 (2014): 650.
49. 30 U.S.C. § 1253(a) (2012); Jason Rapp, "Coal and Water: Reclaiming the Clean Water Act for Environmental Protection," *Tulane Environmental Law Journal* 25, no. 1 (2011): 104–5.
50. *Ohio Valley Envtl. Coal. v. Aracoma Coal Co.*, 556 F.3d 177, 190 (4th Cir. 2009).
51. 33 U.S.C. § 1342.
52. 33 U.S.C. § 1344.
53. 33 U.S.C. § 1344(b)(1).
54. *Nat'l Min. Ass'n v. McCarthy*, 758 F.3d 243, 249 (D.C. Cir. 2014)
55. Rapp, "Coal and Water," 100.
56. *Kentuckians for Commonwealth v. U.S. Army Corps of Eng'rs*, 963 F. Supp. 2d 670, 685 (W.D. Ky. 2013).
57. 33 C.F.R. § 320.4(a)(1).
58. "Federal Actions to Address Environmental Justice in Minority Populations and Low-Income Populations," Executive Order No. 12898, 59 Federal Register 7629, February 11, 1994.
59. Rachel Kalman, "EPA's Mercury Cap and Trade Rule: An Environmental Injustice for Women," *Cardozo Journal of Law and Gender* 13, no. 1 (2006): 113.
60. *Kentuckians for Commonwealth v. U.S. Army Corps of Eng'rs*, 963 F. Supp. 2d 670, 685 (W.D. Ky. 2013).
61. Sara Gersen, "The Potential of State Coal-Purchasing Legislation to Decrease Mountaintop Removal Mining," *New York University Environmental Law Journal* 18, no. 3 (2011): 472.
62. Forman, "The Uncertain Future of NEPA and Mountaintop Removal," 193.
63. Gersen, "The Potential of State Coal-Purchasing Legislation," 472.
64. Rapp, "Coal and Water," 118.
65. Brian S. Clarke, "The Clash of Old and New Fourth Circuit Ideologies: Boyer-Liberto v. Fontainebleau Corp. and the Moderation of the Fourth Circuit," *South Carolina Law Review* 66, no. 4 (2015): 927–28.
66. Andrew J. Taylor, *Elephant's Edge: The Republicans as a Ruling Party* (Westport: Praeger Publishers, 2005), 78.
67. Gersen, "The Potential of State Coal-Purchasing Legislation," 468–69.
68. Rapp, "Coal and Water," 111.
69. *Bragg v. Robertson*, 72 F. Supp. 2d 642, 661 (S.D.W. Va. 1999).
70. *Bragg*, 72 F. Supp. 2d at 663.
71. *Bragg v. W. Virginia Coal Ass'n*, 248 F.3d 275, 297–98 (4th Cir. 2001).
72. *Bragg*, 248 F.3d at 297–98.
73. *Kentuckians for the Commonwealth, Inc. v. Rivenburgh*, 204 F. Supp. 2d 927, 940 (S.D.W. Va. 2002).
74. *Kentuckians for the Commonwealth, Inc.*, 204 F. Supp. 2d at 946.
75. *Kentuckians for the Commonwealth, Inc.*, 204 F. Supp. 2d at 946.
76. *Kentuckians for the Commonwealth, Inc.*, 204 F. Supp. 2d at 946.
77. *Kentuckians for Commonwealth Inc. v. Rivenburgh*, 317 F.3d 425, 445 (4th Cir. 2003).
78. Rapp, "Coal and Water," 110.
79. Gersen, "The Potential of State Coal-Purchasing Legislation," 470.
80. Gersen, 471.

81. *Ohio Valley Envtl. Coal. v. U.S. Army Corps of Engineers*, 479 F. Supp. 2d 607, 631, 636 (S.D.W. Va. 2007).
82. *Ohio Valley Envtl. Coal.*, 479 F. Supp. 2d at 635–36.
83. *Ohio Valley Envtl. Coal.*, 479 F. Supp. 2d at 616.
84. *Ohio Valley Envtl. Coal.*, 479 F. Supp. 2d at 656.
85. *Ohio Valley Envtl. Coal.*, 479 F. Supp. 2d at 660.
86. *Ohio Valley Envtl. Coal. v. Aracoma Coal Co.*, 556 F.3d 177, 198 (4th Cir. 2009).
87. *Ohio Valley Envtl. Coal.*, 556 F.3d at 198.
88. *Ohio Valley Envtl. Coal.*, 556 F.3d at 201.
89. *Ohio Valley Envtl. Coal.*, 556 F.3d at 226.
90. *Ohio Valley Envtl. Coal.*, 556 F.3d at 226.
91. *Kentuckians for Commonwealth v. U.S. Army Corps of Engineers*, 963 F. Supp. 2d 670, 674 (W.D. Ky. 2013).
92. *Kentuckians for Commonwealth*, 963 F. Supp. 2d at 674.
93. *Kentuckians for Commonwealth*, 963 F. Supp. 2d at 684.
94. *Kentuckians for Commonwealth*, 963 F. Supp. 2d at 685.
95. Mark Cherry, "Permit to Poison: The Failure of the Federalist Regulatory Regime to Address the Human Health Impacts of Mountaintop Removal Coal Mining," *Columbia Human Rights Law Review* 47, no. 1 (2015): 216.
96. *Kentuckians for the Commonwealth v. U.S. Army Corps of Eng'rs*, 746 F.3d 698, 708 (6th Cir. 2014).
97. Cherry, "Permit to Poison," 220.
98. Gersen, "The Potential of State Coal-Purchasing Legislation," 481.
99. H.B. 2709, 2007 Gen. Assemb., Reg. Sess. (N.C. 2008), quoted in Gersen, "The Potential of State Coal-Purchasing Legislation," 482.
100. McGinley, "From Pick and Shovel to Mountaintop Removal," 94.
101. Restatement (Second) of Torts § 821D (1979).
102. Gersen, "The Potential of State Coal-Purchasing Legislation," 478.
103. Restatement (Second) of Torts § 821B (1979).
104. Gersen, "The Potential of State Coal-Purchasing Legislation," 480.
105. Gersen, 479–80.
106. Gersen, 477.
107. Baller and Pantilat, "Defenders of Appalachia," 649.
108. *Caperton v. A.T. Massey Coal Co.*, 556 U.S. 868, 872 (2009).
109. Gersen, "The Potential of State Coal-Purchasing Legislation," 479.
110. "Coal Production Using Mountaintop Removal Mining Decreases by 62% Since 2008," *Today in Energy*, U.S. Energy Information Administration, July 7, 2015, https://www.eia.gov/todayinenergy/detail.php?id=21952.
111. "Coal Production Using Mountaintop Removal Mining Decreases by 62% Since 2008," *Today in Energy*.
112. Arathy S. Nair, "Peabody Chapter 11 Tops String of U.S. Coal Bankruptcies," *Reuters*, April 15, 2016, https://www.reuters.com/article/us-usa-coal-bankruptcy/peabody-chapter-11-tops-string-of-u-s-coal-bankruptcies-idUSKCN0XC2KQ.
113. Tom Latek, "Ky. Congressman Wants Health Study on Mountaintop Removal," *Kentucky Today*, April 4, 2019, http://kentuckytoday.com/stories/ky-congressman-wants-health-study-on-mountaintop-removal,18776.
114. Michele Morrone and Geoffrey L. Buckley, "Introduction: Environmental Justice and Appalachia," in *Mountains of Injustice: Social and Environmental Justice in Appalachia*, ed. Michele Morrone and Geoffrey L. Buckley (Athens: Ohio University Press, 2013), xi.
115. Morrone and Buckley, xi.
116. Morrone and Buckley, xii.

117. Morrone and Buckley, xii.
118. Morrone and Buckley, xii.
119. Pierce Greenberg, "Disproportionality and Resource-Based Environmental Inequality: An Analysis of Neighborhood Proximity to Coal Impoundments in Appalachia," *Rural Sociology* 82, no. 1 (2017): 172–73.
120. Robert D. Bulland, *Dumping in Dixie: Race, Class, And Environmental Quality* (New York: Routledge, 2018), 51–53.
121. Bulland, 52.
122. Bulland, 53.
123. Bulland, 54.
124. Erica D. Thomasson et al., "Acute Health Effects after the Elk River Chemical Spill, West Virginia, January 2014," *Public Health Reports* 132, no. 2 (2017), 197.
125. Tribune News Services, "Sentencings Set for Ex-Execs in West Virginia Chemical Spill," *Chicago Tribune*, January 31, 2016, https://www.chicagotribune.com/nation-world /ct-west-virginia-chemical-spill-sentencing-20160131-story.html.
126. "The Appalachian Petrochemical Renaissance," U.S. Department of Energy, https://www .energy.gov/sites/prod/files/2019/06/f64/FE_petrochemInfo%20copy_6.26.19.pdf.
127. Charles J. Denham, "Chemical Industry," e-WV: The West Virginia Encyclopedia, West Virginia Humanities Council, accessed December 5, 2019, https://www.wvencyclopedia .org/articles/1124.
128. Mark Gillispie, "Ethane Storage Seen as Key to Revitalization of Appalachia," *Associated Press*, April 29, 2019, https://apnews.com/8873394dd33647ddb369978bcfdc4e2d.
129. Jim Polson, "West Virginia Gets China Energy Deal That Dwarfs State's GDP," *Bloomberg*, November 9, 2017, https://www.bloomberg.com/news/articles/2017-11-09 /west-virginia-gets-china-energy-deal-that-dwarfs-s-gdp.
130. Sherry Cable, "Natural Gas Fracking on Public Lands: The Trickle-Down Impacts of Neoliberalism in Ohio's Utica Shale Region," in *Fractured Communities: Risk, Impacts, and Protest against Hydraulic Fracking in U.S. Shale Regions*, ed. Anthony E. Ladd (Camden, NJ: Rutgers University Press, 2018), 41.
131. David Matchen and Becky Calwell, "Marcellus Shale," e-WV: The West Virginia Encyclopedia, West Virginia Humanities Council, accessed December 5, 2019, https:// www.wvencyclopedia.org/articles/2334.
132. Philip L. Staddon and Michael H. Depledge, "Implications of Unconventional Gas Extraction on Climate Change," in *The Human and Environmental Impact of Fracking: How Fracturing Shale for Gas Affects Us and Our World*, ed. Madelon L. Finkel (Santa Barbara, CA: ABC-Clio, 2015), 86.
133. Staddon and Depledge, 86.
134. Staddon and Depledge, 90.
135. James M. Van Nostrand, "An Energy and Sustainability Roadmap for West Virginia," *West Virginia Law Review* 115, no. 3 (2013): 883.
136. "Natural Gas and Climate Change," Appalachian Mountain Advocates, accessed December 5, 2019, http://www.appalmad.org/natural-gas-and-climate-change/.
137. Hilary M. Goldberg, Melanie Stallings Williams, and Deborah Cours, "It's a Nuisance: The Future of Fracking Litigation in the Wake of *Parr v. Aruba Petroleum, Inc.*," *Virginia Environmental Law Journal* 33, no. 1 (2015): 4.
138. Heidi Gorovitz Robertson, "Get Out from under My Land! Hydraulic Fracturing, Forced Pooling or Unitization, and the Role of the Dissenting Landowner," *Georgetown Environmental Law Review* 30, no. 4 (2018): 683.
139. Benjamin L. McCready, "Like It or Not, You're Fracked: Why State Preemption of Municipal Bans Are Unjustified in the Fracking Context," *Drexel Law Review Online* 9 (2017): 61.

140. Kate Mishkin, "Pipeline Shouldn't Have Access to Streamlined Permit, Environmental Lawyers Say," *Charleston Gazette-Mail*, February 23, 2018, https://www.wvgazettemail.com/news/pipeline-shouldn-t-have-access-to-streamlined-permit-environmental-lawyers/article_b2451c5d-5224-5f16-a28c-518d7bb8fe10.html.

141. Russell McLenson, "Nature Conservancy Study Shows Appalachian Mountains to Be a Climate Change 'Stronghold,' " *The Huffington Post*, June 6, 2012, https://www.huffpost.com/entry/nature-conservancy-study-global-warming_n_1574671.

142. McLenson, "Nature Conservancy."

143. Chris Swanston et al., "Vulnerability of Forests of the Midwest and Northeast United States to Climate Change," *Climate Change* 146, no. 1–2 (2018): 109.

144. John Abraham, "Fires and Drought Cook Tennessee—A State Represented by Climate Deniers," *The Guardian*, December 2, 2016, https://www.theguardian.com/environment/climate-consensus-97-per-cent/2016/dec/02/fires-and-drought-cook-tennessee-a-state-represented-by-climate-deniers.

145. "What Climate Change Means for West Virginia," EPA 430-F-16-050, Environmental Protection Agency (2016), accessed December 5, 2019, https://19january2017snapshot.epa.gov/sites/production/files/2016-09/documents/climate-change-wv.pdf.

146. "What Climate Change Means for West Virginia," Environmental Protection Agency.

147. "Exposed: Climate Change," *Appalachian Voice*, December 18, 2014, http://appvoices.org/2014/12/18/exposed-climate-change/.

148. "What Climate Change Means for West Virginia," Environmental Protection Agency.

149. "Paris Agreement—Status of Ratification," United Nations Climate Change, accessed December 5, 2019, http://unfccc.int/paris_agreement/items/9444.php.

150. "Remarks Announcing United States Withdrawal from the United Nations Framework Convention on Climate Change Paris Agreement," Daily Comp. Pres. Docs., 2017 DCPD No. 201700373, https://www.govinfo.gov/content/pkg/DCPD-201700373/html/DCPD-201700373.htm.

151. Lisa Friedman, "Trump Takes a First Step toward Scrapping Obama's Global Warming Policy," *New York Times*, October 4, 2017, https://www.nytimes.com/2017/10/04/climate/trump-climate-change.html.

152. Justin Gillis and Nadja Popovich, "The U.S. Is the Biggest Carbon Polluter in History. It Just Walked away from the Paris Climate Deal," *New York Times*, June 1, 2017, https://www.nytimes.com/interactive/2017/06/01/climate/us-biggest-carbon-polluter-in-history-will-it-walk-away-from-the-paris-climate-deal.html.

153. Yong-Xiang Zhang et al., "The Withdrawal of the U.S. from the Paris Agreement and Its Impact on Global Climate Change Governance," *Advances in Climate Change Research* 8, no. 4 (2017): 214.

154. Mark Hand, "EPA Chief Exaggerates Growth of Coal Jobs by Tens of Thousands," *Think Progress*, June 5, 2017, https://thinkprogress.org/epa-chief-exaggerates-coal-job-growth-2ab69ed36b6/.

155. Eric Wolff, "Trump Calls for Coal, Nuclear Power Plant Bailout," *Politico*, June 1, 2018, https://www.politico.com/story/2018/06/01/donald-trump-rick-perry-coal-plants-617112.

156. Doina Chiacu and Valerie Volcovici, "EPA Chief Pruitt Refuses to Link CO_2 and Global Warming," *Scientific American*, March 10, 2017, https://www.scientificamerican.com/article/epa-chief-pruitt-refuses-to-link-co2-and-global-warming/.

157. "Stream Protection Rule," Office of Surface Mining and Enforcement, accessed December 5, 2019, https://www.osmre.gov/programs/rcm/streamprotectionrule.shtm.

158. Warren Cornwall, "Demise of Stream Rule Won't Revitalize Coal Industry," *Science Magazine*, February 16, 2017, https://www.sciencemag.org/news/2017/02/demise-stream-rule-won-t-revitalize-coal-industry.

159. Nadja Popovich, Livia Albeck-Ripka, and Kendra Pierre-Louis, "78 Environmental Rules on the Way Out under Trump," *New York Times*, December 28, 2018, https://www.ny times.com/interactive/2017/10/05/climate/trump-environment-rules-reversed.html.
160. Popovich, Albeck-Ripka, and Pierre-Louis, "78 Environmental Rules."
161. Popovich, Albeck-Ripka, and Pierre-Louis, "78 Environmental Rules."
162. Elizabeth Shogren, "Trump's Judges: A Second Front in the Environmental Rollback," *Yale Environmental 360*, August 28, 2017, https://e360.yale.edu/features/trumps -judges-the-second-front-in-an-environmental-onslaught.
163. Speth, *The Bridge at the End of the World*, 72.
164. "The Causes of Climate Change," NASA, accessed December 5, 2019, https://climate .nasa.gov/causes/.
165. Gavin Buxton, *Alternative Energy Technologies: An Introduction with Computer Simulations* (Boca Raton: Taylor & Francis Group, 2015), 3.
166. "Paris Agreement: Essential Elements," The Paris Agreement. United Nations Climate Change, accessed December 5, 2019, https://unfccc.int/process/the-paris-agreement /what-is-the-paris-agreement.
167. Bob Silberg, "Why a Half-Degree Temperature Rise Is a Big Deal," *NASA News*, June 29, 2016, https://climate.nasa.gov/news/2458/why-a-half-degree-temperature-rise-is-a -big-deal/.
168. Silberg, "Why a Half-Degree Temperature Rise Is a Big Deal."
169. Tom Miles, "Global Temperatures on Track for 3–5 Degree Rise by 2100: U.N.," *Reuters*, November 29, 2018, https://www.reuters.com/article/us-climate-change-un/global -temperatures-on-track-for-3-5-degree-rise-by-2100-u-n-idUSKCN1NY186.
170. David Wallace-Wells, "Time to Panic," *New York Times*, February 16, 2019, https://www .nytimes.com/2019/02/16/opinion/sunday/fear-panic-climate-change-warming.html.
171. "Summary for Policymakers of IPCC Special Report on Global Warming of 1.5°C Approved by Governments," Intergovernmental Panel on Climate Change, October 8, 2018, https://www.ipcc.ch/2018/10/08/summary-for-policymakers-of-ipcc-special -report-on-global-warming-of-1-5c-approved-by-governments/.
172. Helee de Coninck et al., "Strengthening and Implementing the Global Response," in *Global Warming of 1.5 °C: An IPCC Special Report*, ed. Masson-Delmotte, V. et al., 317. Intergovernmental Panel on Climate Change, 2018. https://www.ipcc.ch/sr15/chapter /chapter-4/.
173. Wood, *Nature's Trust*, 155.
174. Ross Gelbspan, *Boiling Point: How Politicians, Big Oil and Coal, Journalists, and Activists Have Fueled a Climate Crisis—And What We Can Do to Avert* Disaster (New York: Basic Books, 2004), 1, quoted in Wood, *Nature's Trust*, 156.
175. Gelbspan, 336.
176. Speth, *The Bridge at the End of the World*, 20.
177. Speth, 38.
178. Speth, 38.
179. "Forests," World Resources Institute, accessed December 5, 2019, http://www.wri.org /our-work/topics/forests.
180. Speth, *The Bridge at the End of the World*, 30.
181. Speth, 33.
182. Speth, 36.
183. Speth, 37.
184. Speth, 34.
185. "Overfishing," World Wildlife Fund, accessed December 5, 2019, https://www.world wildlife.org/threats/overfishing#.
186. Speth, *The Bridge at the End of the World*, 34.
187. Longo, Clausen, and Clark, *The Tragedy of the Commodity*, 8.

188. Stephen M. Meyer, *The End of the Wild* (Cambridge: MIT Press, 2006), 4, quoted in Speth, *The Bridge at the End of the World*, 36.

189. Meyer, 36.

190. Speth, *The Bridge at the End of the World*, 39.

191. Speth, 39.

192. Johan Rockström et al., "Planetary Boundaries: Exploring the Safe Operating Space for Humanity," *Ecology and Society* 14, no. 2 (2009).

193. Rockström et al.

194. Rockström et al.

195. Joseph Stromberg, "What Is the Anthropocene and Are We in It?" *Smithsonian Magazine*, January 2013, https://www.smithsonianmag.com/science-nature/what-is -the-anthropocene-and-are-we-in-it-164801414/.

196. Stromberg.

197. Jason W. Moore, "Introduction," in *Anthropocene or Capitalocene?: Nature, History, and the Crisis of Capitalism* (Oakland: PM Press, 2016), 6.

198. Moore, 5–8.

199. Gerardo Ceballos, Paul R. Ehrlich, and Rodolfo Dirzo, "Biological Annihilation via the Ongoing Sixth Mass Extinction Signaled by Vertebrate Population Losses and Declines," *Proceedings of the National Academy of Sciences of the United States of America* 114 (30) (2017).

200. John Mechlin, ed., "2018 Doomsday Clock Statement," Science and Security Board, Bulletin of the Atomic Scientists, 2018, https://thebulletin.org/2018-doomsday-clock -statement/.

201. Bell and York, "Community Economic Identity," 113.

202. Bell and York, 113.

203. Bell and York, 113.

204. Bell and York, 113.

205. Bell and York, 114.

206. Bell, *Fighting King Coal*, 92.

207. Bell, 89.

208. "Coal Mining," May 2018 National Industry-Specific Occupational Employment and Wage Estimates, U.S. Bureau of Labor Statistics, accessed December 5, 2019, https:// www.bls.gov/oes/current/naics4_212100.htm.

209. Bell and York, "Community Economic Identity," 139.

210. Bell and York, 139.

211. Bell and York, 139.

212. Bell and York, 126, 128.

213. Bell and York, 128–29.

214. Bell and York, 130–33.

215. Bell and York, 130–33.

216. Bell and York, 132.

217. Bell and York, 129.

218. Bell and York, 116.

219. Bell and York, 131–32.

220. Lewis, *Black Coal Miners in America*, 188.

221. Bell and York, "Community Economic Identity," 121.

222. Fraser, *Fortunes of Feminism*, 223.

223. Martin Armstrong, "Women Work More Than Men," *Statista*, March 8, 2019, https:// www.statista.com/chart/13940/women-work-more-than-men/.

224. Duffy, "Making Care Count," 12.

225. Duffy, 17.

226. "West Virginia Poverty Rate Is Up and Has Not Decreased Since the Recession," *WV*

News, September 13, 2018, https://www.wvnews.com/news/wvnews/west-virginia
-poverty-rate-is-up-and-has-not-decreased/article_bbc6689e-99ea-5bc7-983e
-2ffb9b44d734.html.

227. "West Virginia," National Women's Law Center, accessed December 5, 2019, https://
nwlc.org/state/west-virginia/.

228. C. E. Miewald and E. J. McCann, "Gender, Struggle, Scale, and the Production of Place
in the Appalachian Coalfields," *Environment and Planning* 36, no. 6 (2004): 1054,
quoted in Bell and York, "Community Economic Identity," 134.

229. Bell and York, "Community Economic Identity," 134.

230. Bell and York, 134–35.

231. Scott, *Removing Mountains*, 34.

232. Stephanie Alvaro, Jensen Mills, and Politifact, "How Many Oil and Gas Jobs Are There
in W.Va.? It's Surprisingly Hard to Say," *WV Public Broadcasting*, April 8, 2019, https://
www.wvpublic.org/post/how-many-oil-and-gas-jobs-are-there-wva-it-s-surprisingly
-hard-say#stream/0.

233. Ken Ward Jr., "The Coal Industry Extracted a Steep Price from West Virginia. Now
Natural Gas Is Leading the State Down the Same Path," *ProPublica*, April 27, 2018,
https://www.propublica.org/article/west-virginia-coal-industry-rise-of-natural-gas.

234. Nick Wing, "Joe Manchin Shoots Cap-and-Trade Bill with Rifle in New Ad," *Huffington
Post*, December 6, 2017, https://www.huffpost.com/entry/joe-manchin-ad-dead-aim
_n_758457.

235. McGinley, "From Pick and Shovel to Mountaintop Removal," 24.

236. Bell and York, "Community and Economic Identity," 121.

237. Eller, *Uneven Ground*, 232.

238. Eller, 236.

239. Eller, 232.

240. David Koenig, "AP Fact Check: Trump's Vow to Create Appalachian Coal Jobs," AP
News, May 5, 2016, https://apnews.com/2c55cd2496a14bdd98bcf84ccdb34810.

241. Chris Benderev and Kelly McEvers, "In the Coal Counties of Central Appalachia, Will
Trump's Promises Come True?," NPR, May 9, 2018, https://www.npr.org/2018
/05/09/607273500/in-the-coal-counties-of-central-appalachia-will-trump-s-promises
-come-true.

242. Jessica Lilly et al., "Is Appalachia Trump Country?" *WV Public Broadcasting*, March 17,
2017, https://www.wvpublic.org/post/appalachia-trump-country#stream/0.

243. Bell and York, "Community Economic Identity," 139.

244. Abbas Degan Darweesh and Nesaem Mehdi Abdullah, "A Critical Discourse Analysis of
Donald Trump's Sexist Ideology," *Journal of Education and Practice* 7, no. 30 (2016):
92–94.

245. Scott Horsley, "Fact Check: Hilary Clinton and Coal Jobs," NPR, May 3, 2016, https://
www.npr.org/2016/05/03/476485650/fact-check-hillary-clinton-and-coal-jobs.

246. Hilary Rodham Clinton, *What Happened* (New York: Simon & Schuster, 2017), 287.

247. Horsley, "Fact Check."

248. David Leonhardt and Ian Prasad Philbrick, "Donald Trump's Racism: The Definitive
List," *New York Times*, January 15, 2018, https://www.nytimes.com/interactive
/2018/01/15/opinion/leonhardt-trump-racist.html.

249. Scott, *Removing Mountains*, 34.

250. Elizabeth Catte, "Resisting Myths of Whiteness in Appalachia," 100 Days in
Appalachia, March 15, 2017, https://www.100daysinappalachia.com/2017/03
/elizabeth-catte-resisting-myths-whiteness-appalachia/.

251. John C. Inscoe, "Race and Racism in Nineteenth-Century Southern Appalachia:
Myths, Realities, and Ambiguities," in *Appalachia in the Making: The Mountain South in*

the Nineteenth Century, ed. Mary Beth Pudup, Dwight B. Billings, and Altina L. Waller (Chapel Hill: University of North Carolina Press, 1995), 110.

252. Allen W. Batteau, *The Invention of Appalachia* (Tuscan: University of Arizona Press, 1990), 78.

253. Catte, "Resisting Myths of Whiteness in Appalachia."

254. Scott, *Removing Mountains*, 71.

255. Thomas Blake Earle, "No White Man Left Behind: Saving Coal Country Has Never Been about Energy. It's Been about Rescuing White Men," *Washington Post*, October 27, 2017, https://www.washingtonpost.com/news/made-by-history/wp/2017/10/27/no-white -man-left-behind/.

256. Earle, "No White Man Left Behind."

257. Ann M. Eisenberg, "Just Transitions," *Southern California Law Review* 92, no. 2 (2019): 300.

258. Daniel Faber et al., "Trump's Electoral Triumph: Class, Race, Gender, and the Hegemony of the Polluter-Industrial Complex," *Capitalism, Nature, Socialism* 28, no. 1 (2017): 8.

259. Sherrilyn Ifill, "When Trump Attacks One Black Woman, We All Feel It," *Washington Post*, November 13, 2018, https://www.washingtonpost.com/opinions/when-trump -attacks-one-black-woman-we-all-feel-it/2018/11/13/50d77c06-e756-11e8-b8dc -66cca409c180_story.html; Katie Rogers and Nicholas Fandos, "Trump Tells Congress-women to 'Go Back' to the Countries They Came From," *New York Times*, July 14, 2019, https://www.nytimes.com/2019/07/14/us/politics/trump-twitter-squad-congress .html.

260. Faber et al., "Trump's Electoral Triumph," 2–6.

261. Faber et al., 7–8.

262. Dante Chinni and Matt Rivera, "West Virginia: How the Bluest State Became the Reddest," *NBC News*, December 18, 2016, https://www.nbcnews.com/meet-the-press /west-virginia-how-bluest-state-became-reddest-n697491.

263. Faber et al., "Trump's Electoral Triumph," 7.

264. Faber et al., 6.

265. George Packer, "The Corruption of the Republican Party," *Atlantic*, December 14, 2018, https://www.theatlantic.com/ideas/archive/2018/12/how-did-republican-party-get-so -corrupt/578095/.

266. Faber et al., "Trump's Electoral Triumph," 3–6.

267. Elizabeth Catte, "Appalachia Isn't the Reason We're Living in Trump Country," *Literary Hub*, February 8, 2018, https://lithub.com/appalachia-isnt-the-reason-were-living-in -trump-country/.

268. Faber et al., "Trump's Electoral Triumph," 4.

269. Brent Budowsky, "Sanders Lifts Spirits in West Virginia," *Hill*, March 14, 2017, https:// thehill.com/blogs/pundits-blog/lawmaker-news/323921-sanders-lifts-spirits-in-west -virginia.

270. Elizabeth Catte, "There Is No Neutral There: Appalachia as a Mythic 'Trump Country,' " *Medium*, October 17, 2016, https://medium.com/@elizabethcatte/there-is-no-neutral -there-appalachia-as-a-mythic-trump-country-ee6ed7f300dc.

271. Catte, "There Is No Neutral There."

272. Nicholas Carnes and Noam Lupu, "It's Time to Bust the Myth: Most Trump Voters Were Not Working Class," *Washington Post*, June 5, 2017, https://www.washingtonpost.com /news/monkey-cage/wp/2017/06/05/its-time-to-bust-the-myth-most-trump-voters -were-not-working-class/.

273. Lisa R. Pruitt, "The Women Feminism Forgot: Rural and Working-Class White Women in the Era of Trump," *University of Toledo Law Review* 49, no. 3 (2018): 598.

274. Catte, "Resisting Myths of Whiteness in Appalachia."

275. "Appalachia's Population," Appalachian Regional Commission, accessed December 5, 2019, https://www.arc.gov/noindex/research/ACS-infographics2013–2017/Data Snapshot-AppalachiasPopulation.pdf.
276. Schumann, "Introduction," 8.
277. "Appalachia's Population," Appalachian Regional Commission.
278. Matt McKillop and Daniel Newman, "Years of Slower Population Growth Persisted in 2017," *Pew*, June 20, 2018, https://www.pewtrusts.org/research-and-analysis /articles/2018/06/20/years-of-slower-population-growth-persisted-in-2017?utm _campaign=governing&utm_source=twitter&utm_medium=social&utm_content =2017map.
279. Kelvin Pollard and Linda A. Jacobsen, "The Appalachian Region: A Data Overview from the 2011–2015 American Community Survey," Data Snapshots, Appalachian Regional Commission (2017), https://www.arc.gov/research/researchreportdetails.asp?REPORT _ID=132.
280. Bryan T. McNeil, *Combating Mountaintop Removal: New Directions in the Fight against Big Coal* (Urbana: University of Illinois Press, 2011), 9–10.
281. McNeil, 10.
282. Perdue and McCarty, "Unearthing a Network of Resistance," 45.
283. Perdue and McCarty, 35.
284. Perdue and McCarty, 39.
285. Perdue and McCarty, 39.
286. Nicholas F. Stump, "Mountain Resistance: Appalachian Civil Disobedience in Critical Legal Research Modeled Law Reform," *Environs: Environmental Law and Policy Journal* 41, no. 1 (2017): 110–14.
287. Perdue and McCarty, "Unearthing a Network of Resistance," 46–50.
288. Perdue and McCarty, 46; Bell, *Fighting King Coal*, 34.
289. Perdue and McCarty, "Unearthing a Network of Resistance," 48.
290. Perdue and McCarty, 52.
291. *Bragg v. Robertson*, 72 F. Supp. 2d 642, 644 (S.D.W. Va. 1999).
292. *Ohio Valley Environmental Coalition v. Bulen*, 410 F.Supp.2d 450 (S.D.W. Va. 2004).
293. Perdue and McCarty, "Unearthing a Network of Resistance," 54–55.
294. Baller and Pantilat, "Defenders of Appalachia," 649.
295. Baller and Pantilat, 649.
296. Baller and Pantilat, 663.
297. Perdue and McCarty, "Unearthing a Network of Resistance," 50.
298. Perdue and McCarty, 50.
299. Perdue and McCarty, 50.
300. Witt, *Religion and Resistance in Appalachia*, 37.
301. Witt, 37.
302. Witt, 37–38.
303. Witt, 38.
304. Sparki Ran, "10 Arrested in Civil Disobedience at WV Mountaintop Removal and Coal Sludge Impoundment Sites," *The Understory*, May 23, 2009, https://www.ran.org/the -understory/10_arrested_in_civil_disobedience_at_wv_mountaintop_removal_and _coal_sludge_impoundment_sites/.
305. Perdue and McCarty, "Unearthing a Network of Resistance," 53.
306. Perdue and McCarty, 53.
307. Witt, *Religion and Resistance in Appalachia*, 38.
308. Witt, 38.
309. Witt, 38.
310. Witt, 40–41.

311. Emily Shugerman, " 'Frustration, Anger, Helplessness': Virginia Pipeline Protesters on What Drove Them to Live in the Trees," *Independent*, May 5, 2018, https://www .independent.co.uk/news/world/americas/tree-sit-mountain-valley-pipeline-west -virginia-red-terry-franklin-county-protest-a8337311.html?utm_source=reddit.com.

312. Gregory S. Schneider, "Perched on a Platform High in a Tree, a 61-Year-Old Woman Fights a Gas Pipeline," *Washington Post*, April 21, 2018, https://www.washingtonpost .com/local/virginia-politics/perched-on-a-platform-high-in-a-tree-a-61-year-old -woman-fights-a-gas-pipeline/2018/04/21/3b8284b4-435e-11e8-bba2-0976a82b05a2 _story.html.

313. Schneider, "Perched on a Platform."

314. Drew Philp, "America's Tree Sitters Risk Lives on the Front Line," *Guardian*, May 26, 2018, https://www.theguardian.com/environment/2018/may/26/tree-sitters -appalachian-oil-pipeline-virginia-west.

315. Associated Press, "Professor Locks Herself to Pipeline Construction Equipment in Virginia," *CBS19*, June 28, 2018, https://www.cbs19news.com/content/news /Professor-locks-herself-to-pipeline-construction-equipment-in-Virginia-486853821 .html.

316. Barry, *Standing Our Ground*, 63.

317. Barry, 50.

318. Barry, 64.

319. Barry, 53.

320. Shannon Elizabeth Bell, *Our Roots Run Deep as Ironweed: Appalachian Women and the Fight for Environmental Justice* (Urbana: University of Illinois Press, 2013), 171.

321. Bell, 171.

322. Bell, 171–72.

323. Bell, 178.

324. Bell, 178.

325. Anna J. Willow and Samanatha Keefer, "Gendering Extraction: Expectations and Identities in Women's Motives for Shale Energy Opposition," *Journal of Research in Gender Studies* 5, no. 2 (2015): 93.

326. Willow and Keefer, 113.

327. Willow and Keefer, 113.

328. Willow and Keefer, 113.

329. Willow and Keefer, 115.

330. Barry, *Standing Our Ground*, 74.

331. Barry, 74.

332. Barry, 74.

333. Barry, 74.

334. Virginia Rinaldo Seitz, *Women, Development, and Communities for Empowerment in Appalachia* (Albany: State University of New York Press, 1995), 167–68.

335. Seitz, 167–68.

336. Seitz, 167–68.

337. Karen Beckwith, "Collective Identities of Class and Gender: Working-Class Women in the Pittston Coal Strike," *Political Psychology* 19, no.1 (1995): 155.

338. Beckwith, 156.

339. Beckwith, 156.

340. Seitz, *Women, Development, and Communities for Empowerment in Appalachia*, 168.

341. Beckwith, "Collective Identities of Class and Gender," 159.

342. "Inspired by West Virginia Strike, Teachers in Oklahoma and Kentucky Plan Walk Out," CNN Wire, April 2, 2018, https://ktla.com/2018/04/02/inspired-by-west-virginia -strike-teachers-in-oklahoma-and-kentucky-plan-walk-out/.

343. Alia E. Dastagir, "West Virginia Teachers' Victory Shows 'Power of Women' as More Battles Loom," *USA Today*, March 8, 2018, https://www.usatoday.com/story/news /2018/03/08/west-virginia-teachers-victory-shows-power-women-more-battles-loom /403374002/.
344. Strauss, "This Time, It Wasn't about Pay."

CHAPTER 6

1.   Krever, "The Rule of Law and the Rise of Capitalism," 193.
2.   M'Gonigle and Takeda, "The Liberal Limits of Environmental Law," 1113.
3.   M'Gonigle and Takeda, 1113.
4.   M'Gonigle and Takeda, 1115.
5.   M'Gonigle and Takeda, 1110.
6.   M'Gonigle and Takeda, 1115.
7.   Naomi Mezey, "Law As Culture," *Yale Journal of Law and the Humanities* 13, no. 1 (2001): 51.
8.   Mezey, 51.
9.   Mezey, 51.
10. Robert W. Gordon, "Critical Legal Histories," *Stanford Law Review* 36, no. 1 (1984): 109, quoted in Mezey, "Law As Culture," 67.
11. M'Gonigle and Takeda, "The Liberal Limits of Environmental Law," 1110.
12. M'Gonigle and Takeda, 1109.
13. M'Gonigle and Takeda, 1109.
14. M'Gonigle and Takeda, 1109.
15. M'Gonigle and Takeda, 1098–99.
16. Diego Andreucci and Terrence McDonough, "Capitalism," in *Degrowth: A Vocabulary for a New Era*, ed. Giacomo D'Alisa, Federico Demaria, and Giorgios Kallis (New York: Routledge, 2015), 62.
17. Smith, *Green Capitalism*, 47.
18. Smith, 47.
19. Samuel Alexander, "The Optimal Material Threshold: Toward an Economics of Sufficiency," *Real-World Economics Review* 61 (2012): 15.
20. Samuel Alexander, "Voluntary Simplicity and the Social Reconstruction of Law: Degrowth from the Grassroots Up," *Environmental Values* 22, no. 2 (2013): 288.
21. Alexander, 288.
22. Devon G. Peña, *The Terror of the Machine: Technology, Work, Gender, and Ecology on the U.S.-Mexico Border* (Austin: University of Texas Press, 1997), 327.
23. Phillips and Rumens, "Introducing Contemporary Ecofeminism," 3.
24. Phillips and Rumens, 3.
25. Phillips and Rumens, 3.
26. Phillips and Rumens, 2.
27. Phillips and Rumens, 2.
28. Phillips and Rumens, 2.
29. Phillips and Rumens, 3.
30. Robert R. M. Verchick, "In a Greener Voice: Feminist Theory and Environmental Justice," *Harvard Women's Law Journal* 19 (1996): 58.
31. Verchick, 60.
32. Greta Gaard, "Ecofeminism Revisited: Rejecting Essentialism and Re-Placing Species in a Material Feminist Environmentalism," *Feminist Formations* 23, no. 2 (2011): 32–35.
33. Bina Agarwal, "The Gender and Environment Debate: Lessons from India," *Feminist Studies* 18, no.1 (1992): 150, quoted in Gaard, "Ecofeminism Revisited," 35.
34. Agarwal, 150.

35. Agarwal, 150.
36. Gaard, "Ecofeminism Revisited," 27.
37. Gaard, 35.
38. Gaard, 31.
39. Gaard, 31.
40. Ali Young and Scott Taylor, "Organizing and Managing Ecofeminism: Material Manifestations of Spiritual Principles in Business," in *Contemporary Perspectives on Ecofeminism*, ed. Mary Phillips and Nick Rumens (New York: Routledge, 2016), 215.
41. Gaard, "Ecofeminism Revisited," 36.
42. Gaard, 32.
43. Gaard, 27.
44. Gaard, 35.
45. Phillips and Rumens, "Introducing Contemporary Ecofeminism," 1.
46. Christine Bauhardt, "Solutions to the Crisis? The Green New Deal, Degrowth, and the Solidarity Economy: Alternatives to the Capitalist Growth Economy from an Ecofeminist Economics Perspective," *Ecological Economics* 102 (2014): 60.
47. Mary Mellor, "Ecofeminist Political Economy: Integrating Feminist Economics and Ecological Economics," *Feminist Economics* 11, no. 3 (2005): 123, quoted in Bauhardt, "Solutions to the Crisis," 61.
48. Mellor, 123.
49. Gaard, "Ecofeminism Revisited," 28.
50. Michael Lewis and Dan Swinney, "Social Economy & Solidarity Economy: Transformative Concepts for Unprecedented Times?," in *Solidarity Economy: Building Alternatives for People and Planet*, ed. Jenna Allard, Carl Davidson, and Julie Matthaei (Chicago: ChangeMaker Publications, 2008), 29.
51. Bauhardt, "Solutions to the Crisis," 66.
52. Bauhardt, 66.
53. Bauhardt, 64.
54. Bauhardt, 64.
55. Bauhardt, 64.
56. Bauhardt, 66.
57. Mies and Shiva, *Ecofeminism*, 297.
58. Mies and Shiva, 297.
59. Mies and Shiva, 306.
60. Mies and Shiva, 319.
61. Mies and Shiva, 319.
62. Mies and Shiva, 319.
63. Mies and Shiva, 321.
64. Mies and Shiva, 319–21.
65. Mies and Shiva, 319.
66. Mies and Shiva, 319–20.
67. Mies and Shiva, 320.
68. Mies and Shiva, 320.
69. Hans A. Baer, *Democratic Eco-Socialism as a Real Utopia: Transitioning to an Alternative World System* (New York: Berghahn Books, 2017), 137.
70. Michael Löwy, *Ecosocialism: A Radical Alternative to Capitalist Catastrophe* (Chicago: Haymarket Books, 2015), 7.
71. John Bellamy Foster, *The Ecological Revolution: Making Peace with the Planet* (New York: Monthly Review Press, 2009), 277, quoted in Baer, *Democratic Eco-Socialism as a Real Utopia*, 139.
72. Löwy, *Ecosocialism*, 26–27.
73. Löwy, 26–27.

74. Löwy, 27.
75. Kali Akuno, "It's Eco-Socialism or Death," interview by editors, *Jacobin*, Feb. 15, 2019, https://jacobinmag.com/2019/02/kali-akuno-interview-climate-change-cooperation-jackson.
76. Tero Toivanen, "Commons against Capitalism," in *The Politics of Ecosocialism: Transforming Welfare*, ed. Kajsa Borgnäs et al. (New York: Routledge, 2015), 130.
77. Toivanen, 129–30.
78. Toivanen, 124–25.
79. Toivanen, 125.
80. Ariel Salleh and Martin O'Connor, "Eco-socialism/Eco-feminism," *Capitalism, Nature, Socialism* 2, no. 1 (1991): 129.
81. Brownhill and Turner, "Ecofeminism at the Heart of Ecosocialism," 5.
82. Leigh Brownhill, "Earth Democracy and Ecosocialism: What's in a Name?," *Capitalism, Nature, Socialism* 21, no. 1 (2010): 97.
83. Joel Kovel, "The Ecofeminist Ground of Ecosocialism," *Capitalism, Nature, Socialism* 16, no. 2 (2005): 3, 7.
84. Ariel Salleh, "How the Ecological Footprint Is Sex-Gendered," in *Eco-Socialism as Politics: Rebuilding the Basis of Our Modern Civilisation*, ed. Qingzhi Huan (New York: Springer, 2010), 146.
85. Salleh, 146.
86. M'Gonigle and Takeda, "The Liberal Limits of Environmental Law," 1111.
87. M'Gonigle and Takeda, 1057.
88. M'Gonigle and Takeda, 1057–58.
89. M'Gonigle and Takeda, 1057.
90. David Marrani, "Human Rights and Environmental Protection: The Pressure of the Charter for the Environment on the French Administrative Courts," *Sustainable Development Law & Policy* 10, no. 1 (2009): 52.
91. Marrani, 52.
92. Marrani, 52.
93. Marrani, 52.
94. Dinah L. Shelton, "Developing Substantive Environmental Rights," *Journal of Human Rights and the Environment* 1, no. 1 (2010): 98.
95. James R. May, "Constitutional Directions in Procedural Environmental Rights," *Journal of Environmental Law & Litigation* 28, no. 1 (2013): 34–35.
96. Marrani, "Human Rights and Environmental Protection," 52.
97. Gonzalez, "Environmental Justice, Human Rights, and the Global South," 156–57.
98. "African Charter on Human and Peoples' Rights," African Commission on Human and Peoples' Rights, accessed December 5, 2019, https://www.achpr.org/legalinstruments/detail?id=49.
99. Dinah L. Shelton, "Whiplash and Backlash-Reflections on a Human Rights Approach to Environmental Protection," *Santa Clara Journal of International Law* 13, no. 1 (2015): 22.
100. Paris Agreement, multilateral, Dec. 12, 2015, U.N.T.S. I-54113, at 89, https://treaties.un.org/doc/Publication/UNTS/No%20Volume/54113/Part/I-54113-0800000280458f37.pdf.
101. David R. Boyd, *The Right to a Healthy Environment: Revitalizing Canada's Constitution* (Toronto: UBC Press, 2012), 131.
102. "Framework Principles on Human Rights and the Environment (2018)," United Nations Human Rights Office of the High Commissioner, accessed December 5, 2019, https://www.ohchr.org/EN/Issues/Environment/SREnvironment/Pages/FrameworkPrinciplesReport.aspx.
103. "UN Expert Calls for Global Recognition of the Right to Safe and Healthy Environment,"

United Nations Human Rights Office of the High Commissioner, March 5, 2018, https://www.ohchr.org/EN/NewsEvents/Pages/DisplayNews.aspx?NewsID=22755 &LangID=E.

104. David R. Boyd, *The Environmental Rights Revolution: A Global Study of Constitutions, Human Rights, and the Environment* (Toronto: UBC Press, 2012), 77.

105. Boyd, 76.

106. Boyd, 76.

107. Boyd, 77.

108. Boyd, 77.

109. Boyd, *The Right to a Healthy Environment*, 72.

110. Boyd, *The Environmental Rights Revolution*, 91.

111. Boyd, 91.

112. Mont. Const. Art. II, § 3.

113. Barton H. Thompson, "Constitutionalizing the Environment: The History and Future of Montana's Environmental Provisions," *Montana Law Review* 64, no. 1 (2003): 158.

114. Pa. Const. Art. I, § 27.

115. Pa. Const. Art. I, § 27.

116. Dana Drugmand, "Hawaii Joins Trend: Recognizes Constitutional Right to Safe Climate and Environment," *Climate Liability News*, January 5, 2016, https://www.climate liabilitynews.org/2018/01/05/hawaii-climate-environment-constitutional-right/.

117. David Naguib Pellow, *Resisting Global Toxics: Transnational Movements for Environmental Justice* (Cambridge, MA: MIT Press, 2007), 236–37.

118. Pellow, 238.

119. Pellow, 238.

120. M'Gonigle and Takeda, "The Liberal Limits of Environmental Law," 1057.

121. Caroline Bettinger-Lopez et al., "Redefining Human Rights Lawyering through the Lens of Critical Theory: Lessons for Pedagogy and Practice," *Georgetown Journal on Poverty Law & Policy* 18, no. 3 (2011): 350.

122. Avi Brisman, "The Criminalization of Peacemaking, Corporate Free Speech, and the Violence of Interpretation: New Challenges to Cause Lawyering," *City University of New York Law Review* 14, no. 2 (2011): 296.

123. Bettinger-Lopez et al., "Redefining Human Rights Lawyering through the Lens of Critical Theory," 351.

124. Bettinger-Lopez et al., 351.

125. Bettinger-Lopez et al., 352.

126. Anthony V. Alfieri, "Faith in Community: Representing 'Colored Town,' " *California Law Review* 95, no. 2 (2007): 1830, 1877, quoted in Bettinger-Lopez et al., "Redefining Human Rights Lawyering through the Lens of Critical Theory," 353.

127. Ascanio Piomelli, "The Democratic Roots of Collaborative Lawyering," *Clinical Law Review* 12, no. 2 (2006): 544, quoted in Bettinger-Lopez et al., "Redefining Human Rights Lawyering through the Lens of Critical Theory," 353.

128. Bettinger-Lopez et al., "Redefining Human Rights Lawyering through the Lens of Critical Theory," 353–54.

129. Deborah L. Rhode, "Public Interest Law: The Movement at Midlife," *Stanford Law Review* 60, no. 6 (2008): 2064, quoted in Bettinger-Lopez et al., "Redefining Human Rights Lawyering through the Lens of Critical Theory," 354.

130. Avi Brisman, "Reframing the Portrait of Lynne F. Stewart," *Journal of Law in Society* 12, no. 1–2 (2011): 7.

131. Stuart Scheingold and Anne Bloom, "Transgressive Cause Lawyering: Practice Sites and the Politicization of the Professional," *International Journal of the Legal Profession* 5, no. 2/3 (1998): 215.

132. Scheingold and Bloom, 215.

133. Dina Francesca Haynes, "Client-Centered Human Rights Advocacy," *Clinical Law Review* 13, no. 1 (2006): 385.

134. Bettinger-Lopez et al., "Redefining Human Rights Lawyering through the Lens of Critical Theory," 356.

135. Bettinger-Lopez et al., 356.

136. Berta Esperanza Hernández-Truyol, "The Gender Bend: Culture, Sex, and Sexuality—A Latcritical Human Rights Map of Latina/o Border Crossings," *Indiana Law Journal* 83, no. 4 (2008): 1330, quoted in Bettinger-Lopez et al., "Redefining Human Rights Lawyering through the Lens of Critical Theory," 357.

137. Kathryn McNeilly, *Human Rights and Radical Social Transformation: Futurity, Alterity, Power* (New York: Routledge, 2018), 8.

138. McNeilly, 135.

139. McNeilly, 135.

140. Ratna Kapur, *Gender, Alterity, and Human Rights: Freedom in a Fishbowl* (Cheltenham, UK: Edward Elgar 2018), 234–35.

141. Kapur, 235.

142. Dorceta E. Taylor, "The Rise of the Environmental Justice Paradigm: Injustice Framing and the Social Construction of Environmental Discourses," *The American Behavioral Scientist* 43, no. 4 (2000): 511.

143. Taylor, 511.

144. Taylor, 512.

145. Taylor, 514, 516.

146. Joseph Sax, "The Public Trust Doctrine in Natural Resource Law: Effective Judicial Intervention," *Michigan Law Review* 68, no. 3 (1970): 471.

147. Carol M. Rose, "Joseph Sax and the Idea of the Public Trust," *Ecology Law Quarterly* 25, no. 3 (1998): 352.

148. Mary Christina Wood and Charles W. Woodward, "Atmospheric Trust Litigation and the Constitutional Right to a Healthy Climate System: Judicial Recognition at Last," *Washington Journal of Environmental Law & Policy* 6, no. 2 (2016): 648–49.

149. Charles F. Wilkinson, "The Headwaters of the Public Trust: Some of the Traditional Doctrine," *Environmental Law* 19, no. 3 (1989): 429–31.

150. Wood, *Nature's Trust*, 126.

151. Klaus Bosselmann, *Earth Governance: Trusteeship of the Global Commons* (Cheltenham, UK: Edward Elgar, 2015), 181.

152. *Geer v. State of Conn.*, 161 U.S. 519, 534 (1896).

153. *Illinois Cent. R. Co. v. State of Illinois*, 146 U.S. 387, 460 (1892).

154. *Illinois Cent. R. Co.*, 146 U.S. at 460.

155. Hirokawa, "Some Pragmatic Observations about Radical Critique in Environmental Law," 241.

156. David Bollier, "Mary Wood's Crusade to Reinvigorate the Public Trust Doctrine," *News and Perspectives on the Commons*, February 10, 2014, http://www.bollier.org/blog/mary -wood%E2%80%99s-crusade-reinvigorate-public-trust-doctrine.

157. Alexandra B. Klass, "The Public Trust Doctrine in the Shadow of State Environmental Rights Laws: A Case Study," *Environmental Law* 45, no. 2 (2015): 440.

158. Wood, *Nature's Trust*, 138.

159. Wood, 139.

160. John C. Dernbach, James R. May, and Kenneth T. Kristl, "Robinson Township v. Commonwealth of Pennsylvania: Examination and Implications," *Rutgers University Law Review* 67, no. 5 (2015): 1169.

161. *Robinson Twp., Washington Cty. v. Com.*, 623 Pa. 564, 655 (2013).

162. *Robinson Twp.*, 623 Pa. at 689.

163. *Robinson Twp.*, 623 Pa. at 691–92.

164. Dernbach, May, and Kristl, "Robinson Township v. Commonwealth of Pennsylvania," 1169.

165. *Pennsylvania Envtl. Def. Found. v. Commonwealth*, 161 A.3d 911, 916 (Pa. 2017).

166. *Pennsylvania Envtl. Def. Found*, 161 A.3d at 916.

167. *Pennsylvania Envtl. Def. Found*, 161 A.3d at 939.

168. *Light v. United States*, 220 U.S. 523, 537 (1911).

169. Wood, *Nature's Trust*, 133.

170. Wood, 136.

171. Wood, 136.

172. Wood, 140.

173. Wood, 140.

174. Wood, 140.

175. Wood, 15–16.

176. Wood, 16.

177. Wood, 16.

178. Ipshita Mukherjee, "Atmospheric Trust Litigation—Paving the Way for a Fossil-Fuel Free World," *Stanford Law School Blogs*, July 5, 2017, https://law.stanford.edu/2017/07/05/atmospheric-trust-litigation-paving-the-way-for-a-fossil-fuel-free-world/.

179. *Juliana v. United States*, 217 F. Supp. 3d 1224 (D. Or. 2016).

180. "Juliana v. Unites States Youth Climate Lawsuit," OurChildrensTrust.org, accessed December 5, 2019, https://www.ourchildrenstrust.org/juliana-v-us.

181. John Schwartz, "Judges Give Both Sides a Grilling in Youth Climate Case against the Government," *New York Times*, June 4, 2019, https://www.nytimes.com/2019/06/04/climate/climate-lawsuit-juliana.html.

182. Richard Delgado, "Our Better Natures: A Revisionist View of Joseph Sax's Public Trust Theory of Environmental Protection, and Some Dark Thoughts on the Possibility of Law Reform," *Vanderbilt Law Review* 44, no. 6 (1991): 1225.

183. Delgado, 1222.

CHAPTER 7

1. M'Gonigle and Takeda, "The Liberal Limits of Environmental Law," 1110.

2. M'Gonigle and Takeda, 1080.

3. McNeil, *Combating Mountaintop Removal*, 160.

4. M'Gonigle and Takeda, "The Liberal Limits of Environmental Law," 1080.

5. Ryan Wishart, "Coal River's Last Mountain: King Coal's *Après Moi le Déluge* Reign," *Organization & Environment* 25, no. 4 (2012): 481.

6. Nina Gregg and Doug Gamble, "This Land Is Your Land: Local Organizing and the Hegemony of Growth," in *Transforming Places: Lessons from Appalachia*, ed. Stephen L. Fisher and Barbara Ellen Smith (Urbana: University of Illinois Press, 2012), 59.

7. Gregg and Gamble, 59.

8. Gregg and Gamble, 59.

9. Gregg and Gamble, 59.

10. Drake, *A History of Appalachia*, 243.

11. Stoll, *Ramp Hollow*, 271.

12. Stoll, 271.

13. Stoll, 271.

14. Stoll, 271.

15. Stoll, 271.

16. Stoll, 272.

17. Stoll, 273–75.

18. Stoll, 277.

19. Stoll, 277.
20. Cassie Robinson Pfleger et al., "Mountain Justice," in *Transforming Places: Lessons from Appalachia*, ed. Stephen L. Fisher and Barbara Ellen Smith (Urbana: University of Illinois Press, 2012), 237.
21. Pfleger et al., 237.
22. Barry, *Standing Our Ground*, 41.
23. Barry, 127.
24. Barry, 128.
25. Barry, 128.
26. Barry, 149.
27. Barry, 149.
28. Barry, 149.
29. Barry, 149.
30. Stephen L. Fisher, "The Grass Roots Speak Back," in *Back Talk from Appalachia: Confronting Stereotypes*, ed. Dwight B. Billings, Gurney Norman, and Katherine Ledford (Lexington: University Press of Kentucky, 2000), 207.
31. Fisher, 207.
32. Fisher, "Introduction," 12.
33. Barbara Ellen Smith and Stephen L. Fisher, "Conclusion: Transformations in Place," in *Transforming Places: Lessons from Appalachia*, ed. Stephen L. Fisher and Barbara Ellen Smith (Urbana: University of Illinois Press, 2012), 282–83.
34. Carina Millstone, "Can Social and Solidarity Economy Organisations Complement or Replace Publicly Traded Companies?," in *Social and Solidarity Economy: Beyond the Fringe*, ed. Peter Utting (London: Zen Books, 2015), 93.
35. Millstone, 92.
36. Lynn Benander et al., "New Economy Energy Cooperatives Bring Power to the People," in *Energy Democracy: Advancing Equity in Clean Energy* Solutions, ed. Denise Fairchild and Al Weinrub (Washington: Island Press, 2017), 213.
37. Benander et al., 212–13.
38. Benander et al., 203.
39. Benander et al., 203.
40. Benander et al., 213.
41. Renee Hatcher, "Solidarity Economy Lawyering," *Tennessee Journal of Race, Gender, & Social Justice* 8, no. 1 (2019): 25.
42. Priya Baskaran, "Introduction to Worker Cooperatives and Their Role in the Changing Economy," *Journal of Affordable Housing and Community Development Law* 24, no. 2 (2015): 378.
43. Gowri J. Krishna, "Worker Cooperative Creation as Progressive Lawyering? Moving Beyond the One-Person, One-Vote Floor," *Berkeley Journal of Employment and Labor Law* 34, no. 1 (2013): 107.
44. Krishna, 107.
45. Millstone, "Social and Solidarity Economy Organisations," 94.
46. "About Solar United Neighbors of West Virginia," Solar United Neighbors of West Virginia, accessed December 5, 2019, https://www.solarunitedneighbors.org/west virginia/about-solar-united-neighbors-of-west-virginia/.
47. "Repowering Appalachia," Solar Holler, accessed December 5, 2019, http://www.solar holler.com/.
48. "Community Solar in West Virginia," Solar United Neighbors, accessed December 5, 2019, https://www.solarunitedneighbors.org/westvirginia/learn-the-issues-in-west -virginia/community-solar-in-west-virginia/.
49. Solar United Neighbors, "Community Solar in West Virginia."

50. "Community Solar," Solar United Neighbors, accessed December 5, 2019, https://www
.solarunitedneighbors.org/learn-the-issues/community-solar/.

51. Katie Keinbaum, "Rural Electric Co-ops Invest in Community Solar," Front Porch Blog,
Appalachian Voices, January 3, 2017, http://appvoices.org/2017/01/03/co-ops-invest-in
-community-solar/.

52. Brent Bailery et al., "A Windfall for Coal Country? Exploring the Barriers to Wind
Development in Appalachia," The Mountain Institute Appalachia Program, Downstream
Strategies, June 15, 2012, 61, http://www.downstreamstrategies.com/documents
/reports_publication/DS_wind-technical-report-final.pdf.

53. Bailery et al., 45.

54. Bailery et al., 45.

55. Bailery et al., 67.

56. Cecilia Martinez, "From Commodification to the Commons: Charting the Pathway for
Energy Democracy," in *Energy Democracy: Advancing Equity in Clean Energy Solutions*, ed.
Denise Fairchild and Al Weinrub (Washington: Island Press, 2017), 32.

57. Martinez, 33.

58. Weston Berg et al., "ACEEE 2018 State Energy Efficiency Scorecard," Research Report
U1808, American Council for an Energy-Efficient Economy, October 4, 2018, https://
aceee.org/press/2018/10/aceee-2018-state-energy-efficiency.

59. "Why Energy Efficiency Is Critical for WV," Energy Efficient West Virginia, accessed
December 5, 2019, http://www.eewv.org/why-energy-efficiency-is-critical-for-wv.

60. Corneilia Fraune, "Gender Matters: Women, Renewable Energy, and Citizen
Participation in Germany," *Energy Research & Social Science* 7 (2015): 55, 62.

61. Melissa Leach, "Preface and Acknowledgements," in *Gender Equality and Sustainable
Development*, ed. Melissa Leach (New York: Routledge, 2016), xiv.

62. Leach, xiv.

63. Mies and Shiva, *Ecofeminism*, 320.

64. Greta Gaard, "Toward New EcoMasculinities, EcoGenders, and EcoSexualities," in
EcoFeminism: Feminist Intersections with Other Animals and the Earth, ed. Carol J. Adams
and Lori Gruen (New York: Bloomsbury Publishing, Inc., 2014), 225.

65. Henk Renting et al., "Building Food Democracy: Exploring Civic Food Networks and
Newly Emerging Forms of Food Citizenship," *International Journals of Sociology of
Agriculture and Food* 19, no. 3 (2012): 290.

66. Renting et al., 290.

67. Renting et al., 290.

68. Renting et al., 291.

69. Haskell, "Assessing the Landscape of Local Food in Appalachia," 1.

70. Candace Pollock, "Appalachia Identified as Most Diverse Foodshed in North America,"
Sustainable Agriculture Research & Education, July 20, 2011, https://www.southernsare
.org/SARE-in-Your-State/Texas/State-News-and-Activities/Appalachia-Identified-as
-Most-Diverse-Foodshed-in-North-America; James R. Veteto, "Apple-achia: The Most
Diverse Foodshed in the US, Canada, and Northern Mexico," in *Place-Based Foods of
Appalachia: From Rarity to Community Restoration and Market Recovery*, ed. James R.
Veteto et al., accessed December 5, 2019, https://www.southernsare.org/Educational
-Resources/SARE-Project-Products/Books-Manuals-and-Training-Guides/Place-Based
-Foods-of-Appalachia.

71. Haskell, "Assessing the Landscape of Local Food in Appalachia," 1.

72. Haskell, 1.

73. Haskell, 7.

74. Haskell, 9.

75. Haskell, 9.

76. Ryan E. Galt, *Food Systems in an Unequal World: Pesticides, Vegetables, and Agrarian Capitalism in Costa Rica* (Tuscan: University of Arizona Press, 2014), 64–66.
77. Gabriela Pechlaner and Gerardo Otero, "The Neoliberal Food Regime: Neoregulation and the New Division of Labor in North America," *Rural Sociology* 75, no. 2 (2010): 183.
78. Pechlaner and Otero, 183.
79. Jessica Lilly and Roxy Todd, "What Happens When Walmart Closes in One Coal Community?," *WV Public Broadcasting*, August 26, 2016, https://www.wvpublic.org/post/what-happens-when-walmart-closes-one-coal-community#stream/0.
80. Haskell, "Assessing the Landscape of Local Food in Appalachia," 18.
81. Sarah Jones, "Can Local Food Help Appalachia Build a Post-Coal Future?," *Nation*, October 11, 2017, https://www.thenation.com/article/can-local-food-help-appalachia-build-a-post-coal-future/.
82. Jones, "Can Local Food Help."
83. Haskell, "Assessing the Landscape of Local Food in Appalachia," 2.
84. Haskell, 6.
85. Haskell, 6.
86. Tove Danovich, "How a Seed Bank Helps Preserve Cherokee Culture through Traditional Foods," NPR, April 2, 2019, https://www.npr.org/sections/thesalt/2019/04/02/704795157/how-a-seed-bank-helps-preserve-cherokee-culture-through-traditional-foods.
87. Henk Renting et al., "Building Food Democracy," 291.
88. Raquel Ajates Gonzalez, "Going Back to Go Forwards? From Multi-Stakeholder Cooperatives to Open Cooperatives in Food and Farming," *Journal of Rural Studies* 53 (2017): 280.
89. J. Howard, "Solidarity Food Cooperatives?" *Affinities: A Journal of Radical Theory, Culture, and Action* 4, no. 1 (2010): 152.
90. Cristina Grassein et al., "Beyond Alternative Food Networks: Italy's Solidarity Purchase Groups and the United States' Community Economies," in *Social and Solidarity Economy: Beyond the Fringe*, ed. Peter Utting (London: Zen Books, 2015), 196.
91. Grassein et al., 197.
92. Grassein et al., 197.
93. Krishna, "Worker Cooperative Creation as Progressive Lawyering?," 107.
94. Mies and Shiva, *Ecofeminism*, 305, 319.
95. Mies and Shiva, 321.
96. Gaard, "Toward New EcoMasculinities," 225.
97. Gaard, "Ecofeminism Revisited," 27.
98. Lisa R. Pruitt, "Gender, Geography, and Rural Justice," *Berkeley Journal of Law & Justice* 23, no. 2 (2008): 340.
99. Roxy Todd and Jessica Lilly, "Inside Appalachia: What Would You Do If Your Grocery Store Disappeared?," *West Virginia Public Broadcasting*, July 10, 2015, https://www.wvpublic.org/post/inside-appalachia-what-would-you-do-if-your-grocery-store-disappeared#stream/0.
100. "The Project," Women Farmers of Appalachia, accessed December 5, 2019, https://www.wfarmers.com/.
101. Women Farmers of Appalachia, "The Project."
102. "Mission," Blue Ridge Women in Agriculture, accessed December 5, 2019, https://www.brwia.org/about.html.
103. Cristina Maza, "An Appalachian Haven for LGBTQ People," *Week*, February 10, 2018, http://theweek.com/articles/753637/appalachian-haven-lgbtq-people.
104. Maza, "An Appalachian Haven."
105. Maza, "An Appalachian Haven."

106. Alison Hope Alkon and Julian Agyeman, "Introduction: The Food Movement as Polyculture," in *Cultivating Food Justice: Race, Class, and Sustainability*, ed. Alison Hope Alkon and Julian Agyeman (Cambridge: MIT Press, 2011), 10.

107. Alison Hope Alkon and Julian Agyeman, "Conclusion: Cultivating the Fertile Field of Food Justice," in *Cultivating Food Justice: Race, Class, and Sustainability*, ed. Alison Hope Alkon and Julian Agyeman (Cambridge, MA: MIT Press, 2011), 331.

108. Hope and Agyeman, "Conclusion," 331.

109. Ronald D. Eller, "Deep Change the Only Path to Real, Lasting Reform in Appalachia," *Lexington Herald Leader*, February 15, 2015, http://www.kentucky.com/opinion/op-ed /article44554251.html.

110. Vandana Shiva, *Earth Democracy: Justice, Sustainability and Peace* (London: Zen Books, 2006), 63, quoted in Barry, *Standing our Ground*, 149.

111. Herbert Reid and Betsy Taylor, *Recovering the Commons: Democracy, Place and Global Justice* (Urbana: University of Illinois Press, 2010), 22, 42–46.

112. Stoll, *Ramp Hollow*, 271–72.

113. Stoll, 277.

114. Thompson, "Constitutionalizing the Environment," 161.

115. Va. Const. Art. XI, § 2.

116. N.Y. Const. Art. XIV, § 4.

117. Thompson, "Constitutionalizing the Environment," 161.

118. Schumann, "Introduction," 8.

119. Schumann, 8.

120. Schumann, 8.

121. Bettinger-Lopez et al., "Redefining Human Rights Lawyering through the Lens of Critical Theory," 350.

122. Brisman, "Reframing the Portrait of Lynne F. Stewart," 7.

123. Bettinger-Lopez et al., "Redefining Human Rights Lawyering through the Lens of Critical Theory," 351.

124. Bettinger-Lopez et al., 353.

125. Piomelli, "The Democratic Roots of Collaborative Lawyering," 544, quoted in Bettinger-Lopez et al., "Redefining Human Rights Lawyering through the Lens of Critical Theory," 353.

126. Gregg and Gamble, "This Land Is Your Land," 59.

127. M'Gonigle and Takeda, "The Liberal Limits of Environmental Law," 1057.

128. Pa. Const. Art. I, § 27.

129. Va. Const. art. XI, § 1.

130. Tenn. Code Ann. § 68–221–702.

131. Tenn. Code Ann. § 69–3–102.

132. Wood, *Nature's Trust*, 16.

133. Bollier, "Mary Wood's Crusade to Reinvigorate the Public Trust Doctrine."

134. Wood, *Nature's Trust*, 16.

135. "Our Mission," Our Children's Trust, accessed December 5, 2019, https://www.our childrenstrust.org/mission-statement/.

136. "Proceedings in All 50 States," West Virginia, Our Children's Trust, accessed December 5, 2019, https://www.ourchildrenstrust.org/other-proceedings-in-all-50-states/.

137. Petition of Kids VS Global Warming to the West Virginia Department of Environmental Protection & The Division of Air Quality, May 4, 2011, https://static1.squarespace.com /static/571d109b04426270152febe0/t/57859e6fcd0f68284f659f65/1468374641752 /West+Virginia+Petition+.pdf.

138. Our Children's Trust, "Proceedings in All 50 States."

139. Our Children's Trust, "Proceedings in All 50 States."

140. David Takacs, "The Public Trust Doctrine, Environmental Human Rights, and the Future of Private Property," *New York University Environmental Law Journal* 16, no. 3 (2008): 765.

141. Stoll, *Ramp Hollow*, 272.

142. Toivanen, "Commons against Capitalism," 130.

143. Toivanen, 125.

144. Toivanen, 124–25.

145. Toivanen, 129–30.

146. Klaus Bosselmann, "Reclaiming the Global Commons: Towards Earth Trusteeship," in *ResponsAbility: Law and Governance for Living Well with the Earth*, ed. Betsan Martin, Linda Te Aho, and Maria Humphries-Kil (New York: Routledge, 2019), 36.

147. Burns H. Weston and David Bollier, *Green Governance: Ecological Survival, Human Rights, and the Law of the Commons* (Cambridge: Cambridge University Press, 2013), 242.

148. Wood, *Nature's Trust*, 161.

149. Wood, 151.

150. Weston and Bollier, *Green Governance*, 241.

151. Weston and Bollier, 245.

152. Weston and Bollier, 241.

153. Weston and Bollier, 241.

154. Weston and Bollier, 247–50.

155. Weston and Bollier, 252.

156. Weston and Bollier, 241.

157. John D. Echeverria, "The Public Trust Doctrine as a Background Principles Defense in Takings Litigation," *U.C. Davis Law Review* 45, no. 3 (2012): 951.

158. Peter H. Sand, "Accountability for the Commons: Reconsiderations," in *The Role of Integrity in the Governance of the Commons: Governance, Ecology, Law, Ethics*, ed. Laura Westra, Janice Gray, and Franz-Theo Gottwald (Cham: Springer, 2017), 9.

159. Karl Marx, *Das Kapital*, vol. 3 (1865), reprinted in *Marx-Engels-Gesamtausgabe*, part 2 (Berlin: Dietz, 1992), quoted in Sand, "Accountability for the Commons," 9.

160. Echeverria, "The Public Trust Doctrine as a Background Principles Defense in Takings Litigation," 956.

161. Reid and Taylor, *Recovering the Commons*, 43.

162. Robin Celikates, "Rethinking Civil Disobedience as a Practice of Contestation—Beyond the Liberal Paradigm," *Constellations* 23, no. 1 (2016): 41.

163. Ulrich Rödel et al., *Die demokratische Frage* (Frankfurt am Main: Suhrkamp, 1989), 46, quoted in Celikates, "Rethinking Civil Disobedience," 41.

164. Akuno, interview.

165. Stoll, *Ramp Hollow*, 271.

166. Resolution Recognizing the Duty of the Federal Government to Create a Green New Deal, H.Res. 109, 116th Cong. (2019).

167. H.Res. 109, 116th Cong. (2019).

168. H.Res. 109, 116th Cong. (2019).

169. H.Res. 109, 116th Cong. (2019).

170. H.Res. 109, 116th Cong. (2019).

171. "Draft Text for Proposed Addendum to House Rules for 116th Congress of the United States," https://docs.google.com/document/d/1jxUzp9SZ6-VB-4wSm8sselVMsqWZrSrYpYC9slHKLzo/edit#.

172. Resolution Recognizing the Duty of the Federal Government to Create a Green New Deal, H.Res. 109, 116th Cong. (2019).

173. H.Res. 109, 116th Cong. (2019).

174. Sarah Lazare, "We Have to Make Sure the 'Green New Deal' Doesn't Become Green

Capitalism," *In These Times*, December 12, 2018, http://inthesetimes.com/article /21632/green-new-deal-alexandria-ocasio-cortez-climate-cooperation-jackson-capital.

175. Longo, Clausen, and Clark, *The Tragedy of the Commodity*, 32.
176. Resolution Recognizing the Duty of the Federal Government to Create a Green New Deal, H.Res. 109, 116th Cong. (2019).
177. Jan Pytalski, "Where Is Rural in the Green New Deal?" *100 Days in Appalachia*, March 11, 2019, https://www.100daysinappalachia.com/2019/03/where-is-rural-in-the-green -new-deal/.
178. Vaios Triantafyllou, "A Green New Deal Is the First Step toward an Eco-Revolution," *Truthout.org*, February 9, 2019, https://truthout.org/articles/a-green-new-deal-is-the -first-step-toward-an-eco-revolution/.
179. Löwy, *Ecosocialism*, 23–24.
180. Hans A. Baer, *Global Capitalism and Climate Change: The Need for an Alternative World System* (Lanham, MD: AltaMira Press, 2012), 220–21.

BIBLIOGRAPHY

Abraham, John. "Fires and Drought Cook Tennessee—A State Represented by Climate Deniers." *Guardian*, December 2, 2016. https://www.theguardian.com/environment /climate-consensus-97-per-cent/2016/dec/02/fires-and-drought-cook-tennessee-a -state-represented-by-climate-deniers.

African Commission on Human and Peoples' Rights. "African Charter on Human and Peoples' Rights." Accessed December 5, 2019. https://www.achpr.org/legalinstruments/detail ?id=49.

Agarwal, Bina. "The Gender and Environment Debate: Lessons from India." *Feminist Studies* 18, no.1 (1992).

Ahern, Melissa M., et al. "The Association between Mountaintop Mining and Birth Defects among Live Births in Central Appalachia, 1996–2003." *Environmental Research* 111, no. 6 (2011).

Akuno, Kali. "It's Eco-Socialism or Death." Interview by editors. *Jacobin*, Feb. 15, 2019. https://jacobinmag.com/2019/02/kali-akuno-interview-climate-change-cooperation -jackson.

Alexander, Samuel. "The Optimal Material Threshold: Toward an Economics of Sufficiency." *Real-World Economics Review* 61 (2012).

Alexander, Samuel. "Voluntary Simplicity and the Social Reconstruction of Law: Degrowth from the Grassroots Up." *Environmental Values* 22, no. 2 (2013).

Alfieri, Anthony V. "Faith in Community: Representing 'Colored Town.' " *California Law Review* 95, no. 2 (2007).

Alkon, Alison Hope, and Julian Agyeman. "Conclusion: Cultivating the Fertile Field of Food Justice." In *Cultivating Food Justice: Race, Class, and Sustainability*, edited by Alison Hope Alkon and Julian Agyeman. Cambridge: MIT Press, 2011.

Alkon, Alison Hope, and Julian Agyeman. "Introduction: The Food Movement as Polyculture." In *Cultivating Food Justice: Race, Class, and Sustainability*, edited by Alison Hope Alkon and Julian Agyeman. Cambridge: MIT Press, 2011.

Alston, Philip. "Statement on Visit to the USA." United Nations Human Rights Office of the High Commissioner. December 15, 2017. https://www.ohchr.org/EN/NewsEvents /Pages/DisplayNews.aspx?NewsID=22533.

Alvaro, Stephanie, Jensen Mills, and Politifact. "How Many Oil and Gas Jobs Are There in W.Va.? It's Surprisingly Hard to Say." *WV Public Broadcasting*, April 8, 2019. https:// www.wvpublic.org/post/how-many-oil-and-gas-jobs-are-there-wva-it-s-surprisingly -hard-say#stream/0.

Andreucci, Diego, and Terrence McDonough. "Capitalism." In *Degrowth: A Vocabulary for a New Era*, edited by Giacomo D'Alisa, Federico Demaria, and Giorgios Kallis. New York: Routledge, 2015.

Angermeier, Paul L. "Biodiversity in Appalachia's Future." *Appalachian Voices*, December 15, 2008. http://appvoices.org/2008/12/15/biodiversity-in-appalachias-future/.

Anglin, Mary K. "Engendering the Struggle: Women's Labor and Traditions of Resistance in Rural Southern Appalachia." In *Fighting Back in Appalachia: Traditions of Resistance and Change*, edited by Stephen L. Fisher. Philadelphia: Temple University Press, 1993.

Appalachian Magazine. "You Would Not Have Recognized Appalachia 150 Years Ago." January 17, 2017. http://appalachianmagazine.com/2017/01/17/you-would-not-have -recognized-appalachia-150-years-ago/.

Appalachian Mountain Advocates. "Natural Gas and Climate Change." Accessed December 5, 2019. http://www.appalmad.org/natural-gas-and-climate-change/.

Appalachian Regional Commission. "Appalachia's Population." Accessed December 5, 2019. https://www.arc.gov/noindex/research/ACS-infographics2013–2017/DataSnapshot -AppalachiasPopulation.pdf.

Appalachian Regional Commission. "Geography." Source & Methodology. Accessed December 5, 2019. https://www.arc.gov/research/sourceandmethodologygeography.asp.

Appalachian Voice. "Exposed: Climate Change." December 18, 2014. http://appvoices.org /2014/12/18/exposed-climate-change/.

Armstrong, Martin. "Women Work More Than Men." *Statista*, March 8, 2019. https://www .statista.com/chart/13940/women-work-more-than-men/.

Associated Press. "Professor Locks Herself to Pipeline Construction Equipment in Virginia." *CBS19*, June 28, 2018. https://www.cbs19news.com/content/news/Professor-locks -herself-to-pipeline-construction-equipment-in-Virginia-486853821.html.

Baer, Hans A. *Democratic Eco-Socialism as a Real Utopia: Transitioning to an Alternative World System*. New York: Berghahn Books, 2017.

Baer, Hans A. *Global Capitalism and Climate Change: The Need for an Alternative World System*. Lanham: AltaMira Press, 2012.

Bailery, Brent et al. "A Windfall for Coal Country? Exploring the Barriers to Wind Development in Appalachia." The Mountain Institute Appalachia Program. Downstream Strategies, June 15, 2012. http://www.downstreamstrategies.com/documents/reports _publication/DS_wind-technical-report-final.pdf.

Baller, Mark, and Leor J. Pantilat. "Defenders of Appalachia: The Campaign to Eliminate Mountaintop Removal Coal Mining and the Role of Public Justice." *Environmental Law* 37, no. 3 (2007).

Barden, Kimya. "Neoliberalism and African Americans in Higher Education." In *The Routledge Handbook of Poverty in the United States*, edited by Stephen Haymes, María Vidal de Haymes, and Reuben Miller. New York: Routledge, 2015.

Barry, Joyce M. "Mountaineers Are Always Free?: An Examination of the Effects of Mountaintop Removal in West Virginia." *Women's Studies Quarterly* 29, no. 1/2 (2001).

Barry, Joyce M. *Standing Our Ground: Women, Environmental Justice, and the Fight to End Mountain Removal*. Athens: Ohio University Press, 2012.

Baskaran, Priya. "Introduction to Worker Cooperatives and Their Role in the Changing Economy." *Journal of Affordable Housing and Community Development Law* 24, no. 2 (2015).

Batteau, Allen W. *The Invention of Appalachia*. Tuscan: University of Arizona Press, 1990.

Bauhardt, Christine. "Solutions to the Crisis? The Green New Deal, Degrowth, and the Solidarity Economy: Alternatives to the Capitalist Growth Economy from an Ecofeminist Economics Perspective." *Ecological Economics* 102 (2014).

Beckwith, Karen. "Collective Identities of Class and Gender: Working-Class Women in the Pittston Coal Strike." *Political Psychology* 19, no.1 (1995).

Bell, Shannon Elizabeth. *Fighting King Coal: The Challenges to Micromobilization in Central Appalachia*. Cambridge: MIT Press, 2016.

Bell, Shannon Elizabeth. *Our Roots Run Deep as Ironweed: Appalachian Women and the Fight for Environmental Justice*. Urbana: University of Illinois Press, 2013.

Bell, Shannon Elizabeth, and Richard York. "Community Economic Identity: The Coal Industry and Ideology Construction in West Virginia." *Rural Sociology* 75, no. 1 (2010).

Benander, Lynn et al. "New Economy Energy Cooperatives Bring Power to the People." In *Energy Democracy: Advancing Equity in Clean Energy* Solutions, edited by Denise Fairchild and Al Weinru. Washington: Island Press, 2017.

Benderev, Chris, and Kelly McEvers. "In the Coal Counties of Central Appalachia, Will Trump's Promises Come True?" *NPR*, May 9, 2018. https://www.npr.org/2018/05/09 /607273500/in-the-coal-counties-of-central-appalachia-will-trump-s-promises-come -true.

Berg, Weston et al. "ACEEE 2018 State Energy Efficiency Scorecard." Research Report U1808. American Council for an Energy-Efficient Economy, October 4, 2018. https://aceee.org /press/2018/10/aceee-2018-state-energy-efficiency.

Bettinger-Lopez, Caroline et al. "Redefining Human Rights Lawyering through the Lens of Critical Theory: Lessons for Pedagogy and Practice." *Georgetown Journal on Poverty Law & Policy* 18, no. 3 (2011).

Billings, Dwight B., and Kathleen M. Blee. *The Road to Poverty: The Making of Wealth and Hardship in Appalachia*. Cambridge: Cambridge University Press, 2000.

Billings, Dwight B., Mary Beth Pudup, and Altina L. Waller. "Taking Exception with Exceptionalism: The Emergence and Transformation of Historical Studies of Appalachia." In *Appalachia in the Making: The Mountain South in the Nineteenth Century*, edited by Mary Beth Pudup, Dwight B. Billings, and Altina L. Waller. Chapel Hill: University of North Carolina Press, 1995.

Bingman, Mary Beth. "Stopping the Bulldozers: What Difference Did It Make?" In *Fighting Back in Appalachia: Traditions of Resistance and Change*, edited by Stephen L. Fisher. Philadelphia: Temple University Press, 1993.

Blue Ridge Women in Agriculture. "Mission." Accessed December 5, 2019. https://www .brwia.org/about.html.

Bolgiano, Chris. *The Appalachian Forest: A Search for Roots and Renewal*. Mechanicsburg: Stackpole Books, 1995.

Bollier, David. "Mary Wood's Crusade to Reinvigorate the Public Trust Doctrine." *News and Perspectives on the Commons*, February 10, 2014. http://www.bollier.org/blog/mary -wood%E2%80%99s-crusade-reinvigorate-public-trust-doctrine.

Bonds, Eric, and Liam Downey. " 'Green' Technology and Ecologically Unequal Exchange: The Environmental and Social Consequences of Ecological Modernization in the World-System." *Journal of World Systems Research* 18, no. 2 (2012).

Bonilla-Silva, Eduardo. *Racism without Racists: Color-Blind Racism and the Persistence of Racial Inequality in America*. Lanham: Rowman & Littlefield Publishers, 2018.

Bosselmann, Klaus. *Earth Governance: Trusteeship of the Global Commons*. Cheltenham, UK: Edward Elgar Publishing Limited, 2015.

Bosselmann, Klaus. "Reclaiming the Global Commons: Towards Earth Trusteeship." In *ResponsAbility: Law and Governance for Living Well with the Earth*, edited by Betsan Martin, Linda Te Aho, and Maria Humphries-Kil. New York: Routledge, 2019.

Boyd, David R. *The Environmental Rights Revolution: A Global Study of Constitutions, Human Rights, and the Environment*. Toronto: UBC Press, 2012.

Boyd, David R. *The Right to a Healthy Environment: Revitalizing Canada's Constitution*. Toronto: UBC Press, 2012.

Bratt, Carolyn S., and Karen J. Greenwell. "Kentucky's Broad Form Deed Amendment: Constitutional Considerations." *Journal of Mineral Law and Policy* 5, no. 1 (1989).

Brisman, Avi. "Reframing the Portrait of Lynne F. Stewart." *Journal of Law in Society* 12, no. 1–2 (2011).

Brisman, Avi. "The Criminalization of Peacemaking, Corporate Free Speech, and the Violence of Interpretation: New Challenges to Cause Lawyering." *City University of New York Law Review* 14, no. 2 (2011).

Brownhill, Leigh. "Earth Democracy and Ecosocialism: What's in a Name?" *Capitalism, Nature, Socialism* 21, no. 1 (2010).

Brownhill, Leigh, and Terisa E. Turner. "Ecofeminism at the Heart of Ecosocialism." *Capitalism, Nature, Socialism* 30, no. 1 (2019).

Buckley, Geoffrey L. "History of Coal Mining in Appalachia." In *Concise Encyclopedia of the History of Energy*, edited by Cutler J. Cleveland. San Diego, CA: Elsevier, 2009.

Budowsky, Brent. "Sanders Lifts Spirits in West Virginia." *Hill*, March 14, 2017. https:// thehill.com/blogs/pundits-blog/lawmaker-news/323921-sanders-lifts-spirits-in-west -virginia.

Bulland, Robert D. *Dumping in Dixie: Race, Class, And Environmental Quality*. New York: Routledge, 2018.

Burch, John R. *Owsley County, Kentucky, and the Perpetuation of Poverty*. Jefferson: McFarland., 2008.

Buxton, Gavin. *Alternative Energy Technologies: An Introduction with Computer Simulations*. Boca Raton: Taylor & Francis, 2015.

Cable, Sherry. "Natural Gas Fracking on Public Lands: The Trickle-Down Impacts of Neoliberalism in Ohio's Utica Shale Region." In *Fractured Communities: Risk, Impacts, and Protest against Hydraulic Fracking in U.S. Shale Regions*, edited by Anthony E. Ladd. Camden, NJ: Rutgers University Press, 2018.

Carnes, Nicholas, and Noam Lupu. "It's Time to Bust the Myth: Most Trump Voters Were Not Working Class." *Washington Post*, June 5, 2017. https://www.washingtonpost.com /news/monkey-cage/wp/2017/06/05/its-time-to-bust-the-myth-most-trump-voters -were-not-working-class/.

Carson, Rachel. *Silent Spring*. Boston: Houghton Mifflin Company, 1990.

Catte, Elizabeth. "Appalachia Isn't the Reason We're Living in Trump Country." *Literary Hub*, February 8, 2018. https://lithub.com/appalachia-isnt-the-reason-were-living-in-trump -country/.

Catte, Elizabeth. "Resisting Myths of Whiteness in Appalachia." *100 Days in Appalachia*, March 15, 2017. https://www.100daysinappalachia.com/2017/03/elizabeth-catte -resisting-myths-whiteness-appalachia/.

Catte, Elizabeth. "There Is No Neutral There: Appalachia as a Mythic 'Trump Country.' " *Medium*, October 17, 2016. https://medium.com/@elizabethcatte/there-is-no-neutral -there-appalachia-as-a-mythic-trump-country-ee6ed7f300dc.

Catte, Elizabeth. *What You Are Getting Wrong About Appalachia*. Cleveland: Belt Publishing, 2017.

Caudill, Henry D. *Night Comes to the Cumberlands: A Biography of a Depressed Area*. Boston: Little, Brown, 1963.

Ceballos, Gerardo, Paul R. Ehrlich, and Rodolfo Dirzo. "Biological Annihilation via the Ongoing Sixth Mass Extinction Signaled by Vertebrate Population Losses and Declines." *Proceedings of the National Academy of Sciences of the United States of America* 114, no. 30 (2017).

Celikates, Robin. "Rethinking Civil Disobedience as a Practice of Contestation—Beyond the Liberal Paradigm." *Constellations* 23, no. 1 (2016).

Cherniack, Martin. *The Hawk's Nest Incident: America's Worst Industrial Disaster*. New Haven, CT: Yale University Press, 1989.

Cherry, Mark. "Permit to Poison: The Failure of the Federalist Regulatory Regime to Address the Human Health Impacts of Mountaintop Removal Coal Mining." *Columbia Human Rights Law Review* 47, no. 1 (2015).

Chew, Sing C. *World Ecological Degradation*. Walnut Creek: Rowman & Littlefield, 2001.

Chiacu, Doina, and Valerie Volcovici. "EPA Chief Pruitt Refuses to Link CO_2 and Global

Warming." *Scientific American*, March 10, 2017. https://www.scientificamerican.com /article/epa-chief-pruitt-refuses-to-link-co2-and-global-warming/.

Chinni, Dante, and Matt Rivera. "West Virginia: How the Bluest State Became the Reddest." *NBC News*, December 18, 2016. https://www.nbcnews.com/meet-the-press/west -virginia-how-bluest-state-became-reddest-n697491.

Clarke, Brian S. "The Clash of Old and New Fourth Circuit Ideologies: Boyer-Liberto v. Fontainebleau Corp. and the Moderation of the Fourth Circuit," *South Carolina Law Review* 66, no. 4 (2015).

Clemens, Elisabeth S. "The Problem of the Corporation: Liberalism and the Large Organization." In *The Oxford Handbook of Sociology and Organization Studies—Classical Foundations*, edited by Paul S. Adler. Oxford: Oxford University Press, 2009.

Clinton, Hilary Rodham. *What Happened*. New York: Simon & Schuster, 2017.

CNN Wire. "Inspired by West Virginia Strike, Teachers in Oklahoma and Kentucky Plan Walk Out." April 2, 2018. https://ktla.com/2018/04/02/inspired-by-west-virginia-strike -teachers-in-oklahoma-and-kentucky-plan-walk-out/.

Collin, Robert William. "The Role of Government: Fossil Fuel Energy Sources." In *Energy Choices: How to Power the Future,* edited by Robin Morris and Robert William Collins. Santa Barbara, CA: ABC-CLIO, 2014.

Collins, Craig. *Toxic Loopholes: Failures and Future Prospects of Environmental Law*. Cambridge: Cambridge University Press 2010.

Corlett, J. Angelo. *Race, Racism, and Reparations*. Ithaca, NY: Cornell University Press, 2003.

Cornwall, Warren. "Demise of Stream Rule Won't Revitalize Coal Industry." *Science Magazine*, February 16, 2017. https://www.sciencemag.org/news/2017/02/demise-stream-rule -won-t-revitalize-coal-industry.

Council on Environmental Quality. "Environmental Quality 1979." Washington, D.C.: U.S. Government Printing Office, 1979.

Court, Simon Holmes à. "It'd Be Wonderful If the Claims Made about Carbon Capture Were True." *Guardian*, February 15, 2018. https://www.theguardian.com/commentisfree /2018/feb/16/itd-be-wonderful-if-the-claims-made-about-carbon-capture-were -true.

Croix, G. E. M. de Ste. *The Class Struggle in the Ancient Greek World: From the Archaic Age to the Arab Conquests*. London: Duckworth, 1981.

Cunningham, Rodger. "Reflections on Identify and the Roots of Prejudice." In "Appalachian Identity: Roundtable Discussion," by Barbara Ellen Smith et al. *Appalachian Journal* 38, no. 1 (2010): 56–76.

Curry, Janel M., and Steven McGuire. *Community on Land: Community, Ecology, and the Public Interest*. New York: Rowman & Littlefield, 2002.

Czarnezki, Jason J. "Food, Law and the Environment: Informational and Structural Changes for a Sustainable Food System." *Utah Environmental Law Review* 31, no. 2 (2011).

Damstedt, Benjamin G. "Limiting Locke: A Natural Law Justification for the Fair Use Doctrine." *Yale Law Journal* 112, no. 5 (2003).

Danovich, Tove. "How a Seed Bank Helps Preserve Cherokee Culture through Traditional Foods." *NPR*, April 2, 2019. https://www.npr.org/sections/thesalt/2019/04/02 /704795157/how-a-seed-bank-helps-preserve-cherokee-culture-through-traditional -foods.

Darweesh, Abbas Degan, and Nesaem Mehdi Abdullah. "A Critical Discourse Analysis of Donald Trump's Sexist Ideology." *Journal of Education and Practice* 7, no. 30 (2016).

Dastagir, Alia E. "West Virginia Teachers' Victory Shows 'Power of Women' as More Battles Loom." *USA Today*, March 8, 2018. https://www.usatoday.com/story/news/2018/03/08 /west-virginia-teachers-victory-shows-power-women-more-battles-loom/403374002/.

Davis, Donald Edward. *Homeplace Geography: Essays for Appalachia*. Macon, GA: Mercer University Press, 2006.

Davis, Wendy B. "Out of the Black Hole: Reclaiming the Crown of King Coal." *American University Law Review* 51, no. 5 (2002).

de Coninck, Helee, et al. "Strengthening and Implementing the Global Response." In *Global Warming of 1.5 °C: An IPCC Special Report*, edited by Masson-Delmotte, V., et al., 317. Intergovernmental Panel on Climate Change, 2018. https://www.ipcc.ch/sr15/chapter/chapter-4/.

Delgado, Richard. "Our Better Natures: A Revisionist View of Joseph Sax's Public Trust Theory of Environmental Protection, and Some Dark Thoughts on the Possibility of Law Reform." *Vanderbilt Law Review* 44, no. 6 (1991).

Denham, Charles J. "Chemical Industry." e-WV: The West Virginia Encyclopedia. West Virginia Humanities Council. Accessed December 5, 2019. https://www.wvencyclopedia.org/articles/1124.

Dernbach, John C., James R. May, and Kenneth T. Kristl. "Robinson Township v. Commonwealth of Pennsylvania: Examination and Implications." *Rutgers University Law Review* 67, no. 5 (2015).

Drake, Richard B. *A History of Appalachia*. Lexington: University Press of Kentucky, 2004.

Drugmand, Dana. "Hawaii Joins Trend: Recognizes Constitutional Right to Safe Climate and Environment." *Climate Liability News*, January 5, 2016. https://www.climateliabilitynews.org/2018/01/05/hawaii-climate-environment-constitutional-right/.

Duffy, Mignon. "Dirty Work: Gender, Race, and Reproductive Labor in Historical Perspective." *Gender and Society* 21, no. 3 (2007).

Duffy, Mignon. *Making Care Count: A Century of Gender, Race, and Paid Care Work*. New Brunswick, NJ: Rutgers University Press, 2011.

Duggan, Lisa. *The Twilight of Equality?: Neoliberalism, Cultural Politics, and the Attack on Democracy*. Boston: Beacon Press, 2003.

Dunaway, Wilma A. "The Double Register of History: Situating the Forgotten Woman and Her Household in Capitalist Commodity Chains." *Journal of World-Systems Research* 7, no. 1 (2001).

Dunaway, Wilma A. *The First American Frontier: Transition to Capitalism in Southern Appalachia, 1700–1860*. Chapel Hill: University of North Carolina Press, 1996.

Dunaway, Wilma A. "The Incorporation of Mountain Ecosystems into the Capitalist World-System." *Review (Fernand Braudel Center)* 19, no. 4 (1996).

Dunaway, Wilma A. "The Legacy of Social Darwinism in Appalachian Scholarship." Online Archives for *Women, Work and Family in the Antebellum Mountain South*, Virginia Tech University Libraries. Accessed December 5, 2019. https://scholar.lib.vt.edu/faculty_archives/appalachian_women/legacy.htm.

Earle, Thomas Blake. "No White Man Left Behind: Saving Coal Country Has Never Been about Energy. It's Been about Rescuing White Men." *Washington Post*, October 27, 2017. https://www.washingtonpost.com/news/made-by-history/wp/2017/10/27/no-white-man-left-behind/.

Echeverria, John D. "The Public Trust Doctrine as a Background Principles Defense in Takings Litigation." *U.C. Davis Law Review* 45, no. 3 (2012).

Eckersley, Robyn. *The Green State: Rethinking Democracy and Sovereignty*. Cambridge, MA: MIT Press, 2004.

Eisenberg, Ann M. "Beyond Science and Hysteria: Reality and Perceptions of Environmental Justice Concerns Surrounding Marcellus and Utica Shale Gas Development." *Pittsburgh University Law Review* 77, no. 2 (2015).

Eisenberg, Ann M. "Just Transitions." *Southern California Law Review* 92, no. 2 (2019).

Eller, Ronald D. "Deep Change the Only Path to Real, Lasting Reform in Appalachia." *Lexington Herald Leader*, February 15, 2015. http://www.kentucky.com/opinion/op-ed/article44554251.html.

Eller, Ronald D. "Foreward." In *Back Talk from Appalachia: Confronting Stereotypes*, edited by Dwight B. Billings, Gurney Norman, and Katherine Ledford. Lexington: University Press of Kentucky, 2000.

Eller, Ronald D. *Miners, Millhands, and Mountaineers: Industrialization of the Appalachian South, 1880–1930*. Knoxville: University of Tennessee Press, 1982.

Eller, Ronald D. "The Coal Barons of the Appalachian South, 1880–1930." *Appalachian Journal* 4, no. 3/4 (1977).

Eller, Ronald D. *Uneven Ground: Appalachia Since 1945*. Lexington: University Press of Kentucky, 2008.

Elliott, Brian. *Natural Catastrophe: Climate Change and Neoliberal Governance*. Edinburgh: Edinburgh University Press, 2016.

Energy Efficient West Virginia. "Why Energy Efficiency Is Critical for WV." Accessed December 5, 2019. http://www.eewv.org/why-energy-efficiency-is-critical-for-wv.

Environmental Protection Agency. "What Climate Change Means for West Virginia." EPA 430-F-16-050, August 2016. https://19january2017snapshot.epa.gov/sites/production /files/2016-09/documents/climate-change-wv.pdf.

Esworthy, Robert. "Federal Pollution Control Laws: How Are They Enforced?" Congressional Research Service Report 7–5700. Congressional Research Service, 2014.

Faber, Daniel. *Capitalizing on Environmental Injustice: The Polluter-Industrial Complex in the Age of Globalization*. Lanham, MD: Rowman & Littlefield, 2008.

Faber, Daniel et al. "Trump's Electoral Triumph: Class, Race, Gender, and the Hegemony of the Polluter-Industrial Complex." *Capitalism, Nature, Socialism* 28, no. 1 (2017).

Fisher, Steve, and Barbara Ellen Smith. "Internal Colony—Are You Sure? Defining, Theorizing, Organizing Appalachia." *The Journal of Appalachian Studies* 22, no. 1 (2016).

Fisher, Stephen L. "Introduction." In *Fighting Back in Appalachia: Traditions of Resistance and Change*, edited by Stephen L. Fisher. Philadelphia: Temple University Press, 1993.

Fisher, Stephen, L. "The Grass Roots Speak Back." In *Back Talk from Appalachia: Confronting Stereotypes*, edited by. Dwight B. Billings, Gurney Norman, and Katherine Ledford. Lexington: University Press of Kentucky, 2000.

Forman, Isaac. "The Uncertain Future of NEPA and Mountaintop Removal." *Columbia Journal of Environmental Law* 36, no. 1 (2011).

Foster, John Bellamy. *The Ecological Revolution: Making Peace with the Planet*. New York: Monthly Review Press, 2009.

Fraser, Nancy. *Fortunes of Feminism: From State-Managed Capitalism to Neoliberal Crisis*. Brooklyn: Verso, 2013.

Fraune, Corneilia. "Gender Matters: Women, Renewable Energy, and Citizen Participation in Germany." *Energy Research & Social Science* 7 (2015).

Friedman, Lisa. "Trump Takes a First Step toward Scrapping Obama's Global Warming Policy." *New York Times*, October 4, 2017. https://www.nytimes.com/2017/10/04 /climate/trump-climate-change.html.

Gaard, Greta. "Ecofeminism Revisited: Rejecting Essentialism and Re-Placing Species in a Material Feminist Environmentalism." *Feminist Formations* 23, no. 2 (2011).

Gaard, Greta. "Toward New EcoMasculinities, EcoGenders, and EcoSexualities." In *EcoFeminism: Feminist Intersections with Other Animals and the Earth*, edited by Carol J. Adams and Lori Gruen. New York: Bloomsbury, 2014.

Galt, Ryan E. *Food Systems in an Unequal World: Pesticides, Vegetables, and Agrarian Capitalism in Costa Rica*. Tuscan: University of Arizona Press, 2014.

Gare, Arran E. *Postmodernism and the Environmental Crisis*. London: Routledge, 1995.

Gelbspan, Ross. *Boiling Point: How Politicians, Big Oil and Coal, Journalists, and Activists Have Fueled a Climate Crisis—And What We Can Do to Avert Disaster*. New York: Basic Books, 2004.

Gersen, Sara. "The Potential of State Coal-Purchasing Legislation to Decrease Mountaintop Removal Mining." *New York University Environmental Law Journal* 18, no. 3 (2011).

Gillis, Justin, and Nadja Popovich. "The U.S. Is the Biggest Carbon Polluter in History. It Just Walked away from the Paris Climate Deal." *New York Times*, June 1, 2017. https://www.nytimes.com/interactive/2017/06/01/climate/us-biggest-carbon-polluter-in-history-will-it-walk-away-from-the-paris-climate-deal.html.

Gillispie, Mark. "Ethane Storage Seen as Key to Revitalization of Appalachia." *Associated Press*, April 29, 2019. https://apnews.com/8873394dd33647ddb369978bcfdc4e2d.

Goldberg, Hilary M., Melanie Stallings Williams, and Deborah Cours. "It's a Nuisance: The Future of Fracking Litigation in the Wake of *Parr v. Aruba Petroleum, Inc.*" *Virginia Environmental Law Journal* 33, no. 1 (2015).

Gonzalez, Raquel Ajates. "Going Back to Go Forwards? From Multi-Stakeholder Cooperatives to Open Cooperatives in Food and Farming." *Journal of Rural Studies* 53 (2017).

Gordon, Robert W. "Critical Legal Histories." *Stanford Law Review* 36, no. 1 (1984).

Grassein, Cristina et al. "Beyond Alternative Food Networks: Italy's Solidarity Purchase Groups and the United States' Community Economies." In *Social and Solidarity Economy: Beyond the Fringe*, edited by Peter Utting. London: Zen Books, 2015.

Green, James. *The Devil Is Here in These Hills: West Virginia's Coal Miners and Their Battle for Freedom*. New York: Atlantic Monthly Press, 2015.

Greenberg, Pierce. "Disproportionality and Resource-Based Environmental Inequality: An Analysis of Neighborhood Proximity to Coal Impoundments in Appalachia." *Rural Sociology* 82, no. 1 (2017).

Gregg, Sara M. *Managing the Mountains: Land Use Planning, the New Deal, and the Creation of a Federal Landscape in Appalachia*. New Haven, CT: Yale University Press, 2010.

Gregg, Nina, and Doug Gamble. "This Land Is Your Land: Local Organizing and the Hegemony of Growth." In *Transforming Places: Lessons from Appalachia*, edited by Stephen L. Fisher and Barbara Ellen Smith. Urbana: University of Illinois Press, 2012.

Greider, William. *The Soul of Capitalism: Opening Paths to a Moral Economy*. New York: Simon & Schuster, 2003.

Grewal, David Singh, and Jedediah Purdy. "Introduction: Law and Neoliberalism." *Law and Contemporary Problems* 77, no. 4 (2014).

Hand, Mark. "EPA Chief Exaggerates Growth of Coal Jobs by Tens of Thousands." *Think Progress*, June 5, 2017. https://thinkprogress.org/epa-chief-exaggerates-coal-job-growth-2ab69ed36b6/.

Hansen, Roger P., and Theodore A. Wolff. "Environmental Review & Case Study: Reviewing NEPA's Past: Improving NEPA's Future." *Environmental Practice* 13, no. 3 (2011).

Harrington, Michael. *The Other America: Poverty in the United States*. New York: Simon & Schuster, 1997.

Harvey, David. *A Brief History of Neoliberalism*. Oxford: Oxford University Press, 2007.

Haskell, Jean. "Assessing the Landscape of Local Food in Appalachia." Report, Appalachian Regional Commission, 2012. https://www.arc.gov/images/programs/entrep/Assessing LandscapeofLocalFoodinAppalachia.pdf.

Hatcher, Renee. "Solidarity Economy Lawyering." *Tennessee Journal of Race, Gender, & Social Justice* 8, no. 1 (2019).

Haynes, Dina Francesca. "Client-Centered Human Rights Advocacy." *Clinical Law Review* 13, no. 1 (2006).

Hendryx, Michael. "Poverty and Mortality Disparities in Central Appalachia: Mountaintop Mining and Environmental Justice." *Journal of Health Disparities Research and Practice* 4, no. 3 (2011).

Hernández-Truyol, Berta Esperanza. "The Gender Bend: Culture, Sex, and Sexuality—A Latcritical Human Rights Map of Latina/o Border Crossings." *Indiana Law Journal* 83, no. 4 (2008).

Highlander Research and Education Center. "Mission & Methodologies." Accessed December 5, 2019. https://www.highlandercenter.org/our-story/mission/.

Hirokawa, Keith. "Some Pragmatic Observations about Radical Critique in Environmental Law." *Stanford Environmental Law Journal* 21, no. 2 (2002).

Horsley, Scott. "Fact Check: Hilary Clinton and Coal Jobs." *NPR*, May 3, 2016. https://www.npr.org/2016/05/03/476485650/fact-check-hillary-clinton-and-coal-jobs.

Horwitz, Morton J. *The Transformation of American Law, 1780–1860*. Boston: Harvard University Press, 1977.

Howard, J. "Solidarity Food Cooperatives?" *Affinities: A Journal of Radical Theory, Culture, and Action* 4, no. 1 (2010).

Hunt, E.K. *History of Economic Thought: A Critical Perspective*. New York: Harper Collins, 1992.

Ifill, Sherrilyn. "When Trump Attacks One Black Woman, We All Feel It." *Washington Post*, November 13, 2018. https://www.washingtonpost.com/opinions/when-trump-attacks-one-black-woman-we-all-feel-it/2018/11/13/50d77c06-e756-11e8-b8dc-66cca409c180_story.html.

Inscoe, John C. "Race and Racism in Nineteenth-Century Southern Appalachia: Myths, Realities, and Ambiguities." In *Appalachia in the Making: The Mountain South in the Nineteenth Century*, edited by Mary Beth Pudup, Dwight B. Billings, and Altina L. Waller. Chapel Hill: University of North Carolina Press, 1995.

Intergovernmental Panel on Climate Change. "Summary for Policymakers of IPCC Special Report on Global Warming of 1.5°C Approved by Governments." October 8, 2018. https://www.ipcc.ch/2018/10/08/summary-for-policymakers-of-ipcc-special-report-on-global-warming-of-1-5c-approved-by-governments/.

Jackson, Tim. *Prosperity without Growth: Economics for a Finite Planet*. London: Earthscan, 2009.

Jameson, Cade A. "Radical Conservation and the Politics of Planning: A Historical Study, 1917–1945." PhD diss., University of Oregon, 2017.

Jina, Amir. "The $200 Billion Fossil Fuel Subsidy You've Never Heard Of." *Forbes*, February 1, 2017. https://www.forbes.com/sites/ucenergy/2017/02/01/the-200-billion-fossil-fuel-subsidy-youve-never-heard-of/#bafa652652b7.

Jones, Sarah. "Can Local Food Help Appalachia Build a Post-Coal Future?" *Nation*, October 11, 2017. https://www.thenation.com/article/can-local-food-help-appalachia-build-a-post-coal-future/.

Jones, Sarah. "The West Virginia Teachers' Strike Takes Aim at Coal and Gas." *New Republic*, March 2, 2018. https://newrepublic.com/article/147266/west-virginia-teachers-strike-takes-aim-coal-gas.

Kalman, Rachel. "EPA's Mercury Cap and Trade Rule: An Environmental Injustice for Women." *Cardozo Journal of Law and Gender* 13, no. 1 (2006).

Kaneva, Diana. "Let's Face Facts, These Mountains Won't Grow Back: Reducing the Environmental Impact of Mountaintop Removal Coal Mining in Appalachia." *William & Mary Environmental Law & Policy Review* 35, no. 3 (2011).

Kapur, Ratna. *Gender, Alterity, and Human Rights: Freedom in a Fishbowl*. Cheltenham, UK: Edward Elgar, 2018.

Keinbaum, Katie. "Rural Electric Co-ops Invest in Community Solar." Front Porch Blog. *Appalachian Voices*, Jan. 3, 2017. http://appvoices.org/2017/01/03/co-ops-invest-in-community-solar/.

Klass, Alexandra B. "The Public Trust Doctrine in the Shadow of State Environmental Rights Laws: A Case Study." *Environmental Law* 45, no. 2 (2015).

Koenig, David. "AP Fact Check: Trump's Vow to Create Appalachian Coal Jobs." AP News, May 5, 2016. https://apnews.com/2c55cd2496a14bdd98bcf84ccdb34810.

Kovel, Joel. "The Ecofeminist Ground of Ecosocialism." *Capitalism, Nature, Socialism* 16, no. 2 (2005).

Krech, Shepard. *The Ecological Indian: Myth and History*. New York: W. W. Norton, 2000.

Krever, Tor. "The Rule of Law and the Rise of Capitalism." In *Handbook on the Rule of Law*, edited by Christopher May and Adam Winchester. Cheltenham, UK: Edward Elgar, 2018.

Krishna, Gowri J. "Worker Cooperative Creation as Progressive Lawyering? Moving Beyond the One-Person, One-Vote Floor." *Berkeley Journal of Employment and Labor Law* 34, no. 1 (2013).

LaFreniere, Gilbert F. *The Decline of Nature: Environmental History and the Western Worldview*. Corvallis, OR: Oak Savanna, 2008.

Latek, Tom. "Ky. Congressman Wants Health Study on Mountaintop Removal." *Kentucky Today*, April 4, 2019. http://kentuckytoday.com/stories/ky-congressman-wants-health -study-on-mountaintop-removal,18776.

Lazare, Sarah. "We Have to Make Sure the 'Green New Deal' Doesn't Become Green Capitalism." *In These Times*, December 12, 2018. http://inthesetimes.com/article /21632/green-new-deal-alexandria-ocasio-cortez-climate-cooperation-jackson -capital.

Lazarus, Richard J. "Super Wicked Problems and Climate Change: Restraining the Present to Liberate the Future." *Cornell Law Review* 94, no. 5 (2009).

Lazarus, Richard J. *The Making of Environmental Law*. Chicago: University of Chicago Press, 2004.

Leach, Melissa. "Preface and Acknowledgements." In *Gender Equality and Sustainable Development*, edited by Melissa Leach. New York: Routledge, 2016.

Leane, Geoffrey. "Environmental Law's Liberal Roots." In *Green Paradigms and the Law*, edited by Nicole Rogers. Lismore: Southern Cross University Press, 1998.

Leonhardt, David, and Ian Prasad Philbrick. "Donald Trump's Racism: The Definitive List." *New York Times*, January 15, 2018. https://www.nytimes.com/interactive/2018/01/15 /opinion/leonhardt-trump-racist.html.

Levine, Rhonda F. *Class Struggle and the New Deal: Industrial Labor, Industrial Capital, and the State*. Lawrence: University Press of Kansas, 1988.

Lewin, Jeff L. "The Silent Revolution in West Virginia's Law of Nuisance." *West Virginia Law Review* 92, no. 2 (1989).

Lewis, Michael, and Dan Swinney. "Social Economy & Solidarity Economy: Transformative Concepts for Unprecedented Times?" In *Solidarity Economy: Building Alternatives for People and Planet*, edited by Jenna Allard, Carl Davidson, and Julie Matthaei. Chicago: ChangeMaker, 2008.

Lewis, Ronald L. "African American Convicts in the Coal Mines of Southern Appalachia." In *Appalachians and Race: The Mountain South from Slavery to Segregation*, edited by John C. Inscoe. Lexington: University Press of Kentucky, 2001.

Lewis, Ronald L. "Beyond Isolation and Homogeneity: Diversity and the History of Appalachia." In *Back Talk from Appalachia: Confronting Stereotypes*, edited by Dwight B. Billings, Gurney Norman, and Katherine Ledford. Lexington: University Press of Kentucky, 2000.

Lewis, Ronald L. *Black Coal Miners in America: Race, Class, and Community Conflict 1780–1980*. Lexington: University Press of Kentucky, 1987.

Lewis, Ronald L. *Transforming the Appalachian Countryside: Railroads, Deforestation, and Social Change in West Virginia 1880–1920*. Chapel Hill: University of North Carolina Press, 1998.

Lilly, Jessica, and Roxy Todd. "What Happens When Walmart Closes in One Coal Community?" *WV Public Broadcasting*, August 26, 2016. https://www.wvpublic.org /post/what-happens-when-walmart-closes-one-coal-community#stream/0.

Lilly, Jessica, et al. "Is Appalachia Trump Country?" *WV Public Broadcasting*, March 17, 2017. https://www.wvpublic.org/post/appalachia-trump-country#stream/0.

Locke, John. *Second Treatise of Government*. New York: Barnes & Noble Books, 2004.

Lofaso, Anne Marie. "What We Owe Our Coal Miners." *Harvard Law and Policy Review* 5, no. 1 (2011).

Longo, Stefano B., Rebecca Clausen, and Brett Clark. *The Tragedy of the Commodity: Oceans, Fisheries, and Aquaculture*. New Brunswick, N.J.: Rutgers University Press, 2015.

Löwy, Michael. *Ecosocialism: A Radical Alternative to Capitalist Catastrophe*. Chicago: Haymarket, 2015.

Maggard, Sally Ward. "Class and Gender: New Theoretical Priorities in Appalachian Studies." In *The Impact of Institutions in Appalachia,* edited by Jim Llyod and Ann G. Campbell. Boone, NC: Appalachian Consortium Press, 1986.

Maggard, Sally Ward. "From Farm to Coal Camp to Back Office and McDonald's: Living in the Midst of Appalachia's Latest Transformation." *Journal of the Appalachian Studies Association* 6 (1994).

Malm, Andreas. *Fossil Capital: The Rise of Steam Power and the Roots of Global Warming*. Brooklyn: Verson, 2016.

Marrani, David. "Human Rights and Environmental Protection: The Pressure of the Charter for the Environment on the French Administrative Courts." *Sustainable Development Law & Policy* 10, no. 1 (2009).

Martin, Richard. *Coal Wars: The Future of Energy and the Fate of the Planet*. New York: St. Martin's Press, 2015.

Martinez, Cecilia. "From Commodification to the Commons: Charting the Pathway for Energy Democracy." In *Energy Democracy: Advancing Equity in Clean Energy Solutions*, edited by Denise Fairchild and Al Weinrub. Washington: Island Press, 2017.

Marx, Karl. *A Contribution to the Critique of Political Economy*. Chicago: Charles H. Kerr & Company, 1904.

Marx, Karl. *Capital: A Critique of Political Economy*, Vol. 1. Champaign, IL: Modern Barbarian Press, 2018.

Marx, Karl. *Das Kapital*, vol. 3. 1865. Reprinted in *Marx-Engels-Gesamtausgabe*, part 2, Berlin: Dietz, 1992.

Marx, Karl, and Friedrich Engels. *The Communist Manifesto*. Minneapolis: Lerner Publishing Group, 2018.

Mason, Robert J. *Collaborative Land Use Management: The Quieter Revolution in Place-Based Planning*. Lanham: Rowman & Littlefield, 2008.

Matchen, David, and Becky Calwell. "Marcellus Shale." e-WV: The West Virginia Encyclopedia. West Virginia Humanities Council. Accessed December 5, 2019. https://www.wvencyclo pedia.org/articles/2334.

May, James R. "Constitutional Directions in Procedural Environmental Rights." *Journal of Environmental Law & Litigation* 28, no. 1 (2013).

Maza, Cristina. "An Appalachian Haven for LGBTQ People." *Week*, February 10, 2018. http:// theweek.com/articles/753637/appalachian-haven-lgbtq-people.

McCormick, John. *Reclaiming Paradise: The Global Environmental Movement*. Indianapolis: Indiana University Press, 1989.

McCready, Benjamin L. "Like It or Not, You're Fracked: Why State Preemption of Municipal Bans Are Unjustified in the Fracking Context." *Drexel Law Review Online* 9 (2017).

McGinley, Patrick C. "Collateral Damage: Turning a Blind Eye to Environmental and Social Injustice in the Coalfields." *Journal of Environmental and Sustainability Law* 19, no. 2 (2013).

McGinley, Patrick C. "From Pick and Shovel to Mountaintop Removal: Environmental Injustice in the Appalachian Coalfields." *Environmental Law* 34, no. 1 (2004).

McKillop, Matt, and Daniel Newman. "Years of Slower Population Growth Persisted in 2017." *Pew*, June 20, 2018. https://www.pewtrusts.org/research-and-analysis /articles/2018/06/20/years-of-slower-population-growth-persisted-in-2017?utm

_campaign=governing&utm_source=twitter&utm_medium=social&utm_
content=2017map.

McLenson, Russell. "Nature Conservancy Study Shows Appalachian Mountains to Be a
Climate Change 'Stronghold.' " *Huffington Post*, June 6, 2012. https://www.huffpost
.com/entry/nature-conservancy-study-global-warming_n_1574671.

McNeil, Bryan T. *Combating Mountaintop Removal: New Directions in the Fight against Big Coal.*
Urbana: University of Illinois Press, 2011.

McNeilly, Kathryn. *Human Rights and Radical Social Transformation: Futurity, Alterity, Power.*
New York: Routledge, 2018.

Mecklin, John, ed. "2018 Doomsday Clock Statement." Science and Security Board, Bulletin
of the Atomic Scientists, 2018, https://thebulletin.org/2018-doomsday-clock
-statement/.

Mellor, Anne K. "Thoughts on *Romanticism and Gender.*" *European Romantic Review* 23, no. 3
(2012).

Mellor, Mary. "Eco-feminism and Eco-socialism: Dilemmas of Essentialism and Materialism."
Capitalism, Nature, Socialism 3, no. 2 (1992).

Mellor, Mary. "Ecofeminist Political Economy: Integrating Feminist Economics and Ecological
Economics." *Feminist Economics* 11, no. 3 (2005).

Meyer, Stephen M. *The End of the Wild.* Cambridge, MA: MIT Press, 2006.

Mezey, Naomi. "Law As Culture." *Yale Journal of Law and the Humanities* 13, no. 1 (2001):
35–68.

M'Gonigle, Michael, and Louise Takeda. "The Liberal Limits of Environmental Law: A Green
Legal Critique." *Pace Environmental Law Review* 30, no. 3 (2013).

Mies, Maria, and Vandana Shiva. *Ecofeminism.* London: Zed Books, 1993.

Miewald, C. E., and E. J. McCann. "Gender, Struggle, Scale, and the Production of Place in the
Appalachian Coalfields." *Environment and Planning* 36, no. 6 (2004).

Miles, Tom. "Global Temperatures on Track for 3–5 Degree Rise by 2100: U.N." *Reuters,*
November 29, 2018. https://www.reuters.com/article/us-climate-change-un/global
-temperatures-on-track-for-3-5-degree-rise-by-2100-u-n-idUSKCN1NY186.

Miller, Brett A. "Embracing the Water-Energy Contradiction: The Pebble Mine Conflict and
Regulatory Implications Associated with Renewable Energy's Dependence on Non-
Renewable Copper." *University of Denver Water Law Review* 19, no. 2 (2016).

Millstone, Carina. "Can Social and Solidarity Economy Organisations Complement or Replace
Publicly Traded Companies?" In *Social and Solidarity Economy: Beyond the Fringe*, edited
by Peter Utting. London: Zen Books, 2015.

Mishkin, Kate. "Pipeline Shouldn't Have Access to Streamlined Permit, Environmental
Lawyers Say." *Charleston Gazette-Mail*, February 23, 2018. https://www.wvgazettemail
.com/news/pipeline-shouldn-t-have-access-to-streamlined-permit-environmental
-lawyers/article_b2451c5d-5224-5f16-a28c-518d7bb8fe10.html.

Mishkin, Kate. "Without Federal Funding, Study on Health Effects of Mountaintop Removal
Ends." *Charleston Gazette-Mail*, March 21, 2018. https://www.wvgazettemail.com/news
/health/without-federal-funding-study-on-health-effects-of-mountaintop-removal
/article_24a6d16a-faee-59c9-a44b-e1be9494c0ad.html.

Montrie, Chad. *To Save the Land and People: A History of Opposition to Surface Coal Mining in
Appalachia.* Chapel Hill: University of North Carolina Press, 2003.

Moore, Jason W. "Introduction." In *Anthropocene or Capitalocene?: Nature, History, and the
Crisis of Capitalism*, edited by Jason W. Moore. Oakland: PM Press, 2016.

Morrone, Michele, and Geoffrey L. Buckley. "Introduction: Environmental Justice and
Appalachia." In *Mountains of Injustice: Social and Environmental Justice in Appalachia*,
edited by Michele Morrone and Geoffrey L. Buckley. Athens: Ohio University Press,
2013.

Muir, John. *Our National Parks*. Boston: Houghton Mifflin, 1909.

Mukherjee, Ipshita. "Atmospheric Trust Litigation—Paving the Way for a Fossil-Fuel Free World." *Stanford Law School Blogs*, July 5, 2017. https://law.stanford.edu/2017 /07/05/atmospheric-trust-litigation-paving-the-way-for-a-fossil-fuel-free-world/.

Nair, Arathy S. "Peabody Chapter 11 Tops String of U.S. Coal Bankruptcies." *Reuters*, April 15, 2016. https://www.reuters.com/article/us-usa-coal-bankruptcy/peabody-chapter -11-tops-string-of-u-s-coal-bankruptcies-idUSKCN0XC2KQ.

NASA. "The Causes of Climate Change." Accessed December 5, 2019. https://climate.nasa .gov/causes/.

Nash, Kate. *Universal Difference: Feminism and the Liberal Undecidability of "Women."* New York: St. Martin's Press, 1998.

National Women's Law Center. "West Virginia." Accessed December 5, 2019. https://nwlc .org/state/west-virginia/.

Nentjes, Andries, and Doede Wiersma. "On Economic Growth, Technology, and the Environment." In *National Income and Nature: Externalities, Growth and Steady State*, edited by J. J. Krabbe and W. J. M. Heijman. Springer Sciences, 1991.

Office of Surface Mining and Enforcement. "Stream Protection Rule." Accessed December 5, 2019. https://www.osmre.gov/programs/rcm/streamprotectionrule.shtm.

Okereke, Chukwumerije. *Global Justice and Neoliberal Environmental Governance: Ethics, Sustainable Development and International Co-Operation*. London: Routledge, 2009.

O'Loughlin, Ellen. "Questioning Sour Grapes: Ecofeminism and the United Farm Workers Grape Boycott." In *Ecofeminism: Women, Animals, Nature*, edited by Greta Gaard. Philadelphia: Temple University Press, 2010.

Our Children's Trust. "Juliana v. Unites States Youth Climate Lawsuit." Accessed December 5, 2019. https://www.ourchildrenstrust.org/juliana-v-us.

Our Children's Trust. "Our Mission." Accessed December 5, 2019. https://www.ourchildrens trust.org/mission-statement/.

Our Children's Trust. "Proceedings in All 50 States." Accessed December 5, 2019. https:// www.ourchildrenstrust.org/other-proceedings-in-all-50-states/.

Paben, Jeanne Marie Zokovitch. "Green Power & Environmental Justice—Does Green Discriminate?" *Texas Tech Law Review* 46, no. 4 (2014).

Packer, George. "The Corruption of the Republican Party." *Atlantic*, December 14, 2018. https://www.theatlantic.com/ideas/archive/2018/12/how-did-republican-party-get -so-corrupt/578095/.

Pechlaner, Gabriela, and Gerardo Otero. "The Neoliberal Food Regime: Neoregulation and the New Division of Labor in North America." *Rural Sociology* 75, no. 2 (2010).

Pellow, David Naguib. *Resisting Global Toxics: Transnational Movements for Environmental Justice*. Cambridge, MA: MIT Press, 2007.

Peña, Devon G. *The Terror of the Machine: Technology, Work, Gender, and Ecology on the U.S.-Mexico Border*. Austin: University of Texas Press, 1997.

Perdue, Robert Todd, and Christopher McCarty. "Unearthing a Network of Resistance: Law and the Anti–Strip Mining Movement in Central Appalachia." In *Studies in Law, Politics, and Society*, Vol. 79, edited Austin Sarat. Bingley, UK: Emerald Books, 2015.

Perry, Huey. *They'll Cut Off Your Project: A Mingo County Chronicle*. Morgantown: West Virginia University Press, 2011.

Pfleger, Cassie Robinson et al. "Mountain Justice." In *Transforming Places: Lessons from Appalachia*, edited by Stephen L. Fisher and Barbara Ellen Smith. Urbana: University of Illinois Press, 2012.

Phillips, Mary, and Nick Rumens. "Introducing Contemporary Ecofeminism." In *Contemporary Perspectives on Ecofeminism*, edited by Mary Phillips and Nick Rumens. New York: Routledge, 2016.

Philp, Drew. "America's Tree Sitters Risk Lives on the Front Line." *Guardian,* May 26, 2018. https://www.theguardian.com/environment/2018/may/26/tree-sitters-appalachian-oil-pipeline-virginia-west.

Piomelli, Ascanio. "The Democratic Roots of Collaborative Lawyering." *Clinical Law Review* 12, no. 2 (2006).

Pollard, Kelvin, and Linda A. Jacobsen. "The Appalachian Region: A Data Overview from the 2011–2015 American Community Survey." Data Snapshots. Appalachian Regional Commission, 2017. https://www.arc.gov/research/researchreportdetails.asp?REPORT_ID=132.

Pollock, Candace. "Appalachia Identified as Most Diverse Foodshed in North America." *Sustainable Agriculture Research & Education*, July 20, 2011. https://www.southernsare.org/SARE-in-Your-State/Texas/State-News-and-Activities/Appalachia-Identified-as-Most-Diverse-Foodshed-in-North-America.

Polson, Jim. "West Virginia Gets China Energy Deal That Dwarfs State's GDP." *Bloomberg,* November 9, 2017. https://www.bloomberg.com/news/articles/2017-11-09/west-virginia-gets-china-energy-deal-that-dwarfs-state-s-gdp.

Popovich, Nadja, Livia Albeck-Ripka, and Kendra Pierre-Louis. "78 Environmental Rules on the Way Out under Trump." *New York Times*, December 28, 2018. https://www.nytimes.com/interactive/2017/10/05/climate/trump-environment-rules-reversed.html.

Pruitt, Lisa R. "Gender, Geography, and Rural Justice." *Berkeley Journal of Law & Justice* 23, no. 2 (2008).

Pruitt, Lisa. R. "The Women Feminism Forgot: Rural and Working-Class White Women in the Era of Trump." *University of Toledo Law Review* 49, no. 3 (2018).

Purdy, Jedediah S. "The Long Environmental Justice Movement." *Ecology Law Quarterly* 44, no. 4 (2018).

Purdy, Jedediah S. "The Politics of Nature: Climate Change, Environmental Law, and Democracy." *Yale Law Journal* 119, no. 6 (2010).

Pytalski, Jan. "We Have Questions: Seeking Explanation for Halted Mining Impact Study in Appalachia." *100 Days in Appalachia*, October 28, 2017. https://www.100daysinappalachia.com/2017/10/28/questions-seeking-explanation-halted-mining-impact-study-appalachia/.

Pytalski, Jan. "Where Is Rural in the Green New Deal?" *100 Days in Appalachia*, March 11, 2019. https://www.100daysinappalachia.com/2019/03/where-is-rural-in-the-green-new-deal/.

Ran, Sparki. "10 Arrested in Civil Disobedience at WV Mountaintop Removal and Coal Sludge Impoundment Sites." *The Understory,* May 23, 2009. https://www.ran.org/the-understory/10_arrested_in_civil_disobedience_at_wv_mountaintop_removal_and_coal_sludge_impoundment_sites/.

Rapp, Jason. "Coal and Water: Reclaiming the Clean Water Act for Environmental Protection." *Tulane Environmental Law Journal* 25, no. 1 (2011).

Reid, Herbert, and Betsy Taylor. *Recovering the Commons: Democracy, Place and Global Justice.* Urbana: University of Illinois Press, 2010.

Renting, Herk, et al. "Building Food Democracy: Exploring Civic Food Networks and Newly Emerging Forms of Food Citizenship." *International Journals of Sociology of Agriculture and Food* 19, no. 3 (2012).

Reséndez, Andrés. *The Other Slavery: The Uncovered Story of Indians Enslavement in America.* Boston: Houghton Mifflin Harcourt, 2016.

Rhode, Deborah L. "Public Interest Law: The Movement at Midlife." *Stanford Law Review* 60, no. 6 (2008).

Richardson, Benjamin J. *Time and Environmental Law: Telling Nature's Time.* Cambridge: Cambridge University Press, 2017.

Rifkin, Janet. "Toward a Theory of Law and Patriarchy." *Harvard Women's Law Journal* 3 (1980).

Roberts, David. "Friendly Policies Keep US Oil and Coal Afloat Far More Than We Thought." *Vox*, October 7, 2017. https://www.vox.com/energy-and-environment/2017/10/6 /16428458/us-energy-subsidies.

Roberts, Tracey M. "Picking Winners and Losers: A Structural Examination of Tax Subsidies to the Energy Industry." *Columbia Journal Environmental Law* 41, no. 1 (2016).

Robertson, Heidi Gorovitz. "Get Out from Under My Land! Hydraulic Fracturing, Forced Pooling or Unitization, and the Role of the Dissenting Landowner." *Georgetown Environmental Law Review* 30, no. 4 (2018).

Rockström, Johan, et al. "Planetary Boundaries: Exploring the Safe Operating Space for Humanity." *Ecology and Society* 14, no. 2 (2009).

Rödel, Ulrich, et al. *Die demokratische Frage*. Frankfurt: Suhrkamp, 1989.

Rogers, Katie, and Nicholas Fandos. "Trump Tells Congresswomen to 'Go Back' to the Countries They Came From." *New York Times*, July 14, 2019. https://www.nytimes .com/2019/07/14/us/politics/trump-twitter-squad-congress.html.

Romalis, Shelly. *Pistol Packin' Mama: Aunt Molly Jackson and the Politics of Folksong*. Urbana: University of Illinois Press, 1999.

Rose, Carol M. "Joseph Sax and the Idea of the Public Trust." *Ecology Law Quarterly* 25, no. 3 (1998).

Ross, Matthew R. V., Brian L. McGlynn, and Emily S. Bernhardt. "Deep Impact: Effects of Mountaintop Mining on Surface Topography, Bedrock Structure, and Downstream Waters, Environmental Science & Technology." *Environmental Science & Technology* 50, no. 4 (2016).

Roszak, Theodore. *Where the Wasteland Ends, Politics and Transcendence in Postindustrial Society*. New York: Doubleday, 1972.

Salleh, Ariel. "How the Ecological Footprint Is Sex-Gendered." In *Eco-Socialism as Politics: Rebuilding the Basis of Our Modern Civilisation*, edited by Qingzhi Huan. New York: Springer, 2010.

Salleh, Ariel, and Martin O'Connor. "Eco-socialism/Eco-feminism." *Capitalism, Nature, Socialism* 2, no. 1 (1991).

Salstrom, Paul. *Appalachia's Path to Dependency: Rethinking a Region's Economic History, 1730–1940*. Lexington: University Press of Kentucky, 1994.

Sand, Peter H. "Accountability for the Commons: Reconsiderations." In *The Role of Integrity in the Governance of the Commons: Governance, Ecology, Law, Ethics,* edited by Laura Westra, Janice Gray, and Franz-Theo Gottwald. Cham: Springer, 2017.

Sandoval-Ballesteros, Irma E. "Rethinking Accountability and Transparency: Breaking the Public Sector Bias in Mexico." *American University International Law Review* 29, no. 2 (2014).

Sax, Joseph. "The Public Trust Doctrine in Natural Resource Law: Effective Judicial Intervention." *Michigan Law Review* 68, no. 3 (1970).

Scheingold, Stuart, and Anne Bloom. "Transgressive Cause Lawyering: Practice Sites and the Politicization of the Professional." *International Journal of the Legal Profession* 5, no. 2/3 (1998).

Schneider, Gregory S. "Perched on a Platform High in a Tree, a 61-Year-Old Woman Fights a Gas Pipeline." *Washington Post*, April 21, 2018. https://www.washingtonpost.com/local /virginia-politics/perched-on-a-platform-high-in-a-tree-a-61-year-old-woman-fights-a -gas-pipeline/2018/04/21/3b8284b4-435e-11e8-bba2-0976a82b05a2_story.html.

Schneider, Joanne. *The Age of Romanticism*. London: Greenwood Press, 2007.

Schoenbrod, David. *Power without Responsibility: How Congress Abuses the People through Delegation*. New Haven: Yale University Press, 1993.

Schumann, William. "Introduction: Place and Place-Making in Appalachia." In *Appalachia Revisited: New Perspectives on Place, Tradition, and Progress*, edited by William Schumann and Rebecca Adkins Fletcher. Lexington: University Press of Kentucky, 2016.

Schwartz, John. "Judges Give Both Sides a Grilling in Youth Climate Case against the Government." *New York Times*, June 4, 2019. https://www.nytimes.com/2019/06/04/climate/climate-lawsuit-juliana.html.

Scott, Rebecca R. *Removing Mountains: Extracting Nature and Identity in the Appalachian Coalfields*. Minneapolis: University of Minnesota Press, 2010.

Seitz, Virginia Rinaldo. "Class, Gender, and Resistance in the Appalachian Coalfields." In *Community Activism and Feminist Politics: Organizing across Race, Class, and Gender*, edited by Nancy A. Naples. New York: Routledge, 1998.

Seitz, Virginia Rinaldo. *Women, Development, and Communities for Empowerment in Appalachia*. Albany: State University of New York Press, 1995.

Shah, Radhika, and Phil Bloomer. "Respecting the Rights of Indigenous Peoples as Renewable Energy Grows." *Stanford Social Innovation Review*, April 23, 2018. https://ssir.org/articles/entry/respecting_the_rights_of_indigenous_peoples_as_renewable_energy_grows.

Shands, William E. "The Lands Nobody Wanted: The Legacy of the Eastern National Forests." In *Origins of the National Forests: A Centennial Symposium*, edited by Harold K. Steen. Durham: Forest Historical Society, 1992.

Shapiro, Henry D. *Appalachia on Our Mind: The Southern Mountains and Mountaineers in the American Consciousness, 1870–1920*. Chapel Hill: University of North Carolina Press, 1978.

Shelton, Dinah L. "Developing Substantive Environmental Rights." *Journal of Human Rights and the Environment* 1, no. 1 (2010).

Shelton, Dinah L. "Whiplash and Backlash-Reflections on a Human Rights Approach to Environmental Protection." *Santa Clara Journal of International Law* 13, no. 1 (2015).

Shifflett, Crandall A. *Coal Towns: Life, Work, and Culture in Company Towns of Southern Appalachia, 1880–1960*. Knoxville: University of Tennessee Press, 1995.

Shiva, Vandana. *Earth Democracy: Justice, Sustainability and Peace*. London: Zen Books, 2006.

Shnayerson, Michael. *Coal River: How a Few Brave Americans Took on a Powerful Company—and the Federal Government—to Save the Land They Love*. New York: Farrar, Straus, and Giroux, 2008.

Shogren, Elizabeth. "Trump's Judges: A Second Front in the Environmental Rollback." *Yale Environmental 360*, August 28, 2017. https://e360.yale.edu/features/trumps-judges-the-second-front-in-an-environmental-onslaught.

Shugerman, Emily. " 'Frustration, Anger, Helplessness': Virginia Pipeline Protesters on What Drove Them to Live in the Trees." *Independent*, May 5, 2018. https://www.independent.co.uk/news/world/americas/tree-sit-mountain-valley-pipeline-west-virginia-red-terry-franklin-county-protest-a8337311.html?utm_source=reddit.com.

Silberg, Bob. "Why A Half-Degree Temperature Rise Is a Big Deal." *NASA News*, June 29, 2016. https://climate.nasa.gov/news/2458/why-a-half-degree-temperature-rise-is-a-big-deal/.

Smith, Barbara Ellen, and Stephen L. Fisher. "Conclusion: Transformations in Place." In *Transforming Places: Lessons from Appalachia*, edited by Stephen L. Fisher and Barbara Ellen Smith. Urbana: University of Illinois Press, 2012.

Smith, Richard. *Green Capitalism: The God That Failed*. Bristol, UK: World Economics Association, 2015.

Solar Holler. "Repowering Appalachia." Accessed December 5, 2019. http://www.solarholler.com/.

Solar United Neighbors. "About Solar United Neighbors of West Virginia." Accessed December 5, 2019. https://www.solarunitedneighbors.org/westvirginia/about-solar-united-neighbors-of-west-virginia/.

Solar United Neighbors. "Community Solar." Accessed December 5, 2019. https://www
  .solarunitedneighbors.org/learn-the-issues/community-solar/.
Solar United Neighbors. "Community Solar in West Virginia." Accessed December 5, 2019.
  https://www.solarunitedneighbors.org/westvirginia/learn-the-issues-in-west-virginia
  /community-solar-in-west-virginia/.
Speth, James Gustave. *Bridge at the End of the World: Capitalism, the Environment, and Crossing
  from Crisis to Sustainability*. New Haven, CT: Yale University Press, 2008.
Staddon, Philip L., and Michael H. Depledge. "Implications of Unconventional Gas Extraction
  on Climate Change." In *The Human and Environmental Impact of Fracking: How Fracturing
  Shale for Gas Affects Us and Our World*, edited by Madelon L. Finkel. Santa Barbara, CA:
  ABC-Clio, 2015.
Stern, Gerald M. *The Buffalo Creek Disaster: How the Survivors of One of the Worst Disasters in
  Coal-Mining History Brought Suit against the Coal Company—and Won*. New York: Vintage
  Books, 2009.
Stoll, Steven. *Ramp Hollow: The Ordeal of Appalachia*. New York: Hill and Wang, 2017.
Strauss, Valeria. "This Time, It Wasn't about Pay: West Virginia Teachers Go on Strike over the
  Privatization of Public Education (And They Won't Be the Last)." *Washington Post*,
  February 19, 2019. https://www.washingtonpost.com/education/2019/02/20/this-time
  -it-wasnt-about-pay-west-virginia-teachers-go-strike-over-privatization-public-education
  -they-wont-be-last/?utm_term=.7534fb5f0739.
Straw, Richard. "Appalachian History." In *A Handbook to Appalachia: An Introduction to the
  Region*, edited by Grace Toney Edwards, JoAnn Aust Asbury, and Ricky L. Cox. Knoxville:
  University of Tennessee Press, 2006.
Strickland, Ashley. "Earth to Warm 2 Degrees Celsius by the End of this Century, Studies Say."
  CNN, July 31, 2017. https://www.cnn.com/2017/07/31/health/climate-change-two
  -degrees-studies/index.html.
Stromberg, Joseph. "What Is the Anthropocene and Are We in It?" *Smithsonian Magazine*,
  January 2013. https://www.smithsonianmag.com/science-nature/what-is-the
  -anthropocene-and-are-we-in-it-164801414/.
Stump, Nicholas F. "Following New Lights: Critical Legal Research Strategies as a Spark for
  Law Reform in Appalachia." *American University Journal of Gender, Social Policy, and the
  Law* 23, no. 4 (2014).
Stump, Nicholas F. "Mountain Resistance: Appalachian Civil Disobedience in Critical Legal
  Research Modeled Law Reform." *Environs: Environmental Law and Policy Journal* 41, no. 1
  (2017).
Stump, Nicholas F., and Anne Marie Lofaso. "De-Essentializing Appalachia: Transformative
  Socio-Legal Change Requires Unmasking Regional Myths." *West Virginia Law Review* 120,
  no. 3 (2018).
Sturgeon, Noël. *Ecofeminist Natures: Race, Gender, Political Theory and Political Action*. New
  York: Routledge, 1997.
Surber, Sarah J., and D. Scott Simonton. "Disparate Impacts of Coal Mining and Reclamation
  Concerns for West Virginia and Central Appalachia." *Resources Policy* 54 (2017).
Swanston, Chris et al. "Vulnerability of Forests of the Midwest and Northeast United States to
  Climate Change." *Climate Change* 146, no. 1–2 (2018).
Takacs, David. "The Public Trust Doctrine, Environmental Human Rights, and the Future of
  Private Property." *New York University Environmental Law Journal* 16, no. 3 (2008).
Tarlock, Dan A. "History of Environmental Law." In *Environmental Laws and Their Enforcement*,
  vol. 1, edited by Dan A. Tarlock and John C. Dernback. Oxford: Eolss, 2009.
Taylor, Andrew J. *Elephant's Edge: The Republicans as a Ruling Party*. Westport: Praeger, 2005.
Taylor, Dorceta E. "Race, Class, Gender, and American Environmentalism." General Technical
  Report PNW-GTR-534. Forest Service, U.S. Department of Agriculture (2002).
Taylor, Dorceta E. "The Rise of the Environmental Justice Paradigm: Injustice Framing and

the Social Construction of Environmental Discourses." *The American Behavioral Scientist* 43, no. 4 (2000).

Taylor, Dorceta E. "Women of Color, Environmental Justice, and Ecofeminism." In *Ecofeminism: Women, Culture, Nature*, edited by Karen J. Warren. Indianapolis: Indiana University Press, 1997.

Thiele, Leslie Paul. *Environmentalism for a New Millennium: The Challenge of Coevolution.* Oxford: Oxford University Press, 1999.

Thomas, Jerry Bruce. *An Appalachian New Deal: West Virginia in the Great Depression.* Lexington: University Press of Kentucky, 1998.

Thomasson, Erica D. et al. "Acute Health Effects after the Elk River Chemical Spill, West Virginia, January 2014." *Public Health Reports* 132, no. 2 (2017).

Thompson, Barton H. "Constitutionalizing the Environment: The History and Future of Montana's Environmental Provisions." *Montana Law Review* 64, no. 1 (2003).

Tigar, Michael, and Madeleine R. Levy. *Law and The Rise of Capitalism.* New York: NYU Press, 2000.

Todd, Roxy, and Jessica Lilly. "Inside Appalachia: What Would You Do If Your Grocery Store Disappeared?" *West Virginia Public Broadcasting*, July 10, 2015. https://www.wvpublic .org/post/inside-appalachia-what-would-you-do-if-your-grocery-store-disappeared #stream/0.

Toivanen, Tero. "Commons against Capitalism." In *The Politics of Ecosocialism: Transforming Welfare*, edited by Kajsa Borgnäs et al. New York: Routledge, 2015.

Triantafyllou, Vaios. "A Green New Deal Is the First Step toward an Eco-Revolution." *Truthout.org*, February 9, 2019. https://truthout.org/articles/a-green-new-deal-is-the -first-step-toward-an-eco-revolution/.

Tribune News Services. "Sentencings Set for Ex-Execs in West Virginia Chemical Spill." *Chicago Tribune*, January 31, 2016. https://www.chicagotribune.com/nation-world /ct-west-virginia-chemical-spill-sentencing-20160131-story.html.

Trotter, Joe William. *Coal, Class, and Color: Blacks in Southern West Virginia, 1915–32.* Urbana: University of Illinois Press, 1990.

Turner, William H., and Edward J. Cabbell. *Blacks in Appalachia.* Lexington: University Press of Kentucky, 1985.

United Nations Climate Change. "Paris Agreement: Essential Elements." Accessed December 5, 2019. https://unfccc.int/process/the-paris-agreement/what-is-the-paris-agreement.

United Nations Climate Change. "Paris Agreement—Status of Ratification." Accessed December 5, 2019. http://unfccc.int/paris_agreement/items/9444.php.

United Nations Human Rights Office of the High Commissioner. "Framework Principles on Human Rights and the Environment (2018)." Accessed December 5, 2019. https://www .ohchr.org/EN/Issues/Environment/SREnvironment/Pages/FrameworkPrinciples Report.aspx.

United Nations Human Rights Office of the High Commissioner. "UN Expert Calls for Global Recognition of the Right to Safe and Healthy Environment." March 5, 2018. https:// www.ohchr.org/EN/NewsEvents/Pages/DisplayNews.aspx?NewsID=22755&LangID=E.

U.S. Bureau of Labor Statistics. "Coal Mining." May 2018 National Industry-Specific Occupational Employment and Wage Estimates. https://www.bls.gov/oes/current /naics4_212100.htm.

U.S. Department of Energy. "The Appalachian Petrochemical Renaissance." https://www .energy.gov/sites/prod/files/2019/06/f64/FE_petrochemInfo%20copy_6.26.19.pdf.

U.S. Energy Information Administration. "Coal Production Using Mountaintop Removal Mining Decreases by 62% Since 2008." *Today in Energy.* July 7, 2015. https://www.eia .gov/todayinenergy/detail.php?id=21952.

Van Nostrand, James M. "An Energy and Sustainability Roadmap for West Virginia." *West Virginia Law Review* 115, no. 3 (2013).

Veteto, James R. "Apple-achia: The Most Diverse Foodshed in the US, Canada, and Northern Mexico." In *Place-Based Foods of Appalachia: From Rarity to Community Restoration and Market Recovery*, edited by James R. Veteto et al. Accessed December 5, 2019. https://www.southernsare.org/Educational-Resources/SARE-Project-Products/Books-Manuals-and-Training-Guides/Place-Based-Foods-of-Appalachia.

Verchick, Robert R. M. "In a Greener Voice: Feminist Theory and Environmental Justice." *Harvard Women's Law Journal* 19 (1996).

Wallace-Wells, David. "Time to Panic." *New York Times*, February 16, 2019. https://www.nytimes.com/2019/02/16/opinion/sunday/fear-panic-climate-change-warming.html.

Walls, David S., and Dwight Billings. "The Sociology of Southern Appalachia." *Appalachian Journal* 5, no. 1 (1977).

Ward, Ken Jr. "The Coal Industry Extracted a Steep Price from West Virginia. Now Natural Gas Is Leading the State Down the Same Path." *ProPublica*, April, 27 2018. https://www.propublica.org/article/west-virginia-coal-industry-rise-of-natural-gas.

Weston, Burns H., and David Bollier. *Green Governance: Ecological Survival, Human Rights, and the Law of the Commons*. Cambridge: Cambridge University Press, 2013.

Wilkinson, Charles F. "The Headwaters of the Public Trust: Some of the Traditional Doctrine." *Environmental Law* 19, no. 3 (1989).

Wilkerson, Jessica. *To Live Here, You Have to Fight: How Women Led Appalachian Movements for Social Justice*. Urbana: Illinois University Press, 2019.

Williams, John Alexander. *West Virginia: A History*. New York: W. W. Norton, 1984.

Willow, Anna J., and Samanatha Keefer. "Gendering Extraction: Expectations and Identities in Women's Motives for Shale Energy Opposition." *Journal of Research in Gender Studies* 5, no. 2 (2015).

Wing, Nick. "Joe Manchin Shoots Cap-and-Trade Bill with Rifle in New Ad." *Huffington Post*, December 6, 2017. https://www.huffpost.com/entry/joe-manchin-ad-dead-aim_n_758457.

Winkley, Adam. "Corporate Personhood and the Rights of Corporate Speech." *Seattle University Law Review* 30, no. 4 (2007).

Wishart, Ryan. "Coal River's Last Mountain: King Coal's *Après Moi le Déluge* Reign." *Organization & Environment* 25, no. 4 (2012).

Witt, Joseph D. *Religion and Resistance in Appalachia: Faith and the Fight against Mountaintop Removal Coal Mining*. Lexington: University Press of Kentucky, 2016.

Wolff, Edward N. "Household Wealth Trends in the United States, 1962 to 2016: Has Middle Class Wealth Recovered?" Working Paper 24085. National Bureau of Economic Research, 2017.

Wolff, Eric. "Trump Calls for Coal, Nuclear Power Plant Bailout." *Politico*, June 1, 2018. https://www.politico.com/story/2018/06/01/donald-trump-rick-perry-coal-plants-617112.

Women Farmers of Appalachia. "The Project." Accessed December 5, 2019. https://www.wfarmers.com/.

Wood, Mary Christina. *Nature's Trust: Environmental Law for a New Ecological Age*. New York: Cambridge University Press, 2013.

Wood, Mary Christina, and Charles W. Woodward. "Atmospheric Trust Litigation and the Constitutional Right to a Healthy Climate System: Judicial Recognition at Last." *Washington Journal of Environmental Law & Policy* 6, no. 2 (2016).

World Resources Institute. "Forests." Accessed December 5, 2019. http://www.wri.org/our-work/topics/forests.

World Wildlife Fund. "Overfishing." Accessed December 5, 2019. https://www.worldwildlife.org/threats/overfishing#.

WV News. "West Virginia Poverty Rate Is Up and Has Not Decreased Since the Recession." September 13, 2018. https://www.wvnews.com/news/wvnews/west-virginia-poverty

-rate-is-up-and-has-not-decreased/article_bbc6689e-99ea-5bc7–983e-2ffb9b44d734 .html.

Yamamoto, Eric K., and Jen-L W. Lyman. "Racializing Environmental Justice." *Colorado Law Review* 72, no. 2 (2001).

Young, Ali, and Scott Taylor. "Organizing and Managing Ecofeminism: Material Manifestations of Spiritual Principles in Business." In *Contemporary Perspectives on Ecofeminism*, edited by Mary Phillips and Nick Rumens. New York: Routledge, 2016.

Zhang, Yong-Xiang et al. "The Withdrawal of the U.S. from the Paris Agreement and Its Impact on Global Climate Change Governance." *Advances in Climate Change Research* 8, no. 4 (2017).

Zullig, Keith J., and Michael Hendryx. "Health-Related Quality of Life among Central Appalachian Residents in Mountaintop Mining Counties." *American Journal of Public Health* 101, no. 5 (2011).

INDEX

Aberfan, South Wales mining accident in 1966, 94

absentee ownership: about, 25–26, 48; Appalachian elites and, 77, 146; community-based clean energy systems and, 206; public trust doctrine and, 225, 227, 228; regional citizenry's interests versus industrial capitalism and, 198–99; solidarity economies and, 206, 215, 227, 228; subsistence-based modes and, 48, 206, 215, 227, 228

Administrative Procedure Act (APA), 95, 98, 177

African American men: class lines and, 34, 38; coal wars and, 37; company town life and, 30; employment in coal industry, 29–30; hydroelectric project disaster and, 30–31; population statistics in West Virginia, 143; preindustrial Appalachia, 21–22, 24; slavery, 22, 30, 56, 153; white supremacy and, 24, 34, 37. *See also* racism

African Americans: EJ and chemical industry, 129; employment decline and coal industry, 142–43; exploitation of groups, 24; Fourteenth Amendment and, 59; population statistics, 143, 152; poverty rates, 143; racism, 30–31, 37, 83, 148, 150, 151. *See also* African American men

African American women: class lines and, 34, 38; coal wars and, 38; company towns, 33–34, 38; employment decline and coal industry, 142–43; exploitation of groups, 24; gender regimes and, 24, 33–34, 38, 83; paid labor, 33–34, 142–43; poverty rates, 143; preindustrial Appalachia, 24; subordination systems and, 83; unpaid reproductive labor, 33; white supremacy, 24, 34. *See also* African American men; African Americans; white women

Agarwal, Bina, 168–69, 213

A & G Coal strip mine accident in 2004, 156

Agricultural Adjustments Acts (AAAs), 75, 103

agriculture: community-based agriculture, 76, 102–3, 209, 210, 211, 214; decline during twentieth century, 21, 77–78, 210; deforestation and, 42; economic production and, 33; economic use of property and, 66–67; egalitarianism and, 23; industrial agroecosystem, 75, 77, 102–3, 210; industrial capitalism versus, 65, 66–67, 68; intensive modes of production, 42; New Deal era policies and, 75–76, 77–78; preindustrial Appalachia and, 21, 23; private to public land tracts and, 48, 64, 103; property rights and, 68; subsistence farming, 13, 19, 27, 197, 211, 214; surface mining and land degradation, 86; surface rights and, 26, 69; timber industry challenge, 27; treadmill of production model and, 103, 210; women's role, 23

agroecosystem, 21, 23, 75–76, 77–78. *See also* agriculture

Agyeman, Julian, 215

Akuno, Kali, 173

Alabama, 22, 29

Alexander, Samuel, 165–66

Alkon, Alison Hope, 215

alliances, and multi-coalitional interlinking, 11, 82, 91, 152, 153, 154, 155, 160

Andreucci, Diego, 165

Anthropocene, 11, 140

anti-MTR movement: about, 11, 152, 154; civil disobedience, 156–57; common law actions and, 126–27; EJ issues and gender regimes, 119, 199–200; law and policy organizations and, 155–56; materialist approach and, 196, 199; resistance practices and, 90, 154; state laws and, 126; women activists and, 157–58. *See also* mountaintop removal (MTR) mining